T5-ARZ-530

SOCIOLOGY AND LITURGY
RE-PRESENTATIONS OF THE HOLY

Sociology and Liturgy

Re-presentations
of the Holy

Kieran Flanagan
Lecturer in Sociology
University of Bristol

St. Martin's Press   New York

© Kieran Flanagan, 1991

All rights reserved. For information, write:
Scholarly and Reference Division,
St. Martin's Press, Inc., 175 Fifth Avenue,
New York, N.Y. 10010

First published in the United States of America in 1991

Printed in Great Britain

ISBN 0–312–06874–3

Library of Congress Cataloging-in-Publication Data
Flanagan, Kieran, 1944–
Sociology and liturgy: re-presentations of the holy / Kieran
Flanagan.
p.   cm.
Includes bibliographical references and index.
ISBN 0–312–06874–3
1. Liturgics—Sociological aspects.   I. Title.
BV178.F53   1991
306.6'64—dc20   91–24687
                                              CIP

In memory of my father
John F. Flanagan

Contents

Preface

As far as I am aware, this is the first book to be published on understanding Catholic and Anglican forms of public worship, or liturgies, from within a sociological perspective. The neglect of these forms of worship, or liturgies by sociologists is odd. Theologians and liturgists refer much to sociology, and plunder its concepts with impunity. It cannot be said that sociologists reciprocate this interest. With some exceptions, English sociologists ignore the existence of Catholicism and its activities are as unknown and exotic as those of any tribe near or far.

The prime purpose of this study is to show how sociology can enhance an understanding of the dilemmas of liturgical practice. Another ambition is to give the study of liturgy a place within mainstream sociology, but in a way that minimises any misunderstandings about its theological basis. Theologians and liturgists are unlikely to like what they read, perhaps branding the study as too traditional or biased. Certainly, it is not the book they would have written. Another aim of the book is to bridge the gap between theology and sociology at a point where the interests of both merge: the representation of the holy through social means in everyday life. The study operates from within a sociological perspective, but in a way that has theological implications. One has a feeling that liturgists have trivialised their own subject by an excessive use of bad sociology, or versions few sociologists would wish to recognise. A final ambition of the work is to re-sacralise these rites, to give them a more serious aspect, one that recognises their peculiar and delicate relationship to the social form that realises their basis.

One is all too aware of the many philosophical and theological shortcuts that have been made of necessity to realise this sociological argument. Many more competent writers could have written on the subject, but never did, for reasons that seem mysterious. My background is in history not theology. In 1978, I realised that a D.Phil. thesis on the Irish civil service in the nineteenth century, which had imprisoned me from 1971, was not in the centre of debate on modern culture. As a reaction to this exercise in Irish historical sociology I wanted something more up to date and controversial to study.

My movement into a sociological study of liturgy was more by accident than design. A correspondence in *The Catholic Herald* on the

idea of female altar servers aroused my ire (and still does!). In the
course of a heated exchange, one correspondent claimed that liturgy
was sociological after all. This made me puzzled, as I could not recall
any reference to liturgy within sociological textbooks. It was a subject
that did not exist, even in the sociology of religion. This absence made
me interested. Finding out why sociology had neglected liturgy was less
interesting than trying to discover what it could say, and this has been
my concern over the past decade.

Many people have contributed, directly and indirectly, to keeping
me struggling at the wordprocessor on what was often a lonely job. My
department has been kind, supportive and tolerant of my interest in
this odd subject. I should mention three colleagues who helped in
different ways. My principal debt is to Ian Hamnett. In the early stages
of my work, he read, commented, teased and shoved me along the
road, advised me about the erudite and was a foil for most of my
thoughts. An oddity of our department is that it has two practising
Catholics who never agree, but whose failure to do so has made for an
unusually creative relationship over the years. Theo Nichols, whose
specialism is in industrial sociology, has been very kind and supportive, not least in the pub after our weekly game of squash, where the
failings of muscular Christianity were all too apparent to a non-
believer. Willie Watts Miller has also helped in various ways with 'the
book'.

My second principal debt is to Michael Robertson, a fourth year
student at the English College, Rome. Before he started studying for
the priesthood, he worked as a library researcher and was most
generous in chasing up various sources and making a number of
crucial suggestions. John and Alex Farrell have been equally kind and
generous in their support, with Sunday lunches, wit and wisdom and
an ability to enable me to keep things in proportion. They have given
me considerable help with the index.

My colleagues in the British Sociological Association, Sociology of
Religion Group, and at various Universities where earlier papers were
read, gave me many constructive comments and much encouragement.
Mrs Jean Bradford and Mrs Janet Quasnichka, of the inter-library
loan service at the University of Bristol, provided me with an
exemplary and cheerful service.

Although the study is not of the liturgy of the Catholic Cathedral at
Clifton, Bristol, nevertheless this has made an indispensable contribution to the shaping of the book. The Cathedral set a standard for
liturgy that offered a security to this wandering sociological mind. The

Preface — xi

previous administrator, Crispian Hollis now Bishop of Portsmouth, provided much support, wit and spiritual insight and coped admirably with a sociologist about the house. I owe much also to the kindness of the present administrator, Mons. Gabriel Leydon, who wondered why he was blessed with a sociologist, when taking over the plant. On mature consideration, he often told me a sociologist *might* get to heaven. George Hackett, the master of ceremonies of the Cathedral, provided many insights into the nature of liturgy, and I have gained considerably from working with him. One of my more pleasant duties in life is training the altar servers at the Cathedral. This cheerful band of men and boys provided me with much motivation to keep the study going for their future so that they will have a richer and even better liturgy. I owe much to Neil, Hugh, Damian and Blaise Bradley, four brilliant altar servers with wit and style who never made a 'liturgical mistake'.

A large debt of gratitude is due to my publishing editor, Frances Arnold. She has been patient, business-like and supportive and all that one would hope for from an editor handling a nervous writer's first production. I would like to thank also my copy-editor Keith Povey for his care and attention to the detail of the manuscript.

Finally, I must thank my mother, Mrs Maureen Flanagan, for her interest and support over the years. My brother, Brian, and his wife, Joan, and their children have been very tolerant of the sociologist in the family.

Feast of St Dominic   KIERAN FLANAGAN
8 August 1990

Introduction

> Everything in this world is symbolic, everything must serve in some
> way as a spiritual looking-glass; everything has its function and its
> meaning; and everything is a lesson or a warning for us all . . . .
>
> (J.-K. Huysmans to Léon Leclaire 27 April 1896
> quoted in Robert Baldick, *The Life of J.-K. Huysmans*)

Christian religious rituals have attracted oddly little sociological
attention. They lack an image or a literature, seeming to occupy an
analytical limbo beyond the sociological pale. Liturgies, or public
orders of Christian worship, such as the mass, or offices like choral
evensong, appear as less than exotic to a sociological imagination best
employed seeking striking questions elsewhere. As a child of the
Enlightenment, sociology chases more devious prey, those who
operate on the darker side of life. Somehow, the study of liturgy
does not fit easily on a sociological landscape. Christian rites belong to
the childhood of society, the province of the unsophisticated, the
socially immature and unenlightened, who occupy territory the
streetwise sociologists will not enter. Yet these rites persist.

Even in a secular society, such as England, more attend Church on
Sundays than football matches on Saturday. Those attending might be
a small segment of the Kingdom; they join in an activity that has
resonances for the majority. On Sunday morning, many young and
old, rich and poor, men and women, boys and girls will go through the
Church gates as the bells ring out; candles will be lit while the
congregation sit to gather thoughts. Behind the scenes, priests will
struggle into their chasubles, praying not to sink under the detail of the
rite, a multitude of altar servers and choristers will don their clean
white albs and long surplices, remembering their parts again in worried
reflection readying for another performance. A gathered silence will
descend, then as the organ plays and the cross is held high, all will rise
as they enter public view, to represent the holy in a quire and place
marked for worship. Thousands of sermons will be uttered in a variety
of ecclesiastical settings, in majestic Gothic Cathedrals, suburban
Victorian Churches, and in the little Chapels strung out over the hills
and dales of rural England. Heads will bow to pray to say 'Our
Father . . . . .'. Special occasions will shape ritely sensibilities. Yelling
babies will be hatched in holiness, couples will be matched in

1

sacramental union and the dead will be dispatched heavenwards. Receiving communion, many will return to pew to sink and tell God that of which they cannot speak to their neighbour. In privacy in a public place, many will feel strengthened and renewed to holy purpose. At the end, all will rise for the processional hymn, and the altar party will depart, leaving those who remain to disperse. Vestments will be re-hung, chalices will be put away, music re-shelved, and the lights will be put out, as the sanctuary actors depart. They leave the church with a filled emptiness and a wonder as to what passed before.

Churches and Cathedrals strike the imagination. They invite a curiosity as to their social purpose, a puzzlement over the forms of collective activity they have been established to represent. Contemplating the Cathedrals of France, in a future where Catholicism had been dead for centuries, Proust wondered how later generations would view these buildings, 'dumb, alienated from their purpose, monuments, now unintelligible of an unremembered creed'. These Cathedrals represented 'the noblest and most original expression of the French genius'. Men might muse to re-discover their vanished significance, so that 'meaning comes back to carving and to painted windows: mystery, incense-sweet, hangs like a cloud within the temple aisles, and the building takes up once again its ancient song'.[1]

Modern man gazes and parades around the Cathedral aisles. If he lingers just before the liturgical hour strikes, he might discern a solemn spectacle emerging from the shadows, a stately process of surpliced songsters filing out slow and holy to sing the evening office. In their stalls, they fill the building with high and wondrous chant, bringing to life a message for re-inspection. They make present images of angelic holiness that belong more fittingly to the stained glass windows of the building. There is a quality of habit about their act that seems to endow these liturgical actors with an impunity, an absence of worry about the credibility of what is represented. At the end of the rite, these men and boys depart in procession past the observer who might have been struck by what he saw and heard. A witness to a theological truth was given, but there was also a question of sociological interpretation. It would be difficult to deny to this liturgical event the sociological status of a religious ritual. But what was to be understood about this particular rite that would enlighten the sociological mind?

A sociological account, describing literally what was seen at a Catholic mass without reference to interpretative assumptions, or to the theological belief system that governs what is being unfolded, might proceed as follows. A sociologist entering Church before mass might notice a lot of benches filled with all manner of people all facing forward, seldom looking to the side and apparently ignoring each other. To the front stands a marble table, with a white cloth, on a stage that seems to be the focal point for the ritual about to unfold. A bell rings, and from the side door process some oddly clad boys leading an elderly gentleman, even more weirdly attired. At their entry, all stand up, thus obscuring the view. The table is kissed and the boys grovel. Then the old actor waves his hands (to ward off flies?) and a stream of words follow. Everybody sits down and somebody reads without interruption from a box, or podium. Then everybody stands up, and the elderly man moves across the stage to the same spot. He swings a metal object that transmits puffs of smoke at the book stand before speaking. When he finishes, everybody sits down as he moves behind the table to receive some objects from his attendants. More words follow and his hands are washed at the side of the table by the boys. Some songs are sung. Suddenly all around the sociologist vanish, dropping to their knees. After some more words difficult to under-stand, a white object is held up for all to see, apparently causing a bell to ring. Almost immediately an ornate cup is elevated, achieving a similar ringing effect. For a bit, nothing seems to happen. Then everybody stands up. Sociological concentration is disrupted by a request to shake hands. A moment later, all fall to their knees. Silence follows, interrupted by everybody getting up to form a queue to the front to receive an object from the elderly man. Some receive this in the mouth and others take it on the hand and then consume. This token, or gift seems to make everybody ignore each other even more studiously than before. Some washing up is done at the side of the table and materials are removed to the edge of the stage. More words are uttered, and everybody stands up as the boys escort the elderly man to the front of the table, where they bow together and then depart, though the bell is not rung at the door this time.

The ritual lasted about thirty-five minutes and was even more boring than it sounds to the sociologist *not* looking to interpret or to understand the implicit meanings governing this peculiar social transaction. The whole event was brief, predictable and uneventful. It seemed available to sociological scrutiny but in a teasing way that made it unavailable. What could a sociologist say that would add meaning to what was already understood by the participants? A similar dilemma had arisen for one of Margaret Mead's students. Sent to study a Catholic High mass, the student was delighted with the splendour of the form, the sounds and the appeal to the senses. This was a religious ritual, but her sociological imagination jammed to a halt, when she realised 'they do this *every* Sunday'.[2]

At one level, a liturgical event, such as a mass poses few sociological complications. It is a ritual with some form of action, operating in a ceremonial order that bears symbols in a collective transaction that produces a distinctive phenomenon. It is a very elementary form of religious life combining a sacred meal, a sacrifice, and a listening to some texts being read. It is not quite as bizarre as it might initially seem. Other rites, such as those effecting passages of life or those that deal in magic, have generated a vast anthropological literature. The meanings and purposes of these ceremonial orders require subtle negotiation in the course of intensive fieldwork over a few years. They have curious procedures that arouse awe, not least because they violate Western assumptions of common sense. By comparison Christian ritual orders pale into insignificance. They present spectacles that are deemed to 'work' to the degree to which they are uneventful. Their ceremonial orders have a perplexing, ambiguous quality. There is a duality about their enactments that makes them seem both alien and alienating, conveying a mystery but in a mysterious manner of certainty that perplexes. Unlike rituals of the third world, their sequences can be checked in a book of instructions that is available to the public.

Despite being publicly accessible to all, these rites pose numerous problems whose complexity, perhaps, accounts for their sociological neglect. There are so many types or forms of liturgy to select to study, all claiming a capacity to 'work', to deal in hidden meanings produced through ambiguous and indeterminate social means. These liturgies handle meanings in a ceremonial format that operates in the twilight zones of sociological awareness, where faith counts more than reason. Operating on the edge of a secularised society, these rites also seem to express a limit on the capacity of sociology to fully comprehend their performative basis.

In Catholicism, the truth claims of this ritual transaction are enormous. It is believed that Christ is present under the appearance of bread and wine; that the word of God is spoken to those with a capacity to hear its truth; and that the rite represents an instance in a sacred calendar, a moment of immediacy in a timeless order. The mass contains many meanings. It can be conceived as a sacred drama. Like a great work of art, it bears endless re-presentation without its meanings being in any way exhausted. As a ritual, the mass is a condensed expression of a highly complex theology, that regulates and shapes the social contours of what is available for sociological understandings. Liturgical orders operate with a surplus of meanings greatly in excess of what appears in and through their social means of enactment. The proper divisions between theology and sociology become improper precisely at the point where the interests of both converge to understand this apparently simple event, a liturgical performance. Each discipline is incomplete without reference to the other. Theology has no means (nor wish) to deny to this rite a social basis that accomplishes the imperative to re-do and to make manifest what was laid down at the Last Supper. Likewise, sociology cannot give liturgy a complete understanding by detaching the theological layer that gives these social actions their intended meanings. Understanding religious activities has always posed acute problems for sociology. Weber admitted that there was something impenetrable about some forms of religious experience. Furthermore, he suggested sociological efforts to analyse through rational concepts meant a loss of what was distinctive in religious behaviour especially in a mystical form.[3] These difficulties seem to be concentrated in efforts to interpret and to understand liturgical forms. In a routine manner they manage to produce religious experiences through social instruments that 'work' in a mysterious manner all the more puzzling for attracting a sociological attention, but precluding a means of resolution from within its terms of reference.

Sociology faces some formidable and distinctive methodological difficulties in seeking to characterise the social processes that underpin this form of ritual. An uninvolved and disinterested account would be as misconceived as an effort to supply a causal explanation that would satisfy the objective expectations of a positivist sociologist. Liturgies demand an interest and they secure meanings through the hidden, by making the apparent unapparent. They operate in conditions of paradox and delight in the signs of contradiction they display for play. They generate a curiosity, perhaps an awe that something so trivial could produce so serious an effect for their adherents. Participation in a rite mobilises religious sensibilities, a sense of value that is only accessible in complementary terms of understanding that constrain sociological efforts to grasp their essence. An analytical demand is made to go below the social surface of the rite, to reach into its hidden depths to find what is extraordinary about its ordinary apparatus. There is a deceptive quality to liturgy for the sociological eye. As Oscar Wilde indicated in the preface to *The Picture of Dorian Gray*,

All art is at once surface and symbol.
Those who go beneath the surface do so at their peril.
Those who read the symbol do so at their peril.
It is the spectator, and not life, that art really mirrors.[4]

The mysterious and mystifying cast of the rite signifies qualities beyond human manufacture. Despite this constraint, some form of agency is required to effect contact with these mysterious qualities. The form of rite has to be rendered to social account if its unaccountable outcomes are to be secured without presumption. Some mysterious and indeterminate form of relationship operates between the liturgical act and its spiritual outcome. Sociology might be able to understand the act, as a form of social behaviour, but it has no means of gauging its spiritual effect, the element which gives it a deepness of meaning and which suggests a beneficial response from God, who is the object of the ritual exercise. This represents a theological puzzle expressed in the connection between the immanent and the transcendent, that lies at the heart of liturgical transactions with the holy. The social in rite is a condensed expression of the immanent, but in theological terms this can only be understood by reference to the complementary transcendent elements which denote what is apparently unavailable to purely sociological efforts to understand.

Rituals bear subjective meanings in a ceremonial format. They handle a distinctive phenomenon and the actors involved in their reproduction have a tacit set of assumptions that governs what is intended to be revealed and to be understood. To sustain the order of rite in a way that secures its characterising shape, actors have to regulate meanings to secure their stipulated and intended effects. Norms, patterns of expectation, have to be used by actors in liturgical performance. A collusion is required in the use of a social apparatus that allows the rites to repeat and to re-present their incredible messages in a credible manner. Because the resources used are social, imperfections and misunderstandings can arise in performance that no theological formulation precludes. Infelicities and impurities emerge in the use of social means to secure holy ends. Understanding how these emerge, are handled and surmounted, forms a central theme of this book.

The issue of values will arise inevitably in any effort to understand the social basis of liturgy. It arises at two points. There is a problem of bias over the type of liturgy selected for analysis, and then there is the issue of how it is to be understood from within a sociological framework. The former relates to objections theologians and liturgists might make over the form of liturgy selected for analysis, whereas the latter points to methodological difficulties that emerge in efforts to translate the assumptions governing the use of rite into a sociological frame of analysis. This problem of translation between liturgical principles of enactment and sociological efforts to decipher their operating basis gives rise to hermeneutic considerations.

A vast range of permutations of styles of enactment exist in Anglicanism and to a lesser extent, in Catholicism. They range from traditional 'spike' rites laden with bells and smells, to informal charismatic gatherings, to advanced feminist liturgies, to close encounters of an ecumenical kind, to the 'average' parish mass, where the celebrant follows the official instructions as best he can within his limited resources. A sociologist might regard all these as being incredible, or he might have a more selective attitude, giving some liturgical forms a limited credibility, a concession that reflects his own religious prejudices as to which style best expresses his private theological disposition. Biases can be smuggled easily into judgements about particular styles of rite. These can be given a sociological mandate seemingly immune to theological objections. This could reduce an apparently disinterested account of rite to the interested projections of a fervid sociological imagination. Because rites do not produce tangible effects, there is an indeterminate aspect to their interpretation that seems to admit any reading, no matter how plausible or implausible. This presents a difficulty that becomes magnified in sociological efforts to understand. Prejudice can become prescriptive in a theologically unacceptable way, yet some choice of form of rite is required, however subjective and arbitrary, if a study in depth is to proceed. The attractions of a specific tribe, for an anthropologist, are as mysterious as the liturgical styles that manage to engage a particular sociological imagination.

Although sociology cannot certify the spiritual efficacy of a particular form of rite, whether it 'works' or not, it does have a prejudice in favour of liturgical styles that seem to best reflect existing sociological assumptions about how to understand religous rituals. Sociological approaches to civil and secular rituals stress their ceremonial, formal and allegorical qualities. Unfortunately, these sociological emphases conflict with liberal theological perspectives which regard such qualities in liturgy as being incredible and unworkable in contemporary culture. This marks a grey area in the study as to which can claim privilege: theological propositions that are sociologically deficient; or those of sociology which expose the inadequacy of understandings of the cultural which proceed from theology. As this account of rite comes from within, though is not fully confined to a sociological frame of reference, there is an obvious bias *against* liberal theological assumptions regarding cultural elements that impinge on liturgical operations. These latter tend to stress an informality of style so that formal ceremonial aspects are minimised to maximise active participation, to preserve a democratic quality in rite that is culturally sensitive, which includes all and precludes none. Symbols and acts are kept as intelligible as possible and ambiguity is regarded as being counterproductive.

One of the aims of this analysis is to argue against this liberal consensus regarding liturgical styles of enactment and to suggest that it is sociologically misconceived. It ignores the question of *how* the cultural is domesticated and harnessed in a ritual performance that proclaims a distinctive witness. One has to know how liturgical images are constructed and reproduced *within* ritual performance, before one can speak of their external reception and use in a surrounding culture. The internal social mechanism that establishes liturgical forms of ritual has been neglected in debates on the link between culture and faith. In addition, the issue of liturgical praxis, of what emerges in performance when theory and practice converge, has never been subject to sociological scrutiny.

In so far as liturgical values are apparent in this work, they serve to endorse a traditional Catholic position, one heavily influenced by English cultural values and Benedictine nuances. Our interest is directed to theologically unfashionable areas in liturgical thought, the functions of ceremony, the opacity of symbols, the complexity of actions and the qualities of beauty and holiness that give the social form of the rite a distinctive hue. Paradoxically, these aspects of rite, which have been marginalised in recent theological and liturgical thought, seem to offer the richest material for a sociological analysis. These romantic qualities of rite denote images of a homeland, an invisible realm that seems to have vanished in the modern world. One often gets the impression that in the pursuit of relevance, liberal theologians and liturgists have dismantled the sacred superstructure rites are there to service. Notions of the invisible, of heaven and hell, seem to have vanished in earthly pursuits of the relevant.[5] Images of the holy and the angelic are affirmed in the English choral tradition, and this runs as a thread through the work. Men and boys sing in

Anglican Cathedrals and more significantly in Benedictine monasteries, servicing liturgies of beauty and glory that speak eloquently of heavenly things. Perhaps this stress reflects the concerns of another Irishman, John Jebb. As a prebendary of Limerick Cathedral, he re-established a medieval choral tradition and anticipated many of the concerns of the Oxford Movement.[6]

Some form of bias is likely to emerge in sociological attempts to study liturgy. Efforts to connect hermeneutics to sociological theory have drawn attention to the rehabilitation of prejudice which forms a central strand in the writings of the German philosopher, Hans-Georg Gadamer. Presuppositions governing questions are implicated in the answers yielded. This generates the necessity for a dialogue which hermeneutics serves to sustain. Hermeneutics reflects Collingwood's point that question and answer are correlative.[7] The idea of an unsympathetic disengagement in handling subjective meanings is increasingly anomalous in contemporary sociological theory. Critical engagement governs the purpose of many facets of sociological theory, and endorses a moral right to represent those on the margins of society. Feminism argues that the position of women cannot be understood without reference to an ideological belief in the need to emancipate them from structures that reproduce their subordination. Some form of commitment is required to understand and to be taken seriously by the subjects of sociological enquiry. The advantage of hermeneutics is that it stresses the need to gain access through sympathetic understanding in a way that does not foreclose dialogue. It suggests that sociology goes deeper into meanings, that it brackets suspicions to allow the fullness of the subject matter to emerge and that it opens out the widest understanding possible.

How does a similar point apply to the understanding of a religious ritual? If a sympathetic engagement, a prejudice towards understanding, is used to interpret liturgical transactions, some distinctive complications are likely to arise. Will the initial sociological query addressed to liturgy move from a sympathetic understanding to a religious engagement that betokens a confessional affiliation? How far does one advance into understanding the social basis of rite, without at the same time accepting its theological underpinning? What are the limits of prejudice, when a particular form of rite is favoured in a public sociological argument that disguises a private judgement?

Hermeneutics claims benefits in handling conflicting traditions, in deciphering hidden meanings and drawing out a fullness of under-standing of their basis and how they can be reconciled. Clearly, sociology and theology offer differing if not conflicting approaches to the study of liturgy. These reflect contrasting traditions of understanding and use of rite. The purpose of this study is to offer a tentative means of mediation between theology and sociology that minimises a violation of their proper presuppositions in approaching the common question of understanding the social basis of the liturgical act.

Thirty years ago, a sociological interpretation of liturgical praxis would have been neither possible nor necessary. Domestic shifts in sociological theory since the early 1960s, combined with changes in theological assumptions about the link between liturgy and its surrounding culture, make such an analysis more possible. Prior to Vatican II, Catholic liturgy was encrusted in a mass of rubrics which stipulated in a most exact manner the enactment of rite in such a way as to preclude any discretion being exercised, either for cultural or subjective reasons. This objective cast to liturgical operations seemed to remove the form of rite from sociological speculation. Anyhow, sociology did not have an adequate account of ritual in this period that would have been appropriate for understanding liturgy. The form of rite was divorced from the cultural and somehow the question of its sociological analysis never seemed to arise.

Since Vatican II, a theological innocence has been lost in efforts to contextualise forms of rite within cultures, and to link experience with the issue of its efficacy. An implicit sociological agenda operated in the reforms that was seldom understood. Efforts to maximise active participation, to be sensitive to the effects of liturgy on the laity, and to represent their interests in a community of engagement, stemmed from a theology that affirmed the immanence of God in the world. Theology inserted the notion of cultural praxis into its approach to liturgy, but failed to secure the sociological instruments through which this could be monitored and understood. The relationship of rite to the cultural was far more ambiguous and complex than had been understood at the time of the Council. The question of the significance of the social came from within theological efforts to renew liturgical form and not from sociology. Only recently has a form of sociology emerged that could offer a means of understanding liturgical operations in a way that is compatible with their theological basis.

In the late fifties, sociology was dominated by positivist expectations which governed its procedures. Causal explanations, a concern with measurement and analytical detail established a notion of sociology as a science concerned with producing objective disinterested accounts of society. Functionalism, and a grounded empiricism affirmed a sociological tradition that hardly had a benign attitude to religion. Auguste Comte, the founder of sociology, and later Emile Durkheim saw the discipline as a replacement for religion. This meant that sociological interpretations of religion tended to reduce it to what could be analysed within scientific assumptions, but in a way that denied its meaningful basis. Since the early sixties, the discovery of a humanist version of Karl Marx, and the need for a critically engaged sociological imagination have combined to produce a concern with subjective meanings. The recovery of a humanist tradition within sociology led to a more gentle reading of the cultural. Relativism entered sociological efforts to make comparisons between belief systems and their cultural expression. This introduced a certain humility into sociological speculation and led to an agnosticism in its accounts of social actions. A wish to avoid prejudging issues in a pre-emptive and privileged manner became noticeable. The balance of the discipline shifted from an affirmation of the superior knowing of the sociologist to an emphasis on the validity of lay forms of knowledge, those resources of common sense which enable social interaction to proceed. It is in this context, as it is now conceived, that sociology has a benign attitude to religion, simply regarding it as a belief system amongst many with its own social procedures which can be rendered to sociological account. Ironically, the agnosticism that clouds sociological judgement, that gives a veiled recognition to any social transaction that claims credibility, admits liturgical transactions to its remit. Liturgical orders are no more or no less incredible than other forms of belief sociology has to handle. Liturgies are the rituals of just another tribe.

Even if sociology has a sympathetic, if not agnostic attitude to the question of liturgical reproduction, it faces distinctive problems of translation of sociological concepts, from their traditional forms of application in a sceptical secular world, to their unexpected use in understanding how the holy is handled in rituals that affirm and secure belief in the sacred. These sociological insights have been coined for use in more profane fields, to understand worlds rather alien to those dealing in sanctity and holiness. Magic, healing, and circumcision seem to dominate accounts of rituals in anthropology. These practices lie on the edge of missionary territory for Christians, affirming positions ripe for conversion. Concepts relating to role and appearance lie in an equally improbable territory to plunder for instruments for understanding liturgical reproduction. These belong to worldly-wise actors shoring up façades of concern in cosmopolitan society where appearances count even if they sincerely mislead. These arty-crafty mannequins are creatures living at the edge of a world of disenchantment operating in a way that justifies the bleak streak of scepticism attached to sociological ventures into the 'real' world. They confirm the steely gaze of the sociological outsider disbelieving in the beliefs of others, the professional witness to their failure.

To use these theoretical and conceptual terms drawn from worlds alien to religious belief involves a degree of distortion, a translation that almost amounts to a conversion. Liturgical actions shore up belief in the invisible and claim 'success' in realising the holy through social means. In so far as vice is realised through distinctive sociological procedures that embody distrust, the routine production of virtue operates under conditions of trust. There is a black, pessimistic cast to sociology. To use it to ascertain the conditions under which virtue thrives and survives, is to go against the theoretical grain. It is to make an undertaking similar to J.-K. Huysmans, who having written an innovative work on decadence, ended up in Catholicism. He noted that since *La-Bas* (his work on Satanism), 'I have been wanting to write a book dealing no longer with black mysticism, but with white'. [8]

In many senses this present study is concerned with the white side of holy life. It deals with the impression management of virtue, the presentation of innocence in everyday ritual life, and the cultivation of angelic sensibilities. The study represents a sociological venture into an unknown territory: the social construction of piety in public rituals geared to edify actors and onlookers alike. It is concerned with sincerity rather than insincerity, truth rather than deception and edification rather than destruction. The social accomplishment of virtue involves sociology in understanding the dilemmas of impression management in a holy new way. Liturgical actors operate in conditions riven with peril and rife with potential misunderstanding which suggest that if virtue is secured in terms accessible to sociology, it has a heroic cast. The effect of this analysis of the bright side of liturgy, under continual threat from its darker side, is to channel sociology into some odd, if not unexpected, directions.

To some extent, the study involves the discovery of an implicit theology operating within sociology. Many aspects of sociology have metaphorical elements that betray theological debts. The notion of a self-fulfilling prophecy that underlines labelling theory usually has been devoted to studies of deviance, madness and the underlife of society. It contains a self-validating quality, similar to the language of sacramental theology, that can be re-appropriated for holy use in understanding liturgical enactments. Doing is a form of saying that opens up many possibilities for interpreting the performance of rite. Contrasting profane worlds, that form the more usual habitat of sociological concepts, with the theological ingredients governing liturgical transactions, reveals a number of unexpected antinomies that can be understood to operate in a creative tension. Handling these without generating undesirable misunderstandings taps the social skills of the liturgical actor. These point to the degree to which rites represent distinctive social accomplishments. Central to my argument is that an understanding of the social basis of liturgical transactions involves an acceptance in ritual form of the opacity of the cultural resources used to harness the holy. A demand is made on actors enacting the rite to preserve a tacit management of paradox and ambiguity to realise its theological basis in a credible manner. The social mechanism of liturgy must not be allowed to intrude too far. Indeed, it has to be kept at a distance. The containment of potentially dangerous social elements that attenuate possibilities of misunder-standings being amplified forms a crucial aspect of the book. Deciphering these from an alien sociological perspective can lead to a fresh and unexpected reading of some old theological arguments. It is unusual when these are resurrected from within a post-modernist sociological frame of reference. The insights gained re-centre theological approaches to culture to *within* the liturgical frame and with the aid of sociology indicate their crucial importance.

To some extent, this study provides a sociological insight into the plight of the liturgical actor endeavouring to purify his actions, lest they be presumptuous or conceited. The study stresses what the actor *intends* to conceive, even though he might not successfully realise his intention in a particular social transaction. This uncertainty amplifies conditions of deception, whether of the actor or his audience. The cultural resources of rite contain elements whose meaning can be best described as ambiguous, as they can enable *or* disable the realisation of the holy in the re-presentation of rite. The fatal flaw in recent theological readings of the cultural is the slackening of the tension involved in managing these ambiguous facets of rite. This has led to the rise of consumer friendly rites and a demand for loose and lax 'happy clappy' events full of meet and greet transactions. These trivialise the social, preclude deeper meanings being read into the action and skate along the surface of some very thin ice, where all attention to danger, awe and reverence is bracketed. They are rites of the immediate that demand instantaneous theological results.

It was liberal theologians, not sociologists, who argued that a failure to open Christianity to the world impaired liturgical efficacy. They argued that the immanent was restricted in formal rites which denied the realisation of a galaxy of gifts wrapped up in prophetic ideologies of the time, such as feminism. Liberal theologians were also responsible for the notion that the form of presentation of rite in everyday life conveyed images alien and irrelevant to contemporary cultural sensibilities. It was argued that if the cultural arrangements of rite were more authentically grounded in the secular world, then religious belief would become more possible, be fuller and more credible. Such an argument has shaped the more radical aspects of American theology and its attitude to liturgy. But the difficulty with this style of argument is that it advances religious belief into a strand of sociology, where a reductionist reading becomes amplified. It delivers Christianity to a school of sociological thought that regards rituals as social constructions shaped to express and to mirror the ideological sensitivities of the age. This is a familiar argument, that also points to a well noted danger of a spirit of Pelagianism entering theological considerations. This is where the production of rite becomes a man-made venture, an unusual case of a heresy complementing a purely sociological approach, reductionist by default.

This presents a dilemma difficult to resolve. Rites presuppose some selectivity, an element of agency that regulates their enactment, but if this is overstretched, the product that emerges can be regarded, both as heretical and also as a mere projection of the dispositions of the actors involved in the act of worship. Any inductive understanding of rite assumes that the actors believe that their actions *do* make a crucial difference that can be rendered to account. The need to act embodies an imperative to do in remembrance, that is central to liturgy. The difficulty is that they are not sure of the exact theological difference variations in liturgical actions make. Bitter divisions exist in the history of liturgy and theology over this very point. Our concern is not to resolve these, but to supply a sympathetic commentary on how the actor copes with these in performance in a way that has theological and sociological implications. It draws out more finely cast ambiguous elements in liturgical enactments in which the self becomes reflected in a mirror that suggests, unclearly, if not darkly, what the actor ought to become, to realise holiness in this life. This gloomy aspect of the analysis has a redemptive dimension, an eschatological quality that ultimately transcends sociological doubt. Theological understandings of the enactment of rite, as they bear on cultural considerations, have proceeded in a sociological vacuum. This failure to connect to the contemporary condition of man, as viewed in sociological terms, partly accounts for disappointments over the passage of liturgical renewal since Vatican II, and the continual missing of the cultural target. In striving to make liturgy relevant to modern culture, liberal theologians have managed to make it peculiarly irrelevant.

The topics selected for this interpretation of the operation of rite might seem idiosyncratic, if not flawed, to theologians and liturgists wondering what a sociologist might have to say about liturgy. Certain expected aspects of contemporary liturgy are missing. Little attention is given to the issue of active participation of congregations in the rite, and they seem to be awarded a passive role that might seem medieval. There is a pronounced bias towards the male as the liturgical actor. All actions are concentrated on the altar, the sanctuary or the choirstall, and this narrow focus forms the staging ground for the rite. Angels, choirboys, altar servers, bows and vestments form some of the unexpected concerns of this study, pointing up elements hardly on the frontiers of consciousness of liberal theology. Whereas many theologians have sought relevance for the social in rite, this sociological study stresses its irrelevance. When the social appears in this account of rite, it is placed under constraint. It is kept out of the way, hidden and domesticated, lest it gets in the way of petitions for the holy to come. Indeed, the social contributes best to liturgical transactions when it 'fails', and when its limits are marked and transcended. It might seem perverse to write a sociological account of liturgical praxis whose main concern is with the expulsion of the social and the preservation of its invisibility in the performance of rite.

Concentrating on the liturgical fringe, on minor actors and actions, releases sociology from a crippling deference to theological stipulations about the centre of the rite, in areas such as transubstantiation or the validity of orders of a priest. The essential concern of this study is with sacramentals, minor marginal elements that mark grace through actions, clothing and petition, which are instituted by the Church. These involve areas of triviality and slightness of liturgical significance theologians might be happy to abandon to sociological scrutiny.

A sociological concern with the fringe, with what is fragile in rite, might well be accused of exaggerating the inconsequential and of confusing orders of priorities in a way that violates theological judgements about how accounts of rite ought to proceed. But the marginal, and the weak, are areas in which social considerations are most likely to arise in the operations of liturgy. Endless ambiguities

and paradoxes appear in this account of rite that express a limit to the
capacity of sociology to understand and to resolve. By exposing limits
of analysis in what liturgy handles in its ritual procedures, the notion
of the limitless is affirmed. Out of a social incompleteness comes the
possibility of a transcendent completeness that masks and heals the
imperfections, flaws and failures of ritual production that would
otherwise sink efforts to worship in a public and collective manner.
The interpretative focus of the analysis seeks to harness the social into
a form of play with the unknown, so that it is understood to deal
routinely with unspecifiable outcomes. Affirming the incapacity of
sociology to exceed the social limits governing the enactment of rite
leads to an emphasis, by analytical default, on what cannot be known,
what is invisible and beyond understanding. Apophatic or negative
theology most complements this sociological approach to rite.

There are various sociological debts in this work, many of which will
be apparent later. Georg Simmel, Erving Goffman and Victor Turner
are notable influences, whose emphases on social form, or frame, and
on marginality draw attention to another important element in the
account. Form is seen as a temporary enabling device that amplifies
and refracts a holy message that surpasses its objective social
significance. In this context, liturgical form can be regarded like an
icon. To make an image of the invisible in an icon, to mirror the holy
in a perceptible form, is a task that calls for great reverence, petition
and fasting before inscription is to be made. The making of an icon is a
metaphor for understanding how the social form of a rite mirrors the
holy and the invisible and how it establishes a sensibility of what is
beyond the power of man to transcend.

Implicit, tacit elements of rite are considered as being of central
importance in the management and staging of liturgies. In some sense,
this work could be understood as an account of sanctuary manners
and the necessity for mutual consideration in addressing God. This
would miss the point. Our interest in tactful reciprocity is in pointing
to that which cannot be spelt out without misunderstandings emerging
that could corrupt or profane the basis of liturgical praxis. The social
is given a delicate task in the production of the holy, in a ritual venture
laden with risks of generating misunderstandings no matter how
sincere the intentions of the actor.

The vast majority of rites proceed in a routine manner, where the
priest might be on automatic pilot steering his flock through
sacramental promises with ease; choristers routinely sing for their
supper without scruples; and altar servers give easeful attendance. The

form of rite discussed in this book seems to be characterised by unbearable tensions and worry, by scruples that would disable the holiest in the heights of sanctity. The terrors visited on liturgical praxis in this sociological account might make one wonder how any could proceed. Our concern is with a staging of a rite laden with significance, where all counts, and the greatest purity of expression and petition is sought. All elements that bear on liturgical praxis are brought into play in a focused manner that draws attention to what it might be dangerous to neglect. This is an interpretative account of rite, not an empirical description of its enactment. Social elements are pushed as far as they can go in liturgical praxis, in a fine tuning that admits considerations of the holy and the unutterable.

1 Sociology and Theology: A Career in Misunderstanding

... the regular practice of prayer, private or public, is the capital condition of any worship whatever. Far from failing therein, Positivism satisfies it better than Catholicism ....

(Auguste Comte, *The Catechism of Positive Religion*)

Since Comte, sociology has had an uneasy relationship with Christianity. In the nineteenth century, sociology was conceived as a replacement for Christianity, providing a basis for scientific enlightenment, freeing the masses from the illusory grip of religious belief, and applying reason to the strengthening of social bonds and the preservation of morals. For Comte, positivism represented the ultimate outcome of the progress of reason and with sociology he established a new religion of humanity. To Marx, religious belief was based on an illusion. It was an ideological instrument that disguised the interests of capitalists and veiled their ownership of the means of production. Following Comte, Durkheim saw religious rituals as sustaining social bonds and functioning to mirror a collectivity greater than the individual. Simmel, who was Jewish, had a sympathetic, if agnostic attitude to religion, while Weber confessed himself to be tone deaf to the resonances it produced. Sociology was formed outside theology and has had a long career of indifference, if not antagonism, to its truth claims. It is scarcely surprising that the response of Catholicism to the scientific imperialism of cruder forms of positivist sociology was equally hostile.

But these strands of sociology were only part of its origins, and perhaps a distorting aspect. German sociology as it emerged in the nineteenth century kept in full contact with its philosophical relatives. This precluded a naïve endorsement of materialism, qualified an uncritical belief in science and kept open a metaphysical link and the sense of spirit that gave meaning to the human condition. Wilhelm Dilthey, described as the Immanuel Kant of the social sciences, affirmed the distinctive nature of the cultural sciences and the degree to which imaginative re-experiencing was needed to grasp life. The hidden tacit nature of social life required a method, *verstehen*, to disclose what was to be interpreted and to be understood. This made the method of the cultural sciences autonomous from that required by the natural sciences to deal with physical matter.[1] A more provisional form of knowing was embedded in this other sociological tradition, one that presumed a degree of negotiation with the subject, whose intentions had to be taken into analytical account. Max Weber defined sociology as a science whose object was to interpret subjectively meaningful behaviour between social actors and to provide causal explanations of their basis.[2] This interpretative strand never left sociology, even though the quest for scientific respectability and professional acceptance of the discipline in the U.S.A. obscured its existence. The image of the sociologist as a value neutral commentator above the market-place and uninvolved came in for much criticism in American Sociology.[3]

Moral concerns dominated the formation of sociology and some of these still govern critical expectations for the discipline. In its formative years, sociology represented a critical response to the effects of industrialisation and urbanisation, where dislocation fractured a settled social order. Cosmopolitan and impersonal values were embodied in modernity, which loosened the link between the individual and the bonds of community that lent him a sense of place. This need to harmonise relationships between the individual and the collective gave sociology a critical role in assessing social health, in marking pathological distortions of community and in making prophecies about the outcomes and consequences of social change. Sociology has a long tradition of seeking to recentre those who abide on the periphery of society, of amplifying the voices of the under-represented and of being critical of social arrangements that inhibit the human capacity to grow and to achieve. Alienation and anomie characterised the dispossession and dislocation felt by those who paid the price for the development of advanced industrialised societies. Addressing their condition, sociology acquired a prophetic role of witnessing to the fate of these victims of a social pathology, and at the same time seeking a cure for them through a scientifically based diagnosis of the ills of society. This critical interested engagement was somewhat at odds with the disinterested scientific objectivity sociology seemed to cultivate when dealing with rival belief systems such as religion.

This role of enlightening prophecy placed sociology itself on the margin of society, casting it as a critical outsider. There was, however,

a Janus-faced quality to its pronouncements. Sociology affirmed the
need for progress at the same time as it lamented its price. The need for
emancipation from the bondages of domination and distortion were
asserted through critical instruments that dulled the ideals that might
have excited escape. There is a flawed facet to sociological visions of
humanity that makes the discipline more an orphan than a child of the
Enlightenment. Its gaze fits uneasily between literature and science,
giving it incomplete insights into contemporary cultural ills. As a
discipline, sociology cannot quite encapsulate the spirit of life that
gives feeling to the cultural and at the same time it cannot fulfil its
claim to be a pure science.[4] It tends to impose the dead hand of realism
on social ideals, and to freeze what it perceives. Sociological analysis
bears a taxidermal quality that emerges in its efforts to encase in form
that which lives in the ebb and flow of social life. The tendency to
fragment and to dismember in order to analyse makes sociology
symptomatic of the tragedy of culture, a point which Georg Simmel
perceived.[5] Sociology has an inescapable antinomial aspect to its
analysis.

There is a further darkening side to sociology that renders it a
cynical and destructive enterprise. By peeling away in sceptical analysis
the façades, the fronts of culture and civility that give comfort in the
ideological market place, sociology operates as an asset stripper,
robbing believers of their credibility. But in so doing sociology wins
cheaply, for it cannot coin beliefs – it can merely call in the forgeries.
This capacity to render infirm with analytical doubt those who affirm
ideals could represent the arbitrary malices of some sociologists, but
the bias runs deeper.

The destructive powers of sociology emerge also in the fate it awards
non-rational ideals. These are believed to wither before the inevitable
growth of a rational calculating bureaucracy. Modernity brings
dubious gifts and sociology, being its creature, presents a mixed
message to the modern mind, offering liberation and imprisonment.
Weber's dark prognosis of the price of rationality suggested the image
of an iron cage from which there was no escape.[6] The pessimism of
Weber's sociology follows a long career of despair and disillusion that
can be traced back to the Enlightenment.[7]

Sociology seems to assert that in a contemporary civilised society,
ideals are structured to fail and are doomed to fall short. As a
discipline sociology serves to enlighten the mind, but in a way that
destroys the humanity of what it reveals. This dilemma of being caught
on the margin between science and humanity is exemplified in the

career of Comte, who never quite broke free from his Catholic past into the positivism he proclaimed in his writings.[8] There has always been something unsatisfactory about the tart responses the Queen of Reason gave sociology. The arid nature of the replies was all too evident in the early 1960s when sociology became a born again member of the humanities and re-discovered its cousins in history, classics, literature and most importantly philosophy. The humanism embodied in the early texts of Marx, combined with the call for the exercise of a sociological imagination by C. Wright Mills had a profound effect on changing the image and ideals of sociology. The social world where life was lived was found again. Social arrangements for handling meanings, for constructing roles in everyday life and for coping in daily transactions became matters of sociological importance. The issue of common sense took on some unexpectedly important resonances.

A significant facet of this sociological rediscovery of the social world was the uncovering of its underlife, of a deviant culture as exotic as that of any primitive society. Actors who 'failed' society or who were cast off to its margins were given a redemptive sociological reading. Their styles of passing off roles in manners of appearing in a sceptical world aroused awe amongst ethnomethodologists seeking the exotic on the raw side of life. A sympathy for the dilemmas faced by the marginal in society governed this effort to give a human face to the deviant and to underline the poignancy of their plight. This style of sociology was one of involved scrutiny, where *verstehen* became an instrument of endorsement and a means of pleading for recognition of the unrepresented. This concentration on the marginal and the hidden affirmed the role of the sociologist as an outsider, the spectator on the margin, knowing enough to stay out, but not to enter life so lived. Discovery of the 'real' world led to a certain romanticisation of the actor who used all manner of knavish tricks to survive, even if this misled some of the people some of the time. This had a profound impact on the nature of sociological understanding. It suggested that the preconceived superior scientific claims of sociology could distort the nature of the meanings emerging in social transactions, and could neglect the skills that secured their construction. Scientific sociology might miss the point of 'real' life as lived. The balance of the account started to shift from the sociologist to the actor who produced what was to be explained and perhaps had understood it better. Alfred Schutz's comment about sociology being a second order discipline became more apparent.[9] Sociological accounts of social actions handling intersubjective meanings became more provisional, more agnostic and less judgemental to facilitate disclosure of the fullest understandings of what was intended.

This movement towards a relativism in sociological accounts was accelerated by shifts of interest in anthropology, as the impact of ordinary language philosophy became apparent. Paradoxically, the study of the belief systems in primitive societies and the issue of the 'logic' attached to their ritual actions had a profound impact on changing the agenda of Western philosophy of social science. The stress on the internal link between ideas and their context of use led to the notion that social practices, however much they violated Western rational thought, could only be understood from within the non-rational belief systems which regulated their use. A limit to the logic of sociology was encountered, and this came from the margins, from areas it had previously patronised and marginalised as being pre-scientific. [10] This failure to understand has profound implications for the future direction of sociological thought. Relativism has moved from being an issue of angst for philosophers to a methodological conundrum for sociologists. Philosophical issues have become increasingly entwined in sociology as the implications of lay knowledge are being more fully understood and as interests increasingly centre on the actor's account of his actions. [11] Concern with the nature of meaning has given a new twist to the moral purpose of sociological enquiry. Metaphysical issues of Being now hover on the fringe of its business. Hermeneutics has re-entered sociological theory, partly to offset the excessive concentration on objective structures in the late 1970s, but also to clarify the nature of understanding, where the risk of misunderstanding was significant.

Interest in ordinary language philosophy has led also to a concern with the operative effects of actions. This had profound sociological implications for understanding the social construction of deviant labels, moral categories and mental illness. The principle of labelling embodies the notion that the actor adjusts his behaviour to correspond with the expectations of his audience. He confirms their belief in his status by the manner in which he fulfils their expectations. This lends a self-fulfilling prophetic element to labelling, where appearance is linked to an uncertifiable assumption of moral or social worth. This capacity to embody a status and to become that which it signifies, so that the private self responds to its public manifestation, forms a crucial means for understanding the social basis of liturgical performance. It indicates that effects do not have to be visible for them to be believed to be true. It is the belief that is important, however invisible and not the purely visible that ultimately counts for sociology.

Sociology of religion might seem to be the most natural setting to examine a subject such as liturgy, where belief is put into ritual action. It is the branch of sociology that deals with religion as a distinctive social phenomenon and is concerned with its organisation, rates of practice and cultural significance. It is also interested in the social conditions that sustain or impair religious affiliation. To that degree it involves sociology in arbitrating on the 'success' or 'failure' of the Churches in presenting belief in society.

For the past two decades, the interests of British and American sociology of religion have centred on the peripheries of Christianity, on areas where it appears to fail. This concentration on the margins of practice of the main Churches is reflected in the disproportionate interest of sociology of religion in sects, sex and secularisation. These loom large in debates on religion in society, but can become distorting, if they reflect the sole concerns of sociology with the study of religion. The fringe becomes unacceptably magnified if it is not offset by an equivalent investment in the analysis of the core activities of Catholicism and Anglicanism, their forms of worship, their ecclesiastical structures and their theological propositions that are deemed credible by believers. There is a need to offset this implicit sociological bias towards 'failure' in the main Christian religions, with an interest in how adherents secure 'success' in their practices, which survive despite the responses of a surrounding hostile modern culture. The failure of sociology of religion to respond to the efforts of the main Churches to secure their beliefs in modern society partly accounts for the sociological vacuum in which their theologies operate. This lack of interest on the part of sociology in the main Churches in the United Kingdom, combined with the asociological nature of much of their theology, makes the study of liturgy remarkably difficult. An effort to link liturgy to theology through sociological means of analysis has not yet been undertaken, nor has its need even been formulated. For sociology and theology, liturgy represents a marginal subject, underestimated and inadequately understood in its cultural aspects.

Despite efforts to modernise liturgical forms, to shape styles of worship to contemporary social thought, Church attendance for Catholics and Anglicans has fallen quite drastically in the past two decades.[12] The degree to which the mishandling of the modernisation of rites has accelerated this trend is open to debate. The interest of sociology of religion in secularisation is not unexpected. Issues of the definition of religious affiliation, interpretation of church attendance statistics and the relationship between modernisation and pluralism are buried in this debate on secularisation.[13]

The main Churches are failing to keep a grip on their place in civic culture. Whereas in the past, pietism and civil powers enforced an interest in religious practice, now there seems to be a creeping indifference. Indeed, it could be said that liturgy, or religious ritual, is intrinsically boring and uninteresting for many. The public do not like what is routinely presented and falling Church attendance figures confirm this point. But if liturgy is a focal point where culture and theology interconnect in practice, its sociological neglect is all the more perplexing. Theologians assume that cultural elements *do* facilitate the credibility or otherwise of Christian belief, hence the many arguments on Faith in the City, the place of women in the Church, and how far modern thought should count in the formulation of creeds.

A central argument of this book is that this theological strategy of modernisation is misconceived in sociological terms. Modernity is seen as a solution to liturgical problems and not a symptom of them. Cultural elements are given an unambiguous reading, when they are more properly understood to have profoundly ambiguous qualities in liturgical praxis. Above all, there has been failure to establish an argument that tries to understand how liturgies as rituals manage to secure 'success' for some, even though operating in modern conditions. Such an argument has been made before but in terms of the attributes and qualities people bring to rites from the external world. Little attention has been devoted to the internal forms of construction actors employ to make liturgy manifest as a ritual event through social means. Debate on secularisation becomes distorting if it proceeds without a sociological analysis of the internal arrangements of rite and the order of belief it presents to society.

A vast amount of material has been written and gathered on non-Christian rituals, those ranging from the practices of primitive societies, to those of Buddhism and Hinduism. The richness of detail these accounts have produced, of complex ceremonials, symbols thick in meaning, and awe-inspiring ritual procedures, have made their mark on anthropology and sociology. Their penetration into these disciplines compares unfavourably with the almost total absence of sociological interest in Christian liturgy. This suggests that efforts over the past two decades to modernise Christian rites, if anything, have increased sociological indifference to their existence. Modernisation has rendered them uninteresting to the sociological mind. There are, however, domestic reasons within the concerns of sociology of religion that further account for its neglect of the ritual practices of Catholicism and Anglicanism.

Sociological interests in religion have been disproportionately concerned with the rise of new religious movements and with efforts to account for the growth of Christian Fundamentalism. The study of cults has generated a massive literature, that deals with the Scientologists, the Moonies and various independent house groups, which have come to represent the rapid rise of Christian Fundamentalism. Their growth signifies a dissatisfaction with the main Churches, and their failure to tap a spiritual urge that has to be satisfied elsewhere.[14] These cults have attracted considerable publicity, with charges of 'brainwashing' and exotic accounts of the activities of their founders. To that degree the interest of sociology of religion in charting their growth and fragmentation is not unexpected. Furthermore they offer a number of sociological attractions. These cults are usually small in size, have a brief life-span and embody a number of crucial sociological concepts in their activities. Social movements, charismatic leadership and esoteric rituals excite a sociological interest in their activities which runs against the tide of contemporary scepticism regarding the persistence of religious belief. Cults can be examined in the manner of a tribe, with the advantage of conducting the study near the university gates. Their small scale makes them perfect fodder for a research proposal.

But the attractiveness of cults as a field of study has had mixed benefits for sociology of religion. Thomas Robbins suggests that their study has resolved its marginality and has provided a means of reconnecting sociology of religion back into the mainstream of the discipline.[15] Yet interest in these new religious movements has had a distorting impact on the shape of sociology of religion. As suggested above, it has contributed to the persistent neglect of the social issues affecting the 'success' of the main Christian Churches, and has led to an imbalance in sociology of religion where the fringe defines approaches to the centre and misconceives the basis of its operations.

An unexpected effect of this bias towards cults, however, is that it has undermined arguments for the disinterested objective scientific study of religion. This view tends to prevail in religious studies, a somewhat parasitic speciality attached to departments of theology. In an effort to distance themselves from theology, those who operate in religious studies have suggested that confessional positions are unacademic, 'unscientific' and unacceptable.[16] But efforts to examine cults have led to sociology moving away from the uninvolved, objective claims of religious studies, to such an extent that Eileen Barker notes 'students of the new religions have found themselves part of their own data'.[17] The issue of sympathetic attachment does not excite equivalent fears in sociology. If anything, it might be seen as an occupational hazard of the discipline. A famous account of this trend appears in Alison Lurie's *Imaginary Friends*.[18] Functionalism was another expression of scientific analytical disengagement, which has been disregarded, as sociology of religion encounters increasingly an epistemological crisis.[19]

James Beckford argues that sociology of religion is in a state of stagnation if not decline. He suggests that it has concealed the significance of religion from the wider discipline. His arguments bear on our concerns. Little analysis has been made of the way religion is produced and managed in social interaction, with the result that the taken-for-granted qualities of religious occasions and experiences have not been connected to ethnomethodology, which has had such an impact in the remainder of the discipline. Secondly, he suggests that concentration on debates on secularisation and implicit religion have marginalised the issue of belief, have given it a deathwish, and have suggested that it is unworthy of study.[20] Our analysis of liturgy attempts to meet these points. It draws heavily on debates in the mainstream of sociology. One of the aims of the study is to connect the capacity to believe with the ability to act in a liturgical context in a manner that is available to sociological understanding, but also to the theological assumptions regarding the act of worship.

Sociology is far more embedded in an implicit theological debate than many realise. This is not a new argument. Arnold Nash indicated that Karl Mannheim was concerned with the degree to which theology and sociology were interdependent and could not be blind to each other's existence. If theology is socially conditioned, then its propositions can be grounded in a particular cultural or historical context.[21] This introduces a relativism in the relationships between sociology and theology. But relativism is part of a domestic crisis within sociology as a whole and has changed its attitude to religious belief. Older certainties that religion is a form of error have become progressively more uncertain.[22] As Ian Hamnett has observed, 'by making nothing believable, sociology makes everything believable. We are all in it together, and we might as well join Pascal at the betting-shop window'.[23] This shift has important implications for how sociology interprets social practices such as liturgies. It involves sociology in a wager, less whether to believe in the truth or falsity of what is proclaimed in the action of the rite, than in how the liturgical actors involved in its reproduction minimise misunderstandings and charges of deceptive practice. It is their betting practices in handling the holy that give rise to sociological interest in understanding liturgical transactions The uncertainty of sociological approaches to rite perfectly complements the insecurities its enactment breeds amongst the actors, striving to be sincere in circumstances difficult to certify.

In an aptly titled essay 'The Return of the Sacred?', Daniel Bell argued for the persistence of the transcendent as a means of warding off the excesses of modernity. The pressures of disenchantment generate a sense of sociological limit that develops into a compensatory need to find the seeds of enchantment buried somewhere in social processes. These antinomial aspects of the social arise at its limits, where the actors gamble with that which lies beyond their agency to effect. As Daniel Bell notes, 'religions, unlike technologies or social policies, cannot be manufactured or designed. They grow out of shared responses and shared experiences which one begins to endow with a sense of awe, expressed in some ritual form'.[24] This sense of the holy is likely to arise at the limits of sociological speculation, where finiteness is evident, meaninglessness is unbearable and the price of doubt is too great. This is illustrated in the tragic events surrounding Louis Althusser, which have exposed an unexpected insight into the price a denial of religion can demand.[25] There is a sense of absence, of disenchantment and disillusion, that pushes sociology to the theological wall. Such aridness makes the need to find theological meanings beyond social limits not unexpected. There are good reasons why a negative theology best complements sociological efforts to handle Christianity.[26]

Efforts to incorporate hermeneutics into the theoretical concerns of mainstream sociology have led to the discovery of some unexpected theological resonances. Hermeneutics accentuates the open nature of understanding and the need to avoid misunderstanding in the process of interpretation. If it is to have a sociological significance, its traditional interest in deciphering text needs to be moved over into the task of understanding social actions. Because liturgies combine text, symbol and action in a ritual form, these rites offer important sociological opportunities for advancing a particular theoretical interest. A number of theological elements are implicit in the use of hermeneutics in sociology, and these can be used to focus on how liturgical praxis is to be understood. To that degree the sociological study of liturgy meets a theoretical need in a way that it can reconnect sociology of religion back to the main concerns of the discipline.

Attempts to connect sociology to theology, to give it a social basis, are regarded as being most advanced in the United Kingdom.[27] In his effort to establish a dialogue with sociologists, John Habgood acknowledges their lack of impact on ecclesiastical consciousness. The mutual hostility between liberal theologians and sociologists partly accounts for the failure to grapple with the concerns of these Churches, but another reason which he notes is that sociological analysis generates sharp questions and awkward revelations that do *not* necessarily lead to radicalism.[28] Part of the reason for the failure to generate a dialogue is that sociologists, who do comment on Christianity, keep telling liberal theologians what they do not wish to hear.

If there is a bias in sociology towards theology, it operates in a traditional direction. The mutual recrimination between liberal theologians and sociologists is well exemplified in the writings of the Lutheran Peter Berger, who has dominated arguments about sociology of religion for the past two decades. He has shown an affinity between sociology of religion and traditional positions in many of his writings. This is apparent in his critiques of modernity and pluralism. His approach to religion as a social construction strongly influences our interpretation of liturgical praxis. Although Berger has written little on the interpretation of liturgical praxis, the themes in his approaches to sociology of religion have a considerable bearing on the shape of this study of rite.

His stress on locating 'signals of transcendence', on amplifying a rumour of angels, which reductionist liberal theologians had switched off, suggests a form of analysis that can be expanded into an understanding of liturgical operations as they attempt to deal with the holy. His witty effort to relativise the relativisers bears on some of the dilemmas liturgical actors routinely encounter. If religion is to be regarded as a social construction, it has be repeatedly rebuilt in liturgical performances which can have a crucial impact on sustaining the plausibility of the belief proclaimed.

Berger argues that theological thought should follow an inductive approach, beginning with ordinary human experience, within which can be located 'signals of transcendence'. He is very much concerned with the social elements that distort a realisation of their existence. In our study, sociology is given a defensive task of bearing witness to a sacred order that transcends the immediate. Berger regards modernity as corrosive in effecting a movement from fate to choice in religious belief. This capacity to choose is expressed in a pluralism that operates in a market-place and becomes associated with secularisation. Sectors of society and culture are removed from the domination of religious institutions and symbols operate with decreasing effect on public consciousness. The heightened subjectivity that arises in the exercise of choice increasingly makes religious belief a matter of private opinion. Choice saps the capacity of religious institutions to elicit deference to a phenomenon that lies outside the realm of human manufacture, which expresses itself in the experience of transcendence. In Berger's approach modernity erodes the public social basis of religion and impairs the mechanism through which it reproduces its basis of allegiance. The 'plausibility structures' of religion become multiplied making belief incredible for sociological reasons. These 'plausibility structures' are the social bases or worlds that recreate or make real the existence of religion, and in that context they have particular sustaining tasks. They represent the means through which religious belief is manifested and reproduced and therefore have a crucial sociological role.[29] In a pluralist situation where they increase and multiply in competition, the religious contents they bear become relativised and so lose their given qualities. They become private matters and no longer vehicles for public communication and witness. In this context, secularisation generates a 'crisis of credibility'.[30]

Some of these concerns emerge in the question of liturgical praxis, and point to contradictions that can arise in performance. Some form of act is required to manifest its message, yet this must not be characterised by an overdependence on agency; some selection of social resources used in liturgy is demanded, but one that manages to minimise a sense of choice; some plausibility has to be attached to the enactment of rite if it is to secure credibility, but this must not be packaged too much lest what is delivered to the market-place becomes implausible. Something beyond the purely social is required if rites are to overcome a potential 'crisis of credibility'.

Berger suggests that religious experience breaks the reality of ordinary life so that the unuttered is routinely uttered and the supernatural becomes 'naturalized'.[31] The value of Berger's work lies in his efforts to amplify the invisible, to spread rumours about angels, to speak of the awesome and that which lies beyond modern thought.[32] He asks '*How can the nocturnal voices of the angels be remembered in the sobering daytime of ordinary life?*' When the angel utters, the routine business of life pales into insignificance. Berger looks to tradition to domesticate religious experience and to give it a hallowed authority.[33]

In many of his writings, Berger deplored the loss of the transcendent and heavily criticised liberal theologians who sought too much to accommodate religious belief to the wisdom of the world.[34] Effectively harnessed, the social can be used to affirm the possibility of the transcendent, and not to dilute its realisation. Berger is well aware that a deterministic role could be given to sociology of adjusting the mirror to refract the holy in a clearer way. This could produce a form of self-reflection devoid of religious experience. The ambiguous nature of the social when turned to holy use limits this danger. He notes that 'the *same* human activity that produces society also produces religion, with the relation between the two products always being a dialectical one'.[35] If the social produces society and religious belief in a dialectical manner, the problem of interpretation posed is at its most intense in the issue of liturgical reproduction. This is where social resources are utilised to effect, to facilitate, or to bear, in an unobtrusive manner, a sense of God's presence, either in sacrament, or in a phenomenological sense. But it is also where the social is confronted in its most ambiguous expression, and where the liturgical actor experiences the greatest uncertainty over the theological effects of what he proclaims in actions that enable the liturgy to proceed. Plausibility becomes an issue attached to impression management in liturgy and the thrust of Berger's analysis is that both require a degree of social regulation if incredibility in liturgical praxis is to be avoided.

Tradition might well domesticate religious experience and sanction it with authority. But it also embodies a lineage of deceits, and a dubious inheritance for finding the holy in present circumstances. Tradition constrains man's capacity to adjust the limits of action that come down hallowed by time, but in the face of such fixedness, the liturgical actor also confronts an imperative to unfix that which is lodged in the past and to make 'real' through actions in the present, a witness of eternal relevance. For the promise of the Christian charter to be realised, a mark of the sacred has to be made in the immediate if the ritual act is to bear grace and Divine favour. These efforts to realise the holy through social means embody the imperfections of man and his proneness to misunderstand due to a divided nature, the legacy of the first Adam, the only resource available to realise the redemptive fruits of the second Adam.

The 'structures of plausibility', the social bases or forms in liturgy that make religion credible, operate in a dialectic manner with their opposite qualities. These can corrupt rite, corrode sanctity and render its message incredible for the 'wrong' reasons. Actors have to regulate these 'structures of plausibility' so that they produce their intended and desired holy effects. A failure to regulate can lead to the inadvertent production of 'structures of implausibility'. These are likely to arise in liturgical praxis, where unintended and deceitful consequences can emerge that risk profaning the sacred with unholy acts of commission and omission.

The ambiguous nature of the social instruments that secure the holy and the unholy form a central concern of this book. The capacity of liturgies to corrupt and to deceive, but also to edify and to affirm, emerges most clearly when the ambiguous nature of their performance is subject to sociological scrutiny. This is to magnify the divisions within the social instruments of rite and to find a human and theological way of redeeming their imperfect basis. The need to find a passage between plausibility and implausibility finds its most significant point of reference in liturgical praxis, where the demands of theological purity have to be reconciled with conditions of social impurity. The activities that produce the social facets of rite, its obvious qualities, also embody elements of aura that signify its unobvious dimensions, those that give the act of worship its deepest meanings.

2 Liturgical Theology: Some Sociological Implications

A Church is like a reproduction of heaven – only not as good !
(Clifton Cathedral altar server, age 9)

As public forms of worship of the Catholic Church, liturgies utilise visible social resources to convey supernatural gifts of grace. These rites involve actions that effect what they signify by denoting participation in the redemptive effects of the sacred mysteries surrounding the death and resurrection of Christ. Liturgical enactments operate in a narrow divide between the natural and the supernatural. The actor believes that his liturgical actions are spiritually efficacious and this belief is secured by a faith to which God responds through grace and revelation. This Divine response somehow manages to transcend the all too human efforts to use insignificant social resources to seek and to find the holy.

Faith is linked to understanding and grace is believed to enlighten the mind. These enable the actor or his audience to grasp the sacred truths that lie behind appearances, to reveal what lies so concealed. Properties of grace can also become attached to the actor in a way that enhances and makes transparent the holy attributes he strives to incarnate in his liturgical performance. This transparency of virtue, apparent to some, is denied to others present at the same event. Despite being a public engagement in search of the holy, the felt effects of what is perceived and found are interior and private. A random, uneven sense of the holy can become attached to a liturgical performance. If the assembly is charismatic, then the exuberance of uplift is apparent to all. But if the liturgical style is more formal and disciplined, such as at a solemn sung mass, the sense of being acted on is more indirect. The formal, disciplined, ceremonial cast of this liturgical style makes it seem as a holy spectacle that imposes constraints on the congregation. Their restrained attention makes it difficult for an observer, however sympathetically inclined, to decide on the basis of its obvious facets, whether a particular liturgical operation is 'working' or not, in terms accessible to sociology. Despite the many aids to worship used in this liturgical style, such as vestments, symbols and actions, it is difficult for the participants to know which elements will supply cues to the holy and which will 'trigger' sensibilities of its presence. Such rites operate in conditions of unpredictability, where on one occasion the ceremonial apparatus produces a sense of deadness, and on others, achieves a feeling of life that rises above the complex means necessary for its production. This generates an uncertainty amongst liturgical actors about their habitual attachment to a particular form of rite and a worry as to whether it enables or disables the growth of religious sensibility. It is difficult to know if qualities of holiness and edification have been transmitted, and if not, whether the unworthiness of the actor, or a deficiency in the liturgical form itself is accountable for any failure to receive a 'signal of transcendence'. The sociological implications of such failure make the monitoring of liturgical performance hazardous, an endemic condition of uncertainty the sociologist shares with the actor, who strives to be more 'successful' in the next presentation of rite.

Differing forms or styles of rite produce contrasting effects in the way the social is arranged to capture the holy. Informal rites serve to heighten a sense of fellowship of the kingdom being present in a way that binds all together in a common hearing and feeling of God's presence. The minimalism of these ritely arrangements is believed to better facilitate the Spirit in a group freed from the tyranny and burden of a ceremonial apparatus. Something in the simplicity of the shape seems to offer an enhanced promise of locating the Spirit. These communal feelings of the Divine make the participants oblivious to detail, but yet aware of what it facilitates. Later memory might settle on the pattern of the table-cloth, or the cadences of the bidding prayers, or the rather fat, red candles burning brightly. There is an almost apologetic, perhaps accidental quality to liturgical detail remembered. It was not what the transaction was about, but what emerged and was unintentionally marked in memory when the social was domesticated for holy use.

Liturgical performances structure a sense of God in a way that requires an intensified use of its social resources. If 'successful' in realising a sense of the holy, it is easy for the social form to become privileged or blessed. Attachments to aspects of the rite are generated through habitual use. If these are believed to 'work', a brand loyalty to a particular liturgical style will be developed. A particular form of rite is believed to be worthy of investment, commitment and engagement and its 'success' will be defended. The unprovable, illogical, almost random nature of religious experience often leaves the actor incapable of uttering about the unutterable. It is very difficult to put into words why a particular facet of rite struck a chord with such ringing effect. Properties, other than those marked as central to the rite, can take on a disproportionate importance, so that unintended elements can have edifying effects. For instance, at the end of a Faure *Requiem*, sung at a mass on All Souls Night, with a body in the Church, small sounds can come to resonate significantly, speaking of things greater than their slightness might suggest. The creak of the shoes of the altar servers, and the gentle rustle of their albs as they pass by, followed by the choir and the celebrants, complement the receding memory of the *In Paridisum*, so portending more powerfully than the music, heavenly realities that lie beyond earthly unrealities. The detail of the rite has an unpredictable capacity to become a density point for the Divine. The actors involved in the production of rite might not understand themselves why it was 'successful', why it felt as if they were walking under the arches of heaven, but they come to know that it might achieve such an effect on some occasions. With habitual attendance on rites, they develop a capacity to recognise a goodly night's work.

Something has to be done through social means for the sacramental basis of the rite to find its fullest expression. As I. H. Dalmais has noted

liturgy belongs in the order of 'doing' (*ergon*), not of 'knowing' (*logos*). Logical thought cannot get very far with it; liturgical actions yield their intelligibility in their performance, and this performance takes place entirely at the level of sensible realities, not as exclusively material but as vehicles of overtones capable of awakening the mind and heart to acceptance of realities belonging to a different order.[1]

This activating aspect of rite admits a sociological dimension but in a way that arouses puzzlement over what it is supposed to clarify. Clearly, a direct relationship between the social and its invisible effects cannot be established. Their meaning and significance come from outside that which sociology can adequately encapsulate. We might believe in what the actions signify and the properties they contain but we cannot give their use an exact instrumental reading. This raises a dilemma, both for sociology *and* theology. Often the relationships between the two are cast at a speculative level, where each lobs concepts at the other in a war of words. An 'epistemological imperialism' is higher on the agenda than many of the combatants might like to admit.[2] But at some point, the two disciplines have to converge, and the issue of liturgical praxis forces them to confront their mutual limitations. If liturgical forms are regarded as types of 'plausibility structures', sociologists have no means of stipulating which facets convince, which convert and which reach God 'best'. In seeking a fullness of understanding, sociology is also trapped in the social uncertainties that govern the enactment of rite. Certification of the spiritual efficacy of rite lies outside sociological rhetoric. Liturgical forms witness to a revelation of God as mysterious as it is indeterminate. Equally theologians cannot stipulate which specific aspect of the cultural can be manipulated to produce incarnational properties or holy effects. Both theology and sociology are caught in an antinomial dilemma with regard to the social basis of rite, one that is perplexing and at the root of the analytical difficulties its understanding presents. Each layer of rite that is indispensable to one discipline, is dispensable to the other, or so it would seem. Theology might like a pure form of rite, above and beyond the cultural, which is after all, just an enabling complication. The objective status of a liturgy allows them to bracket the cultural underpinnings of rite. On the other hand, sociology might regard the cultural mechanism of liturgy as belonging to its terrain. It might find the spiritual or sacerdotal aura attached to rite as a facet to be bracketed, as existing beyond its rhetoric. This aura can be either ignored or treated as fodder for reductionist speculation. Throughout the book we wish to argue that each discipline becomes implicated with other at the point of understanding the outcomes of liturgical praxis. The social and the spiritual are bound into the conditions of understanding liturgical actors re-present in their efforts to secure the holy. Sociology cannot disregard this intention without a wilful misunderstanding of the purpose and nature of this religious ritual.

The ability of some theologians to bracket the cultural underpinnings of rite often leads them to substitute soft ideological rhetoric for hard sociological analysis. The sacramental certainties of Catholic liturgy seem to permit some liberal theologians to accept the use of almost any cultural wrappings under the umbrella term 'the incarnational'. Giving contemporary culture an undifferentiated theological endorsement, often expressed in demands for indigenisation of rite, can be deceiving. The ambiguities and deceits embedded in human nature, that become embodied in ritual expression, can become obscured in a way that ignores a theological *and* a sociological dilemma. If all forms of rite, that give honest expression to the cultural context of their enactment, are believed to 'work', why bother to make changes in their style of enactment?

A theological endorsement of an unselective use of the cultural resources of rite can de-humanise the actor at the very point where he should confront the limits of the human condition in its most condensed expression in liturgical engagements with God. By denying the actor the need to confront selectively the social detail of liturgical acts, theologians place him above the human condition, where antinomies do not arise and ambiguities do not emerge. Making the actor unaccountable for his liturgical actions denies culture its essential attribute. Some form of human agency is required if meaningful action in an intended shape is to be realised. It is hard to think of a theological argument that could make an exception to this sociological point. Exempting man from the need to struggle with meanings would undermine the imperative to seek and to find God. The opacity of the cultural generates a curiosity, an awe and puzzlement that provides an incentive to delve deep into the dark side of modernity. A bland definition of the cultural veils the dualism of meanings the actor confronts in negotiating a passage into life with God. This dualism of opposites, such as good and evil, and more crucially for our interests, innocence and experience, establishes a tension that forms the basis of mature growth, where the complexity of the cultural can be turned to spiritual advantage, so that the limitless can be known better through human limitations. These dualisms operate in a highly condensed manner in rite and become increasingly problematic when their implications are grasped in struggles to find the holy.

One of the central purposes of this book is to emphasise the ambiguity of the liturgical act as it is perceived from a sociological frame of reference. This sense of paradox and enigma arises in the performance of rite, and is an emergent condition of its basis. The path of liturgical renewal has been bedevilled by a failure to differentiate between productive and unproductive ambiguities. This partly arises from a neglect of sociological resources to scrutinise the detail of rite and the social assumptions that have been used to renew its basis. It also arises from a failure to adequately connect liturgy to theology.

Alexander Schmemann's point still has some force that 'in the West our theology has for a long time been cut off from one of its most vital, most natural roots – from the liturgical tradition'.[3] Liturgy occupies a minor place in theology. It is associated with rules and rubrics, and with details theologians find beneath their dignity to consider. There is an archaeological cast to the study of liturgy that excludes all but the *cognoscente*. This alien and alienating aspect of rite becomes attenuated when liturgists handle their subject rather in the manner of holy stamp collecting and delight excessively in tracing forms of anaphora in the Byzantine rite, or locating varieties of doxologies in the medieval church. Such scholarship has an intrinsic worth, but one that must be offset by an awareness of its implications for current cultural use. There is a disproportion between the effort devoted to the more arcane aspects of liturgical scholarship and the issue of its reception and practice in contemporary society that suggests an unhealthy imbalance. There is a need to re-centre rites in their wider theological nexus and to rediscover age-old dilemmas that seem to have been forgotten. Sociology can offer an unexpected means of accomplishing this task.

There are signs of change in appreciating the theological significance of liturgy. For instance, the Anglican theologian Stephen Sykes observed that 'communal worship, indeed, is a theatre in which doctrine, ethics, myth, social embodiment, ritual and inward experience are integrally related'.[4] This hints at something more than bland references to the place of women in rite, the need to increase cultural relevance, and the demand to throw theological sops to the ideological market place in the hope that some will stick to the spiritually insensitive.

Until some selective criteria is established for interpreting theology at the point where it meets the cultural – in liturgical praxis – efforts to renew are likely to be unsuccessful. There could be some theological argument that suggests that liturgy is exempt from sociological analysis, but such an argument comes uneasily from those who insist its form must be linked to the cultural and the ideological, if it is to be revealed as credible in a modern age. The path of liturgical renewal has run into sociological thickets and this reflects the impoverished concepts used to deliver rite to the cultural. More efforts have been made to correct 'errors' in the enactment of rite than in any other area of Catholicism since the Vatican II.[5] The issue of the link between the cultural and the liturgical has wider theological ramifications than many will admit. It also tells us much about the failure to effect and to sustain a dialogue between theology and sociology in an area of praxis where each can learn from the other.

Reflecting on the decade of turmoil since the Council, an American Anglican liturgist, Urban Holmes, suggested that 'liturgical renewal came to fruition in the church ten years too soon'. He lamented a tragic '"near miss" between a liturgical breakthrough and a turning point in the anthropology of religion'.[6] This change in anthropological approaches to ritual emphasised meaning rather than explanation, and non-rational rather than rational qualities were stressed. The operative effects of ritual, its transformative capacities and its ability to surmount inconsistencies, pointed to a capacity to engage with the transcendent. Rituals were to be judged by the thickness of their symbols, not their thinness. Anthropological concern was less with the social relationships that unfolded in the ritual, and more with the mysterious properties of meaning its performance effected, and which its transaction embodied. Formal structural qualities were stressed in sociological approaches to ritual, whose ceremonial orders carried meanings that had to be understood in their cultural context of use.[7] If this change in sociological understandings of ritual had been understood, the liturgical quest for renewal in the past two decades might have followed a more fruitful path.

The changes in liturgical renewal endorsed in the Vatican II documents were based on a narrowly conceived and inadequate sociology where functional relational aspects of ritual were endorsed. As Luis Maldonado noted, there was an obsessive concern in the key document on Sacred Liturgy of Vatican II, that rites should be simple, brief, facile and clear. The Council sanctioned a deficient set of sociological assumptions and launched these in a society, whose cultural assumptions, in the late 1960s, underwent a revolution that denied what they had endorsed. Efforts to make rites relevant made them curiously irrelevant. The crisis which followed between 1967–1973 was a rather brutal lesson on the problems of the cultural relativity of rite. The price of this failure to understand the complexity of the link between liturgical form and cultural resources was high.

The counterculture of the late sixties discovered an interest in romanticism and mystery that many were unable to find in the threadbare rites that sprang from the thinking surrounding Vatican II. The bare, ruined rites of the late sixties and early seventies gave no satisfaction to many Catholics who sought spiritual meanings elsewhere, in Eastern religions, cults and new religious movements. Those more deeply wounded by the liturgical warfare that broke out, resigned from Catholicism altogether. By 1978, it was observed that many could be found who 'miss rites which are complex, polychromatic, abundant, lavish, rich, long, with elaborate ceremonial'.[8] The tragedy of culture had been unwittingly imported into the question of liturgical form and that which was supposed to supply certainty, gave way to a deepening uncertainty.

At some point sociology would have to be used to clarify the situation. The Council documents did give some recognition to sociology in shaping Catholic thought that was as unexpected as it has been neglected ever since. One of the central documents of vatican

II, *Gaudium et Spes*, emphasised the need to use sociology in pastoral care so that the 'faithful will be brought to a purer and more mature living of faith'.[9] Despite this wish, a dialogue between sociologists and liturgists never came to pass. The reasons for this failure are complex. Sociological responses to liturgy came almost a decade after the reforms of Vatican II. They were highly critical of these liturgical changes. The traditionalist positions expressed in their pronouncements were as perplexing as they were considered unhelpful to liturgists who had hoped for more support from sociologists in their efforts to humanise and to modernise rites, to make them relevant and representative of the people of God. Those sociologists who responded to the changes, they never initiated, claimed that many liturgists were naïve, and misguided in their expectations of the use of the cultural in rite. It was argued that they were grossly insensitive in casting aside the communal and social bonds of tradition that held the Catholics together in a worshipping community. It was further claimed that many actions of liturgists were iconoclastic and that their enthusiasm for a new Puritanism led many to leave the Church, confused and embittered. Sociologists claimed that liturgists at their most progressive and liberal had no basis for their assumptions regarding ritual, symbol, and approaches to the sacred. Oddly, those liturgists most concerned to relate rites to the social patterns of contemporary society seem to have had the greatest misunderstandings of what sociology itself had to say in these areas.

These critical sociological and anthropological responses were highly individualistic. Many liturgists and theologians wondered how representative these criticisms were of the consensus of both disciplines. The issues these sociologists settled on to attack liberal liturgical thought seemed wilfully perverse. Mary Douglas supplied a sound defence of the Friday fast, Victor Turner suggested that the ritual governing the Tridentine mass was perfectly credible to an anthropologist, and David Martin defended the Book of Common Prayer. The difficulty for liturgists was that Douglas, Martin, and Turner (who all complemented the traditional views of Peter Berger) dominated their specialisms in anthropology and sociology and their comments could not be swept aside easily. In dealing with matters liturgical a conservative image of these disciplines was presented to theologians and liturgists. This partly accounts for the mutual hostility that still exists between liturgists and sociologists.

In North America, considerable attention was given to efforts to link sociology to an understanding of liturgical renewal after Vatican II.

A rather anodyne image of the discipline was cultivated that could be tamely adjusted to the liberal assumptions of liturgical theology.[10] The terminology of sociology appeared in many articles in the North American journal *Worship*, which increasingly abounded in references to hermeneutics, symbol, ritual and play. The cultural style of liturgy which emerged in the 1970s seemed to endorse American values of pragmatism, pluralism and consumer rites, with a populist layer of feminism that endorsed a homegrown ideology.[11] If anything, this superficial use of sociology to keep alight the embers of Arcadia first fanned in the late sixties made matters worse. The orphans of this period of hope after the Council gathered around the cooling coals, without heirs or graces for comfort. Somehow, liturgy had become a dead and deadening subject.

Domestic considerations have also arisen in another context that draws on an implicit sociology: the effort to indigenise liturgical forms in the third world, so that local cultures are given ecclesiastical recognition. The question of the link between cultural and liturgical praxis has emerged as a pastoral concern in missionary activities. Arguments regarding the indigenisation of rites reflect demands to adapt their social form to the cultural genius of the people using them. This is so that their active participation will be animated and intelligent, and responses will come from within their own cultural resources and expectations. The issue of the relationship between the cultural and liturgical form has been most clearly expressed on the peripheries of Catholicism, where European and indigenous assumptions governing styles of worship clash, less over theological essentials than over the mode of expression deemed to be most efficacious for the people. Pastoral considerations generate a pragmatic question, as to what particular cultural practice 'works'. Implicit in the arguments of advocates for indigenisation of rite, that its cultural form should be adjusted to the needs of the people, is the notion that social arrangements for worship can and *do* make a difference. To be indifferent to the style of worship would be pastorally irresponsible and insensitive. At some point the cultural basis of rite has to be confronted.

The difficulty with arguments about the need to indigenise rites is that they take liturgists to the edge of a sociological frame of reference, but not sufficiently to allow the discipline to share in their resolution. Terms such as 'inculturation' are unproductively ambiguous and vague.[12] An inductive notion of assimilation of cultural practices into the form of rite generates an unselective and potentially distorting element that concentrates on dispersal of ritual bonds through adaptation. It avoids the issue of what gives them strength. A systematic understanding of ritual seems to be missing from the literature on 'inculturation'. The ambition of representing the fullness of God in the cultural form of rite, qualified by a need to maintain discipline over liturgical essentials, is worthy, but at some point has to confront sociological questions as to what difference these differences in styles of enactment make, and how they are to be understood within their cultural frame of reference and reception. The question cannot be evaded. Indigenisation of rite carries a price of possible syncretism, of admitting unacceptable forms of populist religions into liturgical practices. Unfortunately, a theology of pluralism ultimately fails, for no sociological mechanism for arbitration on liturgical styles has been developed that could indicate how to arbitrate between differing and competing forms of rite.[13] In some senses, it is to ask sociology a question it cannot answer. Liturgists seem to encounter similar problems. The suggestion by Anscar Chupungco that 'the spontaneous reaction of the people is the best measure to gauge the success of adaptation' is hardly convincing. But he does raise an important question which returns us to where we started. He notes that the issue of cultural adaptation represents the second phase of the liturgical reforms, a point understood in third world countries who have been the main beneficiaries of the acceptance of pluralism. Yet he wonders why the issue of cultural adaptation does not generate an equivalent urgency in Western countries.[14] Despite its liberal intentions, such a liturgical quest can unintentionally effect an imperialism, of confirming those Catholics in the third world on the margins of the church. This failure to develop an adequate sociology within the West, that confronts this central question in the life of the Church, of the relationship between the cultural and the liturgical, has left those on the ecclesiastical 'fringe' to work out an unsolvable problem without adequate intellectual assistance from those who first raised the question.

A sociological account of liturgical history has yet to be written that would tell us how the present difficulties arose. There are many classical studies of the development of the rite and the genesis of its parts, the vestments, prayers, and the theological and biblical elements that have affected its shape and use over time.[15] These are no substitute for a history that would plot the development of a social dimension to liturgy.[16] This failure to develop an adequate social history of rite leads to another problem, that belongs to the sociology of knowledge. What were the cultural assumptions used by liturgists in the past two decades in making alterations to forms of rite and how sociologically adequate were these? When rites were ordered according to objective criteria, where discretion in performance was denied, the issue of the social hardly emerged. But if cultural elements were imputed to rites, that indicated how they ought to be shaped, then an exercise in sociology of knowledge is required to investigate the indices used by liturgists that governed their expectations of rite. Many of their ideas were secular and ideological and owed little either to sociology or to theology. The marginal position of liturgists within theology, and their clerical place on the edge of society, has often made them poor judges of what will convince in contemporary cultural circumstances. They managed to back modernity as a winning ticket, just at the point when it became converted into post-modernism. They found a solution in modern culture, just when it failed in sociology.

There is a feeling that recent efforts at liturgical renewal in Catholicism have not worked. Rites have been denuded of their mysterious qualities, they fail to grip and to inspire awe. This point became clear shortly after the implementation of the reforms of Vatican II. Charles Davis observed that 'the general verdict upon liturgical reform is that it has failed to solve the problem of worship in a secular age'. He went on to add that 'the conviction is growing that the chief effect of the reforms has been to uncover an insoluble problem'.[17] This echoes a somewhat plaintive query from Romano Guardini, an astute writer on liturgy, 'Is the modern Christian capable of the liturgical act?'[18] The wish to experiment seems to have run out of steam, and radical enthusiasms of the seventies seem to have given way to a deepening sense of apathy and disillusion.[19] There is a need to re-think some of the cultural elements that influence and shape the credibility of rite.

If secularisation accentuates conditions that draw out the incredible side of rite, and amplifies its capacities for failure, what are the cultural or social elements that can be used in liturgy to render it credible that would enable it to 'succeed' in the contemporary circumstances and expectations of advanced industrialised societies? Vatican II drew attention to a fundamental and inescapable question that has never been adequately answered, yet understood: what is the relationship between culture and rite and how does this affect the theological nature of what is to be accomplished in the liturgical act?

As we have suggested above, the cultural apparatus of rite is ambiguous both in theological and sociological terms. In one sense the cultural is irrelevant in that it ultimately does not matter. As Simone Weil wrote:

> Religious things are special tangible things, existing here below and yet perfectly pure. This is not on account of their own particular character. The church may be ugly, the singing out of tune, the priest corrupt and the faithful inattentive. In a sense that is of no importance. It is as with a geometrician who draws a figure to illustrate a proof. If the lines are not straight and the circles are not round it is of no importance. Religious things are pure by right.[20]

This suggests that the authority of the rite transcends the imperfections of its enactment, but in a way that could be taken to indicate that its cultural expression does not matter. The pure logic of rite makes its impure delivery through cultural means seem irrelevant. But the difficulty with this argument, again, is that it disregards issues of choice and the exercise of the will required to selectively use the cultural to endow it with meanings that manifest holy purposes. The cultural becomes removed from accountability and can no longer be deemed the work, the product of human hands that gives worth back to God.

There is, however, another approach which places the cultural in its fullest use and expression to bind man into an image that transcends his insignificance, where beauty and holiness mix in a gloriously elaborate ceremony. All cultural gifts are mobilised into a giving of worth to God in a public manifestation that marks the imagination and shapes the mind. Often this is seen as a romantic expression of rite, one that corrupts by becoming an end in itself, where its intrinsic worth becomes more valued than its extrinsic task of conveying worship to God.

Each form of use of the cultural bears theological risks, which reductionist 'scientific' accounts of rite fail to perceive. Minimalism suggests a presumption of not needing to act fully to enact rite. The second approach risks amplifying a corrupting degree of self-glorification and over-acting so that the beauty of the rite becomes a mirror for basking in conceit. Despite such risks, this second strand is the one of most sociological interest and the one we wish to explore in this book.

Certain terms have vanished from the liturgical vocabulary and one of these is reverence. This carries notions of deference, and restraint, qualities somewhat at odds with contemporary liberal theological assumptions regarding giving power to the marginal and those who, in ideological terms, can be deemed to be dispossessed. Reverence conveys a sense of awe, of being before something greater than the self. It acts as a defence against the risk of self-glorification in the liturgical act by imposing a sense of humility on the actor. The nature of reverence is well expressed by Dietrich von Hildebrand, who suggests that

> it represents the proper answer to the majesty of values, to the 'message' they convey to us of God, that of the absolute, the infinitely superior. Only the person who possesses reverence is capable of real enthusiasm, of joy in so far as it is motivated by values, true love and obedience. The man who lacks reverence is blind to values and incapable of submission to them.[21]

Reverence involves a sense of limit, a selective use of the cultural, that carries an element of denial of self in the liturgical act, whose purpose is to affirm that which lies beyond the actor's grasp. This involves the liturgical actor in handling a paradox, an element of contradiction, that can be resolved with tact in a way that is available to sociological understanding. The liturgical actor wishes to cast glory on to God in acts of worship that somehow minimise or preclude these elements of worth falling on to himself. Like the self, the social has to be present to enable the act to appear, but it has to disappear if the end of reverence is to be realised. One of the purposes of the book is to explore this apparently odd argument and to justify its sociological basis.

Unless unintended consequences are monitored, and some means are found to separate productive from unproductive ambiguities, the cultural can come to corrupt liturgical engagements with the holy. It is the presumption that the cultural is innocent of a capacity to harm that we wish to attack from a sociological angle. Unless it is properly domesticated, disciplined and harnessed to a specific and distinctive task, it can distort the delivery of rite and profoundly affect what is desirable to accomplish. The cultural basis of rite has to be made explicit, before it can be converted into the implicit to allow the holy to be revealed in all its glory. In itself, such restraint of the cultural might not elicit a revelatory response from God, but it might help as a form of petition, where the means are humbled to secure a mighty end. Whatever happens, the social must not get in the Divine way. Some of these issues are apparent in traditions of worship formulated in the nineteenth century, that were so arbitrarily discarded to legitimise the liturgical styles promulgated by Vatican II. Some of the present problems are due to liturgists forgetting their own history.

The demand for liturgical renewal in the nineteenth century came from the Benedictines and it was a case of one form of community seeking to establish another in a changing society. As a monastic reflection of what good liturgy ought to be, it was an attempt by those who lived on the margin of society to formulate some authentic principles of worship for those who lived on the edge of the Church. This study reflects a sympathetic response to this initial effort in the mid-nineteenth century and suggests that it was more sociologically prescient than later efforts at renewal that became too concerned with establishing parish communities. This suburbanisation of the quest for liturgical renewal obscured the wider philosophical and sociological issues which had led originally to the effort to find some connection between forms of rite and modern cultural circumstances. The original vision for renewal collapsed in efforts to manufacture living communities, which owed more to poor sociology than good theology.

In his defence of a moral tradition in his enormously influential work, *After Virtue*, Alasdair MacIntyre ended with a much quoted reference to the need to build local forms of community to sustain virtue in the face of the 'new dark ages'. Failure to be aware of this need constituted the present predicament, and he concluded that 'we are waiting not for a Godot, but for another – doubtless very different – St. Benedict'.[22] From a different standpoint, this study is concerned with a sociological understanding of how virtue can be secured from within a liturgical tradition, one shaped by Benedictine emphases.

After the first draft of this book was finished, another, perhaps unexpected Benedictine influence emerged in the shape of the art critic, naturalist, Satanist, and later devout Catholic French writer, J.-K. Huysmans.[23] After his return to Catholicism, Huysmans became a Benedictine oblate. There is every reason to think he might have despised sociology as being as soulless as the naturalism of Emile Zola, which he rejected and which had led him into the dark side of spiritual life. His approach to liturgy bears many fingerprints similar to those in this work. He was very much concerned with opposites in meanings, having written the highly influential treatise on decadence, *Against Nature*. Deeply disillusioned with modern life, he was well aware of the pitfalls of interpretation involved in portraying liturgy in romantic, symbolic terms. In his later writings, Huysmans sought to convince his readers that 'God's teaching was everywhere manifest to those who had been schooled in the science of interpretation'.[24] His approach to liturgy and theology was conceived in terms of aesthetics and symbols, which were defined in terms that have a contemporary sociological use.

A symbol was to be regarded as an 'allegorical representation of a Christian principle under a tangible sign'.[25] In speaking of liturgical symbols, he suggests later that visible entities only have value in so far as they correspond to things invisible.[26]

In his unjustly neglected work, *En Route*, the account of his return to Catholicism, he makes a notable point that has a considerable bearing on this sociological approach to liturgical praxis. All his thoughts were embodied in those of the main character, Durtal, who concluded that 'the sacramental darkness of the Eucharist cannot be sounded. Moreover, if it were intelligible, it would not be divine'.[27] In this account, the inexplicable, paradoxical nature of the social is a witness to the theological qualities its use embodies and which it serves. Elements of unknowability pass to the social form of liturgy and it might be tactless to think otherwise, if the theological basis of the rite is to be understood. This is a paradoxical point one wish to pursue in this book.

Many of Huysmans' insights were derived from debate on liturgical renewal in nineteenth-century France. A link between rite and society was conceived and understood but in a way that has since been forgotten. Since the seventeenth century, efforts have been made to adjust forms of rite to engage the laity more effectively in what is being enacted by the priest. Concern with renewal has centred on re-centring the laity into the liturgical action, so that it is more of a collaborative and living exercise, a mutual engagement between priest and people with God. As concern with the pastoral effects of rite increased in the nineteenth century, so did an awareness develop of the social relationships it embodied. The social implications of rite as a transaction were apparent, but in a context where the conceptual apparatus of sociology had not been developed to arbitrate on its fine detail. This need has still not been understood.

The liturgical renewal movement in the middle of the nineteenth century was concerned to make celebrations 'live', to indicate they were not deadening mechanical ceremonies for estranging the laity, who were there to pay and pray. The need to incorporate the laity into the liturgical act developed at the same time as recognition increased of the social basis of the transaction and the relationships it embodied. In the medieval world, the laity often sat outside the rood screen that divided the choir and altar from the main part of the building, so that division between the sacred and the profane was marked in an architectural manner. Despite this rigid separation between the priests and laity, the liturgy gripped the imagination by supplying a ritual order that fed the mind, lit the eye, and marked the soul with heavenly hopes and hellish fears. Modernity and the Reformation managed to kill the stuff of sociological dreams, by leaving bare ruined rites and cold rational orders that freeze the soul.

Somehow the quest for relationships within liturgy has effected a reductionism beyond the ken of the most avid of positivists. The more explicit the social style of the mass became, as it moved from being an objective transaction where relationships were denied, to a new situation where they were to be affirmed, the more it seems to have caused visions of the holy to vanish. Relationships have become incorporated into the issue of efficacy. The meaning and purpose of these orders seem to have become obscured in the quest to relate before God. An awareness developed in the early twentieth century of the degree to which the social structure of the mass was a witness to the truth it proclaimed. The elements of rite became signified and marked to develop an awareness of what they served to effect.[28] This progression was inevitable as a consciousness developed of the social circumstances in which rite operated. Relational aspects of rite were recognised and this is not a point of dispute. The crucial question centres on their meaningful implications and this is one I wish to pursue. The nearest advocates of liturgical renewal came to a sociological understanding of their efforts was in mid-nineteenth-century France.

The social setting of rite became a matter of increasing concern in nineteenth-century pastoral thought, as the context of delivery changed in the face of urbanisation, the break-up of community, increased literacy and the effects of industrialisation. Other factors were also coming to the fore in the nineteenth century. Biblical scholarship and a sharpened awareness of the Eucharist had profound implications for the renewal of rite. The theological demand to purify forms of liturgical enactments merged with the need to make them effective instruments of evangelisation. There was an archaeological cast to much of the early scholarship that shaped the liturgical renewal movement. Sometimes this managed to make that which was alien more so, and to deaden with arcane detail what was after all a form of ritual which only fulfilled functions when it was re-presented as a living expression of the Church.[29] Medieval chants, vestments, and architectural shapes governed nineteenth-century consciousness of rite in a way that seemed to suggest an escape into medievalism. It is easy to mock the ritualism and the fetish about detail that characterised many of the concerns of these nineteenth-century liturgists. The Camden

Society, and English Catholic writers on liturgy, such as Augustus Pugin and Edmund Bishop, struggled to make a medieval mark on the Victorian world. Relics of their efforts still survive and indeed shape our liturgical expectations.[30] In the early stages of the renewal movement, there was a nascent sociological sensibility. R. W. Franklin has uncovered this in an important series of articles on Guéranger's contribution to the liturgical renewal movement in mid-nineteenth-century France. As Abbot of Solesmes, Guéranger is associated with the eradication of neo-Gallican varieties of rite, with a belief in a centralised Roman authority, with the restoration of Gregorian chant and a concern with fostering liturgical piety. In his articles, Franklin draws attention to the cultural context in which Guéranger formulated the liturgical renewal movement, which he pioneered. Franklin suggests that 'we are at the beginning and not at the end of the debate over the origins of the liturgical movement in the nineteenth century'.[31] Through liturgy, expressed as ritual, a quest for community was sought that would insulate ordinary people from the fragmenting effects of industrialisation and urbanisation. Franklin draws attention to the similarity between radical critics of society and Guéranger, who shared an unexpected common concern with defending community against the corrosive effects of individualism .[32] This rediscovery of community was a pivotal issue in the development of sociology as an academic discipline, and a sense of its loss has shaped its moral concerns about the nature of social change.[33] There is an unresolved dilemma in sociology between balancing the concerns of the individual and the community which has been unknowingly imported into the issue of liturgical praxis and which partly accounts for its current difficulties.

In a telling point that has considerable resonances in Durkheim's writings, Franklin comments on Guéranger's 'rediscovery of the liturgy as an instrument for the destruction of individualism. For the first time in centuries there was a definition of prayer as a social act'. Most importantly, the quest for community was tied into mystery rather than rationality. It involved the community in an act of reaching beyond the purely material and human to an order that transcended these elements. One might have reservations about his notion of simplicity, but would agree with Guéranger's argument that 'symbols, gestures and rituals which can be shared by all classes reinforce the community'.[34] Guéranger was concerned with authoritative rites and 'Roman unity was inescapably a part of the liturgical revival'.[35] It is noteworthy from Franklin's account of Guéranger, that community was to be found *in* rites as an emergent property of their disciplined form. This was a distinctive definition of community as the product of a ritual assembly bound into a mystery that transcended the limits of their existence. A sense of transcendence came, not through the loosening of social bonds within rite, but through them being tightened. This comes nearer to a contemporary sociological approach to ritual than one might expect. This approach did not rest on a concept of community based on deciphering local cultures and attaching forms of rite to their values. For Guéranger, liturgy was strong and found its witness *within* its ritual apparatus and not in some vague external image of credibility packaged for consumption outside. It suggests that rites achieve their sense of community less through processes of adaptation, than through the power of the instruments they use. To effect a transformation, these resources of symbol, action and text have to be believed to be credible before they can become so. Thus, in his emphasis on the monastic office, 'the rites and music were perfected so that the beauty of the services would be a witness to the power of the liturgy'. The individual was to find the true meaning of a liturgical community in the subordination of self, in a comprehension of its prayers, in what the priests *do* in the liturgy and in this way it comes to represent the whole Church at prayer.[36]

The notion of community in the liturgical renewal movement always contained an element of contrast. In its early stages, the monastic community was contrasted to that which was to be achieved in a wider secularising and modernising society. In its later phases of liturgical renewal, community became associated with simplicity and this formed a central strand of the parish movement. But the contrast this time was with the trenches, and the experience of mass being said at time of war, or in a variety of social settings such as prisons or concentration camps, where fright gathered a flock into a praying community nearer to the afterlife than seemed either desirable or natural. The fear and terror of these settings concentrated the mind wonderfully and allowed the mass to speak with a simplicity, but in a way unobtainable in suburban settings where indifference and secularism offered a more inhospitable contrast, one that drew few tensions. In this later twentieth-century stage of liturgical renewal, a sense of community arose from the unexpected settings in which the mass was said; later problems developed when efforts were made to apply similar assumptions in expected and predictable settings.[37]

There are few terms in sociology as opaque and as ill-defined as that of community. Liturgists have tried to tie an endemically vague term to a particular liturgical style in a way that excludes its competitors. Thus, it is suggested the term 'community' naturally fits an informal rite, but does not apply to a formal liturgy, such as choral evensong, or a high mass. If community is understood in its use value, then *both* liturgical forms, high and low, can be defined by the term. The concept of community is too vague to selectively differentiate between liturgical styles. Its fundamental use relates to a worshipping assembly, gathered to common purpose despite dissimilar socio-economic backgrounds. They have little in common bar a collective wish to worship and this sense of gathering is as mysterious as it is communal.

Some elements of Guéranger's concerns with community and individualism have had an ironic resurrection in an early critique of the effects of liturgical renewal on American Catholic subcultures.[38] An equally despondent sociological critique of the state of contemporary English Catholicism came later. Anthony Archer argued that the main casualties of the urge to popularise and to democratise liturgies have been the working class. Emphasis on active participation, on undertaking public roles in the new ministries draws on middle class skills of doing and joining. An overemphasis on the behavioural aspect of active participation has inserted class divisions into the liturgical community in a manner difficult to contain. This unintended ecclesiastical embourgeoisement draws cultural elements into rite in a reductionist way. It suggests that if an uncritical rhetoric of populism is used, to justify particular liturgical styles, a price is paid in effects that negate their egalitarian promise. Archer suggested that the Church became bureaucratised, as liturgies were more explicitly planned to secure the most representative communal effects.[39]

With zealous efforts to renew, in the 'spirit' of Vatican II, forms of community in the older culture of worship were dispersed, and the working class drifted away in disillusion to find other forms of communal solidarity. Failure to observe even the rules of enactment laid down in the General Instruction on the Roman Missal, has produced conditions of liturgical uncertainty in which the middle classes, used to dealing with indeterminate situations, have been the main beneficiaries. A condition of anomie effected the alienation of the working class, an ironic sociological effect of efforts to democratise rites. In a special issue of *New Blackfriars* devoted to the book, none of the sociologists who contributed, disagreed with Archer's thesis.[40]

The most creative aspect of Archer's book is the link he makes between sacralisation and egalitarianism.[41] Prior to Vatican II, rites operated in a fixed manner that imposed a ritual authority on all classes, and bound together all individuals in a community of interest, in a mystery that transcended the limits of the immediate. Older forms of rite seemed to have gripped the imagination and provided a sense of being before something worth adoring. For a generation who come to liturgy in the late eighties, folk tales about Tridentine niceties can generate a nostalgia for rites they never saw. It should be said that older rites were often performed in an exceptionally careless and unacceptably meaningless manner that few would care to see revived.

Efforts to make the structure of liturgy more apparent, to draw the people into an active participation in its enactment, worked as long as the form of the rite was encrusted in authoritative rubrics. When these were slackened in the new set of instructions for the mass after Vatican II, the issue of the cultural came to dominate both the principles of reception that affected its use, and also the manner of its enactment. The cultural apparatus of rite moved from being implicit to a more central position that governed increasingly its credibility and incredibility.

A further problem, that has not been adequately resolved, came to the fore in the liturgical movement. It managed to disguise the question of a twofold purpose of the mass that has cultural implications that admit no sociological resolution. The mass is a sacrificial act but its enactment also delivers a sacred meal. It has a vertical dimension but also a horizontal element, one that emphasises a collective engagement which requires some form of social expression. A theological emphasis on the mass as a sacred meal tends to stress elements of dispersal and reception, whereas the sacrificial strand highlights the objective participation in a singular redemptive event, variously understood as *the* liturgical act. Both formulations require reference to vertical and horizontal considerations, but in differing ways that relate to complex theological subtleties. These elements are expressed in the Eucharistic texts and have an indirect effect on the performative assumptions governing the rite and the meanings and purposes its social relationships are supposed to express and to convey.

Vatican II happened, and the abuses that occurred in the late sixties and early seventies are now part of liturgical history, forming part of a long chain of dispute and dissent that can be traced back to the Early Church. At present, we seem to be fulfilling Anton Baumstark's law of liturgical evolution and moving back to richer, more formal rites, where the sacred and the mysterious are re-emphasised.[42] Sacred aspects of the rite were always stressed in the documents on liturgy of Vatican II. Warnings against novelty and wandering from the

directives, norms and structures of the Church appeared repeatedly in
the flood of corrections issued after the Council. It was noted that
those who permitted deviations 'even if alluring, finish in creating
bewilderment in the faithful. At the same time they are killing and
rendering sterile their sacerdotal ministry'.[43] It was repeatedly emphasised that active participation was to be evaluated according to the
degree to which it led to interior assent.

The liturgical instructions of Vatican II were conceived in a climate
of imperfect sociological understanding and this partly accounts for
some of the misconceptions which followed the Council. Repeatedly,
the documents stress intelligibility, clarity, 'a noble simplicity' and the
need to make manifest the sacred properties of rite. A relational
assumption is made that the rites should be delivered in a way that was
in the people's grasp. A theory of reception was assumed, that having
comprehended, the people would assent and believe more deeply. A
functional notion was implicit in some of the directives that was
unambiguous regarding the uncomplicated delivery of sacraments.
These were defined as symbols

> of a sacred reality and the visible form of an invisible grace.
> Consequently the more intelligible the signs by which it is cele-
> brated and worshipped, the more firmly and effectively it will enter
> into the minds and lives of the faithful.[44]

The instruction makes an odd sociological argument. Symbols have
uses to the degree to which they are indeterminate and opaque. To
make them transparent is a misnomer, for they proclaim that which
transcends the conditions under which clarity through intervention is
possible. They embody that which is unavailable to rational manipulation. Furthermore, there is no evidence to indicate that simple rites
convey a sense of mystery. If a mystery is understood, it is misunderstood, for by its nature it pertains to that which is unavailable to
understanding. An element of mystery has to be bound into the social
means that witness to its presence. This point was understood by Odo
Casel, one of the most influential writers on liturgy in the twentieth
century.

Casel has been criticised for his stress on cultic forms of worship and
his deference to ritual modes common in classical civilisation. If he had
been writing today, his material would have been anthropological and
his conclusions regarding the mysterious nature of liturgy would have
been unexceptional. He argued that rationality and mystery did not go
well together. He pointed to a fundamental confusion that has come to

haunt the quest for liturgical renewal: the assumption that changes in outward forms of worship will automatically effect inner spiritual effects. The truth of rite does not lie in its shell, but in its kernel. Thus, he argued that it was 'dangerous to seek first for the outward form and then to build the mind upon it'.[45] He was equally clear that the renewal movement was too concerned with communal forms of worship, with getting people closer to altars. By confusing the husk with the grain, it distracted attention from the mystery represented in the rite. It was the implicit dimensions of rite that were of crucial importance and not their exterior elements. Rites had to carry an image that would mobilise. Thus he suggested that 'the vision the mystery gives awakens our longing for the whole of vision, and at the same time is the pledge of this vision'.[46]

Visions of the holy embody ambiguous elements, some sacralising but some profaning. The beauty embodied in ritual transactions, that proffers visions of the mysterious, carries risks of spiritual and social deception. Because richly allegorical rites resonate with the greatest risks of being misleading, of seducing its participants into a state of narcissism, that subtracts from what ought to be rendered to God alone, their forms are often treated with deepest suspicion. It is feared that they will cultivate aesthetic rather than spiritual sensibilities. Furthermore, they involve an element of concealment in their enactment, a concern with covering and masquerading that seems in excess of what is required for decent, orderly worship. They disguise that which ought to be revealed. Yet mysteries have their functions, as Casel noted:

> many of the difficulties of the liturgical renewal would disappear with a careful observance of the ancient notion of hierarchy. Is it not wisdom on the church's part to have put the *veil* of a ritual language over the liturgy, precisely because the mystery is not to stand in the fierce light of every day? Is it necessary to turn all texts into the vernacular, make every detail of every rite visible? Does not this take away something irreplaceable, the glow of veneration which means more to the people than understanding every detail? The obviously praiseworthy intention of bringing people back to active participation in the liturgy should not fall into the democratic heresy.[47]

Social assumptions regarding what the rite produces of the holy are implicit in the notion of reverence, of veiling and marking a distance. Some defensive ploys and practices are required to maintain a tactful social reticence towards that which comes so indirectly. This point forms a central concern of this account of liturgical re-presentations. I wish to argue that a dialectic operates between the implicit and the explicit which is fundamental to understanding liturgical praxis. It is the management of this tension between the manifest and the hidden that plays a significant and distinctive part in the regulation of rite. A degree of fear, awe, reverence, and interest in the four last things gives velocity and weight to what is reproduced. It supplies an intensity, a felt sense of immediacy that marks the enactment of rite as a prelude for higher matters. There are signs of an emphasis on re-sacralisation in the discussions surrounding the Extraordinary Synod in 1985. A significant contribution to this effort to give weight to liturgical forms has come from the German theologian Joseph Ratzinger, who also is the Cardinal Prefect of the Sacred Congregation for the Doctrine of the Faith.

Ratzinger's comments on the liturgy are important. He suggests that debate would need to be re-started on the nature of the Conciliar reforms, the adequacy of the *Rituale* and the need to secure sacred and holy effects in liturgical praxis. Many of his comments reflect a German tradition, drawing especially from Romano Guardini and Hans Urs von Balthasar, both of whom underwrite this sociological approach to rite. Ratzinger argues that

> the liturgy is not a show, a spectacle, requiring brilliant producers and talented actors. The life of the liturgy does not consist in 'pleasant' surprises and attractive 'ideas' but in solemn repetitions. It cannot be an expression of what is current and transitory, for it expresses the mystery of the Holy. Many people have felt and said that liturgy must be 'made' by the whole community if it is really to belong to them. Such an attitude has led to the 'success' of the liturgy being measured by its effects at the level of spectacle and entertainment. It is to lose sight of what is *distinctive* to the liturgy, which does not come from what *we do* but from the fact that something is *taking place* here that all of us together cannot 'make'.

Later he goes on to add that the Council thought of liturgy in terms of *actio*, while at the same time guaranteeing active participation. Since the Council there has been a fatal narrowing of perspective, so that the latter has come to mean external activities of singing, speaking and shaking hands. Implicit elements also bear on active participation, and the need for silence and stillness can be often neglected.[48] These elements have slipped out of notice in efforts to humanise rites.[49]

In an assessment of the Extraordinary Synod, 1985, the American theologian Avery Dulles noted that its central question was not about the rejection of Vatican II, but how to interpret it and to find a proper hermeneutics of unity.[50] The need to fill relationships once more with a distinctively religious witness led the Synod to re-emphasise the mysterious and to affirm the need for a return to the sacred. This re-weighting of the priorities of Vatican II, to stress the mysterium arose from post-conciliar experiences in the German Church, where dangers of secularisation and the flight of young people into religious sects were apparent. Within the French and German Catholic Churches, this quest for spiritual renewal is evident in various religious movements. Most importantly, the figures for contemplative orders, with a definite way of life and distinctive habits, are showing a marked increase in the numbers of young men and women entering.[51] The Extraordinary Synod, 1985, noted a 'return to the holy' combined with 'a thirst for transcendence'. It seemed to the German Bishops that a profound danger existed of the Church mirroring secular values.[52] This effort to mark a limit, to recover a sense of the sacred, was related to a fundamental question, barely formulated and scarcely understood: how is the holy to be expressed in a way that accords with contemporary cultural expectations?

It might seem as if the sociological hour has come, when theologians – at last – address central questions that draw on the strengths of the discipline. Unfortunately, sociology is caught in its own crisis over the nature of culture and modernity. If the Vatican II documents bore the stamp of innocence in their approach to modernity and culture, it cannot be said that the sociology of the time thought otherwise. Modernity was linked to progress. Culture was a splendid umbrella term that endorsed the need for comparisons between the exotic and the peculiar, the natural and the unnatural and the patterned and the disordered in societies near and far. Edward Tylor's definition of culture was largely accepted with some modifications. Culture was 'that complex whole which includes knowledge, belief, art, morals, law, custom, and any other capabilities and habits acquired by man as a member of society'.[53] For a number of complex reasons, the issue of culture moved from a question of description and classification that dominated its scientific use up to the late sixties to a more reflective metaphysical concern with belief and meaning. The humanisation of Marxism, and the revolt against technocracy in this period, generated a peculiar combination of idealism and pessimism that led to a re-consideration of the nature of culture within modern advanced industrialised society. Belief and relativism flooded into questions of ideology. Margaret Archer is correct to argue that the issue of culture has been neglected in sociological theory.[54] It is not the first time that society has caught sociology by surprise. Culture has become lodged in issues of disenchantment. Sociology, being the prophet of progress and modernity, seems like a symptom of the crisis it strives to resolve. Stress on patterned procedures of negotiation are insufficient in a post-modernist period where meaning and purpose have come to the fore. Earlier positivist definitions of culture are now deficient. Friedrich Tenbruck has argued that the issue of culture requires an adjective if it is to be of sociological use. The term 'representative' relates to beliefs that are married to social actions where ultimate values matter.[55] The question I wish to attend in this study involves a stress on similar words, separated by a hyphen, that convey differing meanings. 'Re-presentation' involves the notion of meanings and beliefs being displayed that mirror higher values; 'representations' relate to the social means through which these are made manifest. There is an ambiguity between the two terms which are mutually implicated in liturgical operations, whose understanding and interpretation bear an intrinsic sociological interest.

3   Sociological Understandings of Liturgy: Some Aspects

> Hast thou with him spread out the sky,
> which is strong, and as a molten looking glass?
> Teach us what we shall say unto him ; for
> we cannot order our speech by reason of darkness.
>
> (Job 37: 18–19)

It cannot be said that liturgies operate at the centre of modern consciousness. To the secular mind, these Christian rites belong to a pre-modern age, relics of past anxieties which technology and modernity have assuaged. Attitudes to liturgical operations relate to wider questions of the value of religious belief in a secular society, where consumerism and instant satisfaction help to keep the flock from the Church door – save at weddings and funerals. Yet, even in a post-Christian society, these religious rituals embody a witness to past cultural traditions not easily dismissed. Aspects of their tradition still attract. Cathedrals draw millions of tourists. It would be odd not to find something appealing about Church music. Even the most devout atheist might be moved by a Bach cantata.

Liturgies relate ambiguously to modern culture: they seem to be in the centre of it, but standing without. In one sense, they present themselves as superficial enactments for the dim in mind, but in another sense, they make highly sophisticated demands on the observer to unpack a remarkably condensed amount of social and cultural material from a ritual that inspires as much as it perplexes.

The opaque and ambiguous wrappings of rite bear a multitude of readings and a plurality of functions. Liturgies operate as rites of passage, acts of commemoration available at differing levels of comprehension to believer and non-believer alike. On sundry civil and secular occasions, these rites can make an exceptional and unexpected mark on those gathered to worship. It is difficult to know what makes one rite more special than another. For the believer, each rite is a stage in a sacred cycle that marks a journey in an annual rotation through the events surrounding the birth and death of Christ.

Colours of vestments and choice of hymns can indicate to the practised eye the point on the sacred clock. The choirstalls, the sanctuary furniture, the transepts and crossing, the windows and arches, convey an architectural sense of the holy that enhances the social performance of rite. These provide a visual setting for the staging of a sacred play that routinely re-presents and realises a mystery. Repetition provides a basis for re-inspection and routine can expose what was inadequately understood before. Liturgies can only present their obvious facets. Their unobvious aspects are to be found only by those who can bracket an estranging suspicion, so that understandings can emerge from what is concealed or is unapparent in the liturgical act. This task of interpreting liturgies involves a wager with the indeterminate, where sociological insight and faith make a precarious mixture difficult to unravel. Faith is required to enter the game; sociology helps to understand some of its permutations. Liturgies present certain quandaries to the sociological mind about how far one should go to understand fully the significance of what is seen. It is one thing to see to understand; it is another to believe to know what was understood. The intangible small ingredients of rite can bring all its aspects into focus.

After his return to Catholicism, J.-K. Huysmans wrote a novel, based on Chartres, called *The Cathedral*, the principal aim of which was to educate and to enhance an understanding of liturgy, Church architecture and symbolism. The main character, Durtal, was the fictitious vehicle for his reflections. Attending mass in a tiny transept in the crypt, he came to understand the beauty and fullness of meaning of the rite. This was learnt through noticing the witness of the choirboy who served the elderly priest. The attention and respect of the boy allowed the meaning of the rite to be revealed anew. He grasped 'truly for the first time what innocent childhood meant – the little sinless soul, purely white'. Somehow at Chartres, the means had been found of 'moulding souls and transforming ordinary boys on their admission to the sanctuary into exquisite angels'.[1] This unexpected capacity of the choirboy to generate awe and emulation led Durtal, later, to ask the Abbé connected to the Cathedral how such reverence came to be instilled. Seeing was not enough. An important critic of French impressionism, Huysmans wanted to understand how that innocence which he had observed in the act had come to be represented. To some extent, he asked the wrong question. The Abbé indicated that the assiduous practice of religion involves a gamble which resulted either in hypocrisy or the purification of the soul to produce 'little priestlings' with 'eyes like clear glass, undimmed by the haze of a single sin', The Cathedral choirboys, the Abbé claimed, were 'dedicated to the priesthood from the time when they can first understand, they learn quite naturally to lead a spiritual life from their constant intimacy with the services'.[2] One can elect to accept Huysmans' account or not. In one sense it seems exaggerated, an odd piece of pious hyperbole, but on the other hand, it could be treated as a sensitive insight from an unexpected source.

Huysmans attributed his conversion to Catholicism to a love of art and a hatred of existence. His life reflected a peculiar movement from a jaundiced experience and interest in decadence to a holy wish to locate and to affirm innocence. He wrote that it was 'through a glimpse of the supernatural of evil that I first obtained insight into the supernatural of good'.[3] This echoes a comment of Friedrich von Hugel that '. . . the highest realities and deepest responses are experienced by us within, or in contact with, the lower and the lowliest'.[4] There is a particular sense of paradox and an awareness of a dualism in modern life in Huysmans that reflects the influence of Charles Baudelaire, who also suffered from a spiritual sickness that led him back to Catholicism.[5]

Poise and an extension of impression management to its limits, are crucial elements in Baudelaire, who was the first to give modernity its modern meaning and expression. His concerns also arise later in Simmel, of presenting the modern interpreter with the task of capturing what is fleeting in the fashion and flux of cosmopolitan life. This effort to find the eternal in the transitory involved an attention to detail, and an awareness of its imaginative potential. The choirboy at Chartres was not the first child to present a theological conundrum to the wise.

In philosophy and literature, the child is often represented as having the capacity to see that which sophistication veils. He sees anew that which has become obscured in the habit of gazing at the familiar. Baudelaire gives an example of the convalescent striving to recollect particular aspects of a former life with the aim of returning to what was lost in illness. This involves an effort to view anew, like the child who 'is possessed in the highest degree of the faculty of keenly interesting himself in things, be they apparently of the most trivial'. He adds 'the child sees everything in a state of newness; he is always *drunk*'. So 'genius is nothing more or less than *childhood recovered* at will' and married to the creative power of the adult.[6] The child seems to have a proximity to the essence of things, to the Divine or to nature. His innocence is believed to give him a directness of comprehension that becomes cluttered, confused and unclear in the experienced world of the adult.

There is perhaps a rather Catholic aspect to this sociological effort to understand. It reflects a similar stress on the child being the father of the man in the writings of Charles Péguy. Again, the child is placed close to genius in his ability to discern and to express with an innocent eye visions denied to the experienced. Darkness and the night are preludes of what is beyond time, of seeking with renewed hope the light of another day. Thus, 'man must each night again become a child, and each night the child draws from the night his strength for the day'.[7] Péguy's poem on innocence and experience presents an image of the sleeping child, praying in a drowsy incompetence, and drifting off into temporary rest to play with the angels.[8] Like Huysmans, the aesthetic was rooted in Péguy's approach to religion. As von Balthasar notes, 'he takes no account of any kind of art other than a religious one, an art of worship. Cathedrals are for him "the prayer of fleshly people, a glory, almost an impossibility, a miracle of prayer"' and these come to be 'embodiments of adoration'.[9] This notion of the child as genius in his relationship to the aesthetic appears also in the writings of Friedrich von Schiller.[10]

The Cathedral and the child merge in the role of the choirboy. In this study, he is the child of the rite, seeing and singing with an innocence that reveals the deepest religious meanings in a fresh manner. Huysmans re-saw through the innocence of the choirboy the familiar structure in the mass in a new way that gave him an understanding he had never known before. The choirboy seems to see heavenly things in a sight denied to the experienced. Their failure of sight points to an issue which will be raised later in the hermeneutic task of understanding embodied in Paul Ricouer's notion of a second naïveté. The key to understanding liturgy lies in its capacity to repeat and to re-present that which has a capacity to be understood anew. It requires a special hermeneutics to grasp this point.

A difficulty is going to arise repeatedly in this study over the difference between a theological and a sociological insight into the basis of liturgy. Both are concerned with realising a clarity of understanding, with grasping the significance of a religious transaction. The problem is not over which has priority in interpretative accounts; the question is how far do sociological understandings have to go to fully grasp the holy essence of the rite? Understanding liturgy is clearly a theological issue; it is unclear what it means to be understood as a sociological issue. Does one accept Flannery

O'Connor's point, as in her case, that belief is 'the engine that makes perception operate'?[11] This would suggest that without belief, one has no way of penetrating below the surface of what is seen in liturgical enactments, to find the deeper meanings that give motion to what is observed. Catholic belief can give sight to the sociologically blind.[12] How can one convey an understanding to those who do not believe in the subject matter to be understood in this account?

O'Connor offers some insights that have a bearing on this sociological problem. As a Catholic in South Georgia, she wrote two memorable novels and a number of short stories, all characterised by a pithy black wit, and a concern with the inexplicable workings of grace, outside sacraments, on the distorted minds of the grotesque.[13] Her concern with the unexpected and the misleading suggest similarities with Erving Goffman, that peculiar American sociologist. Both find a deepness of meaning on the margins of society and the misleading effects of the wary on the unwary. They share a common interest in revealing the precarious nature of manners. There was a theological twist to her vision apparent in her comment that

> the fiction writer presents mystery through manners, grace through nature, but when he finishes there always has to be left over that sense of Mystery which cannot be accounted for by any human formula.[14]

Through exaggeration and distortion, she sought to affirm the mysterious and awesome qualities of Catholicism. For her, the 'prophet is a realist of distances' and this generates a realism 'which does not hesitate to distort appearances in order to show a hidden truth'.[15] Sociological effort to understand liturgy also distorts appearances in its graceless search for a hidden truth it cannot reveal nor can it fully understand. But this theological disadvantage has certain advantages. As O'Connor observes 'the nature of grace can be made plain only by describing its absence'.[16] The graceless nature of sociological understanding allows a peculiar image of liturgy to emerge. To non-Catholics, it is a product of the domestic dilemmas of the discipline, without reference to a grace they cannot share; to Catholics, it speaks of what could be extended into issues of grace. This study is an ambiguous account of a rite riddled with ambiguities.

In view of the dangers regarding a prescriptive approach to liturgy and the degree to which its indeterminate and uncheckable effects admit almost any set of sociological assumptions about how it ought to work, the use of Weber's 'ideal type' might seem ironical. His term refers to a conceptual abstraction, where salient aspects of society are exaggerated to clarify a social world too complex to grasp. It is an arbitrary means of establishing a pure form of analysis and has been used to handle concepts such as bureaucracy, religion, and forms of authority, to name a few areas of application. An 'ideal type' offers a means of connecting elements that lie disconnected in social life. It is a powerful comparative tool for enhancing understandings and for going below the surface of social life.[17] In this analysis, it is used in a number of settings, covering forms of rites, liturgical roles, and situations. Stress is laid on inconsistencies that arise in liturgical praxis, and the means for their resolution, so that attention is directed away from the consistencies that might otherwise provide a 'reasonable' sociological account of the operations of rite. A second advantage of relying on 'ideal types' is that it shelves the problem of locating a typical liturgy upon which to base the analysis. In the Anglican Church, since the Alternative Service Book, 1980, there have been endless permutations of rite, reflecting a bewildering range of styles and varieties of liturgy, High and Low, with little control exercised over their social shape, bar custom, tradition and accommodation to the various vested interests of the Cathedral or parish.[18] Fortunately, the position in Catholic liturgy, which is the main focus of the book, is more clearcut, and rites operate with permutations over a far narrower field.

Because the study of liturgy has been so marginalised within sociology of religion and the mainstream of the discipline, it lies outside debates on methodology and the interpretation of categories of meaning. Those few sociologists who do comment on liturgy have noted how surprising is its neglect in sociology of religion.[19] There are no methodological compass points to use in a sociological exploration of liturgical praxis. Before proceeding to the terms of reference of the study, some of the methodological options that could be used to understand liturgy in sociological terms need to be considered.

Survey and observer participation are two likely methodological options for studying liturgy. Each has drawbacks. There are few subtle surveys of liturgy, its enactment and reception. Bryant produced an interesting and rare account of the implementation of liturgical change in the Church of England. Using semi-structured interviews, he mapped out a complex picture of the liturgical life of a parish Church, and exposed a critical gap between the expectations of liturgists and the unofficial understandings of the laity.[20] A similar discrepancy also emerged in an earlier study in 1963 by Schreuder of attitudes to liturgy in a German suburban parish. He found that the greatest bulwark of church attendance was for utilitarian reasons that expressed individual needs. Many came to find a space in which to re-establish their spiritual equilibrium. The calmness of the rite gave a context in which they could adjust the proportions of a life often confused. Remarkably few formulated their answers in terms of the communal dimensions of rite, or saw it as an instrument for generating group solidarity.[21]

Admittedly, that study was undertaken before liturgy was reformed to stress these points in Vatican II. Nevertheless, the findings are striking, suggesting as they do that the laity, even in Germany, were not thinking in the terminology of liturgists before the Council and came to rites with a wholly different set of assumptions about their social and religious use and interpretation. This might suggest that the reforms proceeded on an illusion, where liturgists attributed to the laity thoughts and attitudes for which there was no sociological basis, and that the laity, who were never consulted, responded in obedience to what they conceived to be Church teaching on how liturgical matters ought to proceed.

Survey methods are unlikely to resolve problems of typicality; if anything, they are likely to exacerbate them. Picking out types of rite for the purposes of stratifying the sample, to make it more representa-tive of the current state of liturgy, is likely to be an arbitrary exercise, given the number of options available in so many settings. Such a study would be very time consuming to achieve a proper depth of analysis. A very small sample of respondents could be interviewed in the case of each liturgical style. This would place a premium on the views of an articulate and perhaps middle-class section of a congre-gation, who might be unrepresentative of the worshipping assembly as a whole. A further problem is that of a methodological individualism arising. This tends to stress the perceptions of particular members of a congregation and pays little attention to the collective experience of worship felt as a group in the process and enactment of rite. Intangible senses of the moment of felt contact with the holy, are difficult to capture through survey methods.

Observer participation also has drawbacks. Being an anonymous member of a congregation will disclose oddly little about how rites achieve their desired effects. A parish study could yield much information about how liturgy is enacted, the planning that goes into its production and the reception of its felt effects. This would be a wider study and would pursue a separate set of questions of which liturgy would be a part. Clearly rites generate affiliations by their style.

Each liturgical style carries a methodological price. A formal rite, with choir and priests, as in a high mass, bears an uninterruptable quality that unfolds in a certainty of manner that defies sociological intervention. If the social seems to disappear in formal rites, leaving the sociologist high and dry, informal assemblies present the opposite problem of potential engulfment where barriers disappear. These evangelical and charismatic rites are believed to be spirit led in a way that allows 'free verbal praise' to break forth, freed from the restraints of ceremony and tradition. Non-participation would become evident, when hands are raised, leaving the sociologist isolated, frigid and rigid, like Lot's wife, gripping the clipboard, the professional's fig leaf, at such high-spirited assemblies. The non-witness of the sociologist might subtract from the sense of holy solidarity found.

Small group assemblies might be more accessible and fit this method better. Unfortunately, this would lead to a bias towards particular styles of rite, such as those of the Charismatics or Pentecostalists. It is of course accepted that every sociological study of liturgy will express a bias, including this one, and each method will seek a form of rite that most matches its strengths. Small groups, usually fifteen or so, are often associated with the house group movement. These forms of worship are high on witness and low on ceremony. There is a pliability to their 'plausibility structures' and these often express the inclinations and compromises of a particular group who have journeyed thus far, before sociological inspection. This makes their liturgical order, in so far as they have one, a matter of opinion, one negotiated in charity. The Spirit that can fill these events, makes these assemblies more private and individual in style than might seem desirable for a sociologist shopping around for the 'typical' Christian rite. There is a further problem of observer contamination. The sociologist cannot sit uninvolved, radiating a professional detachment in a group founded to attach the unattached. Furthermore, as these groups experiment, and adjust the furniture to gain a better view of God, social elements tend to intrude.[22] A sociologist present at such an assembly might be asked for a view and be expected to intervene with comments on small group dynamics. Informal rites exult in a theology of proximity that might entrap the wary sociologist and preclude him escaping to get an analytical distance. Similar problems arise in sociology of medicine, in studies of attitudes to health and illness.[23]

Sociological approaches to rite have to move in more general terms. As Peter Fink noted, the central problem in liturgical theology is one of credibility, and its restoration. In a point that has never been adequately pursued, he notes that this involves a 'shift from a metaphysical to a phenomenological mode of reflection'.[24] Although this study *does* have a prejudice in favour of a particular style of rite, it is suggested that it is one that carries the greatest weight of sociological implication. Formal, ceremonial styles of liturgy are more accessible to sociological scrutiny.

The manifold theological, aesthetic and philosophical complications attached to liturgy make its sociological study unusually difficult. Liturgy is a crossroads for many disciplines, and sociology is a very late arrival at the scene. Any sociological account, however sympathetic, will seem modest and marginal to those most involved in liturgical productions. Drawing from an essay of Wilhelm Baldamus, Robin Williams makes a point that applies very much to this study. He suggests that 'sociological discoveries are not then about the anticipated or unanticipated discovery of previously unknown facts; they are much more about the attribution of different significances to what is already known'.[25] The strength of a sociological contribution is that it is alien, unfamiliar and clumsy in what it selects, but its callow gaze carries an accidental quality of drawing attention to neglected facets and hidden aspects of rite, that can enhance an understanding and appreciation of its endless social use. Any sociological study of rite might start at some unexpected points and yield some perplexing conclusions, but it has to operate on the assumption that it can merely begin a question which theology has to take forward further into its disciplinary remit, if a fullness of understanding is to be realised. A fingerprint in the study is the use of antinomies to draw out polar opposites that pose dilemmas for liturgical actors engaged in their use. It is through an interpretation of these antinomies, as they emerge in liturgical praxis, that an understanding of the social basis of the representation of rite can be discerned.

For instance, innocence and experience have an antinomial quality that poses dilemmas in interpretation that require careful negotiation. Interest in innocence is related to a misfortune of the knowing of evil, a point I will discuss later. It is easy to regard an interest in evil as a figment of the imagination of Christian Fundamentalist sects seeking to drum up trade through the marketing of warnings about spiritual dangers. Yet Huysmans flirted with Satanism, and Baudelaire displayed a keen awareness of external evil forces in his poetry.[26] Paul Ricoeur has written on the nature of evil and draws attention to the need to confront it in philosophical terms.[27] The deadening effects of the Enlightenment have produced a moral wasteland, where distinctions between good and evil have become blurred, and in the lull, it would seem, a fascination with Satanism has crept in, that is profoundly worrying. Various Satanic sects exist, doubtless small in number, which have attracted a sensational and disproportionate interest in the mass media. The market for the occult and the superstitious is well fed in the steady flow of horror films. Equally, contemporary anthropology has developed a widespread interest in magic and spells and has given a credible witness to their unexpected persistence in a post-Enlightenment era. These elements seem part of a cultural movement that is giving rise to a reluctant interest in the existence of evil by the main Christian Churches.[28] Ironically, renewed interest in these dangerous fringes have exposed an odd neglect of their more virtuous counterparts, the bearers of heavenly innocence: angels. Many who profess a lurking fascination with demons, would deny to the hilt a belief in angels. If this study is geared to understanding liturgical 'success', it is partly concerned with the social means through which virtue is secured in public assemblies. It is an account of liturgical manners geared to preserve virtue, to secure 'success' and to realise qualities of the angelic. In philosophical circles we all seem to be after virtue; this is a study of how to stand before it.

There are obvious sociological debts in this work. The emphasis on form or frame of the rite owes much to Simmel and Goffman, as does the concern with managing appearances in habiliments of virtue. The notion of threshold, of marking out the excess of meaning in the social betrays debts to Ricoeur, to Turner's notion of the liminal, and to Rudolf Otto's approach to the numinous. The strain of ambiguity throughout the work points to a dualism that has echoes in Durkheim. The question of deception relates to the most incisive interpretation of liturgy available in the two essays of Roy Rappaport. The dark strands of liturgical performance, its capacity to lie and to mislead, are given the fullest and gloomiest of sociological readings. The issue of ambiguity is most manifest in the question of silence, which ranges from an inner sensibility, to that which shapes social forms, to a metaphysical wager that wobbles between nihilism and holiness, depending on the elective affinities of the actor with disbelief or belief. The stress on paradox, on irresolvable ambiguities and incomplete social elements in rite present sociology as an impaired witness to the passage of rite into holiness. The limits of interpretative account it encounters mark an unexpected witness to the limitless basis of rite. The ambiguous qualities of rite, a deeper sociological scrutiny reveals, suggest some necessary theological connection, one where

failure, absence and incompleteness are redeemed, filled and completed. The trajectory of this sociological analysis of liturgical performance is aimed into an apophatic theology, one where limits are given
a redemptive limitlessness and where darkness is lightened. An
apophatic theology exults in the contradictions sociological analysis
throws up, and can contain that which it analytically cannot, with ease.
The concern of this book is with deciphering rather than with
description, understanding rather than with explanation, and with
balancing opposing elements of revelation and concealment in a way
that the social resources of rite can preserve an opening to the holy.

If sociology is to make a fruitful link with hermeneutics, endless
analysis will end up in conversational circles. At some point a definite
contact with a particular object will have be made if a focus is to be
found for an effective hermeneutic contribution to sociological understanding. Too often, philosophical movements that affect theological
and sociological thought are addressed to social events safely sealed in
a heuristic account, well removed from the untidiness and infelicities a
study of praxis would yield, when dealing with the realisation of a
particular event. When questions are so grounded in an issue of social
praxis and are given an analytical focus, perplexing and opaque
insights are likely to emerge that require a subtle reading to decipher
their nature.

Debates on rationality and relativism, which emerged over the status
of rational and non-rational actions in primitive societies, operate at a
safe analytical distance from equivalent transactions, equally improbable, but 'successful', which occur routinely in advanced industrialised
societies. If hermeneutics is to fulfil its promise, it will have to be
applied to something nearer home. Its familiar terrain of deciphering
and reading texts needs to be given a wider sociological application.
Elements of play, aesthetics, symbols and games lie in aspects of Hans-
Georg Gadamer's *Truth and Method* that suggest possible, but
unfocused, sociological uses. A more definite effort to connect
hermeneutics to sociology appears in an influential essay by Paul
Ricoeur, where action is considered as a form of text.[29] This book
attempts to advance his arguments into a definite object of inquiry:
understanding the social basis of the capacity of liturgies to inexhaustibly re-present the holy. Because liturgies combine text, action and
symbol in a focused form or frame, where the social is given a definite
mark, their study offers much fruit for sociological thought.

The social elements that make up liturgical events constitute a form
to refract heavenly images, to witness, in seen means, ends that are

unseen. The choirstalls, the sanctuary, the surplices and albs of the choir, priests and servers remind in symbols of the heavenly, elements that can be only imagined. Central to the argument of this book is that forms of rite bear revelations of beauty and holiness that refract the glory of God through playful means. This approach links Gadamer to the Swiss theologian von Balthasar. There are two theological reference points in this argument: that the form of the rite is a sacramental or means of grace in itself; and the apophatic theology of the Pseudo-Dionysius. The latter argument will be pursued in Chapter 9. I wish to consider the former, briefly at this juncture.

A Catholic mass is the sacrament of the Eucharist that draws its power from the redemptive effects of Christ's death and resurrection. It is premised on the notion of His Incarnation, that is, of God taking human flesh and being fully man. Visual aids to understanding this mystery are an essential part of Christian tradition. Paintings represent an image of Christ, providing a visual doorway into the invisible. These cues to the holy can also be instruments of grace. Besides sacraments, channels of grace instituted by Christ, the Church also has sacramentals. These are means of grace instituted by the Church and are ancillary sets of signs added to the seven sacraments. They refer to rites or forms of blessings to cover human needs not fully met in the sacraments, which they complement. They are often rites of blessings, of objects, or admission to various offices of the Church, such as that of a Benedictine Oblate, or the consecration of a virgin.[30] Sacraments achieve their efficacy as long as there is no resistance on the part of the recipient. But sacramentals are incentives to further grace, and their efficacy varies in proportion to the participation of the recipient in a life of grace. [31] They are not so much objective conferrals of grace, as in the sacraments, as incentives to invest further in the elements attached to them. This means grace is realised through use on the part of an actor who elects to receive and to find more. Since Vatican II, there has been a renewed emphasis on the presence of Christ within the body of the Church, and also in assemblies of the faithful gathered to seeking and finding Him in worship.[32]

Because sacramentals are part of the sign language of liturgy, denoting efforts to increase and to perpetuate the sanctifying effects of sacraments, they work through means that pre-suppose some understanding, some response to what is manifested. There is some doubt as to whether the forms or ceremonies that surround the delivery of sacraments are sacramentals.[33] In happier days when indulgences were attached to aspects of the ceremonial, the question was more clear-cut. Admitting that the form of rite is itself an instrument of grace has some significant sociological implications. It means that when the form of rite is given a sacramental status, elements on the margin take on qualities of grace where all actions, however trivial, have a singular and possibly blessed effect. They refer to details that count in small part in the economy of salvation of the liturgical actor. This attention to the slight bears on a saying of Christ that 'he that is faithful in that which is least is faithful also in much' (Luke 16.10).

Liturgical actors, engaged in sanctuary play with the holy, attempt to realise an image in a form where grace is conveyed in a way that can be understood in similar terms to the theological arguments governing icons. In sociology, icons refer to elements connected by resemblance, such as blood and red wine.[34] The sacramental use and reverence attached to icons in Christianity is very much associated with the Greek and Russian Church, where they are deeply venerated. These are images or likenesses of God that serve as a mirror on heaven. They operate as a frame that gives a narrow entry to greater things. These visual aids are believed to be channels of grace, eliciting deep reverence, and signifying the response of God to the petitions of his people.[35] Although icons are venerated in terms of what they represent, the making of an image has given rise to schism and dispute. The 'iconoclastic controversy' of the seventh and eighth centuries was partly resolved in the seventh Council of Nicaea in 787. The destruction of these idols or images led to the split between the Western and Orthodox Churches. The theological difficulty with icons is not whether they channel grace, but that they mark a presumption of making an image of the unseen and the Divine that could be deemed idolatrous. The invisible nature of God seems to preclude the presumption of making an image of Him. There is an added danger that the object itself could become the focus for adoration, and not for what it is believed to signify. Man might be made in the image and likeness of God, but he is hardly to construct his maker in like manner. Forming an image of the invisible God seems a contradiction in terms, yet in the light of the incarnation, a tangible form of God appeared as man, whose coming was with the express purpose of supplying a basis of imitation. There is an unexpected account of the theological dilemma this poses in a short story by Flannery O'Connor called 'Parker's Back'.

In a crumbled marriage, Parker decides to have the only spare untattooed part of his body, his back, engraved with an image of Christ to assuage the ire of his devout wife. Reluctant to view the finished image, Parker is propelled by the artist between two mirrors, and is frightened at what he sees. As he moved away 'the eyes in the reflected face continued to look at him – still, straight, all-demanding, enclosed in silence'.[36] When he reveals the image to his wife, she yells 'he don't *look* . . . He's a spirit. No man shall see his face'. At Parker's claim that it's just a picture, she ejects him from the house as an idolator. [37]

Liturgical forms operate in the manner of icons, by opening up a sense of presence of the Divine through social actions that are believed and intended to be endowed with holy purpose. These ritual events are sacred occasions that have to be handled in a holy and becoming manner. They mirror that which is unseen, but also operate to reveal some of its properties in a manner that has to be seen to be believed. Such a vital theological task cannot be handled lightly. In the Orthodox tradition of Christianity, and also in Judaism, great stress is laid on the need for worthiness on the part of the painter or scribe, either in making the image or in copying the Word of God. Fasting, prayer and petition are demanded to make the act of imitation worthy and to preclude any sense of presumption in making a visible mark of that which lies in the invisible.

A tradition governs what can be painted in an icon, if authenticity is to be secured. Only Christ can appear, or the angels and saints. Strict rules govern artistic style, colours and layout used. These give icons an expected, but easily identifiable form. Although this renders these holy pictures profoundly unoriginal, it facilitates an awesome originality that seems inexhaustible. Because icons are so stylised and restricted in what can be inscribed, this narrowing is believed to supply for believers a concentrated window on the infinite. By precluding a number of expected artistic options, the icon manages to include all who gaze in faith. The icon operates as a stereotype that frees.

A similar approach to the use of liturgical form is assumed in this work: that the social has to be reverenced and used with great care in acts of worship; that a selectivity and narrowing of the shape of rite in a stylised, unoriginal and identifiable manner facilitates access to the holy; and that a tactful restraint on the ritual apparatus allows the transcendent to percolate through. Rites work best when they are repetitive, formalised and a total control is exercised over the social resources used. It is suggested that these rituals require a predictable cast if their unpredictable effects are to be secured.

The notion of an icon reveals a dilemma, a sort of theological Catch 22, that forms a crucial strand in the book. To make an image of

God could be idolatrous, a manifestation of what is not yet to be revealed or seen face to face; but not to make such a picture could deny the incarnational qualities of God-made man, in a form to be imitated. To act is to presume, to risk constraining God, or worse to manufacture properties of the Divine. Not to act is to violate an imperative to do in remembrance, to use talents and gifts that secure faith in understanding. The ambiguous properties of acting or not acting within theology spill over into the social actions involved in worship. They require regulation to preclude undesirable and heretical consequences, if fully thought through in theological terms. The social act in liturgy presents an inescapable dilemma which the actor has to confront and to resolve. Handling liturgical instruments that are ambiguous in social and religious terms requires great care in enactment and performance, lest that which is supposed to edify deceives or misleads. Because the social resources of rite are indeterminate in their effects the actor can get away with liturgical murder. This capacity to edify or to disedify generates a sociological issue.

Productive ambiguities facilitate access to meanings best understood in an opaque and open sense. Unproductive ambiguities hinder this task and lead to uncertainties that close off the need to pursue deeper meanings. These latter ambiguities arise when uncertainties become attached to misadventures with the social apparatus of rite itself, and not to the indeterminate phenomenon (the content) the rite routinely realises on occasion. If liturgical good manners are to be secured, performative ambiguities have to be contained within the form of the rite in a way that renders them insignificant. This suppression of unproductive ambiguities that arise in enactment reflects the need to draw attention to larger, more fundamental theological and productive types emerging that reflect the heart of the liturgical matter. The need to cope with liturgical ambiguities that are performative liabilities requires an agency on the part of the actor in the rite. This need to manage social elements in rite admits a sociological consideration but one that points to the antinominal cast of liturgy.

Antinomies are contradictions that cannot be resolved through reason, and indeed in Kant's terminology mark its limits. They express a dialectic quality where each aspect of an act has a truth that contradicts the other and it is impossible through reason to establish the superiority of one over the other. They impose a dilemma. The term has been used in Marxism, especially by Georg Lukacs and Theodor Adorno.[38] In the latter's use, they point to tensions or contradictions that express those of society itself, a point made in his approach to music.[39] There is an antinomial quality in liturgy that fascinates. Antinomies present divisions to the liturgical actor that are endemic in the impression management of the holy. These can give rise to peculiar misunderstandings if mishandled. They do not so much entrap as enable the actor to surmount the weaknesses of a divided human nature.

A liturgical actor who seems to walk with innocent ease through these antinomial perils of rite is the choirboy. He presents a perplexing ambiguity in his all too familiar liturgical part in English society. The service of nine lessons and carols on Christmas Eve represents an invaluable Anglican contribution to Christian liturgies. Broadcast from King's College Cambridge, it is heard by millions. The service starts from the back of the College Chapel with a treble singing solo the first verse of 'Once in Royal David's City'. The plangent, stilling, calming small voice of the choirboy is tailored to the annunciation of the narrative of the birth of Christ. For many, it marks the authentic announcement of the Feast.

A less familiar aspect of the service is the first lesson read by a choirboy, who speaks of the genesis of human nature in verses that indicate the reason for the fall of Adam. The choirboy's innocent reading of the text draws attention to the origins of antinomies and their place in everyday life. Adam and Eve were forbidden to eat from the tree of knowledge of good *and* evil. Tempted by the devil with the possibility of knowing of both, and seeking to be wise, they eat the apple and are expelled from the Garden. This knowledge of good *and* evil suggests a capacity to transcend both, and know each without reference to its opposite. Such knowledge escapes the flaws of antinomenism that have come to divide and to confuse human nature ever since. The choirboy who reads this text in public, incarnates an angelic reminder of what was lost and what can be regained. As Alois Gügler has noted 'genesis is the childhood of man, never wholly lost, which flashes through history time and again'.[40]

Antinomenism has deep theological roots in Thomism, where mystery marks limits to reason and points to contradictions that cannot be resolved from within logic, but by appeal to what lies outside it. The notion of an antinomy proceeds on the basis of double knowledge. By knowing what is opposite, one proceeds to understand what is worth affirming. Some means of discrimination is required to secure the knowing of what is better, to wrest good from evil, the sacred from the profane, and the worthy from the unworthy. This dualism is unavoidable, for as St. Irenaeus warned, 'if anyone does shun the knowledge of both these kinds of things and the experience of this twofold perception, he unawares kills the human being in himself'.[41] Knowing through contradiction is part of the apophatic tradition, of a mysticism concerned with handling paradoxes, where elements of antinomenism are joined together and are transcended. Christianity is riddled with antinomenism, of the blind seeing, the lame walking, of the weak prophesying in ways that unsettle the wise and in such apparent contradictions as revelation operating in hiddenness. The sense of finding deep meanings in what is hidden in contradictions emerges clearly in a comment of Blaise Pascal relating to the veiled vision of man. He sees in between, but not that clearly, and so

> he may not see nothing at all, nor may he see enough to think that he possesses God, but he must see enough to know that he has lost him. For, to know that one has lost something, one must see and not see.[42]

Taken to their highest reaches, theological antinomies signify what is beyond knowing. They witness to that which lies past the human capacity to discern.

Wrestling with these antinomies might seem best suited to mysticism rather than to sociology. Yet, the social basis of rite has an infinite potential to be extended into the limitless, into what can be best reached through contemplation. Ultimate insights are achieved through theology. The purpose of this analysis is to indicate some of the antinomies that emerge in the enactment of rite. These are ceremonial liabilities which the actor confronts in liturgical performance. They disclose ambiguities and potentials for deception and misunderstandings which he would wish to resolve to secure the holiest of deliveries of his part. The enactment of liturgy involves handling dualisms, or polarities of meaning or attributes, some of which are desirable, and others much less so. Distortions that arise in the performance of a ritual refer to those that can be visited on the actors or can give rise to doubts about the sincerity of what they accomplish. These contrasting and contradictory elements bear a possible truth value, an integrity, that might or might not be realised.

Antinomies that arise in liturgy cannot be resolved at the level of the social. Resolution of the difficulties antinomies present necessitates an appeal to that which is beyond the capacities of the social apparatus used to deliver the holy. This need to go beyond the form, or social frame of the rite, indicates its incompleteness and the need to defer to a content that surpasses its limitations. Thus, rites operate in their own peculiar antinomial circumstances and the actors have to deal with dualisms of meaning that are implicated in theological effects. Cultural dilemmas achieve a condensed place in liturgical operations. They denote the constraints and hazards of liturgical enactments and through these tribulations the self secures a higher degree of virtue. An element of choice or decision emerges that permits a sociological understanding of what the actor seeks to wrest from these antinomies, if grace is to be secured. This lends a degree of agency to the enactment of rite. Skills and ploys are required to play this holy game, to rescue the desirable from the undesirable in a distinctive manner of social accomplishment that can be given a sociological understanding. By sympathising with the actor's dilemma, of wishing to edify but through imperfect instruments, that possess antinomical qualities, sociology gains access to the social means through which liturgy accomplishes its goals. Performative infelicities that emerge in liturgical praxis embody layers of implication that need to be deciphered and unpacked. The liturgical actor has to exercise a quality control over the performance if a desired image is to be secured. The staging of rite conveys an image on the sanctuary, a frame set before God, to mirror the holy. Antinomies seem to fracture the glass, but they also permit glimpses of the holy. They are both an asset and a liability whose resolution perplexes and fascinates the liturgical actor.

Some antinomies, such as the contrast between light and dark, transcendence and immanence, relate to wide and fundamental theological issues. But there are others which have a more definite sociological location, such as the contrast between the sacred and the profane and acts that edify or disedify. Social antinomies arise in handling an attribute, a gesture, a role. They point to divided meanings between innocence and experience, the civil and the sacred, the truthful and the deceitful. Antinomies in the liturgical act point to worlds that need to be denied, if truth is to be affirmed. The issues they raise in understanding rite centre on the problem of delivering exclusive appreciation to God in a way that represents the essential task of worship as a social act. Because the social elements being handled in liturgy are indeterminate in effect, they bear corrupting or edifying readings that display profound ambiguities for actor and audience alike. Mishandling of antinomies can have dark and dangerous effects which the actors have to avoid to keep custody over the virtuous in rite.

Antinomies are not peculiar to liturgical praxis. They also emerge in sociology of medicine, in lay representations of health and illness. These form a dualism, where the actor strives to maintain some sense of harmony in dealing with everyday life. The actor struggles to occupy a state of health, and endeavours to resist illness, behaviour that renders him inactive and which can represent an undesirable opposite. Illness and disease are social and physical expressions of sickness and they often require intricate negotiation to secure a satisfactory definition. Minor illness is an ambiguous condition that can denote the serious or the trivial for doctor and patient alike.[43] Although illness is more complex and ambiguous than might be initially assumed, it is certainly more definite than its desired and intangible opposite – health. Claudine Herzlich characterises health as an 'organic silence'.[44] Yet, health represents something more than an absence of disease. It involves an image, a capacity to cope that gives it an ideal state, one rather neglected in recent medical sociology.[45] Health points to an accomplishment, a capacity to maximise autonomy, to be free from engulfment by external social forces. It is an attribute to be preserved at all cost. There is an unreflective quality to health, but once lost it becomes valued as a capacity to be regained. It represents what the self seeks to find and to secure in the conflicts and threats of everyday modern life.[46] Antinomies in medical sociology point to those of the external world, where there is little option but to struggle to survive. In the case of religious antinomies, one is looking at those that operate within the confines of liturgical form in a little world that seems well removed from modern life. The antinomies of liturgical life represent those one can elect to struggle with or not. Both health and sanctity are lodged in antinomies and have to be secured against their disabling opposites, illness and unholiness.

Entering a Cathedral, and seeing an altar set for service, surrounded by a complex architecture, of choirstalls, soaring pillars, stained glass windows, is to find oneself, as did Huysmans at Chartres, in Baudelaire's 'forest of symbols', not in nature but in a crucible built to contain a holy play.[47] All these symbols in stone and wood supply a setting, a backcloth for a sacred drama to be staged that serves to represent a foretaste of heaven on earth. The music, the speech, the stylised gestures, and the white robes of the actors, all denote a condensed expression of what is to be revealed, but which lies presently concealed in symbols. There is an element of beauty about a well ordered rite, the singing of the choir and the careful movements of those in the sanctuary who seem to effect a grace in motion. An

image of beauty and holiness is being cultivated that makes available a
basis to seek and to find connotations of the invisible through social
means.

Gazing at a rite in a Cathedral involves looking at actions that are
initially attractive, but which after continued scrutiny become profoundly uninteresting in their repetitious staging. The ritual frame is
like an icon, not easy to 'see' its point. Similar to a formal staged
liturgy, icons seem 'somewhat rigid, lifeless, schematic and dull. They
do not reveal themselves to us at first sight. It is only gradually, after a
patient, prayerful presence that they start speaking to us'.[48]. There is
an overlap, mentioned earlier, between theology and sociology, over
the notion that beliefs are real in their consequences. Actors or objects
in liturgical use can be 'transformed into the image they contemplate'.[49] Faith permits man to become what he seeks, to incarnate what
he desires, and to recover what was lost in a new image, perhaps one
that embodies a holy innocence. This notion of becoming cannot be
subject to rational proof or explanation. Images have a facilitating use
that enables them to refract the holy. Commenting on Hypatius of
Ephesus, Aidan Nichols notes his view that 'images exist in the Church
by way of a gracious concession to weaker brethren who need such
props to the life of faith'.[50] These material elements offer a means of
identification with the holy and a passage into what is beyond limits of
reason and human endeavour. Because Christian belief depends on
dealing with the unseen, man cannot apprehend deeper spiritual
meanings without some form of social embodiment of those meanings.[51]

Following Cyprian Vagaggini, one wishes to view liturgies as
handling sensible signs that make known a hidden reality. This
involves an element of antinomism for

> the sign reveals the thing signified but at the same time hides it. It
> reveals it in as much as it has something in common with it; but it
> hides it in as much as it is distinct and different from it, and
> expresses it only imperfectly. The sign makes the thing known, but
> at the same time it offers an obstacle to this knowledge because it is
> not perfectly transparent.[52]

The unity between the invisible and visible is expressed in the
combined tasks of the priest and the angel in the enactment of the
mass. Their combined duty was well understood in the Early and
Medieval Church.[53] Artistic representations of liturgies recognised this
point in the Renaissance period and showed a continual exchange

between angelic and social orders. Access to angelic properties is common to men and women, who through will and effort secure these qualities of virtue. Virginity is closely associated with angelic attributes. Huysmans had strong views about the propriety of women singing in Church, and strongly supported the tradition of the highest voice parts being given to boy trebles. Yet in convents of women he noted a purity and beauty of sound that was distinctly moving.[54] An absence of sexual activity seemed to give access to angelic qualities for men and women alike and this was expressed in the voice. A sweetness and innocence in singing was associated with virginity amongst young men and women, and was considered a mark of edification in the Early Church.[55] The image of the angel is most authentically represented in social terms in the young male who most closely fits the part of being an attendant or messenger.

The link between virginity and an angelic state points to the transparent nature of a beauty in holiness, where the attribute seems to emerge from within the actor. There is an indefinable quality attached to such beauty that makes it more than an issue of mere aesthetics. Beauty in holiness achieves its highest state when virtue is allied to spiritual struggle. Detached from virtue, beauty presents a deceiving façade, a mask that misleads. Beauty in holiness bears an antinomial quality. It is a facilitating device that contains the seeds of corruption and possible misuse. Aquinas wrote that 'wisely, therefore, song has been used in praising God, so that the minds of the faint-hearted may be incited to devotion'. The difficulty with music is that it can arouse undesirable sentiments incompatible with religious sensibilities, and for this reason, to secure a division between sacred and secular uses of music, Aquinas prohibited the use of instruments in liturgy.[56] Beauty involves a risk of becoming an end in itself, a mirror in which the actor can come to adore himself rather than God. It is this risk of corruption through the means used to worship that generates a sociological fascination with liturgical enactments.

Despite faith and grace that effect a transformation into the holy, the frailties of a divided human nature remain attached to the most pious of actors in the context of liturgical enactment. Antinomies generate confusion and uncertainty as to which aspect of the social is to be represented to God to secure the most efficacious of effects. In artistic terms, representations refer to images of life framed in an artificial mode of expression, such as in the confines of a painting. In sociological terms, representations have a more distinct meaning. They refer to effects or images drawn through social or ritual means that embody particular collective properties, that could be sacred or profane. Forms of behaviour are used to denote the holy in a transaction geared to express and to realise its basis for public view. There is a quality of imprecision about such ritual endeavours to secure an image of the holy in a social frame. As Durkheim noted, there is a functional indeterminacy and ambiguity attached to such representations.[57] Following Herzlich, representation can be studied at two levels. It refers to the construction of an idea – of health, illness, or holiness. Representation establishes an image of reality. It involves 'the perception and evaluation of an experience, directly influenced by social norms, and thereby serves to influence the orientation of attitudes and behaviour'.[58]

There is a division between artistic and social representations as they apply to liturgy. Whereas the artist can stand back to view the product with an appreciative detachment, the liturgical actor has to bear a price of obliviousness in realising that which edifies through social means. Without risks of conceit, he cannot bask in the reflected glory of his own self-image. In sociology, the notion of a looking-glass self relates to the way the actor adjusts his performance to match the responses of others. In liturgy, elements of adjustment are necessary to monitor intended holy effects, but if the part is to be *fully* realised, a degree of blindness is required on the part of the actor if he is to reflect what is mirrored in holiness. A forgetfulness in his role is required, so that he plays into the part and embodies the possibility of its existence.

Presenting an appearance of holiness involves the realisation of properties whose ephemeral nature can give rise to many misunderstandings. Images so presented embody qualities that cannot be checked – the private spiritual status of the actor – so that prospects of deception and feigning are amplified. Hypocrisy can be rendered with finesse in sacerdotal assemblies in a way that exceeds the scale of deceit possible in civil gatherings. Because there is a discrepancy between meanings expressed in liturgical actions and the spiritual states they signify, actors face endemic difficulties in performance. There is an ambiguous quality in the liturgical act: the actors might be endlessly able to mislead the audience; but they face endless problems of being believed. They are the victims and beneficiaries of the ambiguous nature of the liturgical act. It can deliver the purely social, but the same means are required to deliver the holy. How does one separate the holy from the unholy? Clearly that is a theological question, but hopefully, it is also apparent that it is a sociological one.

Even amongst the holiest of actors there is another form of ambiguity peculiar to the liturgical act. Possibilities of conceit, of self-amplification are especially magnified in the liturgical overachiever, who can reveal too much of what ought to be concealed. The actor can get in the way of the holy act. After all, the purpose of rite is to cast worth on to God, and not on to the actor. The management of this dilemma is another strand in the book that gives liturgical operations a distinctive sociological characteristic. A particular style of tact is required in the establishment of meanings in the liturgical act to preclude misleading implications being spelt out. This becomes apparent in the discussion of innocence and experience. A degree of disguise, of dissimulation, is required to secure virtue. The possibilities for understanding and misunderstanding, and for lies and deceits are endless. Liturgical acts require very peculiar practices if holiness is to be realised and meaningfully established. This book attempts to understand these dilemmas. Gestures, clothing and roles are discussed in antinomial terms in a way that forces the actor to elect to choose between the civil and the sacred. These are dilemmas imputed to the actor with the sole task of drawing out the distinctive and autonomous nature of the liturgical act, one that emerges in a reading of this religious rite that is distinctively sociological.

Another important facet of the book is to draw attention to the precarious and marginal nature of the social apparatus of rite. It requires careful regulation if it is to fulfil its purpose. Competitive assemblies of God operate often within the same Church. Liturgical forms operate in antinomial terms, so that one form of rite is deemed to be incompatible with its rival. This point especially arises in the case of Anglicanism. A spiky ritualist would avoid attendance at a convivial assembly, even if it were the last rite in town on a Sunday. Forms of rite often compete on the basis of mutual denigration of the other's weak points. An understanding of this competition, which we explore later, draws attention to the notion of liturgical boundaries and the need for their regulation and defence. The prime purpose of this aspect of the book is to produce an ironic if not perplexing sociological point. It is argued that liturgies operate best when they manage to make their social apparatus invisible and unsignified. When the social apparatus of rite is domesticated into a state of irrelevance, then liturgies achieve their highest degree of relevance, in theological and sociological terms. The limits of the form of rite are treated in a way that marks them as incomplete and meaningless without reference to the limitless content they embody.

Post-modernism has changed the terms of reference of the debate on cultural studies in a way that might benefit a sociological understanding of liturgy. This somewhat leaky opaque term expresses a movement within understandings of culture that has had a somewhat tyrannical effect on recent sociological deliberations. Problems of mapping mass culture, of facing the limits of modernity characterise the concerns of post-modernism. It embodies an agnosticism about knowledge and culture that justifies the need for artful play with pastiches, with the fragments and ambiguities left in the wake of modernism. A nostalgia, a worry about innocence lost hovers in the background, the price of denial of a transcending bond. When the liturgical act is understood from within a post-modernist frame of reference, it all seems to make theological sense to a perplexed sociologist seeking to understand more. But, he is still caught on the horns of an analytical dilemma. Reductionist accounts of rite would demolish the subject-matter in a way that would be unacceptable for any other issue a sociologist might encounter; accepting the basis of the liturgical act might demolish his discipline. Yet, there is a redemptive aspect to this analytical conundrum.

Leaving sociology at this analytical edge might seem to play a joke on the discipline, confining it to unresolvable antinomies, endless paradoxes, and a welter of ambiguities that would defeat its best efforts to understand. A sociologist might feel perplexed at finding a ritual so near analysis yet so distant, one where trivia could be subject to endless but purposeless speculation but in a way that evaded an understanding of the essentials of what was proclaimed. There is no purpose to the order of rite but to worship, uncertainties of outcome have to be lived with, and the transcendent comes of its own accord, and nobody can change these constraints. But uncertainty of outcome does not rule this rite out of sociological court. Hermeneutics helps us to understand how sociology can participate in this liturgical game, without either winning or losing.

Games depend on the outcome of play not being known in advance. Playing a game involves a wager, a hazarding that has its own attractions, that give this activity an intrinsic worth. Liturgy is a form of holy game, whose indeterminate outcomes permit and indeed facilitate endless re-play. Play arises in Goffman's interests in the wagers involved in impression management, and it forms a neglected strand of Gadamer's *Truth and Method* that has never been put to sociological use in the analysis of a specific event. It is also a concern of the Swiss Catholic theologian, Hans Urs von Balthasar. His interest in formulating an aesthetic theology was undertaken with a vast range of reading, whose extent is truly awesome, ranging from Patristics, to all schools of philosophy, to the Pseudo-Dionysius to a concern with man as actor involved in a sacred drama. Of all the great theologians of the twentieth century, von Balthasar is the most accessible to a sociologist. The notion of play can operate happily with ambiguities and antinomies and for that reason it is a suitable means of characterising liturgical transactions. It is a term that only takes on a use value in enactment within a frame, that limits and excludes. Following Johan Huizinga, play can be regarded as actualisating an image in a representation realised in appearance.[59] The liturgical implications of the term are clear. There is an innocent delight in play that manages to transcend doubt. Play assists an action to surpass itself, to reach for beauty and holiness in a way that transcends the apparent contradictions of the game.[60] It involves a totality, an appropriation, where, as Huizinga tells us, 'the distinction between belief and make-believe breaks down'. [61]

Sociology is going through one of its perennial periods of doubt, when it can be converted to almost anything. Everything seems to be 'post-' everything else, from structuralism, to modernity, to foundationalism, to the Enlightenment itself. Transcendence, a deeper concern with meanings, and indeed an implicit theology seems to be entering sociology from a number of directions. The meaningless void of art devoid of God has received a chilling gaze from George Steiner and this perhaps signifies an effort to find a new direction for European thought.[62] But the most significant contribution to the growth of an implicit theology in sociology has developed from its reference to hermeneutics to resolve problems of incommensurablity generated by the rationality debate.[63]

Initially, heremeneutics was used to affirm the autonomy of the cultural sciences. But its use has spread further into the question of reading any practices, social or textual, likely to give rise to misunderstandings that need to be deciphered to be understood. In using hermeneutics, sociology risks becoming entangled in a surrounding theological baggage attached to its more traditional endeavours, of deciphering texts such as the Bible. Both Ricoeur and Gadamer showed a recognition of the importance of Christianity in their approach to hermeneutics, and their theological interests have been marginalised if not neglected in contemporary sociology. In this approach to liturgy, I wish to exploit the nascent theological overtones of their work to enhance an understanding of rite.

Hermeneutics admits a wider interest in aesthetics, religious language, and in liturgical forms than might be expected. Another aim of
this book is to show that the study of liturgy belongs in the
mainstream of sociology and that hermeneutics helps us to understand that point. Any sociological study of liturgy has theological
implications that are unavoidable. Apophatic theology allows an
approach to beauty, where antinomies operate but in a way in which
they are transcended. This style of theology most closely fits a
sociological approach to liturgy and also the concerns of Hans Urs
von Balthasar.

His efforts to develop a theology of aesthetics, where beauty is a
revelation of the Glory of God, fit with our concern with the
incomplete nature of liturgical form, and the need to find a content
that completes its basis. Hans Urs von Balthasar wrote little directly
on sociology, but what he produced was of theological significance. In
Volume 1 of *Theodramatik*, written in 1973, von Balthasar devotes a
significant section to sociology. His interest in sociology centred on the
relationship between the actor and his role in social worlds. Goffman
and Simmel loom large in his interests, and his main concern is to
pursue the question of identity of modern man before God. He was
interested in the dramatic qualities of praxis, and this led him to view
liturgical enactments in terms of theatre, where the same elements of
re-playing with the transcendent emerge, even if the contexts differ.
The theatre provided an analogy for seeking the Divine.[64]

My concern is less with describing the typical aspects of liturgy and
more with uncovering its atypical facets with a view to giving the topic
a place in the sociological sun. The strands of analyses reflect contours
found in other aspects of sociology. To that extent, one hopes the
reading brought to understanding liturgy is unoriginal in sociological
terms.

There is a danger in this study that the opaque, hazy nature of
liturgical transactions will become excessively mirrored in the rhetoric
of the sociological analysis used. There is an elusive quality to representations of the holy in liturgical productions that seems to
frustrate sociological efforts to understand and to reflect on what is
understood. One is uncertain whether this elusive quality in the
analysis which follows is due to the incompetence of the writer or is
inherent in *any* sociological effort to grasp that which by its nature
eludes captivity within the sociology. At best, one can hope to achieve
a degree of eruditon about the social nature of liturgy in this account.
This is a quality which von Balthasar has noted in *The Sacred Art* by

the Swiss romantic writer Alois Gügler. Erudition is a term usually associated with the fruits of acute scholarship. But von Balthasar cites Gügler's use of the term to refer to a process whereby:

> a person strives to extract or to draw out spiritual and divine life from all the hidden places where it lies concealed. In this way, man is ... filled, animated, and 'made erudite' by the divine life he extracts.[65]

There is, therefore, a theological purpose to this work, a bias in favour of liturgical 'success' that stems from the Catholic interests of the writer.

This study of liturgy is set very loosely against a background of post-modernism and against various movements in philosophy, such as in the writings of Jacques Derrida and Emmanuel Levinas, whose sociological purchase is yet unclear. Issues raised by de-construction yield arguments from a Jewish perspective about the nature of negative theology in modern thought. As these penetrate sociological awareness, theological issues will increasingly attract analytical interest as debates on the limits of modernity gain ground. This account is not to be regarded as an exercise in philosophy or theology, hence the many shortcuts that have been made to flesh out a distinctively sociological account. Equally, it would be premature to sketch out the sociological implications of post-modernity for the study of liturgy. This would require an altogether different account of rite in a separate and later study. The main concern of the study is an elementary sociological question: what are the social processes that enable liturgical actors to re-present the holy in a passage between the obvious and unobvious in a way that minimises misunderstandings?

4 Angels and Surplices: Appearing As Holy Becoming

> The angels keep their ancient places;
> Turn but a stone and start a wing!
> 'Tis ye, 'tis your estrangèd faces,
> That miss the many-splendoured thing.
> (Francis Thompson, 'The Kingdom of God')

The issue of the earthly manifestation of angels in a ritual play might seem to mark a limit to a sociological imagination. The place of the angels in sociology has not greatly advanced since Comte's stress on the need to regard them as 'ministers and representatives of the Great Being' who could be invoked as protectors and models.[1] It is difficult to conceive of a sociology of angels. They belong to a realm of myth and legend. To the secularised mind, they linger as metaphors for states of purity, unreal and irrelevant for the streetwise seeking to survive life in advanced industrialised societies. Liberal theologians regard the idea of angels as a liability, an embarrassing impediment to religious belief in a scientific age. They seek to deny the rumour which Peter Berger has tried to amplify.[2] Somehow the angel seems to have vanished, no longer able to appear in the ideological fogs that swirl around contemporary cultures.

Yet images of these winged messengers persist. Tourists view their likenesses in artistic representations in Cathedrals and art galleries. Angels can be found floating in frescos, or standing guard in statuesque sorrow in graveyards, carved in stone, guardians of the dead, relics of a long-vanished world. They can be found delineated as soft youths in white robes, deadened in sorrow, incarcerated in the leaden contours of a stained glass window, safely lodged on high above the Cathedral nave. Secular culture permits a disbelieving gaze, one that affirms an artistic image, but not the theological reality of what is represented.

Despite these doubts, understanding the social basis of liturgy is difficult without reference to the invisible angelic layer that is believed to hover over this form of ritual transaction. The liturgical actors, the altar servers, the choir and priests incarnate angelic properties in their

84

labour of adoration. This hidden collaborating layer needs to be affirmed if a fullness of liturgical meanings is to be realised. It is easy to lose sight of the invisible in rite. The need to represent the angelic dimension of liturgy in some form of social manifestation was well understood in the efforts to revive the surpliced choir in the Victorian Anglican Church. A white-robed company of men and boys was placed between congregation and altar to remind those present that they shared with the angels a common task of worship.[3]

The voice that comes nearest to the angelic, that persuades most of its existence, emerges from the weakest section of the choir – the boy treble – who also reaches to the highest notes. In a crowded Cathedral, with perhaps over a thousand present, the voices of twenty choirboys in a descant can soar above the singing throng. These choirboys, about eighteen in number, aged between eight and thirteen, are traditionally regarded as the delegates of the angels. They remind the earthbound of what they cannot see, but can only hear. Commenting on the musical establishment of Henry VIII, an ambassador wrote that the 'High Mass was . . . sung by His Majesty's choristers, whose voices are really rather divine than human; they did not chaunt, but sung like angels'.[4] Choirboys singing heavenwards seem to participate in a hidden order, to echo an imagined celestial activity that more fittingly belongs to the angels. In their cassocks, ruffs and long white surplices, they conspire in voice to speak on behalf of the angels. They reflect an obvious angelic image, one all too visible at Christmas in English society.

Apart from their mothers, few believe they are angels, least of all the choirboys themselves. As one wittily affirmed,

> Cassock red, surplice white,
> Mouths wide open, singing right.
> Can you guess? Can you not?
> We look like angels, but we're not![5]

'Real' angels do not appear in long white surplices, in carefully orchestrated rituals, geared to deliver glad tidings of great joy, to tell sweetly of what happened 'Once in Royal David's City'. But the ethereal voice of the choirboy, married to his surpliced appearance, suggests a counterpart to the angel, a hearkener on heaven, authentic in his own rite. He seems to repeat what he hears from elsewhere and passes on the tale. Through some mysterious act of mimesis, the choirboy manages to attach an attribute of innocence to a stereotype and to realise the properties of an angel before a public gaze that oscillates between awe and incredulity at his right to fill the part.

Choirboys appear in expected guises, in rituals that unfold with a happy predictability. They inspire trust that nothing unexpected will occur in their public performance, save a pure and truthful witness to what they cannot see. They act as ciphers for the angels through social resources and in their managed utterances convey a sense of their presence. In their roles, they seem to attract heavenly attention, receiving and transmitting 'signals of transcendence' with disquieting ease. Whereas Huysmans saw monks as lightning conductors attracting the punishment due to sinners, the choirboys seem to gambol in the choirstalls, children of the light, basking in a benign Divine attention.[6] The sense of radiance they convey can be easily romanticised and sentimentalised, leading to predictable misunderstandings. The relationship of the choirboy to the angelic begs many complex questions difficult to understand. Something more is asked of the surpliced songster than a mere capacity to appear angelic. After all, he is not just a small actor with a bit part in a sacred drama. These boys can realise an essence of a religious truth in an unreal manner that has few competitors. Angels seem to have a particular and peculiar relationship to the weak, the marginal and the socially incomplete.

An angelic image can be captured through other means. For instance, William Anderson comments on what the sculptor has achieved in his carved representation in Regensburg Cathedral of the angel Gabriel at the Annunciation. The stance of the statue

> gives out the impulsive joy of a vision that has just appeared. He has chosen the form of an adolescent boy in which to deliver his message; his features, however, are not those of a boy breaking into smile but those played with by the essence of a smile that needed the face of a boy to manifest its nature. His flesh is the medium of the unearthly and the surging uprising folds of his robes, signifying his freedom from gravity and terrestrial constraints, emphasize the active role of his mission . . . .[7]

Angels relate to the timeless, to that which is above and beyond time. Their appearance is usually unpredictable. They tend to arrive unannounced, without much ceremony and with their own rules for coming and going that operate outside the realm of sociological accountability.

Angels are believed to occupy an unfallen state. As pure spirits, they are deemed to have an innocence and a quality of directness in their dealings with God. These virtues are believed to be most naturally expressed by children and to be more difficult to realise in adulthood. An innocent adult generates suspicion in a way a child does not. Man and boy differ in their relationship to the angelic over their access to a crucial defining attribute of its presence: innocence. The child seems to be endowed with this property by right of immature age. This makes it easy for the choirboy to sincerely appropriate this attribute to edifying advantage in his public performance. He seems closest and most receptive to the message he transmits. Sincerity enables him to seem virtuous and also to embody it in the part. He does not have to struggle to be what he appears: the angelic attribute seems to come easefully down from above.

With man, however, the means through which innocence is realised are markedly different. To secure an angelic innocence in adulthood requires the cultivation of heroic virtue, a struggle within a life apart from the world. The choirboy realises his virtue in public; the adult in private, in a monastic calling, where asceticism marks a career of emulation of the angelic.[8]

The angelic is unapparent in the appearance of such adults, shorn of beauty and incarcerated in a monastic habit, witnessing to a life of struggle against the limits of the body. The monk's life can be understood as a calling to a *vita angelic*, a career marked with celestial ambitions, where the timeless is realised in times of service in the choirstalls. The choirboy achieved his closest link with monastic life in the medieval world. Tonsured and with his own habit, some were oblates, boys donated to the monastery. These oblates were often the main source of recruitment to monasteries in the eleventh century. Despite the obvious pitfalls of growing into a life of chastity with little apparent choice, many of these boys grew into adulthood with an innocence and holiness difficult for the modern world to understand. For some it was a life of heaven on earth with an eternal reward. As Quinn notes 'children inherently stood closer to attainment of the monastic ideal than adults'.[9] Choirboys embody a long monastic tradition of seeking and finding the holy.

Acts of worship are earthbound manifestations of angelic endeavours, incomplete now, but to be completed in some unknown future. Altar servers and choristers bear witness to this incompleteness in their robes, and in their marginality on the sanctuary, where they operate best to edifying advantage on the fringes. They play their parts on the boundary of the ritual event, acting as guardians of the periphery, keeping watch over the background of the rite, lest it becomes too significant and too obtrusive in a way that might subtract from the unfolding of a holy event. These minor actors attend to award significance to a sacred drama. Reflecting on the Church's task of replaying the bloodless tragedy of the Crucifixion, Oscar Wilde noted that it was 'always a source of pleasure and awe to me to remember that the ultimate survival of the Greek chorus, lost elsewhere to art, is to be found in the servitor answering the priest at mass'.[10] Those who serve and sing in the sanctuary affirm an implication that something greater is being enacted than their slight parts might indicate.

A belief in angels shapes the task of worship and gives to it an imaginative purpose. But this belief has to be realised and has to be made manifest through social means that bear divided if not contradictory uses, ambiguities most likely to emerge in liturgical praxis. The belief has to be made manifest by way of a paradox: the unexpected that betokens the angelic has to be channelled into the expected to admit a credible social image of something so incredible. Liturgical roles operate to express inexpressible aspects of the angelic imperfectly realised in human form, and for that reason it is easy to find the actors in the rite wanting. Piety might seem unnatural amongst liturgical actors whose efforts mark an 'elevation of man above his natural sphere'. This aspiration is concentrated in a ritual event which achieves its purpose of worship 'if the numbers in the angelic choir are augmented by priests and monks who resemble the angels'.[11]

If a resemblance to the angels is to be achieved through social means, then some form of regulation of appearance is required to secure an intended effect. Characteristics have to be denoted and made manifest for public edification. This process of conversion and transmission involves a social process available for sociological scrutiny. A label has to be established that fulfils an expectation. The social construction of labels in sociology is usually associated with deviance, mental illness, and attributes of vice, that unsettle. Vice need not have a monopoly of labelling theory. The same theory can also be employed to understand the social process through which virtue is realised in public places of worship. Angelic qualities could be regarded as elements of deviance from the concerns of a secular society. The process through which angelic qualities become attached to the actor involves the sacralisation of a self-fulfilling prophecy, that, hitherto, has had secular purposes in sociological understandings achieved in symbolic interaction. It is also related to a dictum of W. I. Thomas that has widespread sociological acceptance, that beliefs are real in their consequences.[12] The appropriation of angelic qualities for ritual use generates a considerable number of distinctive complications. The social actor is unlikely to be able to understand this process, which is as mysterious as it is eventful, and this qualifies sociological efforts to comprehend. Angels are immortal, incorruptible spirits, messengers of God, unaffected by the sin of Adam, which imposes all manner of complications and doubts on a human nature that seeks to appropriate these qualities of purity and innocence for ritual display.

In this chapter, we wish to examine theological approaches to the question of angels, and to assess some sociological implications of a belief in their appearance. Secondly, we want to consider the social purpose of a liturgical garment associated with purity and innocence – the surplice – and to relate its significance to wider issues raised in the sociology of clothing. This leads to the final part, where we suggest that angelic qualities of innocence are riddled with potential misunderstandings and complications. Innocence is a quality associated with the angels and with man before the Fall. It is a deceptively simple characteristic, but one that can be profoundly dangerous, when set in a world of experience where it is to be understood. If mishandled, the innocent can be destroyed as can the beholder who tries to see too much in an attractive, but ambiguous moral trait. The paradoxes involved in dealing with this antinomy have a wider bearing on how liturgy is to be understood in sociological terms. Issues of concealment, of simulation and dissimulation, of lies and mistakes arise in dealing with innocence and the enactment of angelic roles. The antinomies that emerge point to dangers of misleading appearances, and the problems of securing a holy face. Tacit elements can arise, which if drawn to the surface, can lead to misunderstandings. A question and answer is involved in handling innocence, as its facets are deciphered in a public role that generates suspicion, if not scepticism.

A RUMOUR OF ANGELS: SOCIOLOGICAL AMPLIFICATIONS OF THE INCREDIBLE

First Soldier: Why do they dispute about their religion?

Second Soldier: I cannot tell. They are always doing it. The Pharisees, for instance, say that there are angels, and the Sadducees declare that angels do not exist.

First Soldier: I think it is ridiculous to dispute about such things.

(Oscar Wilde, *Salomé*)

A belief in angels, pure spiritual beings, more perfect than man, seems to belong to a vanished era. To the modern mind, they seem incredible. To liberal theologians, they are regarded as the products of a

particular cultural era in which the Bible was written. This view of
angels appeared in the famous Dutch Catechism and led to a dispute
with the Vatican and its subsequent condemnation.[13] For the Anglican
theologian, John Robinson, angels were symbolic means of conveying
the idea of messengers from God. Certainly, they were not to be
regarded as 'real' winged messengers, for he added 'it is no part of the
Christian faith to put one's belief in hitherto unidentified flying
objects'.[14] Angels have been one of the casualties of recent theological
efforts to de-mythologise biblical narratives and to make them more
acceptable for a rational scientific age. They occupy a more secure
position in Catholicism than within Anglicanism. For instance, Karl
Rahner regarded a belief in angels as of central theological importance.
He claimed that 'the existence of angels and demons is *affirmed* in
Scripture and not merely assumed as a hypothesis which we could drop
today'.[15]

In the Bible, angels appear in many guises, undertaking a wide
variety of tasks, both serious and trivial. They are regarded as
instruments of divine retribution, and act as witnesses to central
aspects of salvation and revelation. They often pass unnoticed and
unsignified, hence the famous warning 'be not forgetful to entertain
strangers: for thereby some have entertained angels unawares'
(Hebrews 13:2). An angel was an unrecognised companion and helper
to Tobias.[16] In other circumstances, they are inescapably recognisable
and can be fearsome as was the angel who appeared in a flame of fire
out of a bush (Exodus 3:2) or the one who came with sword to destroy
Jerusalem (1 Chron. 21:27–30). There is an avenging, military aspect to
the manifestation of angels in the Old Testament. Their appearance
often aroused great fear and awe. Gideon cried out with fright to the
Lord on seeing one face to face (Judges 6:22–23). They appear always
in a male form, in whatever role they enact.

In the New Testament, angels come in a less threatening and more
passive manner. They are used to mark four crucial events in the Life
of Christ: the Annunciation, His birth, Resurrection and Ascension
into heaven. The Resurrection was announced by a man whose
'countenance was like lightning, and his raiment white as snow'
(Matt. 28:3). Elsewhere, he is described as being 'clothed in a long
white garment' (Mark 16:5). This accounts for the notion that albs or
surplices are the only liturgical garments sanctioned by Divine
Revelation. They are garments that betoken angelic presence and
have been appropriated to mark this point by man.

In the Old and New Testaments, angels have a common task of supplying comfort and support to those in distress. H. C. Moolen-burgh gives a touching example of this aid in his unique survey of contemporary experiences of the angels. For instance, he mentions a boy, aged nine, who saw an angel who came 'in a sort of shining lustre' and 'accompanied by a tremendous feeling of happiness'.[17] This reflects a Catholic belief that every soul has a guardian angel for protection and to supply hope for future salvation.

The appearance of angels in the New Testament in white garments establishes a means of identification and emulation for actors engaged in liturgical tasks. There is an eschatological aspect to this manner of appearing that is expressed in the verse 'clean and white: for the fine linen is the righteousness of saints' (Rev. 19:8). Wearing of white robes in the sanctuary signifies what the actors wish to appropriate. They operate with the assumption that 'man's understanding of his world is shaped by the presence of the angels'.[18] Angels are liminal creatures who play between the transcendent and the immanent. Some of these qualities also characterise the activities of liturgical actors, who bear witness to what is beyond the social, but also their limitations in so affirming this point. Even though angels are pure spirits, they are believed to share human characteristics of intellect and purpose, but their capacity to take on bodily forms is limited and qualified.

St Thomas Aquinas argues that angelic powers are exercised in using bodily organs as instruments, but these cannot be appropriated or made their own.[19] This would suggest that angels are marginal to and outside the corporal. They appear within the limits of a completeness as a concession to man's frailty. Aquinas suggests that 'angels communicate intelligible truth to men by means of objects apprehend-able by the senses'.[20] Faith is deemed to come through two elements: a will to believe; and a capacity to hear. Aquinas argues that angels assist the latter, acting as instruments of enlightenment. They bear messages not only about what to believe, but also about how to behave. From this one can infer that the message to man from the angels contains an imperative to imitate the qualities and virtues of these heavenly messengers.[21] In this sense, angels are instruments of edification. The manifestation of angels in a bodily shape carries a theological qualification. It is assumed that they act as a 'mover with a body that represents it in its movements'.[22] Because angels service a belief in what is beyond the senses, their form of appearing in 'bodies' has a particular purpose, of signifying 'through human actions and attributes, the spiritual actions and attributes of angels. Indeed it would be less to the purpose if real human bodies were assumed, for then the visible properties would lead the mind to men and not to angels'.[23] This comment of Aquinas on the manifestation of the angels has two important implications for an understanding of the social basis of rite.

Firstly, efforts to call up visions of angels within a liturgy are less to the point than attempts to realise their attributes in human expression. The more the performative basis of the rite is geared to imitate and to establish conditions for appropriation of angelic qualities by all present, the better it is able to concern itself with matters absent, the 'signals of transcendence' that come from outside the social form of the liturgy. Secondly, there is an element of mutual benefit in the relationship between liturgical actors and the angels. Both operate best on conditions of metaphysical limit to each other, but acting together, they produce a holy completeness in liturgical enactment. Each is estranged from a defining aspect of the other. The angel is marginal to a body he can only occupy in an incomplete manner. He operates on the edge of the visible, the tangible and the corporal, and deals with matters he cannot by his spiritual nature fully appropriate to himself. On the other hand, the issue of the angel reveals to man how much of his spirit is hidden to himself, which his body veils. In emulating the angel, man encounters a piece of what is missing in his sense of self. Rectifying this sense of incompleteness bears on the notion of a *Deus absconditus.*[24] By the nature of his fate, man operates on the threshold of the intangible and the invisible, seeking to grasp the essence of a spirit he cannot fully appropriate in life. Within the liturgical act, man and the angel form a complement of body and spirit, where each remedies the deficiencies of the other to form a holy whole, peculiarly able to fulfil the edicts of revelation. The journey of the angel down to life is a temporary reversal of a movement which man has to make towards the eternal. The angel points the way ahead, and the cultivation of his attributes are a reminder of that journey all men will have to make out of life.

St Augustine has noted that 'only through faith do we know the existence of the angels'.[25] Social elements are the means of realising that belief, for they give expression to that which is invisible, and complete meanings in what is visible. The angelic is believed to be 'fused' to the social activities of liturgical actors who become implicated in an effort to realise a sense of its presence. This is where mystery and manners peculiarly combine in liturgical actions, where the angel and man work together as in the Sanctus. Angels are believed to carry forward the efforts of those present in the mass. For instance, in Eucharist Prayer I of the Catholic Church, the priest says 'Almighty God, we pray that your angel may take this sacrifice to your altar in heaven'. Such a plea reflects a wider task of trying to 'transform the worship of the Church into a liturgy which resembles the worship of the angels'.[26]

It is in this context that the liturgical link between angels and angelic appearances mirrored in the actor is to be understood. Liturgical actors strive to arrange their actions to reflect what they believe but cannot see. They attempt to appropriate what they perceive to be angelic attributes in a credible manner of enactment that makes belief in the angels 'real' in its social consequences. Imagined properties are harnessed to holy advantage in a way that gives witness to innocence and purity. In their surpliced roles, the choirboys embody these qualities in their serried ranks in the choirstalls. They operate as resonators of the angelic realising timeless heavenly events in a way that provides an added aura to earthbound activities. Working with the angels they supply through grace and fervour a revelation of what is mysterious and hidden.[27]

In English society, there is an element of stereotype attached to the angelic image of the choirboy that might obscure the wider link between angels and liturgical activities. In a number of areas, angels are believed to be involved in sacramental tasks, such as Baptism. They also complement the social actions involved in other liturgical roles, such as those of deacon and altar server.[28]

Children are believed to have a privileged and proximate relationship to the angels. This is reflected in the warning to 'take heed that ye despise not one of these little ones; for I say unto you, That in heaven their angels do always behold the face of my Father which is in heaven' (Matt. 18:10). Those who are vulnerable to mockery for violating worldly wisdom, who are immature and incomplete, are believed to receive angelic protection. As Ladislaus Boros observes, 'because it is a defenceless creature, a child is a density point for the presence of angels in this world'.[29] The choirboy is a witness to the angelic and in his role cultivates attributes that affirm their existence. He sustains this image of the angelic in a paradoxical manner. He appears to be possessed by what he cannot see and yet to be capable of seeing what he cannot possess. He acts as emblem of the angel delivering a strong message out of weak circumstances. His age and innocence of knowing the full theological implications of what he

sings, give him a natural ease in enacting the part. Choirboys are
believed to be unsullied by a world of experienced knowing. This
makes them obvious and traditional models for the angels, in art, in
music, but above all in liturgical parts.[30]

Innocence was closely attached to the social construction of the idea
of childhood in the seventeenth century. Unfortunately, for some, it is
an attribute increasingly regarded as lost in a contemporary world of
sophistication. The notion of childhood has disappeared, to be
replaced by greedy, grabbing small adults such as seem to inhabit
parts of New York.[31] Innocence amongst children might well be an
illusion, and the choirboy might represent the greatest one of all. But
this would be to miss the point. An imperative is being stressed, that
children ought to have a space to grow in an unthreatened innocence
where the seeds of a spiritual imagination can be developed.

Efforts to appropriate angelic qualities for adults operate under a
different set of considerations from children. Adults emulate the
angelic from a different direction than does the child, from a
condition of loss of innocence, to one marked by a hope of its re-
appropriation from a world of experience. This task of emulation
involves a battle of will to convert what is natural into a link with the
unnatural. Those who remain virgins, or strive to sustain the state in
adulthood are believed to maintain a particular relationship to the
angels, for it is written 'neither can they die any more: for they are
equal unto the angels; and are the children of God, being the
children of the resurrection' (Luke 20:36). The notion of virginity
involves a dying to self, that admits public access to a state of eternal
purity, a form of holy antinomy. The Early Church placed much
value on the calling to a life of virginity, a 'madness' which Robin
Lane Fox indicated was a witness to the pagans. He argues that
virginity was a means of reversing the Fall, and at the same time, of
profiting from the Redemption. A childlike simplicity could be
recovered in virginity that 'encouraged single-mindedness and dependence on God alone'.[32]

Man and boy transmit differing qualities of innocence with
contrasting effects. Whereas the choirboy confirms and comforts in
his part, the adult unsettles by his witness to a folly. Young adult
virgins reveal a paradox, of securing a peaceful identity that is based
on a life of denial of what contemporary worldly wisdom values. By
rendering themselves unavailable, they secure an availability for
devotion to holy purposes. Because they affirm an innocence of life
that seems unnatural, they attract the attention of the experienced and

corrupt, who might seek to violate this odd completeness. This element of antinomy is apparent in pornographic interest in the lives of the virtuous, which speaks volumes for the signs of contradiction they present to the world. Liberation from the contradictions of antinomies is central to Christianity, as for instance in the doctrine of the Virgin birth.

The degree to which the virgin unsettles the compass points of the wise and achieves a contact point with the angelic is beautifully conveyed in Peter Brown's account of the development of the link in the Early Church. Angelic attributes, of freedom to worship God fully and purely, were found in hovels in the desert, in sleepless nights, and by the punishment of the body through fasting and mortification.[33] This imitation of the angelic amongst adults occurred in less than romantic circumstances, far removed from the delicate concerns of sanctuary management of this study. But efforts to pursue angelic qualities in the desert or in the sanctuary have a number of elements in common, however disconnected the social settings of emulation might be.

Both have in common a concern with handling a marginality and traits of ambiguity whose resolution is a witness to higher things. Both arenas point to what lies beyond the antinomies buried in human nature and point to a means of escape where the pain of contradiction can be transcended. Lastly, they combine in a common area of will, and effort to secure understanding against being misunderstood. Even though the boy has an initial natural relationship to the angel, what is secured of these qualities in adulthood lies higher. In one sense, the angel is inferior to the adult virgin, for as Peter Chrysologus noted, 'it is a greater thing to acquire angelic glory than to possess it already. To be an angel has to do with beatitude; to be a virgin has to do with the virtue. For virginity obtains by its own powers, what an angel has by nature'.[34] By striving to resolve the divisions of his nature, man climbs higher than the angel. He achieves this ascent only through surviving testing.

By drawing attention to his wish to appropriate the angelic in his life, an adult pays a price of entering a realm of ambiguity, where deceptions are imputed to him. An excessive emphasis on his virginity in social life might convey a perverse neurosis and witness to a disabling immaturity rather than to an effort to cultivate purity. Amplification of a condition of holy innocence exposes him to the grasp of sceptical experience. But above all an excess of witness to this virtue can nurture a sin of pride at release from the sin of Adam, that can be a prelude to a fall. The purpose of virginity is to free the body and to give an autonomy to a spiritual self.

Virginity, holiness, innocence, purity and virtue are spiritual attributes that require social expression. Male virginity cannot be checked through physical means. Trust and inference are needed to discern this condition. A religious habit allows a claim to be established. It signifies what is to be kept unused and unsignified to find God better. But this quality of holiness would be devoid of purpose, or limited in its effect, if it were kept totally hidden. The virtue of purity has to be made manifest to sustain a witness to what is denied. This is accomplished through a form of witness, the occupation of an image realised through social means. But, if this image is paraded too conspicuously, the bearer of virtue risks encountering undesirable opposites, so that humility becomes pride, innocence experience, and purity corrupt.

Our concern is less with the city, or the desert, or the pursuit of religious life outside Church buildings, than with the way angelic elements become channelled into the sacred drama that concerns the actors in the sanctuary, who seek to play with higher things. It is only in the microcosm of the sanctuary and choirstalls that such a form of social life can be found that would bear a sociological focus. Such an analytical venture means highlighting detail and antinomies that might seem like misunderstood legacies of older codes of Canon Law, where the improbable was codified in an impossibly complex manner where all contingencies were covered. The nature of the sociological gaze will generate theological distortions, but these are the price of an analytical effort to mirror in an alien discipline routine social efforts to refract the holy on the sanctuary by actors striving to be what they are not.

It could be said that a life of virginity is its own witness and that no other signs than the spirit might be required, for its holiness to be discerned. Commenting on the 'angelic' life of Syrian ascetics in the fourth century, Brown noted the way those 'robed in the Holy Spirit' had an absolute freedom to exploit the body and 'to step out of the category of the human by making visible, among one's fellow-humans, the awesome freedom of the angels'.[35] This points to an unresolvable dilemma: how much of the social is required for belief to be sustained? Social markings are aids to belief, which grace can intervene and override.

This makes sociological accounts of activities such as liturgy provisional, for the discipline has no means of indicating how elaborate or simple a rite should be to convince, a point admitted earlier. But assuming that the human condition demands that belief be grounded at some point in a social form of expression, where a fullness of meaning emerges in praxis, dilemmas will emerge that admit to sociological considerations. Some social form of the reminder of the angels is required, however imperfect, that supplies witness to their existence. Some conditions of emulation have to be established in a social arrangement that confers a label and sustains the condition in its desired state. An actor might well know in faith that he is working towards a grace-filled life, but some form of social knowing is required, so that this belief becomes 'real' in its consequences. Appearances can be adjusted to signify and to mark a movement from one state to another, from the unholy to the holy.

Clothing ceremonies in monasteries are rites of passage that signify a translation in status and the conferral of obligations on the initiate. A religious habit supplies a means of expressing a wish to live apart, and to pursue a calling, a venture into a life of grace. It permits the self to be redefined and to be rendered unavailable for particular secular activities. This process of transformation and translation points to the power of the social to yield higher things and to be regulated to achieve openings to the holy. Certain social resources are needed to realise this and clothing is a crucial element in the task.

CLEANLINESS AND GODLINESS: THE ISSUE OF WHITER THAN WHITE SURPLICES

> One rapid and impatient shake,
> (As our own Young England adjusts a jaunty tie
> When about to impart, on mature digestion,
> Some thrilling view of the surplice-question)
> (Robert Browning, 'Christmas Eve')

Clothing is an important means of regulating styles of appearing. In civil society, it supplies clues to identity in the public arena. Habiliment offers a means of gauging social worth, of estimating the status of an actor, his taste and his eligibility to be included or excluded from a particular life style. Judgement operates on the assumption that the mode of dress of an actor indicates how he wants to appear and that his inner social sentiments are married to his external appearance. In cosmopolitan life, it is assumed that the actor does believe and know that his appearance matters. By his clothing an actor can add to or subtract from the intended definition of a social event. Appearances count, but, as in most significant matters, these are ambiguous. Clothing can embody trivial elements, but it can also stand for deeper and more serious meanings. As Wilde has noted, 'the truths of metaphysics are the truths of masks'.[36]

Intentions and meanings are embodied in clothing, which can convey properties of significant sociological worth. There is an elective facet to clothing, where the self can use appearance to lead or to mislead. Disguise indicates a capacity to deceive, whereas other forms of clothing serve to establish trust. Clothing reveals and conceals social properties. It can be used to intensify a claim to esteem and to mobilise degrees of deference. Indeed, clothing is a subtle form of power, a crucial ingredient in the management of impressions. It has a significant bearing on the credibility or incredibility of the actor in the part. Masks are often the means of rendering the incredible credible, of making belief possible in what would be otherwise improbable.

This arises in the case of theatrical actors who use clothing to mask, to supply a means of converting the self into a temporary attachment to a role. Simon Callow writes perceptively on the effects of clothing on the body as a means of entry into the theatrical part. He suggests that 'costume acts exactly like a mask. The costume, as it were, travels inwards. You start to form the bodily shapes of the man that looks like *that*'.[37] The actor's task is to close the gap between his inward sentiment and his outward stance, to minimise any disbelief in his right to occupy the role. He has to appear to believe in what he has temporarily become on the stage. His art lies in making the incredible credible in a way that lulls the audience into believing that there is a truth in the fiction. Success entails a close monitoring of the detail of his clothing to establish a credible image of the part. Sometimes, trivia has to be harnessed to secure dramatic advantage. An actor's clothing indicates a heightened awareness of how he ought to appear, if the part is to be fully appreciated.

This task complements Gregory Stone's effort to link the issue of appearance to self. He uses the term 'dressing out' to refer to the use of clothes as a ticket of entry to a role other than acknowledged to be one's own. Costume acts as a 'kind of magical instrument' that frees the self from the constraints of routine.[38] There is an ambiguous quality to clothing, which can enable or disable the capacity of the self to be as it would wish to appear. This can vary according to institutional setting.

The garb inmates wear in a 'total institution' effects a redefinition of the self. In prison, it marks a civil death and the termination of the right of the individual to regulate his own appearance in public.[39] Like the medieval leper's clothing, it warns of possible danger to the public, should he manage to escape. In other insitutional settings, a uniform, such as religious clothing, can indicate a habit of life that signifies a wish of the self to be free from the cares and woes of the modern world. Clothing can establish a social property, but by itself, cannot necessarily secure it.

In some circumstances, clothing can denote rights and duties that make a total claim on the self. Uniforms convey power and the right to secure compliance in an unambiguous manner. The wearing of a uniform indicates the authority to act. To protect this capacity, the false use of a police uniform is a criminal offence. A uniform signifies a position within an organisation, one that confers rights but also duties. Use of a uniform can render the individual powerless to deny that which his appearance signifies. A military uniform suggests a duty to kill, but also awards to a soldier the risk of being shot. It indicates he cannot be exempt like the civilian from the war game.[40] The actor is bound into his appearance in a way that assumes no exemption.

Clothing also denotes the right to handle with impunity areas that are regarded as morally dangerous. A judge's robes proclaim the right to make binding legal judgments, to preclude demands for vengeance; the doctor's white coat gives a privileged access to parts of a patient's body without the need for negotiation; and a priest's stole signifies a capacity and an intention to administer a sacrament. In settings of use, these garments inspire trust. They secure deference and compliance more easily. Garb transmits indeterminate qualities of competence, and enhances the capacity of the actor to act with credibility in delicate situations. An intention is believed to be marked in the manner and clothing of appearance.

Clothing can be used in an antinomial fashion, where an unclean or clean image is used to mark a contrary private state or disposition. This internal state can be concealed or publicly understood. Andrew Travers has supplied an astute illustration of this point in his account of the contrasting impact of punks and nurses on social settings. He argues that a punk strives to establish a pollution of the social environment in a vileness of appearance that requires a studied construction. But behind this facade lurks a self secure in his knowing that he is more than his appearance. His aim is to mislead, by transmitting greater qualities of discredit than his own self-credit-rating would award. Occupying a narrow ground between normality and appearances that might suggest illegal interests, the punk conveys a knowing of what to violate. As Travers notes, punks are involved in a wager that oscillates 'between the ignominy of not being noticed and their being noticed as ignominious'.[41] By contrast, the calling of a nurse necessitates dealing routinely with often polluting aspects of sickness, such as disposing of human waste, in a dignified manner. Their white uniform serves to sacralise their relationship to these otherwise profaning elements and to protect them from any contamination they might encounter in following their calling.[42] Their uniform enhances their ritual power to deal credibly with tasks which of their nature are discrediting.[43] A similar protection is given to nuns in habit when exercising their calling in areas of moral risk and danger.[44]

Clothing enhances the personality of the individual and makes him more presentable than he might otherwise be. It also conveys a badge of affiliation that marks a group membership. Modern fashion allows identity to be purchased. Clothing represents a commodity that admits access to an enhanced life style, or so the advertising industry would suggest in its marketing. Simmel regarded fashion as having a peculiar characteristic of making possible a social obedience, while at the same time supplying a form of individual differentiation.[45] It supplements a person's lack of importance, 'his inability to individualise his existence purely by his own unaided efforts'. Clothing facilitates a form of collective attachment in a paradoxical manner. It effects a union that is based on segregation, of placing the individual apart, but within a particular context.[46] Clothing also conveys an elective element, by transmitting ambitions or wishes to identify with a particular cultural ideal. For its realisation, a degree of calculation is assumed, of knowing how to present a clothed body to maximum social advantage, so that recognition of worth is instantaneous. Poise, manners and arrangement of the body in gestures complement the social functions of clothing. Social conventions assume an actor so dressed intends to be as he appears. But inferences might be drawn over the discrepancy between expressions intentionally conveyed, and those unintentionally given off. Such miscalculations can lead to embarrassments. To preclude these, the actor exercises a certain custody over his mode of clothing to establish and to control intended effects of his appearance.

This shaping of self into a desired appearance reflects taste and good judgement. The actor knows what to purchase, but, if not, he can shop around to buy an appearance. An assistant in a clothing shop needs a particular skill in estimating how to match his stock to the expectations of the customer, so as to minimise offence and maximise sales. The tailor can be regarded as a unique artist, a decorator of the human frame, seeking to clothe the body in a manner of appearing that will correspond plausibly to a plurality of settings.[47] Both work in an area where gauging the effects of clothing on social settings are crucial. The customer buys access to an aura and by so purchasing, also certifies his discernment in adorning his appearance in such a tasteful manner. The aura of fashion enhances his impact on the public gaze. Thorstein Veblen has argued that the greater part of expenditure on clothes by all classes is less for reasons of protection than for the maintenance of a respectable appearance. Expensive clothing advertises pecuniary advantage, a disengagement from the grime of productive work and the certification of a leisured existence.[48]

Religious clothing represents a witness to a tradition that denies the logic of modernity and all its works. Profoundly unfashionable, religious clothing denotes a disconnection from the values of cosmopolitan life and a wish to affiliate with heavenly realities. It has its own antinomial quality of detachment from the world in a way that attaches the wearer to qualities that transcend it. Perhaps Thomas Carlyle overemphasised its importance when he noted that

> with regard to your Church proper, and the Church-Clothes specially recognised as Church-Clothes, I remark, fearlessly enough, that without such Vestures and Sacred Tissues Society has not existed, and will not exist.[49]

Religious garments effect something more than a mere covering of the actor. The wearer is believed to convey a quality of virtue and dedication to its pursuit. He is believed to express a link to the super-personal, and is given a right of access to handle the holy when so dressed.[50] This relates to a comment of the Pseudo-Dionysius, that the 'priestly vestment signifies the capacity to guide spiritually to the divine and mysterious sights, and to consecrate one's whole life'. The whiteness of a garment, such as a surplice, has a sacramental quality. Grace and virtue are bestowed on the actor, who is expected to live up to the appearances of purity he incarnates when surpliced. This whiteness of a surplice is associated with fire, the cleansing purity and light of the Divine.[51] A white garment can signify a quality of grace conferred, as in the robe worn by infants at baptism. The ethereal nature of whiteness is noted in the reference to the Transfiguration of

Christ, whose raiments 'became shining, exceeding white as snow; so as no fuller on earth can white them' (Mark 9:3).

Grace and virtue are not automatically conferred on the wearer of a sacred garment, nor can the effects of appearance in it be gauged as in a civil society. There is an element of humility attached to the profitable use of a religious vestment that reflects the degree to which the wearer is dependent for holy effects on a source outside his control. A degree of petition is needed to secure a transformation from the ordinary to a condition of being endowed with attributes of the extraordinary. A sense of this quest for spiritual enhancement emerges in the petition of a choirboy, when he vests in his surplice before he goes out to sing to God. He prays:

> Cleanse me O Lord, and keep me undefiled, that I may be numbered among those blessed children, who having washed their robes, and made them white in the Blood of the Lamb, stand before Thy throne and serve Thee day and night in Thy temple. Amen[52]

The above prayer, adapted from the Book of Revelations, reflects an eschatological wish to further a spiritual ambition, and at the same to realise its basis. Besides indicating access to transcendent properties, religious clothing is believed to supply some form of protection in the pursuit of their appropriation. As John Cassian wrote, 'the observance of simplicity and innocence may be preserved by the very character of the clothing'.[53] In former Catholic rites, young men received their surplices when tonsured at a public ceremony. The Bishop said, 'may the Lord clothe you in the new man who has been created in God's image in justice and true holiness'.[54]

The covering of the body in a religious vestment relates to a notion of unworthiness before the numen, the holy. Vestments signify a consecration that enables holy matters to be handled safely with a certain degree of self-depreciation at the awe acts of worship inspire. They signify also an act of atonement and a wish to effect a cleanliness to appear worthily before God.[55] The surpliced are reminded of their deficiencies in Psalm 51:6–7 where it is written:

> Behold thou desirest truth in the inward parts;
> and in the hidden part thou shalt make me know wisdom.
> Purge me with hyssop, and I shall be clean:
> wash me, and I shall be whiter than snow.

Liturgical garments are deemed to be outward manifestations of an inner intention. A surplice denotes a wish to be attached to qualities of

innocence and purity and to appropriate these in an inner commitment, so that the wearer strives to be what he appears. His wish is to
make a holy impact, to edify and to change the significance of what
surrounds him. This means a wish to add an aura of holiness to what is
enacted, so that something greater than himself is secured. The actor
comes to incarnate what he himself wishes to appropriate, and to
exclude that which is unholy and inappropriate. Wearing a religious
vestment means that he clothes himself in an intention, and accepts a
label that binds him to act in a way that realises its basis.

Unfortunately, there are many pitfalls in the way of the humble
wearer of a surplice. His efforts to be attached to virtue can give rise to
a number of misunderstandings. A suspicion can arise over his right to
proclaim such virtue, and also over his capacity to live up to such holy
appearances. Possibilities of deception are amplified beside those that
admit access to virtue. The wearer might not be what he appears, and
the claim to virtue could be misplaced. Misleading claims to virtue that
are confined to the external are often denounced in the Bible, for
instance in the condemnation:

> Woe unto you scribes and Pharisees, hypocrites!
> for ye are like unto whited sepulchres, which
> indeed appear beautiful outward, but are within
> full of dead men's bones, and of all uncleanness.
>
> (Matt. 23:27)

Those wearing religious garments have access to their own types of
vice, infelicities that arise intentionally, or otherwise, in the manner of
appearing laden with virtue. Conceit and self-proclamation can
emerge, where the glory supposedly directed to God falls on the
religious actor instead. J. W. Goethe noted these ambiguous facets
when he observed that those in religious orders can appear

> submissive without abasing themselves, and when they draw
> themselves up to their full height, they are invested with a certain
> self-complacency which would be intolerable in any other profession
> but becomes them rather well.[56]

It is up to the wearer of a religious garment to secure desired properties
of holiness and to monitor the effects of his appearances on others.
Religious clothing simply confers on the individual the capacity to be
holy, if he attends sufficiently to what its wearing implies for his style
of life. As one writer noted, the habit does not make the monk, but it
can conserve him in virtue.[57]

Liturgical garments fulfil particular tasks in this regard. The girdle, the belt or white rope worn around the waist, with an alb, marks a preparation for service. It supplies a reminder to keep the body in check. The surplice, a modified alb, is long, full and white, signifying the charity, innocence and purity it is deemed to express.[58] Despite its apparently innocuous nature, this garment has been awarded a disproportionate significance, especially in Anglicanism, where it signified Romanising affiliations. The rights and customs surrounding its use in Anglicanism were associated with ritualism and led to what became known as the 'surplice riots'.[59] Puritans took violent objection to having to wear a surplice for preaching in the seventeenth century.[60] The complexities surrounding the appropriate or inappropriate use of a surplice or gown in service in the history of Anglicanism would test a fledgeling sociology of clothing to its analytical limits.[61]

Despite potential charges of deceit, if not corruption, liturgical garments fulfil an essential function of providing a covering to go before God. Infelicities and unintended vices can be overcome with grace to fulfil the injunction 'let thy priests be clothed with right-eousness; and let thy saints shout for joy' (Psalm 132:9). Since the Fall, nakedness and shame have been interlinked and this has generated a need for disguise, for the body to be covered. In itself, veiling is insufficient. A covering with a purpose is needed to realise an ambition to return to a prelapsarian state. The clothing ceremony for a monk or a nun not only involves a redefinition of status, but also a carrying forward of the effects of baptism. Being clothed in Christ signifies a notion of belonging, of being attached (Gal. 4:27). This sacrament is believed also to effect a casting off of an old self, and the putting on of a new man (Ephes. 4:22–24). Clothing is the external means, the metaphor, for this change of status.

The need for religious clothing is an artificial necessity in our temporal state. As St Paul wrote, there is a heavenly future for bodies that will be dissolved, but for the present 'we groan, earnestly desiring to be clothed upon with our house which is from heaven: if so be that being clothed we shall not be found naked'. The plea is to be 'clothed upon, that mortality might be swallowed up of life' (2 Cor. 5:2–4). This suggests that religious clothing involves a taking on of an implication, an acceptance of an incompleteness that might be redeemed in a completeness in some future time. Religious garments signify time, but also participation in the timeless. Thus, a surplice denotes a baptismal past, the acceptance of a present obligation to be pure, and a future hope of heavenly membership. It offers a reminder of the possible redemption of innocence, the limits of human frailty, and a witness to a future where these will be cast asunder. Commenting on the process of casting off old garments and taking a religious habit, Maria Boulding observes that prayer and nakedness expose deceits. Stripping involves a notion of redefinition of the self. For her, it represents 'a call to trust and to find anew the confidence of sons symbolised by the stripping and white robes of baptism, which reminded the Fathers of Adam's fellowship with God before his sin'.[62] When Adam indicated to God that he was naked, having eaten the forbidden fruit, he had to be clothed to cover his shame (Gen. 3:7). The recovery of innocence is linked to clothing, to the manner of appearing worthily before God, in a rebirth as a new man. This need to be clothed before God applies even to the martyrs waiting at the threshold of heaven for their brethren to arrive, for 'white robes were given unto every one of them' (Rev. 6:11).

The choirboy is a visible witness to these qualities. Should he walk out from the stalls to sing his solo in full view in the crowded Cathedral, clad in his ruff, cassock, and long white surplice, he does so in the context of the prophecy that those in undefiled garments 'shall walk with me in white: for they are worthy. He that overcometh, the same shall be clothed in white raiment' (Rev. 3:4–5).

EXPERIENCES OF MISUNDERSTANDING THE ISSUE OF INNOCENCE

> How but in custom and in ceremony
> Are innocence and beauty born
> (W. B. Yeats, 'A Prayer for My Daughter')

The choirboy plays in an innocent manner with a deep message, issuing it with an unemotional directness which moves those who attend a religious ceremony where beauty and glory is given to God. As one writer observed 'the chorister boy knows little, and cares less, about effect. He sings as the lark sings his matin song, *naturally*; it is performed as an act coming in the ordinary course of things'.[63]

The image of the angelic is a burden of office for many choirboys, slightly baffled by the assumption that they are holy prigs wholly different from other boys. Most cultivate sports, music, read comics and are all too human. They are less innocent and more knowing of the world than one might expect. Yet, singing, serving and praying

daily does cause some sense of the sacred to stick. The busy routine of
the choir school protects these boys from the harsher side of life. Some
achieve a devoutness difficult to recover in later life. In a collective
grouping, choirboys can be mobilised to pray with awesome power.
The innocence they convey is partly embodied in the music they sing,
the beauty of their voices, but also in the surpliced image they present.
Older boys know they sing on behalf of those present, re-presenting a
message that deeply moves in a way that is as perplexing to them as to
others. They are also puzzled by the quality of innocence they possess
but in a way that does not pose a problem. It seems a question that
belongs to adult life. Somehow, they cannot fully see or grasp the
qualities of innocence they represent.

Schiller's account of the naïve nature of the child and his link to
genius gives some insight into the significance of the choirboy's act.
There is a genius embodied in the naïvety of the child that causes the
adult to attend to his insights. The adult looks upward to the child
from a condition which has encountered limitations. The child has an
unlimited determinacy and a pure innocence. Thus, Schiller suggests:

> the child is therefore a lively representation to us of the ideal, not
> indeed as it is fulfilled, but as it is enjoined; hence we are in no sense
> moved by the notion of its poverty and limitation, but rather by the
> opposite: the notion of its pure and free strength, its integrity, its
> eternality. To a moral and sensitive person a child will be a *sacred*
> object on this account . . . .[64]

The child represents a property somehow lost, misunderstood or
neglected in adult life. He seems proximate to a truth that has become
unclear in later life. The choirboy handles his message with a naïvety
that belies the complex and difficult truths he conveys to an
experienced adult who knows too much to utter so simply. Although
Schiller's point relates to nature rather than to religion, it is apt in this
context. He indicates that

> the feeling by which we are attached to nature is so closely related to
> the feeling with which we mourn the lost age of childhood and
> childlike innocence. Our childhood is the only undisfigured nature
> that we still encounter in civilized mankind, hence it is no wonder if
> every trace of the nature outside us leads us back to our childhood.[65]

Although a small figure, a detail, perhaps noticed or not, in liturgical
enactments, the choirboy exemplifies a wider problem of understand-

ing and misunderstanding the social basis of religious rituals. Innocence and experience have a perplexing relationship that seems to characterise some of these difficulties for a sociological account. The innocent act in a beguiling manner, seeming to have a fortunate blindness to the complications thrown up by a world of experience. They manifest an incompleteness, a lack of knowing of guile and evil, and yet they seem to survive, indeed to thrive on such unawareness. Those endowed with qualities of innocence seem oblivious to the protective necessity of experience. As an attribute, innocence is the improbable quality of the weak, fools and children, those on whom such a valuable capacity to discern seems wasted. The innocent seem oddly blind to the value of the attribute, and the way it could be coined to worldly advantage. Yet this incapacity seems to facilitate a capacity to grasp the essence of nature or of religious belief, to get to the heart of the matter with few complications.

This ability to see, gives rise to an annoying, if not perplexing quality in the innocent. They play with ambiguities and deep truths without apparent metaphysical injury. Having a sight denied to the wise, the innocent possess an uncanny directness the wise, who see matters in a more complex light, find frustrating. Those endowed with qualities of innocence present an injustice to the experienced, of knowing what they could not possibly understand, and of understanding what they could not possibly know – if they are deemed to be innocent.

It is scarcely surprising that literary accounts of the innocent should often be tragic tales of their assassination. They attract misunderstandings, which they do not have the experience to handle, and they fail tests tactlessly made by the wise, who pry to find why things seem so pure. In some ways, the innocent and the experienced seem caught in a dialogue doomed to fail. There is a poignancy attached to innocence, that those who possess the attribute are often blind to its existence. But having no means of valuing the attribute, the innocent are oblivious to threats to their existence. It is hardly surprising that Rollo May wondered 'can innocence, once it becomes involved in action, escape murder?'[66]

This question seems to present an insoluble barrier to sociological understanding. It seems to suggest that when innocence is expressed through social means, it is destroyed, it dies in the experience necessary for its presentation. The price for its ceremonial enactment appears to involve the destruction of the attribute. This would suggest that innocence cannot be known in a world of social experience. It is denied the means of a social manifestation, whether in liturgy or not. For innocence to be delivered through social means, some form of knowing is required to realise the part, so that desirable and undesirable qualities can be stipulated and separated. Some means have to be found to minimise misunderstandings, to order its appearing so that it bears scrutiny again. A certain guile is needed to accomplish this task, one that would seem to be incompatible with the elements that make the attribute so attractive, of seeming not to know what to do when faced with options and demands that arise from the expectations of experience.

An amplification of the contrast between innocence and experience to the point of their mutual destruction, deposits the former concept in an analytical cul-de-sac. It would be more fruitful to suggest that some form of compatibility can be found, that necessitates a degree of tact in understanding the innocent, that strives to affirm rather than to destroy them, that accepts the antinomial relationship operating between innocence and experience, and tries to find a means through which this ambiguity can be turned to meaningful advantage. I wish to argue that an aspect of the vulnerability attached to innocence arises less from its intrinsic characteristics and contradictions than from a failure to understand properly the social means through which it is to be known and understood.

Inversion and paradox are qualities characteristic of many facets of Christianity. The capacity of the foolish to speak wisdom (1 Cor. 3:18–19) can be related to the privileged access of the innocent to the holy.[67] This capacity to reach parts the wise seem unable to enter generates an urge to look closely, to try to imitate the source and to appropriate its qualities. This wish reflects an injunction 'Verily I say unto you, Except ye be converted, and become as little children, ye shall not enter into the kingdom of heaven. Whosoever therefore shall humble himself as this little child, the same is greatest in the kingdom of Heaven' (Matt. 18:3–4). Humility might be a natural quality of childhood, but is a virtue less easy to reproduce in adulthood.

It could be said that the above injunction places a premium on immaturity in a way that makes ignorance virtuous. In this reading, innocence is presented to adults as an attribute involving a path of regression, a movement back to a prelapsarian state. Such an interpretation would involve a misunderstanding of the authentic basis of innocence. If the attribute is to survive, it must do so in the necessary contradictions of human nature, where a pattern of growth is permitted to understand innocence in a healthy manner. Some form of knowing in dealing with innocence is recognised as necessary, for Christians are enjoined: 'be ye therefore wise as serpents, and harmless as doves' (Matt. 10:16). Imputing a total innocence to a child would be to imprison and to deny him the capacity to grow. Anyhow, being so safely placed apart, evil could still lurk within, well hidden behind a beguiling innocence. Such a sentimentalising approach could destroy, for as Leslie Fiedler warns 'like all sophisticated yearnings for the primitive and the inchoate, the nostalgia for innocence and the child is suicidal'.[68] The wish to look too closely, or to keep the attribute 'safe' can have fatal consequences for the innocent and the scrutiniser alike.

The innocent can arouse jealousy at the way they present the quality in a facile and unlaboured manner. The fatal consequences of an envious scrutiny of the innocent are illustrated in Herman Melville's short story 'Billy Budd'. Commenting on the tale, R. W. Lewis noted the way Melville 'took the loss of innocence and the world's betrayal of hope as the supreme challenge to understanding and to art'.[69] The innocence of Billy Budd corrupted Claggart who wondered before such a virtuous young man without satirical turn, for whom to deal in 'double meanings and insinuations of any sort was quite foreign to his nature'.[70] This strange, Christ-like 'Handsome Sailor' appeared as one to whom yet 'has not been proffered the questionable apple of knowledge'.[71] This apparent absence of a sense of ambiguity generated a suspicion in Claggart and led him to resolve the problem by the imposition of a fatal test. Apparently innocent of the fall, Budd was blind before the malign, revealed in Claggart's false charge of mutiny. Seeing suddenly a fatal threat, Budd lashed out and killed his prying accuser. Hung high for this offence, Budd swung dead, a witness to the dangers innocence can pose to the worldly wise. An innocence too far removed from human nature risks being assassinated by its divisions.

Innocence issues a demand, but it also receives one from a beholder curious to know further. It makes an ambiguous demand, for possibilities of deception are enormous, both for the innocent and those who might want to look too closely, a point illustrated in Henry James's short story, 'The Turn of the Screw'. This is a tale of a governess protecting the innocence of her two small charges, Miles and Flora, from the corrupting clutches of two former employees, now dead, whose malign influences live. Attributing a sight to the innocent, and persuading them of what they ought to see can lead to a peculiar form of deception. This occurs when the trait of innocence becomes a figment of an experienced imagination, seeking to believe in a label, whose imposition goes hideously wrong. Because the innocent are unaware of the trait, the possibilities of mis-attribution are greatly enhanced. By making the innocent a repository of what the beholder wishes to believe, the weak wither and die. In their efforts to please, or from the weakness that gives them access to the attribute, the innocent endeavour to confirm what they cannot see. Their tragedy is that they have insufficient experience to protect themselves from what they cannot know. They might, or might not see what they ought.

This was a problem the governess encountered in the case of the boy Miles. Her conclusions regarding the boy bloomed with 'the rose-flush of his innocence' and the belief that he was 'only too fine and fair for the little horrid, unclean school-world' from which he had been expelled. [72] Being so pure, and one who never seemed to have suffered, the governess concluded that 'he was therefore an angel'.[73]

As her fears for the boy's safety increase as she comes to believe in his possession by the ghosts, the slippery nature of innocence emerges. A darker, more dangerous side of the attribute is revealed. At the end of the story, she rushes to protect the boy, who screams 'where' and dies in her frantic clutch leaving an ambiguity in the mind of the reader as to who had deceived whom. A query comes to haunt the governess, who realises that 'out of my very pity the appalling alarm of his being innocent' arose and 'it was for the instant confounding and bottomless, for if he *were* innocent, what then on earth was I?'[74] The scope for illusion and deception in handling innocence is endless for the innocent and the beholder alike. There is a flawless ambiguity in the concept. It presents an image with many misleading layers.

In trying to interpret the concept of innocence in terms of its expression as a social act, we encounter a sociological conundrum. Weber's approach to understanding of action relied on his method of *verstehen*, of grasping the subjective meanings of the actor. The assumption is that a sociological interpretation of the basis of the action can be elaborated in a way that would fit with the actor's own account of what he intended.[75] The interpretation of innocence seems to offer an odd variation on this sociological theme. If an actor is believed to have a quality of innocence, he is deemed to be lacking a sufficient degree of self-understanding to know how to exploit the trait or to defend it in social transactions. Otherwise, he would be presenting a counterfeit product, a feigning that is ambiguous for the 'wrong' reasons. The attraction of the innocent is that they operate with an obliviousness to the boundaries of experience that might imperil the viability of the trait. Yet this incompleteness in knowing is a defining characteristic of its existence. This exemplifies the paradox of innocence, as an image, a moral attribute or a symbol. Much can be said about it but we do not 'have a key to admit us to the state, for it only comes to those who have no inclination to grasp at it'.[76] This point exemplifies the ambiguity of innocence as it lies between usefulness and uselessness.

Innocence seems to admit a bewildering polyvalence of meanings and potential misunderstandings that might seem to defy sociological comprehension. At one level, innocence as an attribute seems to have the potential for moral dynamite, and is a trait that needs to be handled with great care, but at another level it is marked by a distinctive quality of uselessness that is married to a dispensability. This sense of liminality endows the innocent with a wish to escape to somewhere more secure and mature. As Rollo May has noted, 'understandably there seems to be inherent in human life *an urge to get over innocence*', to enter some utopian realm of mature experience.[77] The choirboy will dream of life outside the stall, when his voice breaks and as a young shaveling he casts off his shroud of innocence and so unsurpliced ventures out to find 'real' experience beyond the Cathedral pale. This mutual incomprehension, of the innocent wishing to escape, and of the experienced wishing to recover this quality so wasted on the young, seems to exemplify a peculiar tragedy of culture. Ironically, the innocent seeking to lose the trait, have no idea what they will gain when they enter the world of experience. Herbert Morris has summarised the paradox well. He argues that

> when Adam and Eve eat the fruit, the knowledge they acquire of nakedness is also knowledge of an object the character of which was unimaginable to them prior to the acquisition of the object. Adam and Eve are unable to set out to lose their innocence with a clear idea of what it is that they will lose and what it is that they will acquire.[78]

There is an element of wager presented to the interpreter of innocence, an ambiguity difficult to resolve. So many layers of meaning can be unfolded, between an innocence of knowing and an appearing to be innocent that suggests sociology is not dealing with an innocuous concept. Yet these very qualities of liminality, uselessness and suggestibility indicate that if innocence is given a social setting, it draws attention to a richness in a variety of interpretations. Harnessed to liturgical use, the quality of innocence can be used to embody what it proclaims with great force. We have noted already an aspect of this point in the account of the choirboy as a conduit of the angel. The belief that the weak can deliver potent messages to the strong was understood in the medieval institution of the Boy Bishop.

The *Episcopus Innocentium*, or Boy Bishop was recruited from the choirboys and held office for the day, undertaking his duties either on the Feast of the Innocents, the 28th December, or on the Feast of St Nicholas, the 6th December.[79] This ritual celebration affirmed the words of the Magnificat and reminded those present of the prophetic power of the weak over the strong. The style of the rite bore a resemblance to the principles of the Roman Festival of Saturnalia. It was also associated with the feast of fools.[80] The custom of having a Boy Bishop became widespread in medieval England, France and Germany.[81]

The ceremony exemplified what Yeats might have had in mind in his poem cited above. The purpose of the ritual was to honour the innocent child-martyrs of the Church, to affirm the sanctity of childhood and to draw men's minds to a deeper realisation of the Incarnation.[82] Despite its potential for edification, the ceremony often collapsed into a burlesque, becoming a ritual of mirth that seemed to cater for 'an ebullition of the natural lout beneath the cassock'.[83] As Robertson noted sadly, 'the idea was good: the execution proved weak'.[84]

Much stress was laid on the childlike and imitative qualities of innocence and these were presented in the form of a sermon given by the Boy Bishop. Three of these survive, one of which was written by Desiderius Erasmus for Dean Colet, for delivery in St Paul's Cathedral.[85] The child was regarded as an especially fitting medium for a holy message, as he had dedicated his life to the Church by singing in the choir. It was assumed that some holiness had rubbed off on him in such a career.

A wisdom was embodied in the sermon, which the innocent delivery boy conveyed with fitting earnestness. On Childermas day in 1558, John Stubbs, a choirboy at Gloucester Cathedral, spoke of a feast 'which gyve the child the prerogative this day above men, in token that the innocent childer, which shed ther bloud for the person of the most pure innocent child Jesus'.[86] His purpose in preaching was to emphasise the possibility of moral conversion to adults. His summary of the paradox of innocence is interesting and bears on some points made earlier. 'God!', he proclaimed piously, 'the littill ones have by nature what the elder have by wrestling and stryvyng with their own affections. Thei have humilitie of mynd and sprite, which vertue the lower yt goeth the nerer it approchet the kyngdom of heaven'.[87] Later in the sermon, he asks his congregation to consider the nature of innocent children and suggests that one will perceive in them no manner of malice, envy, sinful affection, pride or carnality, 'but all affections quiet, in all pacience, in all simplicitie, in all puritie, in all tractableness, in all obedience, in all humilitie and in all innocency . . .'.[88] The loss of innocence generated worries, even in the Renaissance period, for Stubbs wondered that so many little ones grow 'so fast owt of this innocent state that it is wonder to me to se amongst yow some many childer in years, and so few innocentes in maners'.[89]

The indeterminacy and ambiguity associated with innocence achieves a condensed expression in liturgical transactions. It is given a focused manifestation in a ceremony, where the actor endowed with the attributes of innocence has to be able to display these in the rite on another day. The viability of the concept in routine ritual orders arouses sociological interest. The representation of the attribute of innocence in endless liturgical engagements with the holy amplifies numerous possibilities for its corruption by those experienced enough to exploit its ambiguous qualities. The prospects for misleading and deceiving seem great. The term innocence in liturgical use expresses the ambitions but also the limits of human nature. The angel that hovers over the rite has a perfection denied to the liturgical actors. After all, the angel 'is an image of God. He is a manifestation of the hidden light. He is a mirror, pure, bright, untarnished, unspotted . . .'.[90] In human hands the polish wears thin, and the mirror can refract more than the holy. It can also reflect lies and deceits buried unseen in what can be seen. The possibilities for deceiving and being deceived seem endless, both for the actor endowed with the attribute of innocence and the experienced seeking to find revelation in what seems so well concealed.

Innocence exemplifies the social conditions under which liturgies operate. They handle slight properties with serious overtones in conditions of ambiguity that involve a struggle between the useful and useless. For their message to be made manifest a process of social construction is required that demands a degree of tact in handling the tacit. The triviality of the social surface of rite, its obvious qualities, make its demands on the onlooker seem slight. But if attention is focused on what lies below the surface, in the unobvious, layers of implication, understanding and misunderstanding seem embodied in this social transaction. The issue of innocence points to a need for social regulation, of not going too close, lest the meaning embodied be destroyed, and of not retreating too far away so that the message fails to stick. There seems to be a mystery of manners involved in handling antinomial qualities of rite that playfully reveal and conceal. Like innocence, liturgies are pointless but are also very much to the point. Revealing and concealing seem to be qualities characteristic of liturgies as a whole, a point we consider in the next chapter.

5 Simulation and Dissimulation: Self-revealing Paradoxes

Oh! if servility with supple knees,
Whose trade it is to smile, to crouch, to please;
If smooth dissimulation, skill'd to grace
A devil's purpose with an angel's face;

(William Cowper, 'Table Talk')

The social instruments of liturgy, whose incomplete qualities produce a truth, can also distribute a lie. Bad faith is not confined to existentialism. The uncheckable nature of rite could allow piety to be feigned, devoutness to be parodied, and deceits to prosper by an actor with sufficient wit to keep a holy face – with the self preserved in a condition of semi-detached doubt. He could be the deceiving beneficiary of what cannot be checked. If so dedicated, he could fool all, especially the credulous sociologist. Bowing and scraping, the liturgical actor could produce all manner of deceptions that might mislead the holy and unholy alike. The problem for the sociologist is that the ultimate sincerity or insincerity of the liturgical act is known only to God. As Romano Guardini has noted 'the liturgy has perfected a masterly instrument which has made it possible for us to express our inner life in all its fullness and depth without divulging our secrets . . .'.[1]

Because the actor can pretend to be what he is not, and could conceal what he ought to be, in a ritual performance that deals with the intangible, deciphering the truth or falsity of his act can pose acute sociological problems of interpretation. Revelation and concealment are qualities embodied in the liturgical act that relate also to notions of simulation and dissimulation. For Steele, 'simulation is a pretence of what is not, and dissimulation is a concealment of what is'.[2] To simulate an appearance is to present something counterfeit, a quality of falseness, feigned to mislead; to dissimulate is to present as a whole an appearance or an attribute whose incompleteness might not even be noticed. Both have a deceiving quality. Simulation reveals too much in a way that paralyses a critical selectivity; dissimulation conceals too

115

much to make a secure judgement. Appearances are ambiguous enough without having to worry about whether they deceive or not. The issue of innocence and experience highlights some of the difficulties that can emerge in the certification of the authenticity of a virtue. Why should simulation and dissimulation be of such interest for an understanding of the social basis of liturgical transactions?

Marxists or Freudians might claim that liturgies are inherently deceiving, anyhow, and that issues of simulation and dissimulation are variations on an ideological theme. They would suggest that these religious rituals are inherently misleading, simply being manifestations of false consciousness, or that they are unconsciously deceiving, regardless of the intentions of the actors. Such privileged interventions conceal more than they reveal about the intentions of the actors. They are not puppets being strung along by some meta-theory, but actors accomplishing the production of a social transaction that happens to be entangled with the holy. A career in liturgical enactment leads to a much more astute awareness of where deceptions lie in rite.

The chances for fooling some of the people some of the time in liturgies are truly enormous. The preacher could sermonise on purity on Sunday and womanise on Monday; the celebrant could lie in his teeth when he utters the words of institution at mass; and the choirboy could come to the sweet conclusion that he does not love God after all. Hypocrisy is endemic in liturgical productions and the scope for simulation and dissimulation is vast. Dissimulation can be a ploy to maintain a smooth surface to disguise all manner of deceiving practices beneath. These discrepancies between faith and appearance point to culpable and obvious forms of dissimulation. Issues of dissimulation arise also in less obvious facets, where problems of accountability for any deceptions are less clearcut. There is, however, an endemic quality of dissimulation neccessary in the liturgical act that requires a tactful response if the actor is to secure 'success' in performance. Liturgical transactions involve a playful art of concealing and revealing. This ambiguity is both an asset and a liability in ritual ventures that deal with the holy. All forms of dissimulation are not necessarily pernicious; some are understandable.

The actors involved in liturgical productions become sensitive to the implications of simulation and dissimulation and the need to accommodate to their existence. Conscience dictates the scaling of these implications and the accountability of the actor for misleading or leading the audience astray. Scruples can become an occupational hazard for the actor, who might feign his appearance for good reason.

Piety might be simulated in a period of doubt, whose disclosure would unnecessarily scandalise; dissimulation might arise for the actor as a means of servicing humility in performance. There are grey areas in liturgical enactments where issues of agency and accountability for simulation and dissimulation are unclear. The even tenor of a well regulated liturgical performance makes recognition of simulation or dissimulation hazardous; they lurk between the obvious and unobvious. Exploring this issue further tells us much about how the actor renders his appearance to account in a way that minimises the harmful effects of simulation and dissimulation.

There are endemic qualities of incompleteness in liturgical transactions, areas of uncertainty the actors can exploit, or have to abide with, if they are to survive this holy life. As liturgical transactions have a quality of hazard in their operations, the degree to which dissimulation characterises the act as a whole is open to question. Firstly, there is an indeterminate relationship between the social form of the rite and the theological content it petitions to effect. Secondly, there is a disproportion between the calculation involved in performing a liturgical act and the incalculable theological effect it is believed to secure. An altar server, who bows low with great devotion, will be unable to estimate the amount of grace such an action confers on him, or on the deeply edified observers attending his liturgical performance. Thirdly, liturgies are peculiarly prone to deceive because the symbols they use can transmit meanings apart from their referents. These symbols service a religious belief in meanings that lie mysteriously beyond what can be seen. The elements that reveal truths can also, perhaps unintentionally, manifest lies. This is the risk of using symbols in a ritual, one especially likely to arise in liturgical praxis. As Rappaport has noted 'lies are the bastard offspring of symbols'.[3] Unintended meanings can be transmitted by the use of symbols in a way that the actor might find difficult to reconcile or to resolve. He has to operate in conditions of theological and sociological uncertainty. The quality control of his message is problematic. Liturgical actions have a peculiar sociological facet that the actor need not necessarily be expected to resolve the difference between intended meanings, and those unintentionally given off in the social expression of the act. Peculiar dilemmas arise for the actor in handling liturgical operations. We shall argue in the following three chapters that these are endemic in the social realisation of the holy basis of rite.

Sociology can merely explore the procedures and social arrangements used by the actors to minimise the risk of unacceptable forms of simulation and dissimulation arising and giving scandal in their witness to the holy. It can only select those facets of the rite that have sociological overtones, that lead to infelicities in production that might or might not have spiritual complications. There are two theological areas which have sociological implications for understanding issues of simulation and dissimulation, and which we will also explore further in the next three chapters. Firstly, it is easy to give the social basis of rite a literal status, where it becomes an end rather than a means. Secondly, there is the problem of presumption in assumptions about how to act in rite. Liturgical praxis generates its own distinctive theological and sociological perils of deceiving or being deceived in the act.

Uncertainty of outcome in the manner of performance points to elements over which the liturgical actor has no control. A reticence is imposed in his dealings where he might not be able to spell out a fullness of what he understands by the ritual task. The liturgical actor has to accept on faith what he cannot know. We have noted aspects of this in our treatment of the interpretation of innocence. Such a reticence that constrains has its own peculiar functions that apply in civil society. As Francis Bacon noted, 'mysteries are due to secrecy'. He went on to add, 'nakedness is uncomely, as well in mind as body; and it addeth no small reverence to men's manners and actions, if they be not altogether open'.[4] This seems to suggest that dissimulation can have a particular function, one of which is sustaining a social order, where an excess of revelation might be counterproductive – the audience might see too much to be able to believe. Civility in manners of appearing in public exchange requires a regulation of the passions. The maintenance of a degree of disguise is expected if politeness is to ensue. Lack of response to a social embarrassment is deemed an acceptable form of dissimulation that certifies a gentility of breeding. Concealment of response precludes a discomfort being signified and amplified. By his *inaction*, the gentleman makes his mark. Commenting on simulating indifference to vice or virtue, Mr Mackenzie noted that since 'very refined people are in a state exactly the reverse of a very rude one, it follows that, instead of allowing the passions thus to lord it over their minds and faces, it behoves them to mitigate and restrain those violent emotions, both in feeling and appearance'.[5] This capacity to dissimulate affects the regulation of social intercourse in a way that sustains the veneers of civility. Dissimulation enables certain forms of social intercourse to proceed, by not amplifying that which is best left unsaid. Some forms of engagement achieve their most potent effects through tacit means. Part of our interest in this study lies in exploring the sociological implications of this point for an understanding of re-presentations of the holy in liturgical enactments. As will have been noticed, our attention has switched from simulation and dissimulation to a concern purely with the latter. Simulation points to a familiar sociological terrain, where finding out, revealing the pretence, is an occupational joy of the sociologist. Locating the feigning liturgical actor would be all too easy a destructive sociological task, one that affirms the notion of the proneness of liturgies to 'fail'. Dissimulation points to a more problematic terrain, where the unobvious facets of rite have to be taken into account. The liturgical actor is part of its hidden message; he might deceive or be deceived by it; but one way or another the sociologist cannot settle for what is presented on the surface of the rite.

Obviously, there are psychological aspects to dissimulation, but these lie outside our remit. Likewise there are moral dimensions to the process which we can only touch on briefly. Immoral efforts to mislead through concealment amount to fraud and these can be discounted. Such arbitrary exclusions beg questions, but our concern is to maintain the integrity of what is after all a purely sociological argument. Our interest in dissimulation arises where it has a virtuous purpose, where concealment is necessary to fulfil a higher calling. The arguments used to defend an idea of virtuous dissimulation bear a resemblance to those that can justify another contradictory term: self-deception. An unexpected effect of such a style of argument might be to marry sociology to casuistry.

At some points simulation and dissimulation combine to mislead. Simulating an expression of interest or of sincerity involves a certain degree of investment by the self in a social appearance. The credibility of an interest is married to a manner of appearing, one where dissimulation is required to bury the 'real' motive. Service workers have to cultivate a manner of interest in customers who might be intrinsically uninteresting. The maintenance of such a façade to earn a living carries a price. To survive, an actor has to pursue a career of private disengagement from the public façade, to leave a space within which the self can pass unremarked. This distancing of the self carries an element of concealment, a detachment that preserves the possibility of sincerity. A degree of insincerity is required to enable the self to move with ease from one social transaction to another. These social fronts appear to work so long as the actor can pass himself off as trustful on the basis of his appearance.

This suggests a cynical social world where the main problem is the successful management of a bundle of ploys sufficient to prevent the self being found out. It is a world very much associated with the American sociologist, Erving Goffman, where social survival is linked to skills in manners of appearing in public rituals. Impression management enables events to pass by, well oiled to preclude insincerity getting stuck. His actors reflect the world of Willy Loman, where 'the man who makes an appearance in the business world, the man who creates personal interest, is the man who gets ahead. Be liked and you will never want'.[6] The self survives in servicing slight engagements in an easy civility sufficient to accomplish a task with the least personal investment. These public encounters, often involve waiters, and commercial travellers, who make a living out of appearing sincere. They operate with all the skills and street knowledge of a 'lumpen bourgeois',[7] earning their daily bread in a world characterised by a 'sociology of soul selling'.[8] Dissimulation is an occupational necessity. In some cases, the structures of life impose an immoral demand; but in others they can generate a moral option. In one context, dissimulation enables and in another, it disables. There is a profoundly ambiguous facet to dissimulation, as it begs a question of who has been deceived: the actor or his audience?

Commercial worlds, where the 'real' action seems to be, involve a life of servicing 'fronts' of brief commercial engagement. An immoral image of manipulation emerges, that concentrates on the stratagems of survival of the morally unfit, engaged in coping with a career of disedification. Certainly, this world seems far removed from that operating on the sanctuary, where impression management is geared to the peculiar concerns of a 'sociology of soul buying', where efforts are made to lead, not to mislead, to edify not to disedify, and to be sincere in conditions where insincerity is easy. This little world of dealing in holiness seems far removed from the deceits and façades governing Goffman's usual and more cynical concerns. Yet the management of piety involves the regulation of appearances. Impressions count if they are to edify. The procedures that secure insincerity in Goffman's world can also be used to understand how sincerity is secured in adverse circumstances in liturgical enactments.

Goffman paid little attention to impression management in religious rituals, yet there are many aspects of his writings that can be applied to the interpretation of liturgical performance. He was concerned with the degree to which sincerity and trust reflected social accomplishments. In his writings, the self is under siege from the social, where it is being continually tested and scrutinised. All the time the actor is engaged in a struggle to maintain a balance of meanings between appearance and self. This tension between appearance and self involves a struggle to emerge credibly in public, to sustain a desired property that confirms expectations of the role. Discrepancies will arise, but these often aid in securing an authenticity in the part. Goffman claimed that 'it is thus *against something* that the self can emerge'. A social consciousness of self arises in the deployment of strategies to deal with discrepancies that emerge as hazards in the ebb and flow of the social, for, as he goes on to add, 'our sense of personal identity often resides in the cracks'.[9]

The feast of the Epiphany, on 6 January, that celebrates the baptism of Christ and His appearance to the Gentiles. It has a richness of meaning, one that encompasses the notion of a manifestation, a descent from majesty to aid and to support believers and worshippers. The term expresses an instance of grace that comes down from above. Shades of the unseen can become attached to the slight, and be discerned in unexpected guises. A characteristic of epiphany is that it operates in paradoxical circumstances. It is an ingredient in rite that saves it sinking into layers of contradiction, and rescues the self from falling into the cracks its habitual use generates for the actor. How is the link between epiphany and the social to be made?

Goffman offers a conceptual means of accounting for this transformation from appearance into the invisible. His concept of 'keying' refers to a systematic transcription of ordinary meanings in the world through play. Thus, 'keying' involves a 'set of conventions by which a given activity, one already meaningful in terms of some primary framework, is transformed into something patterned on this activity but seen by the participants to be something quite else'.[10] In its ceremonial usage, Goffman uses the term to refer to an event in which the performer takes on the task of representing and epitomising himself in a central role in a self-symbolising way.[11] The self is implicated in this process of transformation that links to dissimulation but in an ambiguous way.

If the self wishes to be sincerely attached to what is epitomised in the role, elements of truth might be concealed from him, which the audience, with a greater spiritual maturity, might understand. We have noted how this quality of asymmetry forms a condition of understanding in the case of innocence. In liturgical transactions this incompleteness of knowing has to be added to the incalculable properties of rite. There are layers of hiddenness in what is proclaimed, some that bear on qualities of virtue and holiness, but others on elements of vice and deceit. Something more than equivocation arises in efforts to use the social resources of rite to refract the holy. The more one tries to push past appearances on the sanctuary, the more one encounters profound ambiguities over what is understood by the actors involved in the reproduction of rite. The issue of how much they know, and how much is concealed from them, takes on a mysterious quality, for, after all, they are endeavouring to mirror what can only be imperfectly understood. This failure to perceive a truth that is hidden is reflected in the famous comment of St Paul:

> When I was a child, I spake as a child, I understood
> as a child, I thought as child: but when I became
> a man, I put away childish things. For now we see
> through a glass, darkly; but then face to face: now
> I know in part; but then shall I know even as also
> I am known (1 Cor.13 :11–12).

The liturgical order needs to be kept in continual repair if trust and truth are to survive. This need to protect can involve a masking, a practice of concealment, that enables the holy to be found with the least theological damage. Some form of impression management is required to convey a sense of the holy. It cannot be delivered in a random fashion. In Goffman's writings, there is a concern with the sacredness of the social order, a marking of its limits, and a moral interest in the relationship between the self and its effort to realise meanings in precarious settings. As we have said before, since the actor's spiritual state cannot be checked, the possibilities of lying and deception are greatly amplified. This might seem an asset for those who wish to pursue a career of liturgical deception. But for the actor who wishes to engage his life sincerely in affirming a truth that might edify, the uncheckable nature of liturgical transactions is a mixed blessing. The last thing he would want is to find himself lying in the act, a form of dissimulation with fatal spiritual consequences.

The task of coping with concealments and revelations in the liturgical act bears on similar difficulties that can be found in Goffman's works, where the link between sincerity and the self is problematic. The more secular settings of Goffman draw attention to the peculiar tasks of securing holy impressions on the sanctuary. In the following section we discuss lies and deception, and that peculiar problem of self deception. This leads to the final section on the notion of a virtuous dissimulation, where an acceptable basis for concealing is established. A variation on the theme of self-deception is offered that is linked to the notion of tact.

MEANINGFUL LIMITS TO IMPRESSION MANAGEMENT

> It is only shallow people who do not judge by appearances.
> (Oscar Wilde, *The Picture of Dorian Gray*)

Appearances matter in modern society. The clothes, the gestures, the stance of the actor serve to mark his credibility in a role where initial impressions count. The fluidity and range of relationships in cosmopolitan society place a greater onus on appearance than before, when the actor could be known in a less fragmented manner in more settled stable communities. Aptness in mode of appearing in a sophisticated urban social setting inspires confidence. It confers a credibility on the actor, hence his concern with adjusting appearance with subtlety. The mode of appearing in a role marks an anticipation of what is required for a particular social setting. Behaviour regulated skilfully in a meaningful way confirms what is expected and so secures recognition of the act.

The physical setting for a social event serves to highlight the activities of the actors involved. It supplies a facilitating background to what is being staged. A restaurant, with a rococo ceiling, Dresden china and fresh linen table-cloths, enhances a sense of occasion of a meal in an exceptional public setting. Civility is added to the physiological task of eating, and the crudeness of the act is disguised in the setting. Likewise, the singing of a liturgical office, such as choral evensong, often occurs in the magnificence of a Gothic setting, with carved choirstalls, bracketed candles and a sense of luminosity in the space the Cathedral encloses. When the choir sings, the settings enhance the sound, the text, and intensify the mind to seek a message in an event that is profoundly unmodern. They assist the self to attend to the significance of the event and to decipher the appearances of the actors to find the religious belief they embody and express.

Current interest in Goffman rests on his ambiguous study of ambiguity in social transactions. At one level, he seems to paint modern society with damning cynicism. His sophisticated actors bear social fronts easily through a packaged realm, where triviality is given weight, and sincerity is feigned. Appearances are bought and sold in a manner geared to impress. Plausibility is the ultimate test and to be implausible is to be found wanting. A variety of veneers is presented for inspection in gesture, stance and role that serve to establish meanings and sustain intercourse. Deceits and conceits count and as Alasdair MacIntyre has suggested, Goffman has 'liquidated the self into its role-playing' and has attached it to a peg upon which to play insincerely.[12] There is a perverse aspect to the world of Goffman, of clever puppets fooling audiences who wish to be deceived, who accept the façade to have the service. The audience colludes in the impressions being presented.

But in another way Goffman is a moral critic, one who sees below the surface of social appearances. He chronicles the way the self is tested and violated in conditions where the actor has little control. The actor can also be a victim of the ambiguous nature of appearance made manifest in social situations in an interaction order. A social face exists that embarrasses and entraps the individual in a discrediting front that admits no escape. Such a marred actor is forced to pass tests which his appearance dooms him to fail. Far from being a master of the social setting, where the self can be kept at a safe remove, the actor can find himself doomed by the external world that invades and entraps his soul in a label, that denies him the right to be more than he appears. This vulnerability of the self to such continual testing, distrust, and humiliation suggests a different image to that of the happy puppet who escapes serious moral scrutiny. But even if the self can slide with impunity across a series of social settings, it is likely to face an identity crisis, and a worry about its capacity to be sincere. At some point it will have to decide whether there is more to the self than meets the social gaze.

The responses of others to an actor's actions provide a mirror in which he can gauge his social impact. By monitoring his effect on a social setting, the actor can adjust his delivery, and can reconcile differences between intended meanings and those unintentionally given off in his manner of appearing. Manipulation is the name of the game, with its own distinct set of skills and rules for bending and shaping within the constraints of a public event. The autonomy of the self is realised in this capacity to adjust its impact on social settings. Responses of others to the significant gestures of an actor relate to an internal forum in which the self debates over its social impact. This capacity to monitor points to a process which G. H. Mead has described in terms of a 'conversation of gestures between the individual and the self'. The self uses this dialogue within, to order responses before they emerge in the external world.[13]

This point of Mead has an important implication for our argument. It suggests that an element of the covert and the tacit applies to *all* forms of social interaction, and not solely to those occurring in a liturgical setting. Within symbolic interaction, it is argued that the self has an elective capacity to reveal and to conceal. Admittedly, there are structural constraints on choice that restrict freedom. Nevertheless, a crucial qualification is made to the degree to which external behaviour discloses everything about a particular transaction. There are hidden elements in any social transaction that have to be interpreted. This admits a certain degree of uncertainty in sociological accounts of interaction. Inference rather than causation is the basis upon which sociological understandings are established.

Sociological accounts have become more provisional, and claims to a scientific privilege to know better are increasingly marginalised, if not discarded. A conversational style shapes sociological efforts to understand truth in social reality. [14] In recent years, sociology seems to have become available to hear almost any account of an action with a sympathetic acceptance and a lack of judgement that some might find surprising. As Wes Sharrock and Bob Anderson have indicated, in their assessment of Harold Garfinkel, an 'advanced' ethnomethodologist, there is nothing sacred that cannot be analysed or raised for scrutiny.[15] They argue for a sociological approach that refrains from doubt to yield that which is analytically fruitful. Instead of a sceptical approach to social reality, that emphasises things are not as they seem, they argue for an acceptance of everyday routines. Thus, 'the world of daily life, the world of ordinary experience, is taken by us to be primordially the real world. *Things just are as they appear*' (my emphasis).[16] But if the sociologist is forced to take accounts of social transactions on trust, the same cannot be said of the actor and his audience who have to survive in modern society, where deceptive practices abound, and misleading appearances are all too common. A degree of distrust in appearances is required to survive. Appearances can be genuine, but they can also deceive.

There is a worry that the maintenance of an appearance of dedication is sufficient to pass for success, and a premium is placed on the superficial to effect sincerity. In modern conditions of commercial life, the self must not get too close to the service provided, lest it complicate the appearances demanded for the job. Goffman has given much attention to this problem, but as MacIntyre has observed, ideals are denied in this form of analysis which seeks to deflate 'the pretensions of appearances to be anything more than appearance'.[17] In Goffman's world, the self seems to live in a permanent state of semidetached residence with its appearance. It is close enough to the social front to appear sincerely engaged, but is distant enough to be uninvolved in its implications. It hovers around in a variety of settings, simulating interest to effect entry to a transaction, and dissimulating enough to disguise a departure. The ambiguity of appearance, of engagement and disengagement of the self in its presentation, carries an element of hypocrisy. One needs to be alert to this ambiguous quality in Goffman's world, of being taken in by an appearance, or of being fooled by paying it insufficient attention. But the customers have their own facet of ambiguity in handling appearances. They seem to allow themselves to be deceived by the packaging of sincerity in everyday service life and their collusion is needed for these artificial transactions to proceed. Do they know they are investing in something so insincere, or does it matter?

Emotions, sincerity and interest are packaged as part of the service and these form a commodity which the actor is paid to utilise. The purchase of the self for display occurs with salesmen, and in organisations where a demand is made on the actor to produce a stylised 'front' that sustains the service required.[18] Arlie Russell Hochschild has termed this 'emotional labour'. This refers to 'the management of feeling to create a publicly observable facial and bodily display'. This capacity to 'front' earns a wage and involves a distinctive type of work increasingly common in service industries. It belongs very much to the world of the waiter which we explore later. Some simulation is required to produce the interest necessary to deliver the service in a predictable and acceptable manner. In her analysis Hochschild is concerned with American air hostesses and debt collectors. Dissimulation is the most pernicious aspect of emotional labour, for the self has to be disguised and held back, even in the face of hostile customers. There is a price in this work. The actor wonders where work ends and the 'real' self begins. The structure of the work constrains the self, and regulates what it can produce.[19] Oddly little attention has been given to the sociological study of emotions and their relationship to the social reproduction of values and labour in society.[20] Earning a living by impressing with a capacity to mislead, displaying an interest in the intrinsically uninteresting, make demands on the self that can be accommodated to – at a price. The phoney nature of the life tests the self, and generates a doubt. How many slices of the 'real' self have to put into the social sandwich to entice the customer to 'bite' and take the service?

Many of these dilemmas arise in Goffman's analysis. At one level, he gives the self a degree of autonomy in dealing with social situations. Difficulties can be rescued in ploys that disguise social infelicities, and the self can retreat with a minimum of embarrassment. There is a sense in which Goffman suggests that the role rescues the self, by supplying stratagems that come in a package embedded in the part. Insincerity facilitates the ebb and flow of service life. It allows productivity to proceed in a predictable, uninvolved manner, one that can be packaged and marketed. As Alvin Gouldner suggests, the self is paid to be unemployed, and to be shelved in the interests of service.[21]

There is an illusory element of freedom in some aspects of Goffman's link between the self and a social situation. A space for retreat without damage seems to be allowed in a structure that seems both liberal and pliable. An infinite number of permutations for withdrawal are presented and the self seems safe from harm. But the self so presented seems not only counterfeit, but also artificial, a creature of social settings devoid of emotion, ideals and a past. No deeper meanings emerge in its timeless waltz through a variety of superficially precarious social situations. As Richard Sennett has aptly noted, Goffman's sociology offers an element of drama, of role playing and of theatre, that is devoid of a sense of human engagement. There is no apparent sense of struggle with an identity that lies at a remove from the social.[22] Goffman presents a social game in which the self plays with low stakes, and with little risk of damage if he loses. In some of his works, there is a cut and paste quality to the analysis, as examples are plastered together in a mosaic, filled with the minute detail of telling little ploys that mark the well-adjusted cosmopolitan man who fears no evil and does no good. This static episodic cast to Goffman's work seems to offer little scope for moral speculation. It seems to present a self far removed from religious issues. Yet a deeper, more precarious sense of self emerges in Goffman's later writings.

The self is tested in a way that offers little escape, and the image is less amusing and far more pessimistic. Lofland suggests three important aspects of the self in Goffman's writings that have important implications for our analysis. Firstly, an 'official self' is presented, one that resides in the social arrangements of a group or an institution. Secondly, the self is shown as a performer who is awarded a legitimate retreat from the official demands of the 'front' part of an operation. An area is marked, where the self can emerge in private, out of role and off-duty. Both these official and performing selves combine to regulate a role in a way that precludes discrepancies and indiscretions arising. There is a third aspect of self, of being in opposition to aspects of the social. It is under continual threat of invasion from structural conditions outside its control, that cannot be contained by the self within.[23] An aspect of this emerges in *Asylums*, where the self is routinely violated by intrusive official arrangements that regulate the public life of the 'total institution'. The self is under continual scrutiny in a way that makes privacy a social achievement. Room for retreat becomes a hard won accomplishment. The structure plays on the self with impunity, the converse of the image presented in commercial games.[24] This more moral analysis of Goffman exposes the ambiguous link between the self and its social setting.

A similar lack of escape in a test that is not of the actor's own making appears in *Stigma*. The self lies behind a discrediting mask, an appearance that is doomed to spoil the chances of polite intercourse on initial contact. This flawed appearance is subject to a labelling that encompasses the totality of the self. The actor becomes marginalised to a distance sufficient for the audience to make a civil escape. [25]

The issue of whether the self deceives or is deceived by a social setting that shapes a role is ambiguous. Many times it is unclear who is the victim and who is the beneficiary of this ambiguous game played between the self and the social setting within which the part is enacted. Whatever cynicism might be noted in Goffman's analysis, there is a reverential stress on what he conceives to be the 'interaction order' and the inescapable vulnerabilities its instruments of use generate for the self.[26] One commentator noted that he was 'religious about sociological work' and added that he had a 'deep appreciation of the essential fragility of the self, of the wonder and sacredness of the social magic we invoke collectively so as to shield, nurture, and finally venture it before our fellow humans'.[27] Some definition of the social situation is required if meanings are to be delivered and misunderstandings are to be precluded. Goffman's contribution to sociology has been to uncover the ploys and procedures employed by actors to enable social transactions to proceed. Events do not just happen; they have to be constructed, regulated and controlled if their defining characteristics are to be secured. This point applies to all forms of social transaction, even to liturgies. As Thomas G. Miller has noted, Goffman has shown that 'there is no escape from the circle of social appearances, no break in the cycle of role performances, all of which are on a par *as* performances'.[28]

But the self does have some power to break free of appearances. The self has an internal relationship to its external appearance, that gives it a significant degree of control over the establishment of conditions of trust. For instance, being sick is associated with the right to opt out of social responsibilities in order to occupy an acceptable state of inactivity. The medical profession certify claims to be ill, and this regulates the supply of lay sympathy, which is often scarce. Illness is a negotiated condition and a degree of trust is associated with claims to feeling unwell. Discrepancies can exist between external appearances and an internal physiological state. Hypochondriacs can exploit this discrepancy through false claims to sympathy. Herzlich gives an interesting example of the degree to which appearance can be exploited in relation to claims to be ill. Illness is regarded as a social construction, and some of her sample were adept at manipulating appearances to effect false claims to be sick. One respondent observed that 'if nobody wanted to be ill any more, there would be much less illness . . . I believe very strongly in the possibility of starting off illnesses oneself and misleading the doctor'.[29]

In Alan Dawe's characterisation of Goffman, much play is made of the relationship between the self and the small rituals that involve the maintenance of images that are expressed in performance. These emerge in the management of impressions in a crafty sociological game. Concealment, calculation and gamesmanship are ploys that can be used without limits of sincerity in Goffman's frame of analysis.[30] The social actor strives to appear in a particular way, to present an image in an arena where 'social acting is a category of expressive action'.[31] Thus, Miller argues that in Goffman's analysis, the social actor's only concern is with the social consequences of the image and not its moral effects.[32] This notion of appearing without moral responsibility for the part places Goffman's actor close to his theatrical counterpart in the way he manipulates his audience.

The dramatic metaphor in Goffman's writings is well known, but it requires some qualification, when the theatrical actor is compared with his sociological counterpart. Theatrical actors are expected to appear in images for which their selves are not deemed responsible. They enact parts that may be base or virtuous, which only the most credulous might regard as revealing any aspect of their off-stage 'real' selves. The theatrical actor might have some sympathy for his part, but this is not necessary for its simulation – indeed, in some cases, this could be counterproductive. To realise his theatrical role, to make it 'believable and spontaneous' and to naturalise the presentation of a life in an artificial manner, the actor needs the flexibility of the child and the experience of the adult to become the character.[33] The actor's career is

one of uninvolvement in what he proclaims. Being so absolved from
the moral implications of what he presents, the actor can play his part
with impunity. But, as Richard Sennett notes, this was Jean-Jacques
Rousseau's objection to the theatre, that it promoted the vices of man
in a way that suggested that he did not have to struggle to survive.[34]
Denis Diderot noted that the actor 'excels in simulating, though he
feels nothing'.[35] If the actor's 'real' self is to survive and he is not to
become a chameleon, whose personality is the same, whether on stage
or off, some art of separation is required to effect a distance from his
part.[36] To sustain his off-stage sense of identity, the actor has to
dissimulate his self to simulate the part he is paid to represent.

Acting is a form of transformation that effects entry into the
character of another. Making this appropriation seem natural and
plausible on the stage is the actor's craft. The actor is engaged in an
imagined imitation that involves a paradox: he appropriates the
essence of the part in a manner that requires a distance from it. This
involves a delicate path of working through an apparent contradiction,
of establishing an element of disbelief which at the same time admits
the possibility of belief in the part. There is an occupational skill
involved in bracketing doubt, to let go, in order to fulfil that which
inhibition would disable. A similar form of bracketing doubt, to gain
access, arose in the previous chapter, when we were considering the
issue of innocence in a ceremonial manifestation. The need to believe
in the part to fulfil its basis involves an element of playful risk, a
capacity to let go, and to abandon suspicion. The point has been well
expressed by Callow, when he argues that

> everything that is will-full in a performance comes between the actor
> and the performance, because it is inherently future-stressed. The
> actor must simply be. The character must want, the character must
> will. But the actor must be, with the totality of his being, in front of
> the audience *at this moment*.[37]

There is an artificial cast to acting that precludes the self being
found wanting. Rehearsal, a script, and the formal demands of staging
a part, lend a structural security to the actor, within which he can
regulate a distance between the theatrical role and his 'real' self. His
professional identity, combined with the more mundane practices of
off-stage actors, facilitates this capacity to walk away from the
theatrical part, and to return to it afresh at the next performance.
The actor can dissimulate his own self to preclude it being tested or
being found wanting. The actor's craft demands a capacity to detach

the self to produce the part, to secure an intended meaningful basis to his appearance. Dissimulation, and a division between the private self and a public act, refer to forms of concealing for revealing. Feigning fulfils fantasies in a dramatic package in the theatre in a way that marks it off from the selling of self as a commodity under the duress of 'emotional labour'. Against this background, the trials of the liturgical actor seem more comprehensible. They are partly those to be found in managing any social situation, but they are also those peculiar to the operation of liturgical performance.

The liturgical actor faces the routine problem of securing a definition of the situation, where sincerity matters most, if he is to avoid deluding himself and others. Whereas those who act in the theatre or in the structured world of 'emotional labour' occupy a detached or semi-detached state, where dissimulation preserves a creative or spiritual reserve, a fair retreat for the self, those who work in liturgical practice operate in contrasting conditions. Liturgical actors survive in the public part through efforts to attach the self to the implications of the part, to incarnate in virtue that which it proclaims for public edification. Dissimulation is less a means of survival than a procedure for preserving virtue, for protecting the self against the antinomial slings and arrows that wait in ambush in liturgical performance. The liturgical actor has to secure an authenticity in the rite, where lying and deceit are so easy and so available to cover deficiencies. If 'emotional labour' has its distinctive price in structured commercial settings, where the self is being tested continually, the liturgical actor also faces dilemmas of a peculiar kind, where fear of being found wanting before God and man can haunt horribly. Codes of canon law are now benign on these questions of fear of failure. Theologians place the issue in the context of existentialism and in areas well removed from questions of praxis. In this account, we are looking at the notion of a test that emerges from within sociological understandings of the management of social situations, as it throws light on the efforts to link man to God through cultural means.

The capacity to attach or to detach the self from an appearance is more hazardous in social settings, where there is no script, and where the rules of engagement and disengagement of the self are less clear-cut. In the social world, the self is under continual threat, facing testing in settings not of its own making. There is an open agenda to this risk of failure, whose boundaries are indeterminate. Coping with this reflects a central concern of Goffman. Despite his cynicism and his pessimism, there are some theological fingerprints in his work.

Goffman was highly interested in the problem of being found wanting in a social situation, where its definition *cannot* be secured by the actor. This failure to cope with social discrepancies gives his work a moral quality. Discrepancies in the manner of appearing in a public transaction, that might result in a loss of face, have to be repaired, if a social encounter is not be rendered incredible. Michael Schudson has argued that embarrassment – discrepancies or unfulfilled expectations where the actor is found wanting – exists as a continual threat to social interaction. [38] Public humiliation exposes recesses of the self that the actor could feel are best kept hidden. An unacceptable breach of expectations in a public performance, that is also irretrievable, might amplify an aspect of the actor's character that could be regarded as discrediting. A failure in public performance might force the actor to participate in a test he knows he might not pass.

Paul Creelan argues that Goffman became increasingly concerned with the moral purpose of the relationship between the self and forms of social interaction. The issue of there being more than mere appearance in a frame of interaction increasingly engaged his interest. The limits of the frame generated the possibility of a 'vital test'. This had a capacity to bring the claims of an individual to moral authenticity into doubt in a way that could be fatal to the self. Creelan argues that the social actor can be given an involuntary test in a manner of scrutiny that resembles Job's plight in dealing with the limits of Jewish rituals.

Despite his strict conformity to their rules of enactment, Job appeared to be wanting in his relationship to God. The sufferings inflicted on him, apparently by God, could only be understood by his comforters as reflecting some failure in external performance. Creelan argues that Job encountered the social limits of forms of rites, and his sufferings were a witness to that which lay beyond their manifest boundaries. Forms of rite can be corrupted, and can be subject to a narrowing egoistic corruption that converts them into instruments of self-edification. They become closed to the Divine, and act no longer as openings to an inexhaustible mystery. This raises a point I will develop in later chapters. Creelan suggests that Goffman uses Job as his basis for understanding that

> beyond nature, beyond society, and beyond the individual lies a mystery of Being that continually surpasses, indeed itself engenders the ever-changing outlines of these other finite structures of existence.[39]

In this interesting reading of Goffman, it is noteworthy that the issue of the test is set in the context of the management of a religious ritual, where the sacred, the moral and the authentic all converge on the issue of the ambiguity of appearance, the limits of the social and a doubt that confounds actor and audience alike. The 'vital test' occurs, as one might expect, in a ritual setting. Goffman seems to suggest that the sacred relates to issues that lie beyond the purely social in a way that might have perplexed Durkheim. He confined the sacred to the social and limited ambiguities within it in a way that Goffman seems to deny. Goffman gives an ambiguous cast to appearance and the social order it inhabits. It bears an opening to an inexhaustible mystery, a quality of indeterminacy, so that the social, far from being a master of the sacred, emerges in Goffman's writing as its servant. Forms of interaction are meaningful to the degree to which they effect a sense of transcendence of their social limits. It is when the social form takes on a complete quality that obscures the need to test and be tested that it fails to resonate. Unless a detailed scrutiny is brought to a social event, so that its limits, ambiguities and appearances are magnified, it is so easy to pass on.

This need to look closely at the dubious limits of the social has always been understood in sociology. Ralf Dahrendorf, in his celebrated account of Homo Sociologicus, saw the need to stress the ambiguity of the social role and the dilemma it expressed of joining society, or opting out. Sociology brings to the study of social beings an alienating exactitude that can lead to an unintentional de-humanisation. To offset this threat, Dahrendorf stressed the residual aspect of man, the capacity to stand back from the parts, the masks and other sociological bits and pieces that can be found in the role. These residual elements could be the self, the soul and those areas inaccessible to sociological scrutiny.[40] Dahrendorf marked sociology's need to find an image of man to qualify the artificial constructs it has to use to analyse.[41] Both Goffman and Dahrendorf point to a moral dimension that suggests more than appearing in a social nexus ultimately counts.

Liturgy seems to offer an ideal base to find the inexhaustible in a moral operation that proceeds on the basis of trust, but its study does not get sociology out of its analytical difficulties. Indeed, it seems to compound them. If the social form of a liturgy is indeterminate in relation to its transcendent content and the self has an uncheckable relationship to its enactment, then a contradiction has been established that seems to remove its study from sociological inquiry. The actor could be fooled by the form, but he could be deceiving in its use. This poses an ambiguity for sociology as to which end to start under-standing from: the actor or the social form. As we shall suggest later, the link between action and structure has an accepted quality of ambiguity in sociology. Rather than resist this ambiguity, it might be better to explore the meanings it enables to emerge.

Stress on the ambiguous aspects of liturgy brings in a distortion for sociological purposes. It assumes in a secular age, where there is indifference to religious rituals, that there are polarities operating that are deep, meaningful, and perhaps dangerous to the participants. It establishes scruples theologians would discount and dilemmas that might seem to be sociological inventions to see better, but in a blinding fashion. Theologians would absolve with reference to grace and faith these distortions and scruples that emerge in an artificial sociological gaze. To take such a redemptive path would be to avoid a sociological question. The cultural instruments used in liturgical enactments have considerable potential for lying and deceits, in holy and unholy hands. These lies are the liabilities of liturgical productions and emerge in the use of imperfect means to find God.

LIES AND DECEPTION: HOLY AND UNHOLY CONCEAL-MENTS OF THE SELF

> He that worketh deceit shall not dwell within
> my house: he that telleth lies shall not tarry
> in my sight.
>
> (Ps. 101:7)

To affirm the truth through social means involves a recognition of the possibility of deceiving in the act. As I indicated earlier, the uncheckable private nature of rite gives rise to peculiar possibilities of deceits being practised. There is a fine distinction between that which is incomplete by its nature in rite and which cannot be spelt out, and that which reflects a culpable omission, a misleading state of affairs that deceives.

Counterfeit actions in rite are often difficult to spot. They discredit, because they mislead, and if discovered mark a discrepancy between the holiness proclaimed in public and the inner state of the actor. Some counterfeit actions can be the accidental result of the habitual nature of liturgical engagements. The actors seen on the sanctuary have performed their tasks numerous times before. Repetition can lead to boredom, to dangers of an overfamiliarity with the task of worship that can give it a deadening quality. Few liturgical actors can manage a perfect connection between their inner self and the external holy face they present in every rite they service. An actor, who strives to attach himself to the holy, and to be implicated in the image he presents, but falls short, is different from a person who deliberately cultivates a career of detachment that veils a private contempt for his public part. The actor who lapses in small matters of liturgical detail, who feels himself false, despite his prayerful efforts, is also likely to scruple and worry most about lying, not only before the congregation but also before God. Schooled in liturgy from his youth, he might become all the more aware of the shortcomings in the image he incarnates. Charges of pharisaism hurt the spiritually sensitive most. The man who coins lies with abandon on the sanctuary, who disbelieves in what he enacts, can live lightly with his deceit. His smoothness of manner is unlikely to attract attention. He embodies a lie that the outsider, the disbeliever, is least likely to notice. Because he does not care about any spiritual test rites might throw up, he can dissimulate and fail with impunity. These tests are examinations he has no wish to enter, nor has he any intention of passing. But a holy actor caught in an issue of deception finds himself in a misleading state of affairs, a plight that arises from the pursuit of spiritual ambitions. The unholy feigner is the beneficiary of a false representation of his beliefs. The social substance of a liturgical lie is discussed in the next three chapters. Both actors, the holy man and the feigner, deceive in a way that arouses a contrasting response. The latter might be an oily villain, gaining little or no sympathy, whereas the former arouses compassion for his plight which represents an overdeveloped awareness of the antinomies of the human condition. Both misrepresent their state in differing ways. It cannot be said that each does not have a reason. The question will arise as to whether it is a good one?

The issue of lies and deceits involves questions of ethics that fall outside our remit. We are concerned with incomplete information, with the necessary nature of a degree of virtuous dissimulation in the production of the liturgical act, with elements of denial that can mislead for good reason. There is a fine line between secrecy and mental reservation, between privacy and the public entitlement to know. To omit information could mislead. An omission could be unethical when the person who has concealed is a beneficiary in a way that allows him to gain something he would not otherwise procure if full information had been given. Fraud is an obvious example. But there are often good reasons not to reveal all, for secrets have their justifications as Sissela Bok has indicated.[42]

But if we defend the right to conceal, to be mysterious in liturgical enactments, how do we get around the problem of being misleading? If something is mysterious, we cannot expect the actor to resolve it, to clarify the state of affairs he represents. If he did, it would no longer be a mystery. We would have even fewer grounds to criticise him, if it were to be found that he was equally mystified by that which he so incompletely represented. He cannot be made totally accountable for not revealing that which is concealed from him also. It is no defence of the point to say that some liturgical facets deceive in a way that gives rise to queries about self deception. In some instances, he might have a good reason to cultivate inner sentiments that are different from those embodied in his public appearance. The pursuit of virtue might demand such a misrepresentation. The explicit might destroy that which is best expressed and understood through implicit, if not ambiguous means. The injunction to feign in the practice of virtue has its origins in the warning of Christ who stated:

> when ye fast, be not as the hypocrites, of a sad
> countenance: for they disfigure their faces, that
> they may appear unto men to fast. Verily I say
> unto you, They have their reward. But thou, when
> thou fastest, anoint thine head, and wash thy face;
> that thou appear not unto men to fast, but unto thy
> Father which is in secret: and thy Father, which
> seeth in secret, shall reward thee openly.
>   (Matt. 6:16–18)

I wish to argue that a degree of denial in the social act is required to effect the production of holiness. This is a variation on the theme of the tact required to handle a concept such as innocence, where the excessive pursuit of a demand for revelation can destroy the attribute, which can only be disclosed in precarious circumstances. A misrepresentation might occur, but somehow it seems to have a basis in sociological understanding. Concealments and disguises might seem to negate the need for authentic witness, but they can generate a curiosity, a need to explore, that can draw the puzzled into the realm of a greater truth. The intention is not so much to deceive as to affirm a higher calling.

Innocence conceals but in a way that arouses little curiosity in the case of the child. Rather more unexpected responses occur in the case of the adult, such as he who acts the fool. In the early Church, men became holy fools and behaved in a bizarre manner that bordered on lunacy. Their antics served as a witness to the folly of the world, but also to entice the experienced to follow Christ. Counterfeit idiocy was regarded as an instrument of edification, and for our purposes can be considered as an example of virtuous dissimulation. Holy fools followed a career of intentionally misleading the worldly wise with the aim of doing good, of converting them to a greater truth through the means of a lie.[43] The notion of virtuous dissimulation is in the realm of acceptable paradox, but it is also in the terrain of the lie. The example of the holy fool points to an issue that perplexes. What is to be done with an attribute, which if explicitly spelt out, would fracture the wholeness of a truth being presented through social means? If he acts to proclaim a foolishness, which is other than the truth, should he draw converts through such misleading appearances? In short, do such misleading means justify a holy end? In strict Catholic theological terms, such means that deceive cannot be justified.

A lie can be defined in Catholic teaching as 'a word, sign or action by which one expresses the contrary of what he thinks or wills (usually in order to deceive others)'.[44] This bears a similarity to a recent philosophical definition of a lie as 'an intentionally deceptive message in the form of a *statement*'.[45] Lies have a corrosive effect on social interaction. They undermine the trust that cements social bonds. Transactions have to be continually rechecked before negotiation can proceed. As St Augustine noted, 'every liar in lying breaks faith; for what he wants is that his hearer have faith in him; yet by lying, he himself does not keep faith'.[46] Lying justifies disengagement from social engagements, where the self might not wish to be deceived again.

Social forms whose meanings or implications are incomplete undermine the basis of free and full consent. They are unsafe to trust. For instance, the capacity to effect and to secure domination in the exercise of power relates to an ability to control the flow of information. Secrecy disables, for the dominated lack a knowledge of the basis upon which decisions are constructed, and in consequence their capacity to respond significantly is impaired.[47] Assent cannot be fully given on the basis of incomplete information. Faith speaks volumes for what cannot be said on this issue.

Lying is a denial of the fullness of what we ought to know in order to proceed with a full assent with what is being presented. Deception is a variation on a lie. It relates to an enticement to engage with what is false, or could be deemed misleading, if all its inconsistencies were to be exposed. As a particular form of hypocrisy, deception operates through external manifestations. It conspires to exploit a misattribution in a way in which the deceiver gains and the deceived lose. For instance, deception operates in the context of esteem being falsely awarded to an actor who exploits external qualities that are false, or that are incommensurate with the state of his inner self. The actor is the beneficiary of what he is not, if all were to be revealed about his true state. He manages to exploit this discrepancy in order to enhance his status. This capacity to mislead is easy if there is an uncheckable quality to the attribute he presents. We wish to exclude from our interests certain self-evident forms of deceit, such as fraud, impersonation, or hypochondria. Such deceivers misuse credentials that can be checked. Those engaged in religious forms of deceit pose more complex problems. They are dealing with the social use of religious elements that are deemed to be ultimately uncheckable. Their capacity to deceive or to lead to a truth is endless.

In Christianity (and perhaps other religions) hypocrisy reflects two factors that are interlinked: an absence of holiness and a pretence of its presence.[48] Hypocrisy represents a particular form of deceit. As St Gregory noted 'a hypocrite . . . is a grasping thief who, while acting wickedly, craves to be esteemed for holiness, and so steals the praise due to another way of living'.[49] Hypocrites make a conspicuous display of possessing a virtue that is inwardly absent. They are men who 'make God's interests serve a worldly purpose because by making a show of holy conduct they seek, not to turn men to God, but to direct to themselves the shifting winds of approval'.[50] Fear of misuse of instruments of worship gives rise to scruples amongst the pious as to whether they deceive or are being deceived themselves in liturgical performances.

Self approval carries specific dangers in religious life and needs to be checked. In monasteries, where purity and virtue might flourish to the degree to which few real faults can be found, resort can be made to the controversial practice of 'fictitious humiliations' such as practised at La Trappe by Rancé. This relates to the notion of making oneself available to be punished, even though innocent.[51] Such practices can become corrupting if monks enter the humility stakes, and score points for piety by attracting the most punishment. In such cases, it is difficult to separate practices that damage spiritual health from those that are simply a form of self-delusion. This illustrates again the difficult nature of lies and virtuous dissimulation. For the holiest of reasons the monks feigned offences to elicit humiliation and punishment. Virtue was clothed in the lightest of vices but in a way that did damage. The monks found themselves in a false position. Is our defence of a notion of virtuous dissimulation likely to founder on similar grounds? Do we need such a slippery term? Theologians might say that we have boxed ourselves into a false position.

There are particular reasons why we still need the term and these are sociological and are developed later. Our concern is to draw attention to the dilemmas the actor encounters in handling the antinomial basis of liturgy as he works through social means, where the issue of grace is marginalised. These dilemmas are exaggerated, and are distortions of the hazards of handling rites, but they do provide some sociological insights into its distinctive basis. Actors engaged in the production of rite have to guard against specific deceits being cultivated. Conceit and vanity can be amplified inadvertently so that social rather than spiritual aspects become the objects for display. The most private and spiritual sensibilities are on public display. That which is rendered to hidden account is in some ways more important than that which is manifest. It is written that '. . . the Lord seeth not as man seeth; for man looketh on the outward appearance, but the Lord looketh on the heart' (1 Sam. 16:7). The proportions between the inner culture and its external manifestation have to be regulated so that the former always dominates and matters most.

A degree of self-proclamation is required to make manifest the message of the rite, but if the actor intrudes too far in the part, then risks of conceit can be also amplified. Roger Grainger has expressed this dilemma well when he observes that ritual behaviour is the expression of

> an inner malaise, a codification of feelings that appear to be dangerous to the subject to be expressed openly, but which must nevertheless be expressed . . . .[52]

The pursuit of an authentic spiritual self, that strives to avoid charges of deception, has to pay attention to proper dispositions in a way that confronts certain inescapable contradictions. Inner dispositions have to be expressed even if they risk becoming vain and empty proclamations. The cultivation of liturgical propriety and beauty poses particular risks of deception, unless other matters are given attention. There is the warning of St Paul that 'though I speak with the tongues of men and of angels, and have not charity, I am become a sounding brass, or a tinkling cymbal' (1 Cor. 13:1).

The self is caught in an ambiguous position over interpreting that which might be a deceptive practice. The sense of emptying in the rite might be a test that brings spiritual strength, a form of darkness before the light, or it could express a carelessness, a boredom in dealing with the hallowed. The self is uncertain whether it is before a test, or has been tested and has failed.

There is a specific deceit involved in denying its possibility in a way that has sociological implications. Liturgical practice involves a deference before the holy, a recognition of a degree of incompleteness in the social form of the rite that is harmonised to a theological content that completes its basis. A deceit can arise in a form of rite that is so well practised as to obscure a sense of dependence on the holy from without. This can generate a conceit, a feeling that spiritual perfection has been reached. None are exempt from deceit, for true believers are warned:

> Let no man deceive himself. If any man among
> you seemeth to be wise in this world, let him
> become a fool that he may be wise. For the wisdom
> of this world is foolishness with God. For it is
> written, He taketh the wise in their own
> craftiness. (1 Cor. 3:18–19)

Dealing with the social involves a recognition of the limits of human nature, a point that reflects the saying 'if we say that we have no sin, we deceive ourselves, and the truth is not in us' (1 John 1:8). If the imperfections of human nature are to be contained and if virtue is to be realised, some distinctive form of practice is required, especially in the context of representing the holy in liturgy.

The possibility of a liturgical actor feeling he misleads in a way that comes near to a lie can haunt the spiritually sensitive. An enhanced spiritual awareness makes him conscious of the infelicities that might mar his passage into the holy. His sense of a lie might border on the scrupulous and his deception might be slight. The issue of a liturgical lie takes on a tragic force when an actor confronts antinomial instruments that block his access to virtue. Their use seems to deny what they are supposed to affirm. A young monk seeking to keep his sexual feelings under strict control might be embarrassed to find that his discipline produces thoughts he never knew and pleasures he never wanted. Another might find acts of humiliation produced feelings of conceit and delight at abasing before the proud. Finally, another might find that the music he loves seems to give more glory to him than to God. The actor gets in a muddle, affirming what he is supposed to deny and denying what he is supposed to affirm to possess the good life.

CONCEALING AS A FORM OF REVEALING: A DEFENCE OF VIRTUOUS DISSIMULATION

> But when thou doest alms, let not thy left hand know
> what thy right hand doeth.
>
> (Matt. 6:3)

Virtues such as humility and innocence require a degree of shelter from an approbation that might destroy. Pride stands opposite to humility and represents what it seeks to deny. Those who are humble strive to maintain a lowliness of station, a place on the margins of esteem. As we shall argue later, a gesture such as a bow, that marks a property of deference, encounters particular problems in delivering its intended meanings. The intention to be humble, and to defer, requires attention to social detail, if misunderstandings and unintended consequences are not to arise. There is a defensive, concealing aspect to the practice of virtue, and a need for a custodial rein to be kept on its exercise to realise its spiritual basis. A filtering operation occurs in the use of the social in rite so that a quality of denial is kept in what is affirmed. Certain qualities are not spelt out or signified and this gives to the performance of liturgy a distinctive style practice. Tact and reticence shape the use of the social in rite.

A career in liturgical acting involves an engagement with repetitions, repeated with subtle variation on a weekly or daily basis. The cycle of Christian commitment expressed in the liturgy imposes a demand on the actors and takes a toll on their sensibility. The monk, the priest, the server or chorister all have repeated many times over what they appear to present with a fresh and awe inspiring dedication. Behind the uniformity of their actions, their vestments and their external manifestations of engagement lies the self of each, particular and peculiar in its biographical relationship to rite. Each actor carries the burden of repetition in different ways and the price of engagement is peculiarly variable. Few concepts are as complex as that of the self which lies behind the public front of the actor.

The self finds its identity in a struggle with the social instruments that permit it to express a part in society. But the self is more than a residual concept, the hinterland of sociological awareness. It bears a consciousness, a sensibility of limit where the particular and the unique find a location in the general, the universal and the mysterious. For the Christian, the self finds its realisation and fulfilment in Christ.[53] This involves an opening out to the implications of that relationship, the pursuit of deeper meanings that qualify a sense of place in social space. Such a struggle to reconcile the sense of self with the instruments that facilitate its social expression involves a monitoring of the truth of what is proclaimed. There is a defensive cast to growing in holiness that carries an obligation to regulate and to control the distortions of self with changing social circumstances. Few social arrangements can be found that obviate this obligation. Forms of discipline and control applied to boy oblates in Benedictine monasteries in the medieval world showed an attention to detail that suggests the production of angelic qualities was not a random process. As Patricia A. Quinn indicates, this was a life of sanctity, but one where the divisions of human nature persisted.[54] There is no natural evolution from boyhood into manhood where social means of control do not apply. An unthinking growth into adulthood, a failure to mature and to know the precariousness of angelic innocence can have fatal spiritual consequences. As Erasmus observed, 'it's proverbial that angelic boys become limbs of Satan when they grow old'.[55] Descent into corruption can come earlier, as is shown in William Golding's famous novel *Lord of the Flies*, where the marooned choirboys discover the evil savage side of human nature.[56]

The vulnerability of the self in rite becomes clearer with age, for it is continually at risk of being hoisted on a petard, of being blown asunder in instruments that are supposed to conserve, and to edify it. Few are exempt from these risks; all are rendered open to ultimate account; and those who claim otherwise deceive themselves and others. Increases in awareness of deceits, of discrepancies between appearing and the sense of imperfection of the self, generate a need to accommodate, to come to terms with these flaws. There is a humility in the calling to holiness which strikes even the child caught up in the implications of the liturgical act. The choirboy, sitting down after his solo, might reflect on the tears of compunction his singing wrought on those attending, and wonder why one so little moved so much; and the monk who sits in his choirstall, at a period of meditation, might wonder at the way he has avoided serious tests to his spiritual stability by comparison with others who have been asked more, and failed in a greater manner. Any actor in liturgy comes to see himself in his imperfections, where edification bears qualities of its opposite, an unworthiness, a sense of deceit that the self presented in the social is greater than what is known in privacy. Humility and holiness lead to a self-depreciation, a sense of inadequacy masked in the front of holiness confidently presented for public edification. Hidden layers of worry and doubt lie below the surface of liturgical actions, and hover in the recesses of the actor's mind.

The actor is not called to reveal all. Some reticence in the act is required, for the liturgical actor cannot parade an excess of doubt if belief in his part is to be secured. Some masking, some concealment is required, but how much, and how does it cross into the realm of lies and deception? There is a risk of misleading. As Ilham Dilman has noted, 'I find it difficult to imagine what moral and religious striving would be like if people were not prone to self-deception'.[57]

A degree of imperfection, of failing to live up to appearances, can be tolerated, and a reticence about lapses need not be broadcast. Aquinas argues that a person, wearing a religious habit, who fails to live up to the holiness it embodies, is not bound to broadcast his sin and to discard his habit.[58] In civil society a degree of reticence has acceptable purposes. The actor is not required to reveal all about himself in social intercourse. Good manners permit a level of disguise, and to that degree dissimulation can be deemed a necessary art. It offers a means of preserving a social face, 'a reserve to man's self a fair retreat'.[59] It forms the basis of a withdrawal from the social for the self to disassemble in privacy to re-assemble and to sally forth into the battle of social intercourse with wounds temporarily healed. The innocent seem to present a doubt to the experienced over their powers of dissimulation. How far are they involved consciously in the implications of what they conceal, and to what degree are things concealed from them by nature of the attribute they are believed to possess?

The innocent emerge as vulnerable social actors. They do not have the experience to know when to retreat, when to disguise and when to amplify. The innocent have certain advantages, for as Samuel Johnson noted, 'to dread no eye, and to suspect no tongue, is the great prerogative of innocence; an exemption granted only to invariable virtue'.[60] But in the case of the innocent, it is difficult to know if they are deceiving themselves, or if they are deceiving others in the act. The innocent pose a discrepancy that is ambiguous. They might know, but they might not know the implications of what they utter so innocently.

To render them to experienced account would highlight an area of intentionality that could destroy the virtue. It would be to amplify that which is understood when incompletely rendered. Not to render the innocent to account, would be to risk being fooled, being drawn into a pernicious form of dissimulation, one masked with virtue, the actor simulates. The difficulty is that the innocent present an ambiguity when efforts are made to render them to account.

Innocence can be conceived as a form of self-deception. This reflects a paradox, of how the self conceals that which it knows, and proclaims what it sincerely denies within. An ambiguous message is presented, but one that conveys a meaningful and acceptable form of contradiction, one that has implications for an interpretative approach to liturgical performance.

Self-deception involves an intentional ignorance, a persistent avoidance of an implication. This generates a practice of veiling and editing aspects of the actor's public engagement with the world.[61] Dissimulation relates to a fear of some hidden trait being exposed that would discredit the self or would complicate the passage of social proceedings. The self keeps a custody over those meanings which are to be spelt out and those which are best kept unamplified. The audience also collude in preserving a social front in a performance, and as Goffman indicates, they leave certain matters unsignified to allow the act to proceed. To sustain a dramatic effect and a tension in a theatrical play, an audience will keep silent, while an actor struggles to recover his lines.[62] Inaction can be as important as action in regulating the enactment of rite. A degree of dissimulation can keep the performance going. Concealing facilitates an act of revealing. But dissimulation still relates rather too closely to the possibility of lying. There is a lurking feeling that it affirms something inauthentic and in this context is being given an equivocal defence.

But if we confront somebody who conceals an attribute, and refuses to have it spelt out, we cannot claim to be deceived, if the actor is also taken in by his own lie. If he deceives himself, who are we to complain? This seems to take the issue of antinomy into the heart of the self. Self-deception involves a 'wilful ignorance'. Onlookers have a feeling that the social actor must know in private that which he appears not to know in public. The self-deceiver occupies a contradictory position of appearing to be both sincere and in some way, insincere, for reasons that are unclear to the observers of his actions.[63] Following David Kipp's argument, self-deception can arise where one 'shams beliefs consistent with one's possessing that quality in the hope of deceiving the others into thinking one possesses it'.[64] The issue of dissimulation revolves around the motive, the reason for so concealing, but if the ploy succeeds, this might be unapparent. This hidden agenda to social actions generates a number of complications. If the actor accepts the contradictions of a lie to self, how can a sociologist reason otherwise? Perhaps in revealing the 'real' basis of the action, he might do untold damage. There might be a moral limit to what one feels ought to be known.

Fingarette argues that the self uses defensive and protective tactics to protect these inconsistencies within, and, if necessary, he disavows them lest they become accidentally exposed in his engagement with the world.[65] The self is an accomplishment that strives to overcome contradictions that might impair its social manifestation. Behind its selectivity about what to reveal, and what to conceal, is a wish to sustain a moral integrity in the face of contradictions that would destroy the self. In that context, there is a moral purpose to the self-deception. Fingarette suggests that the greater the integrity of the individual, the greater is the temptation to self-deceive, for 'the nearer to saintliness, the more a powerful personality suffers'. He goes on to add that

> it is because the movement into self-deception is rooted in a concern for integrity of spirit that we temper our condemnation of the self-deceiver. We feel he is not a *mere* cheat. We are moved to a certain compassion in which there is awareness of the self-deceiver's authentic inner dignity as the motive of his self-betrayal.[66]

Even if the motives of the self-deceiver are acceptable, this strategy of engaging so selectively with the world can take on an unhealthy life of its own. This can lead to a failure to become properly engaged with the world in a career of deception that marks an immature wish to escape from its complications.[67] The actor can become entrapped in his self-deceptive practices. By colluding to affirm him in his moral contradictions, the audience can imprison the actor in a cage of illusions in a way that permits no escape.

Self-deception can arise inadvertently. Anthony Palmer gives an interesting example of a woman writing a diary, who moves issues of self-deception that lie below the surface into an actuality that she has to confront.[68] Elements of contradiction often become 'contingently intermingled 'in a way that only becomes clear in retrospection. This is an aspect of self-deception which Dilman brings out in his analysis of Tolstoy's short story 'Father Sergius'.[69] As the self grows in awareness, it becomes conscious increasingly of the need to deceive within, but also of the price being paid for keeping up appearances, without, on such a misleading basis.

Fingarette is concerned with the psychoanalytical implications of the self-deceiver as he tries to make an accommodation to his condition. Little attention is paid to the surrounding social world, which the self-deceiver has to occupy and to present himself with risks of misunderstanding, or worse, a discovery of his paradox in a realm where he cannot rescue himself without massive discredit. I wish to follow Haight in suggesting that self-deception points to an area of social ambiguity in what is released and what is retained by the actor, a selectivity of disclosure that is understandable.[70] The basis of the self-deception could lie in the nature of the relationship the self has to a social world within which he is implicated. Such a relationship carries an element of biography and struggle.

Self-deception carries notions of denial, of wilful concealment, which paradoxically facilitates access to a higher spiritual and moral integrity. It is a strategy that enables the self to survive antinomial divisions that would otherwise disable the actor if they were to be spelt out and confronted in a public setting. There is an unexpectedly emancipatory quality attached to the need to disavow aspects of the self in order to gain access to more desirable qualities. The issue of self-deception raises a question of an elective affinity the actor makes between his contradictions of self and the belief system within which these can be resolved. Kipp notes that Christianity deals with a willingness to believe that leads to a wanting to struggle to become implicated, to be more engaged with the object of belief. Thus, what the Christian faith seems to demand 'is not that one actually *believes* that the Christian myth is true, but rather that one hopes it is true, and *acts as if* were'.[71]

Buried in the issue of self-deception is a question of will, an intention to secure a truth that transcends paradox. In liturgical life, awareness of pockets of self-deception grows with spiritual maturity, as the actor fears what to confront and knows what cannot be spelt out, if his career in dealing with the holy is to develop. Habit in dealing with the hallowed risks boredom and familiarity, but it bears a price of detail being felt too deeply. The liturgical actor can become crucified within by niggling scruples that scar the soul. These can be worries about imperfections in liturgical engagements, the peculiar gap between appearance and inner spiritual reality, or the continual worry of confusing affiliation with the social form, with the spiritual content it is supposed to effect. The effort of the liturgical actor to focus the detail of rite into a concentrated search for spiritual worth risks encountering antinomial elements. These can become mirrored in the soul. The pursuit of spiritual perfection generates a knowing of imperfection. Awareness of this antinomial quality increases as the actor strives to reconcile a private self with its social manifestation in liturgical life, where a collective effort is made to reflect the holy and where the visible is used to mirror the invisible. A priest might have an irritating vanity about a particular chasuble he is asked to wear; a monk may feel his abasements are devoid of meaning; an altar server may feel a sense of embarrassment at acting before his school mates; and a choirboy may worry whether he does love God more than his football. These are all self doubts, divisions that emerge in liturgical activities. There are hidden worries, best denied and kept concealed through a strategy of virtuous dissimulation. Presented in the hard light of public scrutiny, they can become amplified into impairments that discredit, that lay charges of deception against the actor. Colleagues might come to believe that he is feigning in an inauthentic career in liturgical life. These trivial elements can be promoted into a whole batch of discrediting assumptions. Because they are trivial, illogical and odd, the actor might feel embarrassed at even acknowledging their existence. Fears of them being perceived in public by colleagues or by the congregation cause the actor to hope they might not be noticed and that the need for a strategy of self-deception might not even arise. These divisions within can take on a confessional dimension, for the issue of self deception in liturgy can cut that deep. Virtuous dissimulation is the cross of reticence the actor bears, the price paid of delivering worth to God through social means. Feigning piety, when the body speaks internally of other qualities, requires a response of will, an aspiration to enter a better state, where holiness has to be simulated less, because the effects of grace are felt more.

The notion of self deception has a vexatious quality. It seems like an internal holy game with conundrums that conspire to preclude sociological interventions. Simulation and dissimulation present themselves as clever psychological ploys, where the art of the self to beat a retreat reaches a fine state that effects a flight from the social. The issue moves about in a growing inner complexity that seems to become overly detached from sociological considerations. Emphasis on concealment, on the dangers of spelling out meanings seems to subtract from that which is social and manifest. But at some point, this internal forum within which integrity is sought has to be given a social manifestation and form of expression. The actor has to act on his faith in public, if the collective ends of worship are to be secured.

Doubt and dissimulation can disable the need to act and to edify. These qualities can conspire to become the means through which the actor is locked in a timidity of purpose, burdened with a scrupulosity that imprisons. Taken to an extreme, they can justify a total inaction that denies the imperative to act. To edify means to attach the totality of man to shaping a social task, of presenting himself and others before God. It draws on the whole man, in his private and public parts, to invest the self in the act to a virtual point of extinction. Thus, 'a liturgy edifies, so our forefathers taught, when it leads the worshipper to lose himself more easily in all its movements and actions, to forget self in the glory of Catholic worship'.[72] Forms of rite that generate habitual attachments have a sedimenting and securing quality. They generate conditions of trust that the self can be disclosed in public social terms that can be regulated and where a call on the need for a virtuous dissimulation can be kept to the minimum. The stability of the rite permits the actor an acceptable degree of self-deception, an entitlement to mask in an unobtrusive fashion, what are, after all, his own problems. An inner uncertainty can cope in the context of an outward stable certainty of form. The actor can accommodate unfixing private doubts against a fixed public background where he is called to act. In an ideal liturgical world, where stability and uniformity prevail, the deceptions of the self that might arise can be kept untested below the surface.

Unfortunately, the ability to choose, a flawed gift of the Enlightenment, has generated amongst some a quest for alternative forms of rite, types that would express relationships better, would meet liturgical needs more effectively in a modern age and which, somehow, would provide a social arrangement for worship that ought to be more pleasing to God. Such a quest for the 'ideal' liturgical form leads to a destabilising effect, where more of the self is revealed than might be considered productive. Adjustments in liturgical forms unsettle private accommodations and give a public dimension to doubts and to the issue of deception. These are not conditions under which virtuous dissimulation thrives. With a long history of theological and doctrinal dispute stemming from the Reformation, and earlier, this hardly seems a new, if valid point. There is, however, a new dimension to the present quest for the ideal form. Aspects of modernity that have been partly shaped by sociological arguments have been drawn into arguments on the 'ideal' shape of liturgy. Indeed, sociology seems to have been given a mandate by liberal theologians to intervene and to speculate. This has led to some misguided thought on the subject of liturgy, for which there is not a sociological basis.

6 Holy and Unholy Rites: Lies and Mistakes in Liturgy

> Profanations are to be expected, for every religious ceremony creates the possibility of a black mass.
>
> (Erving Goffman, 'The Nature of Deference and Demeanor')

Since the Second Vatican Council, there has been a tendency amongst theologians and liturgists to give modern culture a benign, undifferentiated 'reading', one innocent of the sociological complications such a view poses. A stress on incarnational theology gave a blanket blessing to culture, that was not offset by an awareness of the degree to which it has ambiguous, limited qualities that beg questions of meaning. Theologians seem to have become enchanted with modern culture, precisely at the time when sociologists became disenchanted and began to review its theoretical significance in the light of a growing awareness of post-modernism. A theological failure to specify the use of culture within a particular context partly accounts for the naïveté of many of its contemporary positions and the degree to which it has taken refuge in ideology rather than sociology to shape its presuppositions about religion and society.

Within an inductive approach to liturgy, the implications of a virtuous dissimulation emerge. The actor confronts particular dilemmas in practice that require regulation and disguise, if the social act of worship is to be accomplished in an authentic and intended manner. Some form of collaboration in enactment is required to protect liturgy at its weakest point, where it transforms that which is cultural into the holy, a process as elusive as it is mysterious. To follow Berger, it is to transform that which is implausible into the plausible for believer and non-believer alike. It is in this process that liturgies are prone to generate misunderstandings, and to require a degree of virtuous dissimulation to protect their basis, both for the actor and the definition of the situation sought. Representations of the sacred involve risks in the task of transferring indeterminate meanings into a determinate ritual event. This bears on a point of Niklas Luhmann. He regards religion as effecting a sacralising task through 'ciphering', where the indeterminate is replaced and hidden in a social act that incarnates what it proclaims. The unreal nature of the religious act is disguised.[1] I wish to argue that virtuous dissimulation is a means of understanding this process from a sociological point of view in a way that links the actor to the structure of what he re-produces in the performance of rite. A similar form of transposition, that also requires a degree of defence arises in the context of Goffman's notion of 'keying', which I mentioned earlier.

If liturgies operated under a sense of a steely Divine gaze, so that dissatisfaction was registered all too clearly, the sociologist would have little to worry about. An altar server, passing the altar, bowing ever so slightly, might hear a loud voice booming out 'deeper boy, deeper, or I'll have you up on the second commandment'. Unfortunately, there seems to be a Divine reticence about what is liked and disliked in rite.

A certain agnosticism seems have settled into contemporary liturgical life. A degree of liturgical pluralism is now sanctioned (within limits in Catholicism) without any great certainty as to what arrangement 'works' best, or what difference all these differences do make. The only difference this climate of liturgical agnosticism over forms of worship has effected, is a continued fall in attendance rates at Church in the United Kingdom. Those who have taken diversity of rite the furthest, such as the Anglicans, seem to have lost the most in terms of weekly attendance at Church, which presumably is not the purpose of the experiment.

At some point, a limit to liturgical pluralism has to be stipulated, otherwise the act can become, eventually, an oddly random exercise. Far from generating conditions of plausibility for belief, pluralism has had the unintended effect of increasing levels of implausibility about religion in modern society. Agency and choice are not solutions but problems that can undermine the need to believe.[2] Few theologians, liberal or otherwise, have understood the implications of relativism as it bears on issues of liturgical praxis.[3]

Pluralism generates indifference towards religion in the wider society, but in a way that disguises intense competition within, especially between liturgical forms seeking scarce believers. Liturgies operate in the manner of rituals of the tribe, defending territorial practices against the hostile imputations of their neighbours. Boundary maintenance in rite is less about defence against hostile charges of the wider society (which is usually too indifferent to bother) than against fellow Church members who adhere to a rival form of rite. Breaches in the wall of liturgical practice are to be precluded at all costs. Each

form of rite tends to give its rival a fatal test that shows it to be
wanting before God. This notion of a liturgical market-place reaches a
state of perfection in contemporary English Anglicanism.

In the Church of England, Anglo-Catholic Eucharists and Evangelical assemblies operate in a free and largely unregulated market. There
are an endless set of permutations of liturgical form permitted,
operating with a variety of veneers, Tractarian, Charismatic or
feminist, whose borrowings are barely discernible even to a liturgist.
All forms seem to operate with their own set of rules for engagement.
No rules for ceremonial enactment are stipulated in the Alternative
Service Book (ASB), 1980. A diversity of rite, reflecting accommodation to local circumstances is not only tolerated, but seems to be
enjoined in modern Anglican thoughts on liturgical use. In its response
to *Faith in the City*, the Liturgical Commission of the Church of
England rejoiced in the new era of flexibility brought to pass by the
ASB. It called for liturgies to reflect local cultures to meet the needs of
Urban Priority areas. It felt that more engagement and liturgical
relevance were required so that congregations would have some sense
of affiliation with the rites they had constructed. The Commission
indicated that

> the congregation can be involved in both drama and dialogue
> readings. It might mean changing the visual presentation, removing
> distractions by putting all lights out apart from a spotlight on the
> reader, or signalling the fact that a story is being read by using a
> Jackanory armchair, or that a proclamation (for example Amos?) is
> being made by using a soapbox.[4]

These suggestions attracted some rather ungrateful comments in the
mass media and exposed an ambiguous attitude towards rituals in
Anglican liturgical tradition. There is a stereotype in Anglican
theology regarding rituals that lingers from the Tractarian period
and the debates which followed in the nineteenth century. Adherence
to ritual form in liturgical enactment is equated with 'ritualism' and
the deadening hand of the 'spike', who kills the spirit in deadening
ceremonials. The Liturgical Commission went to the opposite extreme
in striving to establish 'living' rituals for local cultures, but without
reference to any anthropological thought on the subject.

Most anthropological studies of ritual concentrate on the meanings
they fulfil, the belief systems they embody and the functions their
orders effect. Ritual forms use complex social arrangements cast in
ceremonial form and the more odd and arbitrary these are, the more

they are likely to attract anthropological scrutiny. Rituals function to cope with conditions of uncertainty, or unsettlement. Somehow, they manage to render these definite and stable. This accounts for the way many rituals deal with healing, with magic to handle spells, with rites of passage to mark transitions of age, or death, or to cope with the arrival of the stranger with the least social disruption to a settled order. Rituals enable the weak to handle anxiety by domesticating their worries in a social order that harmonises and heals. They can also serve to communicate qualities of deference, and to confer rights and obligations in an elaborate manner that signifies an event of crucial political importance. The pomp and circumstance of a coronation follows complex rules hallowed in tradition. It is a majestic social means of marking dignity and the right to marshal symbolic forces to rule dutifully in a credible and accepted manner. Deference is secured through the solemn demeanour that characterises the style of the rite. Regal ceremonies confer properties of grandeur and power on their object of dedication, providing an unmatched means of enhancing a public claim to rule. The social resources of a ritual are used to consecrate objects or actions that would be otherwise insignificant and the manner of dedication secures their credible redefinition.[5]

We are concerned with examining ritual in liturgical use in a way that unmasks its social base, and reveals that which the actors strive to keep concealed. When a form of rite becomes unsecured, deceptive possibilities arise that are peculiar to the style of worship. This unsettlement forces the actors involved in the social construction of rite to look closely at the assumptions governing its enactment. As one young altar server noted, 'it is only when things go wrong that things get really interesting'. Infelicities and mistakes of a significant kind have to be regulated out lest an unproductive uncertainty emerges. Tacit assumptions over how the rite ought to proceed can be breached by a failure on the part of the liturgical actors to monitor their performance. Desired liturgical outcomes can easily be unsecured. This need to regulate the shape and order of rite points to a distinctive concept in this study: the notion of a 'liturgical mistake'. This indicates how the autonomous defining qualities of this form of ritual have to be serviced and kept secure in a tactful manner so that tacit assumptions can be protected. These are deemed to be vulnerable and are associated, crucially, with the intended definition of the situation.

Some means of regulation of liturgical performance is required, lest its enactment collapses into a series of unprofitable ambiguities and paradoxes that would estrange even the most curious of sociologists.

Failure to regulate a form of rite can give rise to lies and deceptions in its performance. These are believed to be culpable and are of a type which liturgical actors ought to avoid. These mistakes are usually about the detail of the rite and its mismanagement.

Gestures, vestments, symbols, and actions are minutiae in a collective effort, details in the ritual mosaic, that provide a structured means of coping with the holy in a public place. In Catholicism, rubrics or ceremonial guidelines help to keep the detail of rite in its proportionate place, so that the whole of the liturgy always exceeds its parts. If the details of a liturgy are adjusted with careless disregard, the shape of the rite takes on an unfruitful unpredictability that also impairs its claim to be a public order of worship.

Because liturgical forms represent habitual modes of linking with the sacred, forms of rite take on a brand loyalty. They establish orders of trust, that elicit a congregational response, an investment on their part that often represents a career in dealing with the holy through the social means. The detail of the rite also services an order of predictability. It confirms a sense of expectation that the use of detail in the rite *can* yield particular qualities of the holy. But such a belief is arbitrary, intuitive and difficult to defend in public. Liturgical details are ambiguous and a scaling of their significance is problematic. Small points of detail can take on disproportionate value, such as the way the bell is rung at mass, or the form of introduction used by the priest, or the way the altar server makes the sign of the cross. These minor elements of style can offer comforting means of identification, points of recognition that give the form of the rite a certainty against which the self can lean to find the uncertain.[6] These cues become part of a liturgical biography of the actor. As David Martin has noted aptly, 'the liturgical order belongs to these familiar rhythms and ways of doing things. All the buried selves of innumerable yesterdays are reactivated in the order of worship'.[7] A sense of the detail of a rite can make an overwhelming impact, as is indicated in the recollections of the main character in *Sinister Street* serving an Anglo-Catholic high mass for the first time.

During the Elevation of the Host, as he bowed his head before the wonder of bread and wine made God, his brain reeled in an ecstasy of sublime worship. There was a silence save for the censer tinkling steadily and the low whispered words of the priest and the click of the broken wafer. The candles burned with a supernatural intensity: the boys who lately quarrelled over precedence were hushed as angels: the stillness became fearful; the cold steps burned into Michael's knees and the incense choked him.[8]

Detail moved from one liturgical context for display to another tradition of worship can give rise to profound unsettlement and a sense of threat difficult to articulate. Such an arbitrary action can break a precarious sense of liturgical order. A sense of affiliation with an order of completeness is broken by the inclusion of a point of detail from an alien rite. A deep bow to the altar, or table, of a United Reformed Church could cause as much consternation as a Catholic priest turning up with lace, biretta and maniple to a Eucharistic gathering of liberal theologians. The displacement of detail signals affiliations at odds with the domestic assumptions of a particular congregation as to what ought to happen in the rite. The transplantation of detail to an alien rite generates an ambiguity. At one level, detail ought not to count, and a concern with it might seem obsessive, but at another remove, it might be felt to be of crucial importance, being considered a defining characteristic of a particular style of rite. Detail has an ambiguous relationship to the form of a rite. Not only does it signal badges of ritual affiliation, it also secures a relationship between the part of a rite and its whole. In this latter task, it also has an ambiguous role that needs regulating. It has to be kept in a proportionate place, lest it becomes promoted to a disproportionate rank that might limit the credibility of the rite and warp its shape. Because detail poses a potential but uncertain threat to a ritual order, furious disputes can arise. As Weber noted,

the greatest conflicts between purely dogmatic views, even within rationalistic religions, may be tolerated more easily than innovations in symbolism, which threaten the magical efficacy of action . . .[9]

The structure of rite supplies a context that can contain its detail. This does not resolve the question of ambiguity that detail gives rise to within liturgy. Rites are polyvalent in effect and this capacity to generate many meanings increases the subjectivity of response of those present, as actors or in the congregation. A mosaic of detail is presented as offering a variety of cues and passages into the holy, but the price of this availability is that it is difficult to stipulate which minute aspect counts most. There are theological rules that try to order and to settle matters of detail. Our concern is with the way these details, often insignificant, can emerge as ambiguous in the performance of rite. They take on a disproportionate significance for some as entry points into the façade of the rite, to find what lies hidden. The actors and the audience come to rites with a variety of expectations. They handle the uncertainty it generates with differing procedures. Competitive assemblies of God operate in a liturgical market through an amplification of the weaknesses of their rivals, and that which they wish to escape from.[10] There are incommensurable antinomial elements of meaning and action operating in liturgical forms that can threaten their desired image. Choral evensong can descend into a concert, and a conceited choir might get a clap after the canticle from some disedified born again Christians. An envangelical service might get so convivial in its praise, that a displaced 'spike' might faint under the pressure of the joy, overcome less by the Holy Spirit than outrage.

Hostile and reductionist overtones can be imputed to any form of rite by its rivals. Amplification of undesirable aspects of a particular liturgical style can give comfort to rivals, thus confirming their worst fears regarding its 'real' basis. Despite their purity of intention, liturgical actors can face charges of impurity arising from the styles of rite they proclaim. Antinomial facets of a particular liturgical style can be given a one-sided reductionist reading by adherents of rival assemblies, that ignores the dilemmas of the actors in its production. Thus, rites that use beautiful Church music in elaborate ceremonial orders can generate a sense of the glory and wonder of God, but they can also convey an intrinsic aesthetic quality that appeals to the secular mind. This represents a dilemma of witness and enactment for the actors, but to those of a Puritan cast, the whole exercise is deceptive, idolatrous and self-serving. The response of actors to these potential charges of deception and impurity of practice point to procedures governing the production and enactment of liturgical performances.

The social procedures upon which custody of a particular liturgical form is secured involve a degree of disguise of its mechanism of reproduction. If the mechanism intrudes too far into the quest for the sacred, the ritual can fail. As Durkheim has noted, 'when a rite serves only to distract, it is no longer a rite'.[11] If the liturgy is to 'work' in sociological *and* theological terms, the social form of the rite has to produce a sensibility of something greater than the ceremonial mechanism that realises its basis. This need to affirm through denial points to an antinomial aspect of rite that continues the problem we examined earlier in terms of the concept of innocence and also the need to exercise a virtuous dissimulation.

Any form of rite that denies having some procedures for the management of holy effects deceives. Some means of regulation of rite is required if it is not to lapse into that which it fears and so produce effects it would wish to deny. A charismatic assembly, which denies having a stage-managed form, could find its clapping getting out of hand, producing hysteria rather than ecstasy. We wish to argue that as long as ambiguities are domesticated and contained within a form of the rite, meaningful paradoxes can be handled without damage. The liturgical form operates to enhance a sense of the uncertain, to quicken the spirit to engage with the indeterminate. But if uncertainty becomes attached to the form of the rite itself, focus on the indeterminate switches to the mechanism, and doubt ensues over the nature of the message proclaimed by its enactment. Such doubt disables and subtracts from efforts to deal in a certain manner with the uncertain. The rite never quite manages to escape the form used to produce the holy, and in being so limited it imprisons those present in the purely social. There is an ambiguous quality attached to the use of the social in liturgical forms. Too much attention produces a reductionist effect, but too little can generate an uncertain witness.

There is a necessary ambiguity operating between action and structure as this relationship is conceived in sociological terms. This is apart from the ambiguity of the message proclaimed as it emerges between the manifest and hidden aspects of rite. Actions and structures are mutually implicated in a rite in a way that relates to Anthony Giddens' notion of 'structuration'. This concept suggests a duality operating that enables an event to occur, but also constrains its enactment.[12] Actions are bound into structures in a way that disguises the ambiguous link between the two. Liturgies handle a sense of contradiction, between the need for rules that will enable them to have a predictable cast, and the affirmation of a sense of play that transcends the requirements for an orderly enactment. As Gilbert Lewis suggests, rituals present constraints that paradoxically free the individual to explore indeterminate meanings and playful effects.[13] Somehow the liturgy binds its form in a way that surpasses the totality of its contradictions and so releases the individual to pray and to worship.

In this chapter the functional nature of ambiguities as they operate between action and structure will be examined. I wish to suggest, not very persuasively, that formally cast rites are less prone to social misunderstandings than informal rites. To understand this point, I will examine Rappaport's approach to the obvious aspects of rite. Finally, I will look in a little more detail at the idea of a 'liturgical mistake' in relation to liturgical rules.

ACTION AND STRUCTURE: AN AMBIGUOUS INTER-CONNECTION

Therefore, one exposes oneself to grave misunderstandings, if in explaining rites, he believes that each gesture has a precise object and a definite reason for its existence.
(Emile Durkheim, *The Elementary Forms of the Religious Life*)

In seeking the truth from those who deceive and lie, one assumes that their intentional wilful statement that misleads can be rendered to account. It is believed that the actors are responsible for disclosing the true state of affairs and that they can rectify that which so misleads. Unfortunately, liturgical enactments are characterised by a certain degree of ambiguity. Liturgical actors can lie and deceive, almost with impunity, in bad faith, in a wilful manner, for the ultimate effects of their acts are known only to God. Yet it is also the case that actions which give rise to charges of deception are not completely the responsibility of the actor, but derive from the indeterminate poly-valent nature of the social basis of rite. There is an ambiguous facet to the issue of liturgical ambiguities. The actor is using ambiguous instruments but in a way that suggests his relationship to these can be characterised by an ambiguity that lies in the link between action and structure. It is argued that sociology has to live with such ambiguities but that the liturgical actor has to find some means of coping and resolving these, if he is not to be doomed to deceive and mislead in his part. In some senses this is an artificial theological dilemma. Despite the potential deceits, as long as he wills a sincerity in the liturgical act, grace will enable him to achieve a purity. Yet he still has to find a social means of understanding of how doubt can be overcome in the liturgical act.

Ambiguities seem to have a disabling and negative function in social transactions. They hinder the pursuit of a fullness of understanding, but they also have a facilitating task. Ambiguities have definite functions within a liturgical form, of precluding a reductionist closure, and maintaining an opening, an availability, to the sacred. Some ambiguities, however, amplify an uncertainty within the mechanism, and are unproductive, whereas others are more productive and necessary, especially when handling the limits of rite, the meanings it produces and the symbols it handles. It should be possible to provide some sociological means of distinguishing between the two.

Ambiguity seems to present an area of failure in sociological theory. As Robert Merton has suggested, the discipline has a bias towards symmetry and tends to avoid areas dealing with uncertainty. He goes on to suggest that this has narrowed the range of meanings sociology can take into analytical account.[14] The scientific claims of sociology press it to resolve meanings in a precise and checkable fashion, to minimise uncertainty and to maximise freedom of choice. Elements of ambiguity represent either a potential for conversion into rational clarification, or exist as failures that bear witness to the limits of sociological intervention. In the study of liturgy, a subject riddled with ambiguities, sociology seems to have become caught in an ambiguous position. Failure to accept the ambiguities buried in liturgical praxis would remove the subject from sociological scrutiny. Yet acceptance of these liturgical ambiguities which sociology can make no claim to resolve, simply amplifies their number into endless permutations. It is scarcely surprising that liturgy has been a neglected area for sociological study.

Donald Levine argues that, with the exception of Simmel, sociology has had a career of struggle against accepting the implications of ambiguity and the polyvalent meanings it presents.[15] As Levine suggests, the acceptance of ambiguity in sociological interpretations draws attention to social processes that depend on a quality of vagueness and indeterminateness to fulfil their functions. For instance, a political order might be insulated against conflict by keeping potentially contentious matters ambiguous and unresolved. Inconsistencies and ambiguities preserve an openness to meanings, whose political effects cannot be excluded from sociological examination.[16] In his examination of jokes and riddles, Ian Hamnett shows the way ambiguities preserve social arrangements by allowing certain facets of action to be left implicit and unresolved.[17] A similar argument has been made by Patricia Greenspan concerning the ambivalence of emotions. She argues that this can motivate behaviour unlikely to arise from detachment and a resolution of ambiguity.[18] Acceptance of an ambiguous aspect to particular forms of action, allows sociological access to what an excessive concern with rationality might preclude. Because ambiguity relates to elements of uncertainty in social transactions, that are also implicated in their meaningful basis, a particular style of negotiation in the way they are handled can be uncovered.

Inconsistencies in analysis might stem from a carelessness that can be resolved with further thought. But they might also be characteristic

of a particular style of ritual. In his study of the social and symbolic
functions of circumcision rites amongst the Ganu in New Guinea,
Gilbert Lewis argues that these rituals are structured to facilitate
openings to meanings as broad as those of the nature of life itself. The
public issue of blood facilitates an opening to a sense of tribal
continuity, and a sense of enrichment that binds past struggles with
present engagements.[19] A tolerance of imprecision in meanings also
serves a moral purpose. As Alan Dawe has suggested, ambiguity
maximises agency, by keeping options of choice open. Sociological
interventions could be *too* successful in amplifying a deterministic
strand of rationality within advanced industrialised society, thus
further advancing Weber's most pessimistic fears. An overemphasis
on predictability and clarity can overly stress the significance of
rational calculation, thus marginalising meanings whose outcomes
are indeterminate.[20] Sociological difficulties with ambiguities arise in
some unexpected areas.

Sociology has a striking incapacity to resolve the ambiguous link
between action and structure. This seems to pose an antinomial
problem for sociology. Interpretations that apply to accounts of
action are often contradicted at the level of structure, and vice versa.
Despite these interpretative difficulties, ambiguities can be regarded as
assets rather than liabilities in sociological analysis. Dawe suggests that
'ambiguity remains essential to any serious conception of the self – and
socially creative capacities and possibilities of human agency. It
remains the only possible basis for the translation of the actual into
the ideal'.[21] An attempt has been made to link accounts of action to
structure, through the concept of 'structuration'. Anthony Giddens
approaches structures in terms of rules and regulations that operate as
the medium through which actions are re-produced and constituted.
Thus, action and structure are deemed to operate in an interdependent
manner sociology has to take into analytical account.[22] There is an
excessively heuristic cast to his conceptualisation that seals ambiguity
within, and precludes a meaningful indeterminacy arising without. A
rather vacuous interdependence is posited, and there is a circular cast
to an argument that never seems to be grounded in a meaningful
content or praxis.

I would wish to argue that the ambiguous link between action and
structure places an onus on the actor to effect a passage into deeper
meanings. The ambiguity of the ritual facilitates this advance, and
indeed forms its basis. This bears on a point of Durkheim, that rituals
have a necessary quality of indeterminacy, a functional ambiguity, a

point that especially applies to forms of liturgy. Thus a funeral mass represents a commemoration of the dead, but also facilitates a religious affirmation of life and hope.[23] Unresolved paradoxes and ambiguities give forms of rite a motive force. These form the basis of the rite's capacity to reproduce, in a way that arouses awe and curiosity. Because nothing determinate is effected, produced or resolved, a sense of the indeterminate can be sustained that also forms the distinctive basis of the rite's capacity to be repeated. The form of the rite facilitates access to a religious content, one that transcends its social basis and also amplifies its insignificance.

Simmel's approach to the relationship between form and content provides a sympathetic basis for a sociological understanding of liturgical practice. Although of Jewish background and a religious agnostic, his emphasis on paradox and opposites of meaning, is a useful sociological resource for handling liturgical transactions in a way that allows their 'success' to be understood. There is an overlap of interest also between Goffman and Simmel, in their approaches to social interaction.[24]

Social forms represent the means through which a content, theological or aesthetic, is clothed and presented in an objectifiable manner. These forms are stable, identifiable and have to be related to their context of use. They are incomplete and artificial social means of handling a content of meaning or phenomenon that is ephemeral and perhaps indeterminate.[25] There is a dualism involved in Simmel's approach to form, a contrasting of opposites, such as the sense of proximity and distance that occurs in response to the arrival of a stranger. His coming represents an ambivalent encounter, one that necessitates particular social procedures to effect hospitality, but also to minimise disruption of the settled affairs of the tribe.[26] Rites of passage are often used to handle the visit from the marginal and to contain the uncertainty the stranger generates in his visit.[27] Because Simmel relates forms to context, and grants them an equivalence in terms of the meanings they embody, his analytical approach carries an element of relativism. This generates a wager, to chose between nihilism or belief, and the need for choice emerges from within sociological speculation. Lukacs noted a modern tendency towards 'religious atheism', an alienation of intellectuals from established churches, that led to an experience of disorientation and emptiness, that could generate some sort of religious need.[28] The pursuit of sociological enquiry can cause it to arrive at some odd theological stations along the route.

Simmel grants religion an autonomy and a dignity of social form. He manages to avoid a reductionist interpretation of religious belief, such as Durkheim makes. Firstly, Simmel places the issue of the truth of a religion beyond empirical inquiry. Religion is regarded as an emergent property of social relationships, but is in some way independent of them. This bears on a point suggested earlier, that Goffman regarded social forms as being incomplete and incapable of exhausting the religious beliefs they served to denote. Secondly, Simmel approaches religious forms (of practice) in terms of products of piety and faith that are grounded in social relationships. Religious forms fulfil emergent functions. Furthermore, he regards religion as a totality that transcends forms of contradiction in other styles of life. Although Simmel admits an ambiguity between form and content in his approach to religion, nevertheless this is given a benign status. Religion is seen as providing a means of resolving conflict rather than generating it. Thus he argues that 'it is almost solely in religion that the energies of individuals can find fullest development without coming into competition with each other . . .'.[29] We would wish to criticise this point, and suggest that forms of liturgical practice *are* in conflict. Although religion does give comfort, its imperfect instruments of worship often lead to profound discomfort. Simmel approaches the issue of social forms in a way that has crucial implications for our approach to liturgy.

Oakes gives a valuable reading of Simmel that shows the way social forms have an incommensurable quality that makes each distinctive, thus securing their analytical autonomy. At the same time, he notes the incompleteness of social forms and their incapacity to exhaust the meanings they convey. This incompleteness presupposes access to a content that completes what is in the social form.[30] I have noted this point earlier in commenting on the link between the choirboy and the angel.

This approach to social form precludes a reductionist account and at the same time admits transactions, such as liturgies, to sociological consideration. Guy Oakes argues that Simmel does not give any social form a privileged ontological, epistemological or logical status. But social forms that operate to express ephemeral aspects of life demand a price. They can render meanings in an artificially exact form that disguises their ambiguous and indeterminate nature. Simmel notes a curious result in the evolution of culture that 'as man becomes more cultivated, his life becomes more oblique and opaque'.[31] A similar problem emerges in the case of liturgy when its cultural apparatus is subject to close analysis. There seem to be endless ambiguities attached to the social form of rite, which an effort to achieve exactness could distort. It is easy to concentrate excessively on the social form and to lose sight of the content it strives to embody. This point represents a particular arena in which deceptions can arise in dealing with liturgical transactions.

The duality that operates between form and content has a playful cast. The opacity of the game yields deeper meanings. As Tenbruck suggests, social forms 'have a dual character, at once superior to the actors and subject to them. They operate on the actors, and the actors operate on them'.[32] This ambiguous interdependence suggests an element of wager, a risk of the form dominating, but also of the actors being dominated in a way that effects the release of a distinctive content. In a point that has significance for the later application of hermeneutics to the understanding of liturgical performance, Simmel links ambiguity to the interpretation of a written text. He argues that determinateness and ambiguity are interdependent sociological categories of the first rank in regard to all utterances between man and man. Significantly, this point is made in the context of a discussion of written communication and the issue of secrecy.[33]

In an ideal world, the social form of a rite should always be kept in a subordinate place and should never be allowed to dominate the pursuit of an engagement with a holiness of content. The difficulty is that the form of the rite can take on a life of its own, where its beauty and order can become inherently attractive in a way that renders the performance an end in itself. The actors involved in the liturgical performance can become overly concerned with the means, and can be carried away with an interest in self proclamation and so

> the musician will sense the musical beauty and lose the purpose; the actor will love the dressing-up, the sonorous language, the ballet-like movements and miss their import; the slothful will allow the sheer sonority of the prayers to drug him into an intellectual sleep.[34]

It is easy to confuse an overpowering sense of the collective, in a Durkheimian meaning, with a feeling of edification that relates to the spiritual. The liturgical actor can find himself engaged in a peculiarly sociological form of self-deception, where the servicing of the social means obscures the sacred end they are supposed to exemplify. The difficulty is that the link between social action and spiritual effect is profoundly ambiguous. By its theological nature, the link is a matter of mystery. Gareth Matthews is correct to argue that the mere motion of the body in ritual inculcates and intensifies a sense of religiosity in a way that cannot be explained. His attempt to resolve the dilemma by reference to 'the sincere and understanding performance of rite' moves the dilemma to the liturgical form itself.[35] There is a necessary ambiguity between an outward action and its inner effect in liturgy. This is a problem of central importance in understanding liturgy, which will emerge more fully in later efforts to interpret and to distinguish between civil and sacerdotal abasements.

To a large extent, the ambiguous nature of liturgical transactions is a sociological problem rather than a theological issue. Because sociology is concerned with a social apparatus, whose meaningful nature lies outside its remit, the risks that arise in its use may be exaggerated and in consequence the deceptions involved in its production may become needlessly amplified. Because sociology does not have resource to grace to resolve issues of deception, it has to understand the issue from within its own terms of analysis. Nevertheless, there are some theological qualifications that need to be taken into account in the case of Catholic liturgies.

Firstly, the validity of the mass is not a function of the personal disposition of the celebrant, otherwise its theological effect would be an extension of his spiritual state, which could be low. The theological outcome of the mass is facilitated by the actions of the priest but is not to be understood as being manufactured by them. Nor is the theological efficacy of the rite to be understood in terms of some magical instrumental intervention that produces an invariant 'felt' effect. It is an objective transaction whose validity is derived from the orders conferred on the celebrant. Any subjective effects are matters of grace and the indirect results of intention. Secondly, the most incompetently performed rite imaginable could be deemed to 'work' in a spiritually efficacious manner. Assuming the intention to consecrate on the part of the celebrant, the mass would be valid. Deficiencies in presentation could be absolved by a belief that the rite is stronger than the man. The Mystery re-presented could be even more mysterious by being understood to emerge from such an incompetent performance. Thirdly, one has to assume that the link between form and content is of its theological nature inexact, ambiguous and indeterminate. To claim an exactitude of relationship would be presumptuous, and heretical.

Grace makes determinate that which might seem indeterminate in effect. But one cannot presume that grace will always redeem that which is ambiguous nor does it exempt the liturgical actor from knowing of issues of lies and deceptions in the practice of rite. Having accepted that ambiguities do not necessarily disable, that they can have positive functions of admitting access to that which might not otherwise be understood, the crucial question to which we now turn is the vexed area of accountability in competing forms or styles of rite. Forms of rite operate in the context of theological and sociological risk, of heresy or culpable deceit, and to that degree have to find some means of avoiding such unintended outcomes. Roy Rappaport offers a purely anthropological solution to a theological dilemma. It does not resolve the problem of deceit, but it does place it in a context where the issue of the actor's accountability for what occurs can be examined.

DARK AND DUMB CEREMONIES: FIBS IN FORMS OF RITE

> This our excessive multitude of Ceremonies was so great, and many of them so dark, that they did more confound and darken, than declare and set forth Christ's benefits unto us.
>
> (Preface – *The Book of Common Prayer*)

The vast majority of rites are uneventful events, marked by a security of tenor. The main threat to participants is boredom. Occasionally the social base intrudes and disruption follows. Although the social apparatus of rite lies below the surface, when matters become unstuck, and infelicities emerge, the actors attend to provide ceremonial repairs, and strive to re-dedicate the transaction once more to holy purpose. Profaning errors in enactment reveal the accounting practices of the liturgical actors and their assumptions as to how the rite ought to proceed. Every form of rite has its own endemic social corruptions. Through experience and habit the actors learn to recognise what is undesirable so that it can be masked and disguised. What is feared in rite reveals much about what is desirable to affirm. When implicit social assumptions are breached and become intrusively explicit, the issue of the social form and its management emerges as a serious consideration.

Because forms of rite compete within denominations, particular conventions become apparent when comparisons are made. Invidious comparisons often point to hostile social assumptions being made about how rival rites proceed. This mutual denigration allows access to the social base of rites and gives a practical twist to the question of whether these forms lie and deceive. The liturgical act bears divisions and these arise both within *and* between forms of rite. There is an antinomial element buried in the theological act, which Ian Hamnett has exposed and discussed. This has a bearing on how rival forms compete and manage to mutually misunderstand each other.

Hamnett has argued that styles of worship have theological implications in terms of their use or non-use of social resources. An excess of deference to the ritual form can generate problems of idolatry. Pelagianism is the characterising heresy of Catholicism, where actions and symbols are too closely related to human agency in terms of delivering their outcomes. God becomes constrained to respond by the admirable order of rite presented. An opposite theological vice is that of High Calvinism, where the distance of God is stressed in terms of any responding action by man being deemed presumptuous. Any intervention by man to affect the course of his ultimate salvation could be regarded as subtracting from the will and glory of God. Hamnett regards Docetism as the characterising heresy of this position. Both extremes present a dilemma over the basis of actions in liturgy. Pelagianism suggests that actions can become presumptuous by over reliance on the social, and so leaving little space for God to respond. On the other hand Docetism, as he points out, by denying the efficacy of actions, subtracts from the incarnational notion of God and His relationship to the world.[36]

For 'success' in theological terms, liturgical practice involves the management of a mean between overdependence and underdependence in the use of the social resources of rite. This fine line between assumption and presumption points to an ambiguity over which theological end to start from to effect a sociological study of rite. Theological positions dictate how elaborate or simple the social resources of rite ought to be to produce a good and holy effect. Yet these share an uncertainty with sociology over how the social links with the Divine. The history of Christianity is littered with disputes over this question of which social arrangement in worship best pleases God. Any sociological intervention into this debate is likely to be odd, arbitrary and inconclusive.

To establish an interpretative means of characterising liturgical form, two extreme versions are posited in terms of Weber's 'ideal type'. There are implicit value judgements involved in the elements selected for analysis. When an 'ideal type' is applied to an understanding of liturgies, there is an implicitly prescriptive element that contains a bias towards a particular form, the one most available to sociological analysis. It is important not to confuse the availability of a liturgical style to sociology, with the issue of its theological efficacy, an issue which lies outside a sociological remit. It also should be admitted that there is an element of caricature involved in the way that these two opposite forms of rites are handled.

It is assumed that the liturgical forms being contrasted contain elements of detail that are deemed to be incommensurable. Both forms represent the high and low ends of the liturgical market-place. They operate with notably different 'plausibility structures' that impose contrasting expectations and tacit assumptions of procedure about the nature of the liturgical performance. At the higher end are forms of rite that can be characterised as operating under a mode of 'spiky privatisation'. These rites are executed with a rigid impersonal ceremonial exactitude under strict and checkable rules that order and control the use of symbols, actions and gestures in a highly stylised manner. A strict division is kept between the actors on the sanctuary and the congregation, who are deemed to participate in an equally anonymous fashion. The privacy of the laity is respected under a consensus that prohibits social intercourse, to maximise the interior sensibilities each member of the congregation is striving to cultivate. There is a formal, impersonal cast to the ceremony. One has in mind an Anglican Choral Eucharist in a Cathedral or a Catholic High Mass in a Benedictine monastery. The service is rigidly controlled in its management of time and sequence, and lasts about an hour and fifteen minutes.

By contrast are informal rites. Their style of enactment can be characterised by a 'convivial puritanism'. Rules of engagement are kept to a minimum. Procedures for worship are kept as simple as possible to maximise social relationships in the production of the rite. This minimalism is used to sustain a relaxed atmosphere, where all may informally participate and contribute. Hierarchical arrangements and ceremonial rules are believed to deaden the spirit and to kill the production of a happy sense of belonging. There is an emphasis on holy mood music, use of gesture, and an effort to bind all together. These informal rites have a puritanical cast towards symbols, complex actions and rules, which are regarded as unnecessary corruptions that get in the way of direct relationships to God. The assemblies one has in mind are those that can be found amongst Christian Fundamentalists, or charismatic assemblies. Scaled-down versions operate with greater emphasis on personal relationships within house groups, where utterance is high and gestures are kept low. These assemblies are open-ended in terms of the management of time, and their sequences are not rigidly adhered to, but are adjusted as the Spirit moves the gathering.

There is much competition *within* these forms of rite. There are subtle variations in practice that can unsettle the committed. For instance, an Anglican Eucharist, with female servers, deacon and girl singers, with a male for the 'magic bits' might affront a devout Anglo-Catholic, who would settle for something lower, but more authentic in liturgical style. Equally, there are implicit rules regulating competition between house groups, who have to be careful to avoid poaching or 'sheep stealing'.

Each form of rite imposes an etiquette of behaviour on its participants. They are assumed to accept the house rules of a rite, and not to import rival customs or practices that would unsettle and give discomfort to those attending habitually. Those attending a particular form of rite have an implicit contract which assumes that the 'plausibility structure' of the rite will not be rendered implausible by counterfeit gestures or actions being imported that imply alien affiliations. It is not only the disruption that is feared, but the degree to which that which is imprecise is given an unfruitfully definite basis, one that draws the conventions of the rite into question. Such intrusions draw attention to the frailty of the social mechanism and the degree to which its conventions are arbitrary, and have no logical basis. A proof is invited that cannot be rendered, as to why a particular gesture is acceptable or is unacceptable. Given this uncertainty and accepting that the outcomes of liturgical enactments are indeterminate in their social effects, how is sociology to discriminate between these two artificial 'ideal types' to secure an understanding of the performative basis of rite ?

A stress on the operative basis of rituals can make *any* form of enactment 'work' in sociological terms. To sincere believers, any authentic liturgical form is believed to have an efficacious cast, a capacity to make present an event in a way that does not exhaust its mysterious basis. Rites are believed to be successful in their enactments for non-sociological reasons. This gives them an ambiguous quality of making them accessible and inaccessible at the same time. Sociology can affirm that the rite 'works' but it has no means of access to the mysterious elements that fill it with grace and Divine favour. This quality of ambiguity lends a tautological cast to many sociological accounts of operative ceremonies, where that which is stated or done accomplishes what it marks to effect. Operations are described in terms of a 'success' stemming from the authority of a practitioner uttering words, or performing an action, in a particular context that secures its authority. There is an internal, self-sustaining characteristic in accounts of ritual actions that provides a defence of their basis. An attempt to use these words or actions outside their normal ritual context would render them meaningless and useless. Paradoxically, the uselessness of liturgical instruments, such as vestments, or other material objects, for any other purpose than use in rite, helps to secure their meaningful basis. Maurice Bloch regards ritual enactments as rather like a song, as following a sequence that is above and beyond argument. He suggests that

> the experience of the ritual is an experience fused with its context and therefore only an attempt to explain what this event as a whole is for is an explanation of the content. An attempt to link the context of ritual to the world or society directly does not work because in secular terms religious rituals are mis-statements of reality.[37]

An analytical stress on the successful basis of ritual actions incorporates an acceptance of their 'fused' basis. This refers to the degree to which form and content are mutually implicated in a way that does not admit separation, for the meanings being effected can only derive their basis from such an interdependence. This might be an acceptable constraint on a sociological attempt to characterise the social basis of liturgy in general, but it becomes more problematic when used to arbitrate between differing forms of rite, both of which are believed to be 'successful'. If adherents of a 'spike' rite and a convivial assembly both claim that their social arrangements success-fully reach God, who is the sociologist to state otherwise ?

Rappaport offers a highly subtle account of liturgical deceits that draws their management and resolution to within the ambit of sociology. The thrust of his analysis is directed towards formal ceremonial rites, where implications do matter and where the actor is made accountable for what he reproduces. Interest in Rappaport is less directed to point scoring off convivial assemblies than indicating that if there is a sociological route, it moves mysteriously in a 'spike' direction. If the actor has to pass through a social form to find the holy, this is the best sociological account, and it is one directed to the issue of lies and mistakes that can emerge in liturgical operations. One cannot see how Rappaport's form of analysis could be applied to a convivial assembly and to that degree 'spike' rites win by default in this sociological game.

Rappaport is dealing with the obvious aspects of ritual, 'those of its features that, being most apparent, lead us to identify events as instances of rituals'.[38] There are three important elements in Rappaport's approach to liturgy. Firstly, he establishes a link between the mysterious (the unquestionable) and the invariant performance of liturgical orders. Secondly, he examines the relationship between private intention and the effects of its public expression. Acting in a rite involves a transformation of the actor, who accepts the obligations which he has constituted as effecting a redefinition of status, one embodied in the liturgical order. Thirdly, he examines the ambiguous capacity of rituals and symbols not only to effect santification but also to manifest lies. His primary concern is with the emergent qualities of the sacred that are effected by the ritual's structures. His term 'liturgical orders' refers to the sequences of formal acts and utterances that are enacted in specific contexts. These have a predictable routinised cast. The link between the particular and the general is expressed in terms of the 'canonical' and the 'indexical'. The former refers to the durable and the immutable, and this complements the immediate and variable nature of the latter. Both operate within the liturgy in an interdependent manner.

Sanctity is the quality of unquestionableness imputed by a congregation to postulates they regard as neither verifiable nor falsifiable.[39] He argues later that 'to sanctify messages is to certify them'.[40] The system of ritual effects a transformation of doubt into a principle of certainty. Thus, the invariant performance of liturgical orders transforms messages that seem dubious and arbitrary, into communications that are necessary and natural. This process of transformation, through which sanctity affects the actor through what he effects, has a quasi-sacramental aspect. Rappaport argues that

> by drawing himself into a posture to which canonical words give symbolic value, the performer incarnates a symbol. He gives substance to the symbol as that symbol gives him form. The canonical and the indexical come together in the *substance* of the *formal* posture or gesture.[41]

There is much to agree with in Rappaport's approach to liturgy, which contains elements implicit in our analysis so far. It also relates to John Skorupski's approach to operative ceremony, that it not only signals, but in so doing, effects a change, so that the object of the rite is redefined.[42] This reflects a variation on J. L. Austin's approach to performative utterances, where deeds rather than words accomplish their intended effects through ritual enactment. It also bears on S. J. Tambiah's approach to ritual, which he argues constitutes a distinctive activity with a meaning and an effect. The repetition of ritual produces a sense of heightened and intensified actualisation of a message deemed to be regarded as sacred and dramatic.[43] A sense of constraint is imposed on the actors involved in a liturgy that effects access to a liberating message. This bears on another aspect of Rappaport's approach to liturgy that has important implications.

Crucial to Rappaport's argument is the acceptance by the actor of the public implications of what he has privately imposed upon himself by performing the ritual action. The ritual operates to convert a private aspiration into a status that is given a public form of certification. He goes on to argue that 'it is the visible, explicit, public act of acceptance and not the invisible, ambiguous private sentiment that is socially and morally binding'. The effects of enacting a liturgical performance in public are powerful, for it makes it 'possible for the performer to transcend his own doubt by accepting in defiance of it'.[44] The social resources of rite not only certify and re-define the actor's relationship to the rite; they also effect a conversion of his position. Rappaport argues that acceptance is not synonymous with faith, nor does it necessarily produce an inward state. Nevertheless, acceptance of obligations in a public social act involves the imposition of a standard on the actor, which he has consented to make. This point relates to earlier arguments on the social functions of religious clothing. Their public use betokens the acceptance of a state of being unavailable for particular activities. In this regard, they fulfil a protective function for the wearer by precluding him from activities that might give public scandal.

There are some difficulties in Rappaport's argument. His interest in the obvious aspect of rite leads him to stress particular instances, such as circumcision, where a boy becomes man. A less clear cut transformation operates in the case of religious rituals. These admit the candidate into a career of struggle to secure the deeper and ambiguous meanings signified in the event. It is part of the definition of these religious ceremonies that social infelicities will not be absolved at the level of the obvious but in the unobvious. Rappaport has supplied a point of departure into the latter realm, which marks a limit to the social, and the degree to which it can bind and heal. A further difficulty with Rappaport's position is the implication that liturgical orders not only ameliorate infelicities, but make them irrelevant. In our approach, these take on a heightened significance in rite, for the actor takes it upon himself that he will struggle with these difficulties to secure virtue. Rappaport's argument resolves social doubt, not spiritual uncertainty. But the value of his position is that he has moved uncertainty from the social form to the content that gives it shape. He has provided a means for resolving uncertainty in rite, by transferring it away from the social instruments to the content constituted. In his argument, faith has been made irrelevant at the level of the social and the obvious, for doubt is transformed out of existence. He places the question outside the social form of the rite, the liturgical order that conveys the obvious. That is why he admits considerations of the numinous and the transcendent. The theological bias of his position, that lies implicit, is directed to a position where the social, being invariant and formal, does not count. It is irrelevant, for it has been so cast in his analysis as to overcome doubt, which being domesticated releases the individual to pursue what lies outside the form of the rite. His approach to liturgy is wholly at odds with the domain assumptions regarding renewal since Vatican II. While Victor Turner has made a notable if not misunderstood contribution to liturgical thought in North America, Rappaport's arguments regarding the obvious aspects of rite have been virtually ignored. They are also arguments difficult to defeat from within a sociological frame of reference. His approach to liturgy assumes a high degree of concentrated ceremonial power to overcome doubt. Social bonds have to be definite and controlled to achieve their effect. Liturgical instruments must be secured and cannot be left to chance. It is difficult to see how informal rites have a place in his analysis.

Liturgical activities have a hidden, invisible dimension of meaning, whose task is to bear witness to the unobvious. The unverifiable nature of sanctity is partly realised through social performance, in a way that contains doubt not so much over the efficacy of the act, as over the worthiness of the actor to accomplish it. The performer acts as if the social element he incarnates is true, and so it seems to become. But when this element is given a Christian dimension, the unverifiable only takes on a meaning when it becomes attached to an interior state, one that the social resources of the rite cannot penetrate. The social offers a means of changing the spirit, but is not to be confused with it. A clothing ceremony for a monk marks the beginning of a journey, not its end.

Rappaport's concern with the issue of liturgical lies and deceits, gives analytical access to some means of arbitrating between our two 'ideal type' forms of rite. The ambiguous capacity of rites to sanctify and to lie represents a dilemma that has to be handled *within* each form of rite. Because their outcomes are unverifiable, worries will always arise over the liturgical form drifting into dealing in what Rappaport has termed 'vedic lies'. These refer to incorrect states of affairs that do not conform to the specifications they are supposed to meet.[45] These misrepresentations can be due to failure of the liturgical actors to regulate the enactment of the rite. These lies can also reflect misattributions by rivals who seek to amplify the deficiencies of a particular liturgical style in a way that affirms their brand loyalty. Spelling out too much in rite and making the social too manifest can miss the liturgical point. Informal rites deceive by denying they have a mechanism to be regulated. There is too much of the obvious in their style for the unobvious to be recognised. As Rappaport suggests, 'it is important, if a proposition is to be taken to be unquestionably true, that no one understand it, and it is not surprising that ultimate sacred postulates are often "mysteries"'.[46] This relates to a similar point of Odo Casel on the need to protect the mysterious aspects of liturgy.

Despite his emphasis on the invariant quality of rite and the degree to which its public nature can resolve doubt, Rappaport admits that some form of regulation of enactment is required. He notes that 'if authorities wish to maintain their sanctity they must keep the operations of the regulatory structure they administer in reasonable working order'.[47]

The need to control the shape of the rite admits a sociological consideration as to what are the assumptions these actors use to deliver the correctly understood message. Even though the enactment of liturgy transforms obligations, and admits a form that sanctifies the social, the actor still has to attend to the servicing of what has been accomplished. Part of the obligations he has accepted, and that are constituted in the liturgical order, bear on the need for him to attend if presumption and deceits are not to emerge. The public state he affirms assumes some form of impression management, some criteria of judgement that admits an element of agency. As I have suggested, there are antinomial and ambiguous qualities buried in the liturgical act that have a potential to entangle the actor. He deceives himself if he feels he is in some way precluded from attending to the possibility of a 'liturgical mistake'.

RITUAL MALAPROPOISMS: HANDLING LITURGICAL MISADVENTURES

> as little public attention as possible is to be called to the occurrence
> of the defect, it is to be remedied briefly and quietly, and without
> any unnecessary repetitions (as the details of the remedies, given in
> the rubrics . . . show).
>
> (J. B. O'Connell, *The Celebration of Mass*)

Hugh Vickers has collected accounts of some dreadful mishaps in performance in his book *Great Operatic Disasters*. Mistaken entries and cues, the firing squad shooting Tosca instead of Cavaradossi, are mixed with accounts of scenery collapsing and the audience rioting.[48] These tales form part of the other operatic tradition, one sustained with relish by singers and agents and house managers, to keep the mighty in their place. Great liturgical disasters also happen, and these form part of the subculture of the sacristy or vestry, passed on between priests, servers and choir members. These disruptions range from the serious to the trivial: surplices catch alight; funerals get mixed up with weddings because of a slip in booking arrangements; the sermon gets lost; or the music comes in at the wrong time. Such ceremonial failures are hardly unexpected. What is of interest, is the response of actors to them. The management of such infelicities tells us about the regulation of the social base of particular styles of rite.

Operatic mistakes are rare, and can usually be resolved easily. The audience might laugh and the dignity of the singers might be dented. A mirthful response to a mistake at a solemn part of the liturgy would be a different matter. It might border on blasphemy and the actors might be visited with Divine wrath. Responses to mistakes on the sanctuary are usually muted. The actors try to disguise lapses, either by implying that they are part of the ritual process, or by not signifying them. Mistakes are handled in the hope that they have slipped God's attention. This muteness before anything presented in Church reveals an odd passivity amongst congregations before what they see and hear on the sanctuary. Commenting on the lack of a response to Mr Slope's admirable sermon, where feelings of hostility were not vented within the Cathedral, Anthony Trollope mused that

> There is, perhaps, no greater hardship at present inflicted on
> mankind in civilised and free countries, than the necessity of
> listening to sermons. No one but a preaching clergyman has, in

these realms, the power of compelling an audience to sit silent, and be tormented. No one but a preaching clergyman can revel in platitudes, truisms, and untruisms, and yet receive, as his undisputed privilege, the same respectful demeanour as though words of impassioned eloquence, or persuasive logic, fell from his lips.[49]

It would be perverse to go shopping around operatic and liturgical happenings to find a mistake that would characterise what the actors wish to avoid having spelt out in performance. One cannot commission 'liturgical mistakes' to test the dissimulating powers of those present, to see how far disattention can go for a particular congregation.

The shape and sequence of a formal rite can be checked. As a public order of worship, its form of enactment is accountable to an ecclesiastical discipline, a set of rubrics or ceremonial guidelines. Highly detailed staging instructions were given in Tridentine manuals, where every movement was stipulated, codified, and rendered to exact account in a code of canon law. Often these rules seemed very legalistic, and bore more of a resemblance to a chess manual than to a ceremonial directory. But as Adrian Fortescue, the author of one of the most widely used liturgical handbooks of the Tridentine rite, observed, 'actions are far less conspicuous when done than when described in words'. He went on to add that

> when each person knows exactly what to do, when they all agree and do their parts confidently and silently, the effect of the ceremony is immeasurably more tranquil than when there is doubt, confusion or discussion.[50]

Liturgical manuals are often used like cookbooks. Priests and servers will check the rules for particular rites, such as on Holy Thursday, to find if bells are to be rung during the consecration, as normal, whether the Easter candle is to kept on the altar until Pentecost Sunday, or how to perform a baptism and confirmation of a mother and baby child, without getting things mixed up. Procedural rules are listed as well as those that offer a means of redress should a mistake occur. 'Liturgical mistakes' in enactment are most likely to occur amongst the altar servers, the minor ministers who attend on the priest. As the authors of one liturgical guide observed:

> experience has convinced us that well instructed inferior ministries play a very large part in the good order and dignified appearance of episcopal ceremonies.[51]

Formal prescriptive rules do not capture the spirit of collusion and the sense of worship the enactment of a rite conveys to its participants, on or off the sanctuary. Although they were often described as ritualistic, older manuals seldom conveyed a sense of ritual, or indeed how it was constructed by the actors involved in its reproduction. Older rubrics were ceremonial details on procedure that paid little attention, not unexpectedly, to the sociological significance of rules, and the assumptions these reveal about the social basis of rite. The issue of theological and sociological rules for the staging of liturgies is highly complex, and represents an area that requires much further exploration.[52] Between the rise of ethnomethodology, and changes in the interpretation of the rituals of primitive society, rules have taken on an increased sociological significance, which few theologians or liturgists have understood. They reveal much about how rites are to be understood as unfolding in enactment and use.

Peter Winch has argued that the idea of following a rule is logically inseparable from the notion of making a mistake.[53] Adherence to a rule pre-supposes an accountability for a social outcome. Rules reflect an attempt to regulate that which is intended to be realised by a public event. Rituals operate according to regulative and constitutive rules, and these govern the context within which practices are to be understood. Emily Ahern has made a useful comparison between rules of enactment of games and the Azande's use of *benge*. The Azande, a tribe in Sudan, were studied by E. E. Evans-Pritchard in terms of their forms of social accountability. Poison oracles were used to resolve disputes. *Benge* was a substance fed to chickens, whose fate determined judgements of right and wrong. This means of arbitration has fascinated philosophers. The constitutive rules of such an odd ritual have clear implications for an understanding of liturgical procedures of enactment.[54]

Theological rules govern the validity of what is enacted, but also regulate what can be discerned in liturgical use. There is a sociological bias towards rules, not so much to affirm their regulatory functions, as to use them as a means to understand how the rites proceed, and the assumptions that govern their enactment. As Rom Harré has observed, constitutive and regulative rules do not explain rituals or ceremonials. Like staining a cell for microscopical examination, the application of concepts, such as those of rules, have the effect of forcing an opaque reality to reveal its structure.[55] Thus, in sociological terms, ceremonial and ritual rules do not have a prescriptive function so much as an enabling task of giving analytical access to understanding the artificial form or mechanism used to realise an indeterminate content. This would relate to Simmel's point noted earlier, on the analytical distinction between form and content. Liturgical transactions are governed by formal rules of accountability, that give rites a rather fixed and mechanical characteristic. These have a somewhat artificial relationship to the more informal procedures actors use and encounter in the process of performance. Accommodations and adjustments are made by actors who have a career of enacting a particular style of rite. These govern how the obvious in rite becomes so, and are of fundamental sociological interest.

The term 'liturgical mistake' refers to a breach in settled arrangements of practice, where the tacit structure of the rite is exposed in a discrediting way. The error is irretrievable, and to minimise the potential amplification of embarrassment, it is left unsignified. The 'flow' of the rite is disrupted and attention is drawn to the ambiguities and frailties of the social mechanism of representation in an unproductive manner. These mistakes are rare, but such is their effect that actors involved in the production of rite guard against their repetition as house practice. Contingencies are kept in mind to preclude or to smother such mistakes. An example of a 'liturgical mistake' can be drawn from another form of ritual: the graduation ceremony.

Names of students are called on the stage by the Dean from the left and candidates move across from the right, escorted by a university ceremonial officer. They stop in front of the Chancellor, present joined hands with a small bow and the degree is conferred. The risk of a mistake arises if the ceremonial officer finds himself moving across the stage with a large, heavily-built male, when the dean has called out a female name. The embarrassment inflicted on all parties can be great, and for the young man it could be a deep humiliation. To preclude such a mistake happening, each candidate is checked and rechecked as they form in batches to be taken up. A further worry is that a quasi-sacramental element operates, so that degrees imposed in a public ceremonial cannot be rescinded. An incorrect class might be conferred. Degree congregations are fragile events, and could crack under the discrediting weight of the 'wrong' candidate being conferred. Disrepute could reign for an embarrassing but not to be forgotten moment.

A 'liturgical mistake' arises when an uncertainty is unintentionally transferred from the content, which is indeterminate, to the mechanism or social form that ought to carry a quality of certainty to secure a credibility of engagement with the incredible. If an agnosticism overtakes the mechanism, then the delivery of the message becomes impaired and incredible for the 'wrong' reasons. The actors involved in a liturgy are not responsible for the uncertainty of outcome of the rite, that is a defining condition of its basis; but they would be regarded as responsible for guarding against corrosive doubt arising due to malapropoisms emerging in its performance. Rites operate to cast off uncertainty, and not to have their mechanisms clogged with it. Mistakes violate a sense of use and habit. This bears on David Babin's notion of 'liturgical use'.

'Liturgical use' refers to the customs of a particular worshipping community, its domestic style of ceremonial action, vestments, furnishings and accommodations that make up the biography of a parish. Babin argues that congregations are deeply sensitive to variations or alterations in the detail of 'liturgical use'. Part of the reason for the hostility of response relates to my earlier point, that apparent trivialities can become disproportionately significant. Because cues to the holy are so subjective in 'use', so variable in effect, and so difficult to defend or to articulate, changes in the liturgical order can have a disproportionate effect which is hard to estimate. Perception of the significance of a 'liturgical mistake' is highly variable.

Taste, availability of resources, and competence greatly affect the style of worship of a particular parish. The strength of character of the parish priest is another important influence in shaping patterns and styles of 'liturgical use'. A further complication is that perception of the quality of a parish liturgy depends on the amount of knowledge of the principles of worship in a particular community. This can be unevenly distributed within a congregation.[56] Discernment of what is happening in the sanctuary can range from a pious blindness to a list-taking of infelicities, flaws in liturgical manners, and breaches of major and minor rubrics. This variability of knowing what ought to happen makes assessment of perception and understanding of liturgical praxis by the congregation difficult to evaluate. Equally difficult to assess is the significance of the discrepancy between official liturgical rules, and the more informal and implicit principles that govern 'use' within a parish.

The issue of liturgical rules of enactment and their sociological assessment has become more complex since Vatican II. This might seem paradoxical, in view of the current emphasis on a quasi-sociological aspect to rite, where terms such as 'community', 'active participation' and a concern with relationships would seem to favour sociological interventions. The difficulty is that constitutive rules have become entangled with regulative rules in a way that generates sociological confusion. Terms acceptably vague in theology become unacceptably precise in sociological analysis, and this grounding gives a false precision to elements that have an indeterminate basis. Furthermore, sociology imperialises by setting prescriptive rules for the realisation of these quasi-sociological properties in a way that confuses their constitutive basis, which is based on theological arguments.

Tridentine rites had an exhaustive and exhausting number of detailed guidelines that governed the way mass was to be celebrated. Any variations were prescribed and limited, and infringements led to ecclesiastical penalties. The issue of 'use' hardly arose, as every mass was supposed to be celebrated in an exact and checkable manner that admitted no parochial discretion to alter practice. Oddly, the detailed stipulations for the performance of rite, which many liturgists regarded as an impediment to practice, had a certain ritual logic which anthropologists, such as Victor Turner, found attractive.[57]

Custom and tradition gave the rubrics of the Tridentine rite a timeless, objective cast, one above human intervention, that endowed its enactment with a sense of absolute certainty. Every detail of the rite could be rendered to exact rubrical account. These rubrics were divided between those deemed substantial and those regarded as accidental. The former referred to those affecting the validity of the rite, in its matter and form, an example being the imposition of hands at Ordination. These rules were regarded as immutable, binding in conscience, and were believed to be based on Divine law. Accidental rubrics were concerned with the ecclesiastical regulation of rite, and issues outside the validity of its enactment. The distinction could be expressed in another way. Preceptive rubrics bind in conscience; those described as directive refer to approved ways of carrying out a liturgical action; and those marked as facultative allow for choice or omission. Considerable dispute arose over the binding nature of accidental rubrics, and whether a mortal or venial sin applied to their breach. The rite was less changeless than it seemed, as concessions and prohibitions were added continually to a mosaic of ritual law after the Council of Trent.[58] The gestures, stances, and tones of the priest and his servers were all subject to the most exact account. Equally detailed laws applied to cover all manner of contingencies or defects that might arise in the celebration of the mass. These ranged from provision for the death of the priest in the midst of the celebration of the mass, to poison being discovered in the bread and wine, to the Host disappearing by accident, such as wind, or the intervention of an animal, or through a miracle.[59] However odd some of these rules were, they did provide a guidance to a sociologist and a scaling of priorities difficult to establish in the new code of canon law.

The liturgical renewal movement led to a greatly simplified rite that maximised lay participation, simplified rules of enactment, and gave a distinct recognition to the cultural basis upon which rites were received and understood. Indigenisation of forms of practice, and a stress on the sense the rite conveyed, led to an emphasis on subjective and cultural factors. Increasingly, the 'success' of the rite was being gauged according to the degree to which these factors were recognised, a reversal of the principles of the older code of canon law that sought to preclude such subjective cultural elements entering considerations of rite. Maximising and engaging the community in the task of worship became a matter of increasing concern that led to an emphasis on a recognition of the place of the laity in the enactment of the rite. As John Huels noted, 'liturgical law must enhance the spiritual and pastoral good of the worshipping community by promoting effective celebrations of the saving mysteries'.[60] Pragmatic considerations that deferred to communal sensibilities increasingly governed rules and expectations for liturgical performance. This change in emphasis provides a remarkable contrast to the invisibility awarded to the social base of rite and the relationship of the laity to it in liturgical enactments before Vatican II. For instance, in J.B. O'Connell's monumental work, *The Celebration of Mass*, the rules for the participation of the laity in a high sung Tridentine mass were given two pages –in the final appendix.[61]

Our interest in 'liturgical mistakes' centres on the degree to which these expose the accounting practices of actors involved in the presentation of rite in a public arena. It also gives us access to the social assumptions actors wish to make in enacting rite in a credible manner. These errors must be regarded as exceptional, otherwise the loyalty of adherents might be strained by such a mistake prone order of rite. 'Liturgical mistakes' are discrediting features that give unholy comfort to rivals, and confirm them in their brand loyalty to particular styles of worship. It could be argued that few rites operate with an obsessional concern with avoiding 'liturgical mistakes'. They are usually explicit, but can often be implicit, representing a worry as to what the form might sink into, if care in regulation were not maintained. Every liturgical form bears an image that is often too close to parody. A 'spike rite' can become embedded in an enactment more akin to a military parade, where the altar servers click their heels when they bow, and everything is done with a self-conscious air, somehow devoid of a sense of spirituality.

'Liturgical mistakes' bear on Goffman's approach to embarrassments arising in social encounters. In his account, embarrassments reflect unfulfilled expectations, revelations that discredit, and which are difficult to contain. They present an unacceptable sight that gives rise to uncertainty as to how to proceed without amplifying the offence, or causing further loss of face. They have to be managed in a tactful manner. The discrepancy exposed has to be resolved, if the encounter is not to sink into irredeemable discredit.[62]

An example of a 'liturgical mistake' might arise in the case of a witness at a Charismatic service. He might speak of private sinful matters in public, and might disclose that which is best left unsaid. The embarrassment of possibly interrupting the Spirit speaking through this witness has to be offset by the discrepancies disclosed that utter what is best left unspoken, at least in public. If this trend continued, of candid disclosure, those organising such assemblies might find all manner of voyeurs turning up to hear lurid disclosures. Contingency plans can exist to preclude such discrediting incidents arising, by having 'safe' witnesses at the ready, to hijack the sin into a more sanitised and creditable version and if the worst comes to the worst, the background music can be turned up. Convivial assemblies dissimulate these managed procedures in performance.

Another facet of a 'liturgical mistake' arises in the case of failures in face-work. 'Spike' rites are specially prone to such errors. In Goffman's terms, this refers to the image of self the actor shows to display approved social attributes.[63] Since modern Catholic liturgies have to be staged to be seen by the congregation, in all its aspects, the management of face-work has become far more important than when rites were performed in a way that ignored those off the altar. An altar server is employed to maintain a holy face, to sustain an image of dedicated involvement. If he slackens in his maintenance of the role, by revealing in the act a total boredom at the consecration, it is hard for him to recover face later in the mass, in a credible manner. Loss of face bears on hypocrisy and deception. Discrepancies exposed bring other aspects of appearing into disrepute.

'Liturgical mistakes' have a further important task, of drawing attention to the need to manage the social resources of rite to preclude unproductive ambiguities emerging. Each ritual has a sense of 'flow' that has to be 'paced' so every aspect of the social is kept subservient and is never allowed to present a fruitless uncertainty. A tension exists between actions and inactions. Not all rites are subject to this, but when they are shaped to cope with exceptional occasions, such as the funeral of an important personage, where many believers and non-believers alike will be in attendance, it is inevitable that a heightened awareness, a sense of alertness will reign over the rite, that could be regarded as filling it with a tension. Inactivity needs to be marked as a space in the action to meditate on the holy. This should be distinguished from cessations in activity, where the actors are uncertain as to how to proceed to the next stage in the ritual. An uncertainty in procedure can give rise to a sense of embarrassment that is contagious and that subtracts from a sense of the sacred.

Liturgical forms operate in the manner of a game, with its own odd set of rules and sequences. When these are bound together in performance, the enactment of the rite takes on a certain logic or coherence, that protects the detail and implies the trivial is something more meaningful than its apparent insignificance would suggest. This wholeness supplies the context in which the rite moves forward. Thus, following Turner, 'flow' denotes 'the holistic sensation present when we act with total involvement' and where the action follows a logical sequence to sustain that end. Ambiguous and contradictory aspects of the performance are concentrated into a confined frame of reference that enhances a sense of meaning. The term 'flow' is derived from the work of Mihaly Csikszentmihalyi and is used by Turner to suggest the way structures can be transformed and transcended.

In an earlier work, he raised the possibility of 'anti-flow'. This refers to that which breaks or arrests the 'flow' of a ritual action. Interruptions in the 'flow' of the Good Friday liturgy mark periods of contemplation that are therefore deemed productive.[64] Where unintended inactions occur, the 'flow' of the rite is impaired for unproductive reasons, which Turner did not explore. Goffman offers a concept that relates to this point. His idea of negative experience arises when the sense of concentration in the act is broken, and the actor comes to lose his capacity to dominate the proceedings.[65]

Goffman suggests a crucial variation on the notion of the definition of the situation, a term we have used a number of times. He suggests that actors do not create definitions, but rather assess what they ought to be, and then act accordingly.[66] Andrew Travers has supplied a useful notion of a ritual realm as a context of interaction in which the actor finds his maximum social importance.[67] In his comments on ritual roles, Goffman gives the self a dual definition. One is of the 'self as an image pieced together from the expressive implications of the full flow of events in an undertaking' and the other is of acting 'as a kind of player in a ritual game who copes honorably or dishonorably, diplomatically or undiplomatically, with the judgemental contingencies of the situation'.[68] This broadens the role of the actor in handling a symbolic order, given ritual expression, but allows a greater range of accountability to arise. In the duality which Goffman expresses, it is the latter aspect we wish to develop, where the self is involved in a ritual game. The self is engaged in handling layers of implication laminated in a ritual order. The main task of the actor is to prevent these layers becoming unstuck. Unaccounted-for gaps or inactivities in a ritual order can cause uncertainty to arise, and can attract attention to a failure in the mechanism.

A 'liturgical mistake' introduces a notion of responsibility for the 'flow' of the rite, and the need to check against breaches of its sequence. 'Liturgical mistakes' amplify that which is deemed to subtract from the sense of wholeness which the enactment of rite petitions to yield. If a rite is to 'work' credibly, it has to appear just to happen in a way where human agency is disguised. It seems to unfold of its own accord. For this reason, the 'flow' of the rite needs to be protected. Every gap in the ritual sequence or period of action has to be rendered to potential account. These can mark a prelude to a more significant part of the rite or they could be used to prepare the next stage of the liturgy, the movement from the Word to the Eucharist. If inactions are to have a significant effect, they must not be spoiled by gaps that are insignificant. Fruitful gaps need a monopoly of inaction if they are to bear significant and intended meanings. 'Pace' represents the means through which the sense of 'flow' is maintained and is kept to account in the performance of the rite. It is the means through which actors adjust the tension of the ritual form to keep the sequence running in a smooth coherence, where the parts of the rite seem to 'flow' into a meaningful whole. Fruitful inactions call attention to what is beyond the limits of the liturgical form; unfruitful gaps cast significance on that which is insignificant in the performance.

The finesse involved in the regulation of rite points to procedures that can take on an excessively domestic, if not neurotic, quality. A sociological amplification of deception, linking the actor to the staging of a particular liturgical style, risks becoming lodged on a holy stage and being placed too far apart from the 'real' world. Stress on 'liturgical mistakes' in terms of warding off reductionist misreadings by rivals point to antinomial qualities that operate between rites. Plurality breeds competition between forms of rite but in a way that can also distract attention from the antinomial problems of operating between the small holy world of the sanctuary and the larger universe of modern culture, where other ambitions and manners prevail. Spiritual emphases in Catholicism stress the need for detachment from the world of goods and services within which liturgical actors operate more routinely. Such an emphasis, however worthy, can accentuate the unreal nature of liturgy in a way that suggests it is above and beyond the need for any form of social regulation. Unless they are monks, or living in a boarding school, most liturgical actors also have links to the modern world with all its pressures to consume, to acquire and to be fashionable. If they do not feel the antinomial dilemmas on the sanctuary, they know of them out of it. Representing them involves a routine conversion that sets a distance from modern life. The division between the sanctuary and the modern playground has an antinomial quality which even the youngest liturgical actor can feel deeply.

Modern theologians have fretted over the link between theological belief and modern culture, where far larger antinomial issues loom. Tensions between civility and sanctity, between modern and traditional cultures, and between belief and disbelief, seem to enable or disable religious belief. The question of how to harness these tensions to sustain a capacity to believe seems to have evaded modern theological thought. As indicated before, the issue of culture achieves a condensed and structured expression in liturgical engagements with the holy. It is in this context that the question of the link between culture and belief needs to be put, if theologians are to make progress.

Any examination of liturgical form has to be selective, arbitrary and artificial in the analysis it produces. Liturgical bows and the activities of altar servers might not seem to be obvious staging posts for great sociological debate on the nature of the link between culture and belief. The purpose of the next two chapters is to show that such minor aspects of rite can be amplified in an antinomial way to mark distinctions between the civil and the sacerdotal. If this work were to have an indefinite length, other minor aspects of liturgy could have been selected for analysis.

Acts of abasement and the role of the altar server draw attention to the mystery and manners of the sanctuary. Both point to the rescued quality of holiness the actor can achieve on the sanctuary. Bows are a mannered aspect of civility, servicing a world of politeness in which the sophisticated can shine forth. But the same actions also convey worship to God on the sanctuary, a world apart from the realm of the civil. Equally, the altar server suggests to the liberal puritan a ceremonial role that more belongs to the world of the waiter. Indeed one role is a metaphor for the other. This gesture and this role point to an insight of Berger made earlier, that the same human activity that produces society also produces religion. Similarly the same gesture and role that produces liturgical enactments also produces significant ingredients in notions of civility. There is an antinomial quality to both gesture and role which, if neglected, reduces the sacred to the civil in a way that suggests a deceptive practice. Our next concern is to establish some sociological means of interpretation that allows these mutually incompatible meanings to be kept apart, in a way that affirms the autonomy of the holy gesture and role.

7 Sacred and Profane Abasements: The Management of Esteem

> the Lord had made a covenant,
> and charged them, saying, Ye shall not fear other
> gods, nor bow yourselves to them, nor serve them,
> nor sacrifice to them.
>
> (2 Kings 17:35)

Sitting in a darkening abbey waiting for vespers, one might notice a monk coming out with lighted taper. Clad in his black habit and scapular, he glides silently by. Before the altar, he bows deeply from the waist, lights the candles and departs equally gracefully.

This simple gesture is easy to describe, but is more difficult to interpret as to what it means or signifies. Despite the gesture being manifest, the meaning conveyed seems unapparent. The context of the act does indicate that religious rather than civil or theatrical properties were being expressed by this monastic gesture. Of course, one could ask the monk what this action of the body meant, but in some ways this would miss its point. After all, it is an act that is supposed to speak for itself, not in words, but in another form of language, one all the more powerful for being imprecise.

Unfortunately, the grammar for deciphering bows is neglected in a contemporary culture that uses other more elementary forms of appreciation. Bowing is a mannered antique act rarely used in Western social intercourse. Few people bow, and those who do, generate a suspicion at worst, and a curiosity at best. There is something alien, exotic, if not artificial about those who bow. It presents a spectacle. The Japanese bow at tea parties; fawning fops abase madly in a plenitude of gesture and appreciation in Restoration dramas; and head waiters give artful little grovels in the better class of restaurant. These little marks of deference lie on the edge of our society.

Bows are forms of gesture, stylised acts that are risky, less for their insignificance than for their capacity to be misunderstood. Because gestures are handling that which is not stated in words, they are very likely to produce misunderstandings. They have an ambiguous cast. This arises from their capacity to express definite sentiments, but in a way that can seem indefinite. Their indeterminacy can give rise to unwarranted inferences. Sir Alec Guinness records a visit to a Trappist monastery, prior to his conversion to Catholicism in 1955. Walking across the fields, he encountered an elderly tonsured monk, who sprang from a workman's hut and gesticulated wildly. Thinking such an excess of gesture reflected the strains of monastic silence, Sir Alec was a little surprised to discover from the guestmaster later that the monk had been stationed to warn him to stay away from the quarry as gelignite was being exploded on that day.[1]

The presentation of the body for social intercourse establishes tacit distinctions and expresses a diversity of attributes. The manner of gesturing certifies a civil credibility in a wide range of subtle nuances. As Lord Chesterfield noted, 'in good breeding there are a thousand little delicacies, which are established only by custom; and it is these little elegancies of manners, which distinguish a courtier and a man of fashion from the vulgar'.[2] Gestures serve to denote the moral character of an actor, who presents an implication for judgement. As meaningful and intended actions, gestures convey sentiments of politeness, religious feelings and shared sensibilities in an unstated manner that speaks louder than words. They supply a basis for inference and social judgement that operates through tacit means. Writing to his son, Lord Chesterfield observed:

> if you would either please in a private company, or persuade in a public assembly, air, looks, gestures, graces, enunciation, proper accents, just emphasis, and tuneful cadences, are full as necessary as the matter itself.

Later he wrote:

> if you have any sagacity, you may discover more truth by your eyes than by your ears. People can say what they will, but they cannot look just as they will; and their looks frequently discover what their words are calculated to conceal.[3]

Gestures are trivial aspects in forms of appearing in social inter-action which can be promoted into acts of great significance that transcend the slightness of the act. For a head of state to bow at the grave of a former enemy after his funeral, might convey an honour and a respect which those who survived the war might feel unable to share.

Bows can be innocuous acts of appreciation, but if they are set in a ceremonial context they can take on a velocity to deliver meanings, whose significance cannot be adequately appreciated in mere words. They can be used to denote or to mark qualities of commitment in a way that makes the act irretrievable. Because a gesture can have a symbolic purpose, it bears the mark of a belief system, and its use signifies an affiliation that is undeniable. To make the sign of the cross in public in a country governed by Islamic fundamentalists could have a deadly effect on the actor making the gesture.

Gender status, religious beliefs, and standards of civility are mediated through the language of gesture. Fingers, hands and all parts of the body can be mobilised in the service of a variety of belief systems.[4] Some form of regulation is required if the use of gestures, their meaning and interpretation is not to get out of hand. An indiscriminate employment of gestures without attention to their suitability can lead to all sorts of misleading impressions.

Because they service so many forms of meaning, the use of gestures has to be stipulated in a context, and arbitrarily given a capacity to bear a particular quality of meaning. Yet even with some form of control, gestures still have a distinctively ambiguous quality for the following reasons. As gestures express meanings indirectly, there is often a discrepancy between intended effects, and those which might be unintentionally realised in the meanings given off in the act. Secondly, gestures have a potential for promotion to a significance out of all proportion to their apparently trivial and observable functions. Thirdly, a gesture, such as a bow, can carry a number of conflicting messages bound together in a way that generates an uncertainty as to what exactly is being said. Fourthly, meanings of great significance might be read into an action that are disproportionate to what the actor intends. A degree of ambiguity exists between the actor and his intended audience in the delivery and interpretation of a gesture. Sometimes this can be resolved through calculation of purpose and effect, but at other times it cannot be rectified by the nature of the act.

The qualities a gesture affirms are often as indeterminate and as diverse as the act itself. Ephemeral qualities of civility, and of 'good manners' are transmitted by an abasement. But the same gesture can be used to effect religious intentions in another context. This gives an act such as bowing an antinomial quality. It services two incompatible constituencies. A bow in a drawing room at a state reception clearly marks qualities of civility different from those of sacrality accomplished before an altar. This is not where the problem lies. The issue to be explored is how the act of abasing, so easy to describe, services two incommensurate belief systems.

The separation of meanings in a common act poses a particular sociological difficulty. In civil society, the act of bowing effects the demands of good manners, but in a religious ceremony, such an assumption would be quite reductionist. In the latter use, more than an issue of good manners is involved. The bow fulfils the second commandment, to render honour only to God. It forms part of an effort to worship in a setting where 'the liturgical gesture is faith in action'.[5] Because gestures embody condensed signals of belief in an economy of movement, much disagreement can arise over their significance and use in liturgy. Indeed, the act of bowing before an altar, in some Protestant eyes, is idolatrous and corrupting of true faith. They would point to the injunction

> Ye shall make you no idols nor graven image,
> neither rear you up a standing image, neither
> shall ye set up any image of stone in your land,
> to bow down unto it: for I am the Lord your God.
> (Levit. 26:1)

In this chapter, I wish to examine the interpretative dilemmas a gesture, such as a bow, poses for actors and their audiences within civil society, and to compare these with the problems that arise over their use within religious ceremonies. Many gestures could be examined within civil society, that transmit manners. Shaking hands in a way that signifies trust; standing up to show respect; and sitting down to suggest ease in relationships, are all gestures that could be fruitfully analysed. Equally, within liturgical orders, a large number are used that bear on the detail governing the use of the body in worship. Kneeling, genuflecting, making the sign of the cross, are but a few. Each of these actions has a complex lineage and a web of justifications that mark their significance. A gesture, such as a bow, poses less of a problem for description than of interpretation of the meanings it conveys. It serves to realise properties of civility or sacrality in a peculiarly efficient manner that belies the slightness of the act. As an action, it can bear a large amount of theoretical and interpretative baggage.

A bow is an intentional inclination of the body that conveys reverence or appreciation. It represents a form of attention that has an intended focus on an individual or an object. An element of trust is assumed in this act of deference, that the actor means what he does. How is the recipient of this form of appreciation to know that the act is sincere and is not feigned? The sincerity of the bower relates to interior sentiments that are not fully disclosed in the act, and the effects of its issue are equally indeterminate. The capacity of the recipient of a bow to check the sincerity of the bower is limited, for the properties conveyed in the act disclose meanings that are diminished if they have to be translated into verbal terms. It would be graceless to check every bow. To some extent the recipient of a bow is powerless before the compliment. Indeed, he might not be the object of the act. A fulsome grovel might suggest an amplification that falls less on the object of deference than on the actor so deferring. But fawning abasements that fall with abandon can fill the recipient with a profound distrust of the bower. Some economy of grovel is required. Bows entice but they can also generate suspicion as to whether a reservation lurks in the self of the actor that subtracts from the external act of deference. An unselective use of bows can convey, unintentionally perhaps, a discrediting insincerity in the bower.

We wish to argue that the self is implicated in markedly different ways in civil and religious ceremonies. Contrasting intentions are expressed in this act of deference, that illustrate differences in meanings presented in two worlds, that seem adjacent but need to be marked as distant. A mannered bow in a court might appear similar to the careful bow of an altar server in a Cathedral, but the belief systems being serviced are remarkably different. The act of bowing effects a regulation of the social form of a transaction. It permits distinctive qualities of meaning to be disclosed and to be realised in the act. In a liturgical setting the prospects for deception are great, but the only person perhaps being fooled is the insincere bower. It is precisely because he can feign so easily that he has to explore the sincerity of the act to avoid potential corruptions becoming embedded in habitual acts of deference.

The style and manner of bowing clearly affects the credibility of the act. Some bows can be graceful acts that enhance; others can be incompetently performed, jerky inclinations whose purpose might be unclear. One is less concerned with the art of bowing than with the worlds of civility and sacrality it services. It is the properties of meaning the act embodies that generate interest. Both worlds assume a sense of occasion, something to be marked in the staging of ritual events. An element of spectacle is involved that relates to an expectation that onlookers will gaze, either to be confirmed in their sense of gentility, or to be edified by what they observe. In both worlds, appearances *do* matter and there is an evident interest in the quality and the right to act. Abasements performed by those with no title, whether civil or spiritual, subtract from the sensibility the rituals serve to enhance. Bowing is simply a tiny but noticeable ingredient in these worlds. Because a bow is a public expression of a private sentiment, the bower allows himself to be checked and to be subject to a scrutiny that varies in intensity, depending on the significance or otherwise of the act. To survive such tests, he needs to attend to the quality of his acts of deference. Following Rappaport, if the actor bows sincerely, he is using a public means to affirm a private sentiment. A spirit of calculation is necessary in civil circles that would be unholy in the realm of the sacred.

DEFERENTIAL GESTURES: THE ART OF BOWING

> He seldom comes in till the prayers are about half over; and when he has entered his seat, instead of joining with the congregation, he devoutly holds his hat before his face for three or four moments, then bows to all his acquaintance, sits down, takes a pinch of snuff, if it be the evening service perhaps takes a nap and spends the remaining time in surveying the congregation.
>
> (Richard Steele, 'On improper behaviour at Church')

A bow amplifies the significance of an action or an event. It serves to embellish an activity that might otherwise be regarded as trivial or insignificant. Adding bows into the fabric of rite dignifies an event with a sense of occasion. As an episode in a ceremony, a bow marks a warning of the significance of what is to come. It might amplify an entrance to a chamber where a ritual of appreciation is to be enacted. Bowing can also effect a graceful exit from a social event, where delicate departures are required to preserve the civil fabric. The capacity to know when to bow with grace in civil society in the seventeenth and eighteenth centuries certified gentility. It demonstrated an ability to grasp an implication and to acknowledge it in a subtle response. The ability to know when to bow, to gauge its angle accurately according to rank, signified breeding and a capacity to engage in tacit relationships, where the unspoken was more important than what could be spoken.

Bows implicate the bower into a closer and more deferential relationship to the object of his appreciation. They effect a proximity, an intimacy in transaction, but they also serve to exclude and to mark a social distance. They form part of the defensive basis of manners, and mark distinctions in a subtlety the unsubtle might fail to perceive. They can be an important facet of social intercourse, for as Lord Chesterfield observed, 'all ceremonies are in themselves very silly things; but yet a man of the world should know them'. He went on to add that they

> are the outworks of manners and decency, which would be too often broken in upon, if it were not for that defence, which keeps the enemy at a proper distance. It is for that reason that I always treat fools and coxcombs with great ceremony; true good breeding not being a sufficient barrier against them.[6]

Karen Halttunen illustrates the way bows were used to regulate proximity and distance in social relationships in nineteenth-century American society. A welcome social acquaintance was to be greeted with a 'cordial bow', whereas an unwelcome person was to receive a 'cold bow', one that effected a studied non-recognition.[7] The act of bowing pre-supposes a capacity to discern its intended purpose, otherwise it would be a meaningless movement. Indiscriminate bowing can bring discredit. To bow presumes the right to do so. Thus, it was suggested in a late-nineteenth-century etiquette column that 'casual conversation at an afternoon party does not establish a bowing acquaintance . . .'.[8] In civil society, bows are mannerly instruments that effect and sustain the gracious cordiality in social relationships that are presumed to characterise the upper classes. They are mannerly inclinations that form part of the civilising process outlined by Norbert Elias. Courtesy is related to a growth of self-consciousness and a capacity to regulate the self in an unobtrusive manner that conveys a delicacy of response to a variety of social situations.[9] Used well, bows magnify the insignificant in a pleasing way that smooths the passage of social intercourse. Qualities of judgement in use of gestures are affirmed in a manner that heightens a mutual sense of esteem amongst those gathered at a civilising event. This imposes a demand on the self to attend to the way the body is presented for public mannerly display and to preserve a heightened consciousness of the effects of its movements in gesture.

In civil society, politeness and moral disposition are partly confirmed by stance, by the knowledge of how and when to incline the body. Honour and esteem are certified in the use to which these inclinations are put. These can be deemed to be base or civilised. Social movements should generate few apparent waves. A sense of propriety over how to gesture denotes breeding and certifies the benefits of a liberal education. This produces a gentleman who has a 'cultivated intellect, a delicate taste, a candid, equitable, dispassionate mind, a noble and courteous bearing in the conduct of life . . .'.[10] An awareness of the impact of one's presence in social company marks a training in the management of implication. A lack of awareness of how to move gracefully can form the basis of exclusion from civil society. Social infelicities were believed to mark defects in character. As Lord Chesterfield noted 'awkwardness of carriage is very alienating; and a total negligence of dress and air is an impertinent insult upon custom and fashion'.[11] Errors of civil deportment can be culpable and need not be taken seriously. For instance, Americans travelling in foreign parts were warned against failures to understand the timing and angle of a bow. Misplaced obeisances could generate confusion 'offending everyone who is forced to keep smooth on the outside while convulsed with inner laughter'.[12]

A well-cast bow delivers esteem to a recipient in a way that enhances his sense of honour and worth. It mirrors gracious properties. In civil society, a bow is founded on a social paradox: that those who lower their body with effect are raised up in social esteem. Indiscriminate abasements betray a lack of sincerity, or skill in knowing where to deliver one's grovels with the maximum of gentility and the minimum of effort. A knowledge of the craft of abasement magnifies the bower and at the same time confirms his judicious nature. It elevates the self in public esteem. To be so rewarded, the self has to display an attachment to the act and its implications, if the deference so presented is to be sincerely received. An interest is required, if the act is to accomplish that which it expresses: the conferment of honour on another. Bows form an aspect of Goffman's notion of 'status rituals', a term that arises in his account of deference and demeanour. He was solely concerned with acts of subordination between individuals.[13] Where bows form part of an issue of public manners between equals, the qualities of the self are amplified and confirmed. In so deferring to his equals, the self becomes elevated and its claims to gentility become enlarged.

Bows in a liturgical context impose contrasting conditions on the self. The purpose of the act is not to magnify the self and to proclaim its worth. These are qualities that are not intended to be attached to the actor, but are to be cast off and given to God who represents the purpose of this act of deference. If the self is too far detached from the civil act of abasing, it faces charges of insincerity, which is the reverse of the case in the sacerdotal use of the gesture. In liturgy, the self is to be distanced from the act of abasement to preclude charges of self-glorification and insincerity. In civil society, by lowering the self, the actor is raised in social esteem. In a religious context, the self has to be lowered, and has to remain so, in a way that defers to God's mercy to raise him up.

In his lessons on civility for a boy, Erasmus noted that at Church 'the entire bearing of the body should accord with nature of the rite'.[14] Such an injunction suggests a selective care over what is presented by the body in worship. Particular gestures are marked out for distinctive and exclusive use. Thus, there is the call 'O come, let us worship and bow down: let us kneel before the Lord our maker' (Ps. 95:6). Actions in a liturgy, such as bowing, kneeling, or walking are believed to bear sacred meanings. In enacting them, the actor affirms a belief in holiness, and in so doing, he manages to incarnate a sensibility of its existence. This liturgical task makes a difficult demand on the actor, of constantly aiming at expressing in 'his own bodily acts what he realises in his soul'.[15] In some way the body has to be used to intensify a sense of prayer and to generate a capacity for awe and worship. As Origen noted, 'the posture of the body images the qualities of the soul in prayer'.[16] The actor not only acts in terms of a looking glass self, that monitors the social shape of what is produced, but also he tries to mirror and to reflect in his soul how he acts and appears in liturgy before God. In this sense, the actor in his performance strives to effect a quality of grace in the act. By bowing sincerely, he transmits qualities of grace to his beholders, which seems to be embodied in his act of homage.

There is an element of petition involved in liturgical gestures that underlines their hazarding nature, for their determinate nature distracts attention from their indeterminate effects. Even if the effect of the act of bowing is unclear, this does not absolve the actor from certain minimum standards in the control of his posture on the sanctuary. This need was well understood in older liturgical manuals covering matters of deportment. For instance, in a section on rules for 'Ecclesiastics in Choir' one liturgical manual stated that clergy ought to comport themselves in silence, modesty and self-possession, abstaining from everything that would indicate frivolity or irreverence, such as reading letters, talking, giving snuff to each other, gazing about, sitting cross-legged, lolling in their seats, and other acts of this nature.[17]

The issue of bowing poses a number of pitfalls for even the most pious of liturgical actors. If he renders his bows too well, and bends in an ostentatiously holy manner, he might be implying that his fellow altar servers are inclined to the worst in their abasements. Conspicuous styles of abasement can betray a conceit that might cause a liturgical actor to forget the warning that 'whosoever shall exalt himself shall be abased; and he that shall humble himself shall be exalted' (Matt. 23:12). An element of corruption might arise, of knowing how to bow so well as to place a constraint on God to defer to this expertise in humility.

Bows signal implications in the social, and the same gesture can disclose remarkably contrasting meanings within a single event. An illustration of this appears in *The Brothers Karamazov*, when the elder Zossima is visited in his hermitage attached to the monastery. The elder was greeted with deep bows and kisses by his monastic brethren, a collective abasement that aroused mixed feelings from the other visitors, much to the annoyance of Alyosha, who was a novice at the monastery at the time. Miusov, profaned by these sacerdotal obeisances, made a rather deep and dignified bow, a distancing act that denoted the response customary in polite society; Ivan signalled reservations by bowing with his hands at his side; and Kalganov was so flustered by the whole event, that he did not bow at all.[18] All recognised that a bow carried an element of sincerity, a pledge that implicated the actor. The same act signalled a variety of sacred and profane meanings to affirm or to deny esteem for the monastic elder. The differences are subtle but significant.

By effecting what they are deemed to signify, bows convey meanings that can have significant social effects. They transmit messages that have a potential to make a mark on the social, to present implications 'in operative actions . . . performed in order to create or cancel a set of rights and obligations'.[19] Bows have a potentially irreversible quality. They bind the bower to the object of his appreciation. Thus, 'these marks of devotion represent ways in which an actor celebrates and confirms his relation to a recipient'.[20] There is a contractual element implied in a bow. For our purposes, bows re-define an actor's relationship to another person or object in a way that qualifies private reservations about the act. When he bows, the actor seems to accept the public implications of the act. He allows himself to be considered bound by the rules of deference for the particular context that expresses the belief system to which he is supposed to be affiliated.

This draws us back to a familiar question in the work so far: the tactful management of meanings that are by their nature antinomial. The act of bowing is used in both civil and sacred settings. The context of use denotes the intention of the act, and supplies a clue as to the meanings a bow embodies. The difficulty with liturgical bows is that they represent an action that is isolated and is oddly artificial in a culture where manners are far more simple and direct. With the decline in the civil use of abasements, except in public and academic contexts, bows in liturgy take on a heightened significance. In civil society, the actor can render his abasements to account. He can calculate inclination according to person and object, and judge the grace of the deference to a fine degree. The liturgical actor, however, faces a distinctly different problem. Since he is dealing with the incalculable, how is he to calculate the degree of his abasements on the altar?

THE ART OF PLACING A PROFANE GROVEL

> Bow, Bow, ye lower middle classes,
> Bow, Bow, ye tradesmen, bow ye masses,
> Blow the trumpets, bang the brasses,
>   (William Schwenck Gilbert, *Iolanthe*)

Bows express forms of appreciation. They also describe a social order, and the hierarchy within which respect is to be shown. Bowing is a means of marking the unequal allocation of honour and prestige within a group. As a form of deference, bows establish conditions of entitlement, to receive respect, but also to confer it. Civil forms of abasement have their own forms of ambiguity. They serve to express a humility, but also a superiority by denoting the right to abase. The use of a bow conveys tacit assumptions regarding the status of a bower. In complex social circles, where orders of civility are consciously arranged, a superior claim to gentility is involved in the accurate delivery of a bow to the correct addressee. A finesse in abasement is required to surmount a delicate paradox: that the lowering of the body acts to confirm the social superiority of the bower. The capacity to bow credibly without social injury to the superior claims of status of the bower requires a judicious touch. A mis-spent obeisance can debase the value of a bow, for like currency, the bower can run out of social credit by spending his abasements unwisely. A social incompetence is displayed, and an incapacity to confer honour would be revealed that could be discrediting. As Lord Chesterfield observed 'an awkward address, ungraceful attitudes and actions, and a certain left-handedness . . . loudly proclaim low education and low company; for it is impossible to suppose that a man can have frequented good company, without having catched something, at least, of their air and motions'.[21]

In the seventeenth and eighteenth century, bows were linked to deportment, to graceful movements that certified a gentility of breeding. These abasements were taught to the nobility by dancing masters. To make an entrance, or to effect a departure with the least social disruption, required a schooling in graceful inclinations.[22] The angle and number of bows varied according to rank and title, and a complex etiquette governed the degree of abasement required lest a misdelivery occurred. The exactness required in abasing with credit is indicated in the exchange between Mr Jourdain and his dancing master, in Molière's play 'The Would-Be Gentleman'. Asked how to bow to a countess, the dancing master tells Mr Jourdain

> if you wish to show great respect you must make your bow first stepping backwards and then advance towards her bowing three times, the third time going down right to the level of her knee.[23]

Failure to calculate the requisite number of abasements to impress could generate misunderstandings. An unchecked flow of bows could convey, perhaps inadvertently, an insincerity of appreciation, and could bring the basis of the act into doubt. Since bows bear polyvalent meanings, all manner of implications could escape if the actor is not on guard. An ironic acknowledgement could easily be confused with a hesitant, but apologetic inclination; a religiously cast bow could be misread as a civil and graceful accomplishment; and a deeply mannered obeisance might be interpreted as a hypocritical grovel.

It might be thought this analysis is making a sociological mountain out of a molehill on the landscape of social action. But trivial actions can have serious political consequences. They can come to signify conflicting demands of loyalty, a point that worried Lord Macartney on his trade mission to China in 1793. To gain access to the Emperor, a ritual kowtow was required, of three kneelings and nine knocks of the forehead on the floor.[24] This was in excess of the abasements required from ambassadors to gain entry to the English court, where only three simple bows were demanded.[25] Macartney felt he could not spend on the Chinese Emperor a quantity of abasements in excess of the entitlement of his own monarch. If the number and inclination of bows are not calculated, misattributions can occur. For instance, the gradations of abasement at the end of an artistic performance require a fine calculation. An excess of bows might seem presumptuous, but equally a deficit in expected abasements could seem ungrateful. In another context, a surplus of bows could present an unredeemable pledge to the recipient, one that might suggest the beginning of a career of dependence and obligation to the bower, who bestows an excess of honour for no good or apparent reason.

A plenitude of bows abroad could generate suspicion. As H. R. Haweis observed, perhaps, 'one of the most agonising incidents of foreign travel is the practice of universal salutation'. He wondered at an early sociological survey amongst the readers of the Paris *Figaro* about the question of whether one bows on entering a railway or an omnibus. The survey revealed divided views on abasements and their use in public transport. One reader acidly observed that one no more bowed in a railway carriage than in a circus, and added 'notice people who bow; they either look nervously timid, silly, or like people afraid of the police'.[26] Indiscriminate bowing generates suspicion of motive. An excess of abasement can remove an actor from the sphere of respectability and suggest he is intending to deceive and to defraud by so manipulating. Character can become confused with social incompetence. Some sort of custody is assumed, if the actor and the act are not to be brought into disrepute.

Bows in polite society involve aspects of Goffman's notion of facework. If they are delivered correctly, they save face, and preserve an even tenor of deference; misdelivered, either in quality or quantity, and discrepancies emerge that effect a loss of credibility. Errors in abasement reflect infringements of Goffman's notion of a 'ceremonial rule . . . which guides conduct in matters felt to have secondary or even no significance in their own right'.[27] But as Goffman observes later 'the gestures which we sometimes call empty are perhaps in fact the fullest things of all'. Goffman awards a sacralising quality to civil ceremonies, seeing them as effecting a distribution of social indulgences throughout society. He goes on to add that the self is in part a ceremonial thing, a sacred object which must be treated with proper ritual care and in turn must be presented in a proper light to others.[28]

Gestures are an important facet of this need to convey respect, but also to embody it in civil ceremonies. The ambiguity of civil gestures, the degree to which they are empty or are filled with meaning relates to the issue of their intended use, and the meanings actors choose to channel into them. If they are deemed significant, then they bear a pledge of the sincerity of the actor, and the accountability he imposes upon himself for the action. This also places a demand on the actor to exercise a custody in gesture, to be aware of its impact in delivery. A capacity to calculate is assumed if the gesture is to deliver its intended effect. What form of self-accounting can be understood to operate in a liturgical context?

SACRED BOWS AND UNHOLY DELIVERIES

I beg of you to forebear giving him any account of our religion or manners till you have rooted out certain misbehaviours even in our churches. Among others, that of bowing, saluting, taking snuff, and other gestures. Lady Autumn made me a very low courtesy the other day from the next pew, and, with the most courtly air imaginable called herself *miserable sinner*. Her niece, soon after, saying, *Forgive us our trespasses*, courtesied with a glouting look at my brother. He returned it, opening his snuff-box, and repeating yet a more solemn expression.

(Richard Steele 'Indecorums at Church')

Civil bows regulate the ebb and flow of social intercourse. They make only partial demands on the actor's self, sufficient to maintain an appearance of courtesy and grace, and enough to lubricate sentiments of appreciation. The self can remain detached from the gesture, and be a beneficiary of that distance, in the esteem conferred on him for being able to abase so gracefully. In religious terms, the actor bows to express an inward sentiment in an outward manifestation, to make an act of worship in a way that admits a total claim on the sincerity of the self. Furthermore, this is done in a way where the self strives to avoid any glorification being attached to his action. This denial of self-esteem is a condition imposed by the actor to effect as pure an appreciation of his Maker as possible.

In theology, a bow services a relationship of dependence, reverence and adoration in a way that is intended to implicate the soul of the bower into a bodily action. The process through which the soul is bound into the body, in such an act, is partly an issue of grace, but it is also one of intention. Gestures represent a distinctive language of theological purpose which 'not only expresses but can also intensify the sentiments that inspire it and can transmit them to others'.[29] The need to direct a bow exclusively to God, does not so much resolve problems, as open up a new field of difficulties. Profane bows presume a certain degree of calculation, if they are to effect the delivery of their intended meanings of honour and appreciation, and not to dilute these in an artless form of flattery. But such a spirit of calculation in the case of religious bows would be alien to their purpose. An anthropomorphic consideration would arise, that carries an implication that one *knows* how the body combines with the soul, so that spiritual outcomes can be exactly calculated. Sacred bows service the incalculable, but if that is their purpose, how does one become aware of their effectiveness, as sincere self-denying acts that edify?

The act of bowing in liturgy is the social expression of a spiritual impulse to worship God. An inner intention is imposed on the body to act to express deference to God. Given the dualism believed to operate between mind and body, gestures represent imperfect instruments to express a deep seated need that lurks in the mind. Writing on the use of the hand in liturgy, Guardini suggested that 'we must not make of it an idle, artistic play; but it must speak for us, so that in very truth the body may say to God what the soul means'.[30] Somehow, this is easier said than done. Gestures represent a social means of expressing an obligation to God, and even though they are slight and artificial, they are indispensable and necessary. Whatley's point is good, that 'mankind are not formed to live without ceremony and form: the "inward spiritual grace" is very apt to be lost without the "external visible sign"'. Thus he argues, removing the ceremonial form is like taking away the 'crutches to cure the gout'.[31]

Despite these indeterminate characteristics, liturgical bows have a predictable use in the rubrics or ceremonial directions. They occur at the same place and in the same part of the sequence of the rite. Gestures act as preludes, marking the sequences of the rite; they solemnise aspects that might appear trivial and insignificant; and they dignify that which might otherwise seem slight. They are cues to meanings holier than those who enact them. The formalised style of rite carries an element of studied repetition rather different from the unstudied obeisances that characterise orders of civility.

Rubrics on bowing might seem to have vanished since Vatican II, but a profound or low bow to the altar is stipulated, representing a tradition older than the genuflection.[32] Three forms of bow still apply: a slight inclination of the head at some prayers; a moderate abasement, such as at petitions, when the altar server presents the bread for consecration; and a deep bow before the altar, when moving past it. Despite the closely regulated rules on bowing in the Tridentine rite, disputes could arise over whether the Bishop gave a deep bow to a cross on the altar.[33] This capacity to check when bows ought to occur removes any quality of spontaneity in the act. Indeed, at a formal rite, it would cause embarrassment, perhaps even deeper at an informal assembly, if a member present were to take it upon himself to abase deeply according to what he felt were impulses from the Holy Spirit. Formal rites tend to eradicate individuality amongst liturgical actors, so that bows are part of a standardised collective effort to worship.

The liturgical act of bowing involves a sociological paradox that arises at the point of its delivery. An altar server is trained to bow deeply on passing the altar, whether a vast congregation is present, or nobody is in the Church. In enacting this gesture, his social self is implicated in what he spiritually strives to accomplish. This can become unintentionally magnified. It might seem as if he is called to do something impossible – to present a gesture in a way that renders himself absent from what he delivers. Expressed in another way, the altar server becomes involved in a performative contradiction: to bow sincerely, he has to attach his self to the action in a way that expresses a totality of deference, but at the same time he has to manifest a certain self-obliviousness that involves a degree of detachment lest esteem fall on him rather than on God for whom the act is intended. A degree of social interest is required for the sacred to be revealed, and this necessitates a fine discernment to deliver the act without spiritual injury. A good liturgical actor strives to be a conduit on the holy, so that in his actions he acts to be acted on.

Although the instruction to bow deeply on passing the altar might be understood by a server, and his intention to worship might be clear, a number of misrepresentations can be cast on him. If he bows too deeply, he might be signifying a piety beyond his spiritual station in this life. A deepening series of abasements before the altar by a Catholic server might betoken an unhealthy interest in Orthodox practices. To bow with grace and dignity might seem to reflect a hankering by a server for a Benedictine way of life. If the bow is too low, it might suggest a competitive element operating between the servers in the edification stakes. If the bow is too rapid, a presumptuous acquaintanceship with the Holy Spirit might be implied, which suggests that the second commandment could be fulfilled with a speedy grovel. If the bow is made too slowly, an effort to re-convert the congregation to better practices of worship might be suggested. Styles of bows reflect brand loyalties for those able to discern these matters. Other believers have less benign attitudes to such differences in styles of abasement.

For some Christians the mere idea of bowing before an altar is deemed a scandal and also an affront to the Almighty. High Calvinists would go to the stake rather than abase before a graven image. Disputes on bowing in Church gained an unexpected significance during the Reformation and after. Acute problems over the scale of reverences before the altar arose in seventeenth-century England amongst Anglicans. Objections were raised against some members of the Chapter of Durham Cathedral in 1630, for standing too close to the altar, and abasing themselves ten or twelve times in an hour. Furthermore, they were charged with teaching others 'so to doe, going backwards with ther faces towards the east and making legs to the Altar, so low sometimes, that ther noses touch the ground'.[34] Archbishop Laud's defence of the practice of bowing before the altar is interesting.[35] Puritans regarded bows as forms of cringing or ducking likely to offend 'sincere or well-affected Christians'. The term 'to make low legs' before God was seen as a form of profound inclination. In another observation on Durham, in 1650, it was noted that the choristers were taught

> to make legs to God when they light the tapers, and when they have done them to go backwards with their faces towards the east, and looking on the altar make legs to God; at every approaching near it, and every departure from it, at the taking up or setting down of any thing upon the altar, ever and anon to make a low curtesy . . . . .

Such practices were regarded as 'vain, superstitious and idolatrous'.[36] Puritans claimed that an object, such as an altar, was being given a disproportionate amount of reverence over the Word of God. But if bows were to be so discounted, how was the second commandment to be fulfilled? Prohibitions on bows to graven images presupposed that the act of deference should be solely directed to God. The act of bowing was not condemned, rather its false use was prohibited to preserve the integrity of this act of worship for its stipulated purpose. If the act of bowing was so enjoined, in what direction was it to be made? One could hardly accept the idea that any direction or form of abasement would count, for such an unselective practice would render a crucial gesture in worship meaningless. Some order in abasing had to be assumed, otherwise to cast bows into the realm of the random could be deemed to be a sin of presumption, a belief that God could be edified by something so formless and nude of witness. In other traditions of Christianity, bows were considered a particularly effective means of reaching God.

In a manual on monastic rule, written as a model for nineteenth-century Russian Orthodox monks, Bishop Brianchaninov made frequent references to the spiritual benefits of bowing. He felt that prayers 'have quite a different taste when they are read or said after bows'. Although a great number of bows (mainly from the waist) are demanded in his approach to monastic prayer, he warned frequently of the dangers of confusing quantity with quality, of developing a Pharisaical attitude to the frequency of abasement, and of cultivating 'the fatal passion of conceit'. He suggested that bows can inadvertently stimulate excessive mental activity by heating the blood. It was recommended that bows should be made 'extremely unhurriedly, for the bodily labour must be animated by mourning of heart and prayful cries of grief on the part of the mind'. A reverent attitude was crucial, if the bow was to secure the mercy it petitioned. 'Humble advice' was given on the number of bows and prostrations required. A form of 'spiritual gymnastics' was suggested of a more uplifting variety than the muscular Christianity fostered in the English public school.

Abasements performed in public or in the monastic cell were deemed to generate purity, alertness of mind and compunction of heart.[37] Reverence required a regulation of the body and its strict control. To avoid spiritual perils, monks were instructed to remember that 'the church is heaven on earth'. They were to stand in it in 'an orderly manner, like the Holy Angels' and not to lean against the wall, nor should their arms be folded, nor should they rest on one leg, but on both.[38]

The link between 'devout posture' and prayer is given a very original reading by Richard Trexler in his study of medieval practices. Postures formed a pattern of imitation for the young, and many examples were set down on how to place oneself before God in the most spiritually advantageous manner possible. Illustrations of prayer posture were of particular importance in a largely non-literate society. Peter the Chanter attempted to set down a form for submission gestures and bodily postures that could be deemed to penetrate to God. As Trexler indicates aptly 'praying was a type of profession, and professions required knowledge: body prayer had as much need of study as military action'. These 'devout postures' were marked by fine, if not arbitrary distinctions between actions that were regarded as conducive to spiritual engagement and those that were felt to be insulting to God, such as partial genuflections or sitting at prayer. Despite the intrinsic humiliations of some suggested actions, such as prostrations, it was argued that these gestures could confirm interior efforts at reverence. These acts of abasement also generated a sense of shame, a feeling of grovelling before men. This limited the value of his recommendations, and in the end Peter the Chanter came to regard private prayer as 'better' than public forms, which often led to hypocrisy. Although his effort failed, Trexler suggests that this did not invalidate his attempt. It related to a persistent 'fundamental property of humans in groups to *know* what is sacrilegious without daring to ask why'.[39]

Jean-Claude Schmitt examined the nature of a 'gestural grammar' in illustrated representations of St Dominic at prayer. These 'spiritual gymnastics' formed the basis for imitation by novices, for it was assumed that outward expressions of belief *do* have some connection to the internal workings of the soul. The body could not just be ignored, but had to be mobilised in some particular way that would facilitate the spirit to pray. Some form of fine judgement was required to avoid some of the pitfalls mentioned earlier. It was felt that 'virtuous gesture' should be 'both gracious and severe, but gracious without slack, which would be a sign of laxity, and severe without any disturbances which would signify impatience'. Illustrations of a Saint at prayer suggested that gestures could show the state of the inner soul on the outside of the body.[40]

This attempt to link external gestures to internal spiritual states raises a number of perplexing and fundamental theological issues. In the Cistercian Usages (1964) the section on the function of bows draws on a comment of St Augustine that 'those external and visible bodily movements intensify the interior and invisible movements of the soul without which they are impossible'.[41] It is difficult to see how a social act can surmount a dualism between body and soul. It might be believed to be the case, and could be a way grace 'works' but not in a way that is accessible to sociological scrutiny. Matthews has argued that St Augustine has raised a false distinction between body and soul.

In themselves, bodily movements have no significance. These actions only become meaningful when they are placed in the context of a 'sincere and understanding performance of ritual' and are put to public relational use for collective engagement with the Divine.[42] This brings us back to Rappaport's point that public rituals can enable private doubt to be overridden.

To some extent, the problem of civil and sacral abasement is resolved by its context of enactment. Throughout the analysis I have emphasised the liabilities involved in the public expression of worship. These have an antinomial quality, one exemplified in the issue of abasement. There is a fine line involved in the act of bowing in religion, between humiliation and conceit, superiority and inferiority, adoration and idolatry, truth and deception. All these have an antinomial cast that calls on a refined private judgement by the actor over what to deliver in public. Doubtless some religious bows will be automatic and unreflective, but others will not be so easy.

In her discussion of Norbert Elias, Joanne Finkelstein pays attention to the degree to which his idea of civility involves the art of concealment, regulation and control. The public arena makes a demand to reflect intelligently on what is being reproduced. There is a paradox to manners. She notes that

> they provide us with mutually understood techniques which prepare us for social engagement and, on the other hand, they are devices through which we have learned to conceal our sentiments and moral positions from the other in the hope that we may gain some purchase on their behaviour.[43]

If civility assumes control and restraint, it does so to achieve a particular manner or style of appearing, one that enables desires to be fulfilled, affiliations to be formed and ambiences to be secured. Civility operates through the capacity to dissimulate in order to disguise baser emotions. As Finkelstein, aptly, notes 'manners mask natural vice'.[44]

The qualities that enable civility to be accomplished have a striking similarity to those needed to produce piety, but with some significant differences. The need to dissimulate and to regulate is also required but for different purposes. Concealing is a restraint that enables virtue to be found and humility secured. Good liturgical manners presuppose a degree of calculation to act in a meaningful and reflective manner, but in a way that admits an antinomial consideration that the actor affirms the incalculable nature of a truth whose fullness is concealed from him.

Civil manners fulfil worldly desires; sacral manners deny them. Civil manners affirm the veneer of appearance that can be purchased, packaged and presented with impunity; sacral manners penetrate below the surface of appearance, affirming what cannot be bought, and what cannot be appropriated without a total demand being made on the self.

Liturgical manners are structured to witness to contradictions, but also to overcome them. They appropriate elements of modern culture not so much to mislead, but to lead to a truth that lies beyond 'manufacture'. These differences can be further understood in the world of the waiter and the altar server. They attend to implications, but from contrasting sets of meaning. Both roles service an ambience, attending to the dedicated management of an implication. The higher the quality of their dedication the more intangible is the product.

8 Altar Servers and Waiters: Serving in Worlds Apart

> Anybody can wait at table, but it requires a high degree of skill to perform the duties thoroughly well.
>
> (A prosperous head waiter, *Waiting at Table*)

The Catholic mass is a sacred meal enacted for the community of the faithful. It is also a liturgical act that re-presents through sacramental means the sacrifice of Christ on the cross. These two theological strands merge in the liturgical actions of the mass. They might not be apparent if too much attention were to be given to the obvious aspects of the ritual. Both govern the theological basis of the rite.

Entering the sacristy before a mass, one might notice cupboards open, and the long white albs of the servers hanging on their hooks like butchers' overalls ready for a bloodless sacrifice. These servers attend on the priest, fetching and carrying, and marking points of the rite with gestures, or actions, such as incensing. They supply a link between the congregation and the priest, bringing gifts forward from the offertory procession. Properly trained, altar servers contribute to the atmosphere of the rite. In their actions they solemnise a routine event. Altar servers can add to the gravity of the rite, dignifying and embellishing what could be otherwise an uneventful transaction. Following Richard Sennett, one can regard roles as embodying codes of belief and behaviour that activate a set of values.[1] The task of serving can give rise to some misleading assumptions. Despite their holy intent, good altar servers can remind a congregation of service elsewhere, in the restaurant, where a more profane meal is eaten. In their roles, altar servers might seem like holy waiters.

The waiter services the ebb and flow of a meal, facilitating a sense of occasion for the customers and enhancing their sense of participation in something special. The role of the waiter involves serving in a diplomatic and unobtrusive fashion. He exercises a discreet control over the stages of the meal as it runs through the courses of the menu. The ambience of the restaurant, the white linen table cloths, the china, the fittings, such as the lighting and the curtains, all provide a fitting backdrop to this dedicated service. Customers are aware of their position as objects of a dedicated attention, the recipients of an unobtrusive craft of deference. The devotion of the service can give the occasion a quasi-religious cast, a sense enhanced by the food and the wine, which is poured with reverential care by the waiter.

If the event fulfils its promise, the customers relax, increasingly oblivious to the artificial nature of the transaction, and the cash nexus that governs its basis. The waiter becomes absorbed in the 'emotional labour' of producing well-satisfied customers. He hopes they will tip well, thus confirming his professional skills and the particular nature of his calling. Simulating and dissimulating, the waiter conducts his table with the manners of a magician, converting the nervous into the settled, and discreetly dethroning the brash who might disgrace an occasion of grace. He structures and regulates the event in a tacit manner, sufficiently distant to disguise the stage-managed nature of the transaction. With guile and diplomatic skill, a good waiter can transform a mundane act of eating into a memorable event. The dedication of his service confirms the distinctive purpose of dining out, of enhancing a sensibility of civil values, which are available for purchase by all with money to spend, and especially by those who are deemed to be discerning.

Although the tasks of attendance for waiters and altar servers bear a superficial similarity, it is important for all interested parties that their manner of operating does not generate a confusion in terms of the civil and sacred constituencies they represent and present for public display. A waiter with a sacerdotal gait might serve with a solemnity that could sink a meal with a gravity of presence those dining might wish were absent. Equally, an altar server, who struts about the sanctuary with a profaning casualness, might convey a disedifying disregard for his holy part, acting like a bored waiter serving inferior tables with all the hallmarks of bad faith. There are antinomies buried in the parts that require a subtle filtering and separation if civility or holiness is to be achieved. The two worlds are near, but need to be kept afar, if their respective ambitions are to be realised. The restaurant is a setting for the massaging of the egos of the preening classes, a civil place to confirm the mighty on their thrones by waiters who service worldly vanities in an unworldly manner. Sanctuaries are the battleground for the altar servers, who parade piously in artful dedication, squashing their vanity for other-worldly interests of preserving the sacerdotal classes in their labour of securing God's presence for all the gathered flock. Each role makes a contrasting demand on the sincerity of the actor who simulates and dissimulates in the part, striving to find a happy or a holy mean in the antinomies each world presents for negotiation. There is an elective affinity involved in securing intended definitions in serving these separate tables, where each embodies contrasting values of the civil and the sacred.

There are obvious dissimilarities between the worlds of the waiter and the altar server which can briefly be noted which need not detain us. The waiter is dealing with customers, who might express their gratitude in tips. He is the intermediary between the kitchen and the tables in the restaurant, and his role involves moving in and out of public view. The altar servers, usually boys, sometimes men, attend the priest on behalf of the congregation. They act as exemplars for them in terms of gestures and actions. Their role facilitates the ebb and flow of the rite on the sanctuary, and except when a mistake occurs, they seldom disappear from public view. They are unpaid amateurs, unlike waiters who are professional workers. Any tips these altar servers receive are usually of grace and Divine favour.

There are however, some crucial similarities between the parts. Each world being served, the civil and the sacred, embodies meanings that are best secured through implications that have to be managed, if intended impressions are to be delivered successfully. The restaurant and the sanctuary denote worlds, or settings, on which ritual occasions occur that heighten sensibilities. These civil and sacred worlds have boundaries that are fragile and indeterminate. As suggested earlier, religious rituals need to be kept in good repair if they are to 'succeed' in their purpose. Keeping the holy and the civil fenced into the ambience of these worlds requires a dedicated maintenance, a duty that falls, in part, on the altar servers or the waiters.

Both roles involve service of a meal or an event, whose central basis is provided by another actor – the chef or the priest. Without the activities of either, neither event could proceed. They make possible the defining attributes of the transaction. Yet the altar server and waiter, despite their subservient ancillary roles, can have a crucial impact on the atmosphere of the event they service. The quality of altar serving can make or mar a sense of the holy in a way that is disproportionate to the theological insignificance of the part. In a similar way, despite his inferior status, the waiter has an unexpected capacity to make a meal a profoundly uncivilised event, if he should so wish.

In analysing the role of altar servers in the production of liturgy, it is not intended to amplify their theological status. Instead, it is argued that altar servers have an important sociological role in servicing fragile social aspects of liturgy. Altar servers, who unobtrusively police its rims, are custodians of the rite. They embody a marginality but also represent it in their actions, coming and going from the edge of the rite. They bear witness to the boundary between the social and the sacred, tipping the balance of the rite in favour of the holy. There is an element of threshold in liturgical performance that involves a play between the sacred and the profane, where a sense of the holy can be secured. This can become unsecured by the inept performance of those operating on the fringes of a priestly authority. An atmosphere of pious ease in coping with the complex can be destroyed by the carelessness of the attendants on the sanctuary, who can attract attention for the 'wrong' reasons. Items can be dropped, and failures of attention can generate a rich crop of 'liturgical mistakes'. A considerable amount of face-work is required from altar servers if their 'emotional labour' is to succeed in appearing to find the holy in a way that communicates a sensibility of its presence to a congregation.

Waiters and altar servers usually form part of a team. They collude to produce an intangible quality of service in an atmosphere of commitment that inspires trust. Their dedication can establish a reputation for a particular building. A restaurant renowned for its service attracts a clientele capable of discerning and appreciating this dedicated service. The ephemeral nature of the waiters' service carries a sense of being beyond calculation, serving those who do not need to calculate to pay. Equally, a Cathedral with a well-trained set of altar servers can gain a reputation for the quality of its serving. In their guardianship of the ritual contours, they can give weight and credibility to a rite in a way that enables it to betoken the incredible. Waiters and altar servers who contribute to the aura of an establishment share a paradox: despite their dedication, they occupy roles which are redundant to the strict requirements of the event they service.

A mass could proceed without altar servers; a meal in a restaurant could be self-service, or worse, could employ a 'dumb' waiter. Despite being surplus to the strict requirements of the event, both altar servers and waiters manage to convert a dispensability into an indispensability. They manage to convey a suggestion that the event would lack an underpinning, a quality of enhancement, which only their presence could supply. Their uselessness seems to give them access to the very indefinable qualities that characterise a memorable event. Both roles magnify implicit elements in the event, but in a way that is unobtrusive.

They accomplish what they signify in a tactful manner that seems to deny their presence. The less they are noticed the better their performance is deemed to be. Somehow, the altar server and the waiter convey a sense of being present that is marked by a well-regulated sense of absence. Even their inaction seems to convey a quality of activity. These roles share an accomplishment, a skill in making unobtrusive intrusions in a public domain, which can be fraught with private worries. A funeral mass can be a tense affair, and the altar servers have to move stealthily to preserve a ceremonial order geared to soak up grief. Many of those present at funerals are not Catholics. Some will look to the servers as exemplars of what they ought to do, to join in the rite.

This capacity to amplify the uneventful into a memorable event requires a particular tact to preserve the object of dedication in its superior position. The server is inferior to the priest. Likewise, the waiter has to sustain a credible subservience to the customer's wishes. Both roles confront an ambiguity that requires tactful handling in a peculiar balancing act if misunderstandings are not to arise irretrievably. The actors have to appear to be significant in the role, otherwise they could seem dispensable, but they have to exercise the part in a way that preserves its insignificance lest it subtract from the object of their dedicated magnification – the priest or the customer. This element of concealing for the purpose of revealing has arisen in other parts of the book: the understanding of innocence; the handling of the social basis of rite; and the problem of bowing without amplifying a disabling conceit. A degree of tension has to be sustained in handling these ambiguous liturgical instruments to secure their meaningful theological basis.

Restaurants and Churches are arenas in which familiar actions are handled in an unfamiliar public context. They suggest exceptional use for a transaction that might be otherwise unexceptional. A meal could be eaten at home; prayers could be said in one's bedroom. Handling the familiar in unfamiliar surroundings generates an uncertainty. There is a worry about how to proceed in a public arena with a transaction that is so easily accomplished in private. Waiters can amplify this uncertainty with a view to increasing their indispensability before the customer. Both the altar server and the waiter act to entice a commitment on the part of those attending to invest an interest in the event, and to act with a security of belief that it will accomplish that which it promises. Other actors in the rite, such as the priests and the choristers, have their own contribution to make to the felt qualities of rite. Apart from their central theological role, priests can sink a rite with a bad sermon, a careless demeanour or a weak faith. Because contemporary Catholic liturgical thought stresses the need to show forth and to display the symbols and actions used, the performance of the actors can have a crucial impact on the cultural credibility of the rite. Its obvious aspects are on display for reasons that bear witness to its unobvious qualities. Liturgical actors have an enhancing task, and altar servers, especially, need to be alert to the implications of their vocation.

In this chapter, we consider the history and duties of the altar server before moving on to assess the qualities of the 'good' waiter in the next section. This forms a background for the final concern of the chapter with the link between the altar server and the 'flow' of the rite. The altar server has a crucial role in masking and minimising 'liturgical mistakes'. The demands made on the altar server, in fulfilment of his role, provide a basis for considering how aspects of the regulation of rite are accomplished. Some of the previous considerations will be brought together to look more closely at what everybody is being tactful and tacit about in the performance of rite.

ALTAR SERVING: A MARGINAL TRADITION

> The service in which they assist is no common service but sacred and solemn, and . . . . therefore must the server constantly remind himself of the presence of God and His holy angels if he would serve well.
> (Anon., *Servers' Manual of the Archconfraternity of Saint Stephen*)

Meals and masses have a quality of repetition, but one that makes marks in a biography, where the expected can become surprisingly memorable. Altar servers perform mundane actions in rites that become hallowed in habit and dedication. Their role embodies a career that advances in understanding and awareness of the significance of what their service accomplishes. Liturgical habits can breed awe. A sense of this is conveyed in the recollections of a young boy serving a Christmas mass in an Irish convent before the First World War. This priest's attendant, clad in his white surplice and cassock, reflected on his task of providing a 'perfect service. Not once would he sink on to his heels or droop his back. Not once would he fiddle with the bell, nor scratch his knees, no matter how weary they became'. 'Carefully following each sequence of the service' the boy enacted his part before the nuns with a care, 'timing his slow walk to bring him at just the correct moment to just the correct part of the altar, gratefully making each bow and movement respond to Father Riordan's care and dignity'. He moved in a mood 'and served in a kind of rapture'.[2]

Servers in the sanctuary stalk God in a manner that conveys a self-obliviousness; they seem unworried by the intangible outcomes of their all too tangible dedication. They fulfil their parts according to age and experience, and most importantly the type of liturgy being serviced. If he is good, the altar server facilitates the 'flow' of the rite, and sets its tone by his dedication and attendance to the detail of the ceremony. He is trained to be alert, to anticipate and, above all, to assist the priest. Many of his tasks service a hidden order of belief, such as pouring water over the priest's hands as an act of purification, or standing with a colleague at the lecturn, for the reading of the gospel, remindful of the angels awaiting the Word; or swinging a thurible, whose smoke rises to heaven as the prayers of the congregation should.

Because the effects of his activities are indeterminate, it is often difficult for the altar server to estimate the consequences of his actions. Even the most trivial of actions can have profound sociological and theological implications. A misplaced gesture can make a vast difference. When 'Uzzah put forth his hand to the ark of God, and took hold of it; for the oxen shook it. And the anger of the Lord was kindled against Uzzah; and God smote him there for his error; and there he died by the Ark of God' (2 Samuel 6:6–7). In the belief that gestures, demeanour and his actions *do* make some difference, and can edify a congregation, the altar server imposes certain constraints on his manner of appearing. Profaning aspects of behaviour are omitted in a studied effort to be available to the holy. The style of moving, of holding hands joined, with right thumb over left, and clad in his white robes, the server seeks to realise a quality of epiphany in his act. He strives to incarnate the angelic, and to be a prism for its presence in the rite. Marked movements serve to sustain a sense of predictability in the rite. They underwrite its repetitious functions, and sustain a sense of stereotype. These repetitions facilitate an attachment, an investment of belief in what is being presented in such a fixed manner. The altar server services this sense of predictability in a way that strives to transform the expected into a means for handling the unexpected.

Despite the slightness of his task, the altar server has a long biblical lineage. Thus, it is written: 'whosoever will be great among you, let him be your minister; and whosoever will be chief among you, let him be your servant' (Matt. 20: 26–27). Serving involves a long-standing belief in the inversion of the weak before the strong, a point most clearly expressed in the washing of the feet of the disciples at the Last Supper (John 13:4–20). The first server was the boy Samuel, who acted as a servant of the sanctuary and ministered before the Lord in a white robe (1 Sam. 2:18–19). His heirs in the New Testament are the boy who supplied the five loaves and two fishes for feeding the five thousand (John 6:9); the man with the pitcher of water on his head who was the peculiar sign for the disciples of the location of the upper room for the Last Supper (Luke 2:10); and the young men who carried out and buried Ananias and Sapphira (Acts 5:6–10). The confinement of altar serving to males complements a similar tradition in the terms of the priesthood in the Catholic and Orthodox Churches. The role of attending at the altar goes back to St Stephen, the patron saint of servers. According to tradition, he was the first deacon and martyr. Stephen was one of the seven men of 'honest report' who were approached by the twelve Apostles to 'serve tables' to release the Apostles for more preaching and other good works (Acts 6: 1–6). Arrested and tried for his own preaching and miracles, Stephen was placed before the council, who 'looking steadfastly on him, saw his face as it had been the face of an angel' (Acts 6:15). The link between the angelic and liturgical roles has been discussed in Chapter 4.

Unfortunately, there is no adequate history of the altar server. Nevertheless, it is a role with a secure place in Church tradition. The tradition of using laymen and boys goes back to the medieval church. Altarists were often choirboys, whose voices had broken, and who were kept on with a view to stimulating a monastic vocation.[3] The greatly increased number of chantry and monastic masses in the medieval world required a vast army of altar servers to deputise for priests and for those in minor orders. Joseph Jungmann notes that it was the tradition of the monasteries to choose young boys as servers 'whose innocence can, in a measure, substitute for the clerical character'.[4] The custom of laymen and boys serving represents an anomaly. Efforts were made by the Council of Trent, 1570, to confine serving to those in minor orders, or who were training for the priesthood. The last formal condemnation of the custom of using laymen and boys came from the Congregation of Sacred Rites in 1847.[5] The practice of using laymen and boys has become the rule rather than the exception. In 1955, it was ruled that every mass had to have a server, and this can be assumed in the Introduction to the current Roman Missal, where the part is stipulated for a private mass. By 1972, the minor orders were abolished, and ministries of acolyte and reader were opened out to laymen. There are public rites of dedication, where men and boys receive their albs, surplices or medals, according to the custom of the guild or the diocese.[6] This sacramental rite of passage marks out in public the obligations of the part, and blesses the server with the grace to fulfil these tasks. There are many ambiguities in the part of an altar server.

Despite being a layman, or a boy, and not in orders, custom and tradition allows him to wear a white alb or surplice, bestowing on him marks of priestly service. He represents the priest to the congregation, but is also their delegate on the sanctuary. At one level, the altar server could be considered as an apprentice to a priest, a student in minor orders, or he could be a man or a boy with no particular clerical ambitions. Many of the tasks of an altar server could be undertaken by a priest, assisting another, or by a deacon. A man serving might seem to be usurping a role a boy ought to perform, hence the common term 'altar boy'. Equally, it could be argued that a boy serving is undertaking a role that belongs to the acolyte, to a man preparing for ordination.

The duties and functions of a server depend on the simplicity or complexity of the form of rite he is attending. This will also bear on whether he is serving by himself, or as part of a team on the sanctuary. For some forms of rite, a white robed army of servers was required. For instance, the Sarum rite demanded serving of the first division, with acolytes, cross bearer, thurifers, boat and water boys and a lot of processing. Movements were stipulated in a rite which admirably reflected the English genius for orderly processions. The rank of the feast day affected the complexity or simplicity of the rite.[7] For instance, the singing of the Gradual demanded surpliced boys, clerks in silken copes, with or without rulers, in the pulpitum or at the quire-step, depending on whether it was All Souls Day or Maundy Thursday.[8]

Some of the rules for serving in the Tridentine rite, made an uncommon demand on intelligence. For example, the thurifer had to remember that an assistant bishop received three (double) swings of the thurible, but that all dignitaries, such as a Minister of State, or Lord Mayor, receive one swing less in the presence of a Cardinal, the King being an exception.[9] A knowledge of the rite, and a sense of collusion in its movements, reflect teamwork, and experience. Many servers have worked together before. They have often been promoted from menial tasks such as boat boy, to what is regarded as the most prestigious role, that of cross bearer. He leads the processions, and establishes a solemnity in movements on and off the altar.[10]

Modern Catholic rites make varying demands on the altar server. For an ordinary mass, one or two servers are required, but for a more solemn occasion, in a Cathedral, a team of eight would be used. Unfortunately, rules in the new rite for a solemn mass are not sufficiently specified for adequate checking. Many actions of the older rites have been carried over, and even in Catholicism, some practices reflect the traditions of the house. Altar servers are trained in liturgical practices, and need a good understanding of the mass, its ceremonial shape, its theological significance, and the various customs that make up the tradition of the rite.[11]

Waiters and altar servers are accountable for assisting in a way that secures the desired definition of the situation. They facilitate an enactment that is fragile, that can be fraught with risk for all parties, and which requires a delicacy of judgement to succeed in the part. These roles of service demand a degree of 'emotional labour' that makes contrasting demands on the self. They also service implications of civility and holiness that have to be structured in a way that conceals the artificial basis of the transaction. Issues of good and bad faith arise over that which is concealed that tell us much about the enactment of religious rituals. Both roles have a skill that is deceptive.

AN UNOBTRUSIVE PRESENCE: THE ART OF GOOD WAITING

> The child plays with his body in order to explore it, to make an inventory of it; the waiter in the café plays with his condition in order to realize it. This is not different from that which is imposed on all tradesmen. Their condition is wholly one of ceremony.
>
> (Jean-Paul Sartre, *Being and Nothingness*)

Waiters believe they have rare qualities in their occupation that mark them out of the ordinary. As Morley Roberts noted, 'the good waiter, foreign or English born, takes a pride in believing that not every one with ordinary outfit of legs and arms is adapted for the task'.[12] A manual dexterity, combined with a grace in movement, tact, a good memory, and a knowledge of food and what the well-bred customer *ought* to want, are some of the attributes, which come together in a rare combination. The capacity to intrude at a delicate moment without being intrusive; to defer but not to grovel; to be interested, but not excessively so; and to be sincere, but not overly concerned, are some of the fine points involved in the waiter's craft. Failure to surmount these can affect his living, for his wage is heavily dependent on the customer's discretion – the tips that are left. His qualities of tact are given a monetary expression. Part of the waiter's stock of occupational knowledge is to know how to calculate the relationship between his presence, and that of the customer. Successful judgement, and a capacity to grasp the definition of the situation have a crucial bearing on the economic rewards of the occupation.

Anticipation and discretion are of central importance in establishing an unobtrusive presence. 'Reading' the customer's wants requires a dedication to observing detail. The capacity to anticipate needs is of crucial importance in accomplishing his role. Success rests on the ability to allow the 'flow' of a meal to proceed without interruption. His service just seems to happen. The waiter seems to grasp the point of the customer's wishes even when they are implied and not stated. The customer's interests are paramount. Meeting these requires a skill in coping with uncertainties in a calming manner that inspires trust. Handling the unexpected is an important part of the waiter's skill. His career gives him access to a number of contingency plans, should mishaps occur. As Gerald Mars and Michael Nicod note, the customer's emergency is the waiter's routine. The waiter and the customer come to the meal from differing perspectives. For the customer, the meal is a special event, an occasion that is exceptional and is to be remembered. But for the waiter, this meal is one of many that form part of an occupational routine. If all goes well, it should be for him a quite forgettable occasion. To enable the customer to feel that the event is special, the waiter has to simulate a sense of interest in what is routine, and is perhaps instrinsically uninteresting. Thus, Mars and Nicod note that 'the art of service often lies in creating an impression that there is something of a struggle involved in supplying satisfaction'.[13]

The amount of 'emotional labour' an employer can demand in a restaurant varies from the total dedication required in a high-class establishment, to the instant smile which has to be worn all day behind the counter in a fast food chain. In these hamburger establishments, a small amount of the self can be spread widely around a lot of customers in such thin slices as to make few calls on the private

Sociology and Liturgy

sincerities of the actor. The little 'emotional labour' required for the task allows his authentic self to hang out elsewhere. In higher-class establishments, a more complete call is made on the self to engage heavily in 'emotional labour' to deliver a sincere and dedicated service. As part of his job, the 'real' self of the high-class waiter has to be requisitioned in the interests of good and credible service. Moods need to be regulated to sustain an evenness of impression. First impressions are deemed to be crucial. Training manuals advise waiters to be courteous, efficient, interested and friendly, simply because it pays well. This well regulated flow of pleasing deference can generate a puzzlement about the waiter's 'real' identity. It seems that there are 'mysteries connected with him as yet impenetrable. The deepest obscurity pervades all that appertains to his past, a gloomy uncertainty hangs over all that relates to his present, upon his future we dare not speculate'.[14] It is scarcely surprising that the waiter has become an object for existential speculation.[15]

In the better-class hotels, waiters are denied all forms of personal adornment, and their individual autonomy is restricted. Eating or smoking, or lounging about, is not allowed before the customers in the restaurant. Being in the role of a waiter makes the actor unavailable for certain forms of behaviour in public. His uniform serves to remind him that his self is on hire to his employer and that he has to regulate his appearance accordingly.[16] These restrictions render the waiter an object for the part, and serve to make his presence as invisible as possible. Such limitations bear on a point of Veblen, that a capacity to employ a servant to be useless is an indicator of the wealth and status of an employer. Footmen standing in draughty halls in picturesque poses confirm the ability of an employer to engage in conspicuous consumption.[17] A retinue of waiters who come forward with differing stages of the menu to be carved and served, suggest a high-class restaurant where the service will be total and impeccable. There are far more waiters about than are strictly required for the task of waiting, or so it seems to the customer.

The customer in a restaurant is buying a concentrated amount of dedicated service. He is purchasing a large amount of 'emotional labour' that should justify the ritual of dining out for the evening. The commercial basis of the transaction needs to be disguised, and should it be exposed inadvertently, the artificial nature of this civil relationship would protrude, wiping the magic out of the event. A crude request for a tip might make one wonder whether the service of a restaurant was all it should be. As long as the monetary basis to the relationship between the waiter and the customer is dissimulated, the civilised basis of the transaction can be simulated smoothly. In so accepting this totally dedicated service, the customer becomes an object, a passive recipient of the waiter's attention. He becomes the centre of a service that involves a complex division of labour between waiters, each with rights of access to serve particular dishes, or to cut certain portions. This hierarchy of deference operates to fulfil an order of service, one that follows a strict ceremonial routine. Paradoxically, the restaurants that place the most restrictions on the waiter's manner of appearing, are also those in which the greatest amount of manipulation of the customer can be exercised.

Waiters exercise power through implication. They seem to have a capacity to confer grace on a customer, or to withdraw it. They can imply his taste is fraudulent, or they can indicate how worthy they are to serve this discerning customer. The capacity of the customer to respond to slights can be limited by the waiter's power to ignore him in the restaurant. Rules of redress for customers are often unclear, and the exceptional nature of a meal for many leaves them uncertain as to the nature of the rules of the establishment.[18] The waiter is the person dealing with the customer directly and regardless of any crisis in the kitchen, he has to present a smooth front, even if chaos reigns in the rear. A large amount of 'emotional labour' can be involved in dealing with moods in the kitchen. Uniquely, the restaurant combines production and service. The relationships involved in securing and delivering the meal to the customer can be complex.[19] With a difficult customer, the waiter can play all sorts of delaying games with impunity.

Although the waiter's role is geared to maximising income, through tips and service charges, there are difficulties, as we suggested above, in balancing the manner of appearing in proportion to the beneficial economic rewards that can be gained. Under-performing the role might suggest a presumptive casualness, a familiarity with the customer that might be unacceptable; over-performing could secure an impression bordering on the satirical that might infuriate. The more individual and exacting the service is expected to be, the more the waiter has to resort to discretion and judgement in the interpretation of rules, that are tacit and indeterminate. Delivering more service than the customer might expect involves the supply of satisfactions deemed implicit in the definition of 'good service'. As Mars and Nicod observe, 'often service is judged on the most intangible aspects of customer satisfaction, especially in highly prestigious hotels and restaurants'.[20]

In such establishments, the waiter shares with the altar server a concern with sustaining an indeterminate quality of service, one whose basis is secured through a tacit acceptance and understanding of its existence. The customer defers to the waiter to receive intangible benefits of 'good service'; the congregation accept the actions of the altar server as marking the social with indeterminate qualities of holiness. Both must occupy a public realm in a dignified manner. Predating Goffman's concern with impression management, and with front and back regions, where the self appears on and off duty, George Orwell commented on how instructive was the sight of the waiter going into a hotel dining-room. As he moves through the door 'a sudden change comes over him. The set of his shoulders alters; all the dirt and hurry and irritation have dropped off in an instant. He glides over the carpet, with a solemn priest-like air'.[21]

The waiter maintains a social mask, an image for ceremonial use to effect the part, to present a tacitly understood service. As Goffman observes, the demeaned individual operates through deportment, dress and bearing to express an image, that exists not for himself, but for others, those who are the objects of his dedication.[22] The image has to be regulated and controlled to bear repeated presentation, where a freshness of interest is required to inspire trust from the customer. The skilled management of appearance to elicit confidence from the customers is a particular occupational requirement of the waiter. His demeanour suggests a control of the definition of the situation that enables the customers to relax in unfamiliar circumstances, so that in a mutual endeavour, both parties make a meal memorable. This collusion reflects a form of civil manners where each needs a degree of faith from the other to produce the event.

Notions of civility and refinement are affirmed in the restaurant, and the waiter strives to sustain these elements in the performance of his role. Although his contact with the table he serves is brief and to the point, it is nevertheless significant in sustaining the desired image of the establishment. By surrounding his customers with attention, the waiter manages to insulate them from any intrusions that would violate their sense of privacy in a public place. Embarrassment and uncertainty can damage a veneer of civility, which rests on the notion that the 'distasteful is removed behind the scenes of social life'.[23] The raw and the uncooked are converted into the acceptable and the civilised. The waiter is an agent of this transformation, presenting the cooked for inspection in a manner that garnishes the mundane with a delicacy of presentation which sustains the magical sense of a good meal. His bows and manner of serving confirm the impression that the raw is safely disguised.

Conversation and a heightened awareness of the delicacy of the occasion add to the significance of the meal as a special event. The waiter fulfils his part by keeping the boundaries of the meal intact, so that space for the privacy of the customer can be secured in a public arena. The tension that exists, between the need for privacy and the urge to display the self in public, forms one of the essential attractions of a civilised meal in a restaurant. This custodial duty involves the waiter precluding anything being amplified that might detract from the relaxed surroundings of the customer who mixes the private and public according to whim. This defensive function grants the waiter a quality of indispensability in the exercise of a tactful craft. The waiter serves to insulate an event of great delicacy from risks of embarrassment, and manages with a mysterious skill to keep the meal within the confines of sensibility.[24] He adjusts the form of the event to maintain a focus on the customer, who is the object of dedication in the event. His task is accomplished if the customer does not notice these subtle little shifts and changes in the ebb and flow of the event.

An eventful meal is characterised by its uneventful nature. The waiter operates to keep disruptions at bay. Particular problems can arise between the kitchen and the customer, where mistakes can occur over the timing of orders. As these mistakes can disrupt the natural 'flow' of a good meal, the waiter strives to prevent such mishaps. This need to co-ordinate the resources of preparation with those for presentation in the public arena is another facet of the waiter's need to manage impressions of a civilising smoothness in the operation of the restaurant. Any frictions that might arise in this task of co-ordination must be kept from view of the customer. Gordon Marshall has aptly indicated the peculiar nature of the contact between customer and waiter as involving a contact between leisure and work. There is a playful characteristic to the job of the waiter.[25]

At an elementary level, waiting involves serving. But it also involves participation in sustaining a ritual event in a restaurant, whose ambience can vary from the convivial and the informal to the sleek and the ceremonial. Bound into the elementary tasks of waiting are the need to secure an intended definition of the situation which the restaurant strives to present as an ideal. There is an indefinable quality of atmosphere in a fashionable restaurant. This can be due to the quality of the waiting. A meal in a restaurant carries many redundancies and embellishment of ceremony and action, that wrap a mundane act of eating in layers of social implication which the discerning can note. As Pierre Smith has suggested, 'rituals are particularly elaborated cultural creations, and one can hope to clarify their incredible complexity and their captivating strangeness only by trying to find the principles of their own specific elaboration'.[26]

RULES FOR SERVING THE SACRED IN A PIOUS MANNER

while serving, his whole demeanour will show that he duly appreciates what he is doing; on no account is he to stare about him, to stand when he should kneel, to lean against the altar, or place his hands upon it, or walk about the Church in a hurried or unseemly manner.

(Domenico Luigh Cesari, *Manual for Serving Boys at Low Mass*)

In some ways, the comparison between the altar server and the waiter is misleading. The restaurant is a setting where the waiter deals directly with the customer on behalf of a proprietor. In the kitchen, the waiter can disassemble his serving face and seek relief from service by relaxing into his 'real' self. A breathing space to relax from the public part is necessary, lest he comes too close to the role. As Sennett aptly observes, 'an actor who believes in his own tears, who governs his performance according to his sentiments, who has no distance from the emotions he projects, cannot act consistently'.[27] Too much sincerity would drown the waiter in the part. Relief from the stress of the 'emotional labour' of waiting can be obtained in the backstage or region, where, Goffman observes, 'the impression fostered by the performance is knowingly contradicted as a matter of course'.[28] This capacity to escape from the burdens of 'emotional labour' is necessary to sustain the act of bad faith in the public part.

But the altar server's tale is different. Part of his role is to fetch and carry like a holy waiter, but the more important duty is to edify. This demands a spiritual labour that needs to be exercised in good faith, if the actor is to survive as an altar server. He serves before and on behalf of the congregation, by acting as an intermediary but also as an exemplar in the gestures he performs. The symbols embodied in these gestures are a small but crucial ingredient in an image the ritual serves to represent. His act provides an example in gesture for the congregation to imitate. Unlike the waiter, and with the exception of the thurifer, he seldom leaves the altar, unless some mistake has occurred and some item that was forgotten has to be brought out. The altar server is called to give all of himself in the part. As his career develops, he comes to know more of his contribution to the tenor of the rite. His part has a subtle effect on the quality of the atmosphere of worship in the liturgy. To some extent, he is a manager of the frame, with the priest in the centre, as his object of dedication. As in the case of a good restaurant, he manages the background of the rite, filtering out and suppressing infelicities.

There is a certain mysterious anonymity required for the part. Like the waiter in the higher class of restaurant, the altar server is shorn of personal qualities, and appears in his cassock and white surplice or alb. His tactful management enhances the foreground, the altar area where the priest operates as a passive recipient of his attendance. By his dedicated attendance, the altar server supplies a concentrated focus on the priest, who is kept passive and secured in the centre of the ritual. He can be raised up by the quality of the attendance of the server, whose spiritual sensibilities are amplified in the act of deference.

Whereas the waiter places his self in a semi-detached state to the role, the good altar server strives to achieve the fullest attachment of the self to the part so that the transparency of his act will glow in all its holiness. The waiter can adjust his face to elicit the maximum of tips, and this capacity is derived from an experience of calculation in the part. But the altar server has to maintain a holy face, without prospect of economic reward and in a way that copes with a paradox that has emerged before, of calculating how best to deal with the incalculable. There is a mode of being caught up in the part that he might not be able to perceive himself. It is very difficult for an altar server to know whom he affects by the quality of his serving. God might be pleased, and his priest might be edified, but after that it is difficult to know. Too close attention to the part could corrupt the capacity to edify, as a spirit of calculation would enter the soul of the server. He cannot bask in a reflection of himself, if he is to refract an image of grace in the part, one that reaches others.

In some respects the issue of defining a good server is beside the point. A similar problem can arise over the definition of a gentleman. Sennett quotes an example of a Russian visitor to the Jockey Club, who asked his hosts to define the attribute of a gentleman. Was it an inherited title, a caste, a question of cash? The answer he received was that a gentleman disclosed his qualities only to those who had the knowledge to perceive them without being told.[29]

Those with the gift of discernment will know a good server by his dedication and the degree to which he transmits a self-absorption in the part. It will be obvious he cares deeply and he shows it. The issue of the good server is partly resolved in the qualities of grace he transmits unwittingly to the priest, or to those in the congregation, who might just attend to his actions at a moment that edifies. It could be the way the actor bows, or prays after communion, or washes the hands of the priest. Some gesture or action might catch the eye and impress. All manner of things can emerge in the slightness of the act, and there is a random, polyvalent quality to what can be transmitted. It might be felt that this emphasis on the capacity to edify reflects wishful thinking, a self-confirming belief in the goodness of an altar server who does his best. But this is no less naïve than the customer's belief in the benefits of the attention of a good waiter on his somewhat deflated ego. The altar server has less power to command attention than the waiter who serves the few. But because the mass is a repetitious action with often the same congregation, those present come to notice and to believe in his capacity to edify – should they notice at all. Like the waiter, a good altar server achieves excellence by being unnoticed, by attending without attracting attention.

As is the case with some restaurants, there are altars that are served with excellence and others where the quality of the serving is on a more modest scale. One might go to small rural Catholic Church and find two small boys doing their best to serve on a small sanctuary where the priest is close and supportive, and where it would be uncharitable to expect too much. But in a Benedictine monastery with a school attached, or a Cathedral, one does expect excellence in serving. The sanctuary is likely to be so large that 'liturgical mistakes' will resonate. Furthermore, they have the resources to use teams of servers to cover ceremonies that do not normally occur in parish Churches, such as the blessing of the oils for Maundy Thursday, or a religious profession or ordination. Usually, there will be a choir of men and boys whose musical excellence should be complemented by equally high-quality serving. Should the two strands get out of gear, liturgical chaos can follow, as for instance, if the Gospel procession moves off too fast and reaches the lectern just when the choir have started to sing the acclamation. An experienced team of servers will work with the celebrants and choir to produce a solemnising atmosphere, where sight and sound are married to a holy effect.

An important part of the tradition of the altar server, that marks him off from the waiter, is that it provides a means of education for boys and young men into handling sacred mysteries. More crucially, there is an element of anticipatory socialisation involved in the role, that might convert the altar server into a priest. The acolyte is still a minor order that marks a stage in the training to the priesthood. Very few priests have not been altar servers. One study indicated a close relationship between family religiosity, altar serving and a favourable image of the priesthood.[30] An altar server operates in a close and confidential relationship with the priest. Seeing the stresses and rewards of the vocation, a young man might decide to further his career more permanently on the sanctuary. This partly accounts for the way the server operates in the ambit of clerical discipline. Altar serving still carries an element of clerical apprenticeship.

This can be expressed in terms of the control exercised over the appearance of the server. Training manuals stress the link between cleanliness and godliness, by demanding that the servers have a clean face and hands, shoes that do not squeak, and the possession of a handkerchief to use when sneezing.[31] Victorian Anglican manuals were particular on the issue of cleanliness. One suggested that servers washed their hands *after* vesting. The object of this exercise 'is *partly* to guard against any dirt having settled on your hands in the course of vesting or changing your shoes; but chiefly to put you in mind of the purity of heart required of those who minister before the Lord'.[32]

The sanitary aspects of sanctity signify the preparation of a disposition, one that also involves vesting prayers (rarely used nowadays) and prayers said together by the priest and his servers in the sacristy before going on to the altar. Unlike the waiter, who uses the kitchen to dissemble the self, the server uses the sacristy to assemble a self, to recollect, and to develop an interior disposition that complements his external activities. A server runs a particular risk of becoming overly familiar with holy objects through habitual use. To guard against this danger, servers have to be trained to treat liturgical actions and symbols with a seriousness that allows them to survive handling that which would be otherwise mundane.

After the reforms of Vatican II, the role of the altar server seemed to have become truly dispensable. Much stress was laid on active participation, and on the removal of hierarchical elements that would hinder engagement of congregations in what was increasingly being presented as a collaborative effort between priest and people, united in a worshipping community. A sign of this effort to release the rite to the congregation was the removal of the altar rails, which formed a boundary between priest and people. More significantly, the use of the vernacular and the opening out of the responses of the mass to the people seemed to diminish the role of the server. In the Tridentine rite, he made the responses on behalf of the congregation who followed the mass silently in their missals. With the development of the vernacular mass, all laity present join with the server in making the responses to the priest. His role seemed to have been further reduced in the simplification of rubrics governing the mass. In former rites, the demands made on the server were truly complex. Not only has his role been reduced but other laymen now participate in ministries, such as reading and distributing communion. They enter the sanctuary to undertake their tasks, which formerly he occupied alone with the priest. There is an illogicality in these new ministries that amplifies the ambiguity of the role of the altar server as hovering somewhere between the laity and the priest. Despite these reforms which have reduced his role, his part has become *more* significant in sociological terms. To understand this paradox, one has to understand changes in the rules governing his part in the rite.

In the Tridentine rite, a high degree of skill was required to serve. Not only had Latin responses to be learned off by heart, but movements had to be drilled in, so that they seemed to occur automatically. A canonical exactitude applied to posture and move-ment, that governed all aspects of the presentation of the body for liturgical use. The way hands were to be held, the form of kneeling, bowing, sitting, were all subject to exact stipulations. Older guides to serving supplied rubrics or ceremonial directions that rendered all actions of the altar server subject to account in canon law. A total demand was made, binding under pain of sin. The sincere server had little option but to obey. Disputes often arose over the most minute of detail, for instance over whether the server was to move on the steps of the sanctuary or across the floor when carrying the missal.[33] There were prohibitions on what the server could touch. He could not open the missal on the altar, nor could he cover or uncover the chalice. The order of lighting the candles was also stipulated. Those on the Gospel side of the altar were to be lit before those on the Epistle side, and if two servers were employed they had to perform their actions simultaneously, a point that also applied to the candles being extinguished. Even ringing the bell at the consecration could be a complex exercise.[34] In the absence of a sacristan, the server had to prepare the altar. The complexity of the server's task greatly increased at a high mass. Working as part of a team of servers, involving a minimum of five, a complex sequence of instructions had to be remembered. The brunt of Adrian Fortescue's stipulations was borne by the master of ceremonies, who was sometimes a layman.[35] Habit and practice enabled these complex instructions regarding use of the thurifer, and the movements of the cross-bearer, to be carried off with ease. As they grew older, servers were promoted to more complex positions, and were likely to be deployed at the more solemn ceremonies, where ordinations occurred, or where the Bishop was making a visitation.[36]

Altar serving pre-supposes a growth in religious and liturgical knowledge developed over a number of years. A server gains a degree of expertise, not only governing the rubrics that relate to the enactment of the rite, but also a sense of how it ought to be performed. A boy who serves develops an attachment to his part, that shapes his growth into manhood. To that degree he tends to have a traditional bias towards the mass, and a sense of awe as to what ought to be preserved. Habit becomes married to custom and the server, as he grows older, develops a proprietorial attitude to altar matters. A sense of what can go wrong is also cultivated, as also is the need to have to hand a stock of contingency plans to cope with minor liturgical disasters.

In the Tridentine rite, the server was the enactor of an objective set of rules, that stipulated what he was accountable for in the enactment of the rite. Little provision was made for a sense of 'feel' in the performance, that would require a monitoring of self to gauge the effect of what had been presented. Ritual was a term seldom used. Rubrics were established to place the outcome of the rite above the intentions of the actor.

With mass now being said facing the people, and with an emphasis on opening out the rite so that a subjective sense of active participation is stressed, the movements of the altar server are more manifest and, intentionally or otherwise, they make a greater impact on the congregation. In a subtle way, this has expanded his role, and has compensated him for the loss of his former exclusive right to make the responses on behalf of the congregation. The actual tasks of serving mass have not greatly changed from those in former rites, although the rules governing their performance have been minimised and simplified. The new rites place a premium on areas that are accessible to sociological scrutiny. Stress is now laid on the obvious facets of the rite. The altar server is there to be seen to make a difference. Even if there is an element of stereotype, and unoriginality attached to his gestures of bowing and kneeling, these take on an added significance as a means of evoking a sense of participation amongst the congregation in the action of the rite, and in the mystery of what is presented. Whereas in the older rites, the server was a puppet on a string of rubrics, in the newer liturgical forms he has a more conspicuous role to play, where discretion and interpretation are required to secure the desired public qualities of the rite.

The freeing of the form of rite from exact rubrics that governed every detail has expanded the role of the server in another unexpected direction. Because parishes develop a house practice, within the general confines of the present rubrics, the method of saying mass will vary in subtle details from place to place. Because the altar server is familiar with local rules of liturgical 'use', he will be expected to advise a visiting priest. As one American manual for younger altar servers noted, 'you can be a big help to him'.[37] In the Anglican Church, where there are numerous permutations of ceremonial practice, and no agreed set of instructions equivalent to those governing the Roman rites, the discretionary role of the altar server as an interpreter of local practice could be unexpectedly amplified, although the congregation, the vicar and the parish council could limit what he can do.[38]

A further complication in the Catholic Church is that directions for serving mass are given in a rather general way. The roles mentioned in the General Instruction apply both to a solemn *and* a simple mass. In the absence of a more definite set of instructions, some traditional practices of serving mass have been carried over into the new version of the rite. Disagreements can often arise over the mixture of old habits and new customs of serving appearing in a mass. Only those with a detailed grasp of the rubrics of the older rites, and the more enabling rules of the reformed version, could discern the distinction in the manner and style of serving, and the implications being presented for diverse interpretation.

Earlier, we examined the way rites compete and can be understood in terms of handling 'liturgical mistakes'. Unacceptable signals can be transmitted that give comfort to liturgical rivals. Because altar servers move about the sanctuary so much, and attend to obvious aspects of liturgical production, they can have a disproportionate effect on what is noticed. To a degree that is easy to underestimate, altar servers have a peculiar capacity to manage, or to mismanage the obvious facets of the rite. They can also have a profound effect on the style of the rite by their manner of serving. As Fortescue indicates, there is a need to find 'the right mean between slovenliness and affectation'. Prior to this comment, he cites Pius Martinucci who commented on the behaviour of servers. He noted that they should avoid too much precision or affectation, or such a bearing as befits soldiers on parade rather than churchmen. They must certainly do all gravely and regularly; but if they behave with too punctilious a uniformity the sacred functions look theatrical.[39]

The server has to sustain a marginality in his task besides that which is imposed on him by the nature of his duties, yet he has to act with discretion when something goes wrong. The priest is confined to the altar, or to the chair at the side, and cannot vary his set movements without causing a considerable amount of puzzlement and distraction to the congregation. Many ceremonial repairs have to be left to the server. Elementary forms of mismanagement can arise in the staging of the rite, such as failing to light the altar candles, or omitting to put out the consecrating host, or not lighting the charcoal for the thurible adequately, so that it goes 'dead' at a critical liturgical moment. These might seem trivial, but can be significant, if they bring the whole rite to a halt whilst the 'mistake' is rectified. Often slips can pass unnoticed, and with really good servers, and a skilled master of ceremonies, the 'liturgical mistake' can be disguised, and made to appear as if it is part of the ritual practice of the Cathedral or monastery. If slips occur, they should not be amplified. Part of the ability of a good serving team is to smoothly disguise and leave a 'mistake' unsignified.

Where the server makes a mark on the enactment of rite is in the cumulative area of timing. Every rite carries a certain tension. A slackly managed rite can appear to be inadequately regulated and virtually meaningless in effect. It is unlikely to make an impact. Absence of a tension can denote a failure to attend, and can betoken an unfitting carelessness in the act of worship. It can also indicate a failure to attend to elements much neglected in modern theology – a fear and awe of God. A tension in the enactment of rite conveys a sense of walking before God, and good servers can manifest this property in an indefinable manner that governs their activities in other parts of the liturgy.

A sense of tension has a crucial function in the management of the performance by the servers: all social resources of the rite are kept in play and are rendered to account in the rite. A concern with a dignified order is also conveyed, so that the performance is worthy of the intended object of dedication in the rite: God. Any movement that occurs has a significance and there are no unproductive and puzzling gaps. It is in the management of the 'pace' of the rite, that the quality of the serving shows. Water for the washing of the hands arrives exactly when the celebrant turns to present his fingers for purification; the thurifer comes out just before the end of the second reading, so that no unfruitful pauses occur; and the crucifer and acolytes move just when required for departure at the end of the rite. If gaps are precluded, it means that a cessation of activities in the rite serves its purpose, of drawing attention to the need to contemplate what is past the action, to the silence that fills the space and to the opening that has been so regulated to make way for a Divine response. Good servers, knowing the distances required for actions to be performed, will time their services to a clinical exactitude, not drawing attention to themselves, but to the significance of what they are endeavouring to attend to – the worship of God.

These elements of style reflect implicit judgements, an experience of life in a holy house seldom mentioned in liturgical manuals. These subtle elements of managing the 'pace' of the rite, and the amount of tension there is on the altar, bear on another point: the way the servers tune their actions to a sense of atmosphere in the Church. They endeavour to 'pace' their actions to the felt phenomenon of the rite, the sense of threshold conveyed, and above all the qualities of silence that can be most closely felt on the sanctuary. If it is realised there, it can become available elsewhere to all present in the building, listening to hear. These qualities of style govern a sense of contact with the holy and affect the 'flow' of liturgical actions accordingly. There is a subtle but inescapable element of collusion between the celebrants and servers and the choir, who work together to produce a 'good thick' rite.

The differences between the world of the waiter and the altar server are obvious and involve intentions that are mutually exclusive. There are apparent similarities in the procedures both employ to secure the requisite atmosphere of these sacred and civil worlds, but there are also crucial differences. These tell us much about the autonomous nature of liturgical reproductions in a way that links with modern culture. Although liturgies re-present that which seems detached from the world, their actors use cultural resources that belong to it, even in advanced industrialised societies.

Civility and modernity are values embodied in the restaurant. It is the contemporary setting for relief from the turmoil of life, where discontents can be masked, and the mundane self can be tuned into the indulgent. Restaurants are settings in which the actor can be transformed, where esteem is enhanced, and where self-importance is amplified, however briefly. On the other hand, the sanctuary calls for a more self-denying ordinance, a straining to refract the heavenly in a way that marks the finite nature of life and the vacuity of the modern. Actors service the margins of the altar and the restaurant. Both roles of server and waiter require a tact in handling antinomies of proximity and distance, where the self is best attached or detached according to sacred or civil circumstances to procure an intended definition of the situation. They share a common task of colluding to sustain a desired ambience, that is both fragile and felt. In addition, they share the need to cope with a dilemma, that the pinnacle of 'success' in the exercise of service lies in the intangible, a quality that can be discerned but which eludes definition. The sophisticated and the spiritually advanced know this quality of service when they perceive it.

Far from being a liability, this indefinite quality residing in the ritual of good eating or holy worship is a spur to the actors to strive for a greater service, if they so will. There is, however, a contradiction between the good or bad faith desirable in the part, which can enable or disable the actor and which also influences his chances of survival. The waiter glides along the surface, steering clear of sinking deep. He is not called to believe in his encounter with the customer in a religious sense. On the other hand, the altar server tries to become caught up in the ritual 'flow' in a way that binds his self to the act. He seeks to drop the self deep into the implications of what he facilitates. The waiter seeks to avoid being implicated in the act, to preserve a detachability, whereas the server has the opposite task, of achieving a state of attachment.

Part of the problem with the analysis of the restaurant is that the issue of 'emotional labour' is ambiguous. In the American literature, there is a commercial etiquette attached to the notion. It represents the demand for a corporate face-work which actor and customer collude in sustaining, but in a way that deceives few. But in Marshall's recollection of his Scottish restaurant, the line between work and leisure, waiters and customers, and proprietor and staff, seemed remarkably thin. If there was any 'emotional labour' involved in waiting, the demands were remarkably light. The restaurant seemed to have been a centre for drama, for gossip and scandal, so that work and play mixed together. The staff came back to the restaurant on off-nights to drink and also hired the place for their own functions.[40]

The rise of service industries to cater for taste and recreation point to dramatic changes in modern culture, where identities are packaged, and where civility and gratification can be bought without reference to the moral worth of the purchaser. Tone, ambience and excitement mark the allure of the fashionable settings for service, where the ego is massaged and enhanced in a way that re-fits the actor for struggles with modern living. Time is bought to stand back, but in a way that affirms modernity, yet disguises its price. The self becomes part of a package deal, full of credit, but no worth, left lying between being sufficiently enchanted, but just distant enough from any disenchantment that might spoil the dream. In civil life, the self has its own antinomial struggles. The intangible nature of a civilised dream, exemplified in the restaurant, is an asset rather than a liability. It allows efforts to achieve authenticity to be postponed. As Finkelstein has argued, higher-class restaurants offer a deluding form of escapism, one where civility is dependent on the artificial construction, regulation and control of wants, that render the self inauthentic in such settings. These forms of dining out present a capacity to blunt sensibilities, which the customer colludes in sustaining.[41] Restaurants exemplify the world of dreams, where the *flâneur* can sit happily in the frame of dedicated service, musing in his amusement at the mix of dissimulation and simulation, where it is good manners not to look too closely behind the façade. Tensions are masked as the diner sits in the cage peering out at the spectacle of other lives passing by.

There are superficial similarities between the sacral and the civil world, where similar ploys sustain the social construction of significant events, marked with contrary meanings. But as I have tried to suggest, they operate with crucial differences. The self of the liturgical actor is bound into the antinomial implications of what is being presented, if he wishes to cultivate a dedication to the holiness he incarnates. The liturgical act exists less to blunt sensibilities, than to rough them up. It involves taking on a burden that is inescapable, as the actor becomes implicated in the act of presenting a witness, but denying a conceit in the action, of adjusting social means for incalculable ends. Like the waiter, the altar server is a spectator of a drama, but of a sacred kind, where different subtleties of tone and ambience prevail. Whereas the waiter has a definite contribution to this indefinable quality of good service, the altar server has a more facilitating function in the sense of sanctity his act procures. He has to work to establish conditions that will enable others to impute to him qualities that lie outside his own manufacture. He is the conduit of a holy act, not its agent.

The altar server's game is played on the sanctuary in little movements and acts of deference that might or might not be noticed. He cannot command attention; he can only attract it, if people are willing to notice it. The tentative condition of his act exemplifies the social basis of the rite as a whole. It has an enabling quality that plays at limits. A subtle reading is required to find the meaning of what lies below the surface, which returns us to a familiar point.

In the final chapters, I wish to explore this issue of the limits of rite, the boundaries it handles and the ephemeral nature of what it produces that gives liturgical transactions such an ambiguous, but fulfilling quality, that fascinates as much as it seems to estrange. Hermeneutics allows a fullness of understanding that other approaches cannot achieve. It facilitates a sociological entry into a holy game.

9 Liturgy as Ritual: Playing on Social Limits

> Behold now, an evil spirit from God troubleth
> thee. Let our lord now command thy servants,
> which are before thee, to seek out a man, who
> is a cunning player on an harp: and it shall
> come to pass, when the evil spirit from God
> is upon thee, that he shall play with his
> hand, and thou shalt be well.
>
> (1 Sam. 16:15–16)

Habitual engagement in liturgical productions leads often to its actors feeling there is something unmysterious about the ritual transaction as a whole. A day filled with offices takes on a life of its own. The choir monks barely reflect as they file in for compline; the choirboys struggling into their surplices after rehearsal for vespers, think perhaps of football after, but of little else; and the servers light the candles again, as part of a holy routine in the evening, with flickering worries about unfinished homework. There is something uneventful about servicing such holy events.

It is easy for these actors to overlook the mystery they hallow by their dedicated actions. The celebration of a mystery, however, is a central facet of the rites they enact. As Casel notes, 'the mystery of worship, therefore, is a means whereby the Christian lives the mystery of Christ'.[1] The mysterious aspects of the social wrappings of rite serve another purpose, of drawing attention to that which might seem to be unmysterious and easily misunderstood through the routine handling of this theological core. Reflecting a point made earlier, Casel claims 'the mystery was formed for man; it is to bring about in him an inward change'.[2] Any mysterious qualities attached to the social form of rite, and the image it cultivates, serve to service the interior life of the actor and to transform it into a deeper spiritual basis.

The re-play of rite gives access to elements of mystery that can redeem the contradictions that might otherwise divide and distort its capacity to bear credible meanings about matters which of their nature are incredible. Hans-Georg Gadamer makes a helpful point about the symbolic in art that can be applied to an understanding of liturgical performance. He suggests that symbols involve an 'intricate interplay of showing and concealing'. This teasing antinomial quality can develop a sense of self-recognition, an enhancement of the self *before* what is presented through these symbolic means of expression. By participating in such a simple but complex ritual task the actor realises an image in the form, and in what he produces can catch an intimation of the Divine. This is where the social form married to a theological content creates an icon. Harnessed to its holiest of purpose, the social becomes a crucible to contain what drops down so unexpectedly from above. This relates to Gadamer's notion of *mimesis*, when he suggests we are not dealing with a matter of imitation, but with a capacity to re-present 'in such a way that it is actually present in sensuous abundance'.[3] The capability of transforming the mundane into the service of the mysterious is a peculiar gift of religious rituals, a point that puzzled Péguy, who wrote in a letter:

> Sunday afternoon I entered the church of . . . without noticing that I was doing so. They were saying vespers. What an amazing thing it is, when one comes to think of it; these three or four urchins of the Ile de France, who meet every Sunday, dressed up as choir boys, to say the psalms of your King David . . . .[4]

This capacity of liturgical actors to engage and to be transformed in a ritual that addresses a sacred mystery is at odds with worldly wisdom. The vast majority of the population in a secularised society do not go to Church, hence the perplexing nature of those foolish enough to go, to act a holy part. In the action of rite and its easeful re-presentation is a 'scandal of particularity', a stumbling block to belief. The scandal lies in the folly of the social act, and the belief it proclaims, that it can attract the attention of God and can fulfil incarnational promises. More usually, the phrase refers to the incarnation of Christ as God in a particular era, a specific event that is as mysterious as it is scandalous in the demand it makes on the intellect.[5] In our context, the phrase expresses a continuity with the incarnation realised in liturgical performance. The capacity of rite to re-play endlessly represents a scandalous assumption, that God comes in a particular time and place, in a liturgical instance. The style of enactment of the liturgical actors conveys this sense of walking before a holy mystery, whose mysteriousness attaches to them as they strive to find the holy in a public arena.

This tacit mysterious basis to rite operates in an ambiguous fashion. It might justify the suspicion that it is about nothing in particular, and if so, this could be deemed the ultimate scandal about liturgy. But on the other hand, it might denote the property of experience, the mysterious phenomenon, that links the social to the sacred. This felt property of rite poses numerous pitfalls. It places the analysis in the context of a fledgeling sociology of emotions and the vexed area of religious experience. The more dramatic aspects of experience, such as involved in conversions or in ecstasy are often discussed. Less exotic forms of religious experience are neglected in sociology. There is, perhaps, too much of a difficulty involved in endeavouring to track the quickening of the spirit that emerges from quiet, disciplined orders of worship, such as choral Evensong, or a solemn mass, where silence and gentleness lurk in the pauses of what is proclaimed.

This chapter prepares the way for the use of hermeneutics in understanding rite as a form of play. There are mysterious tacit facets of rite that suggest a game is being played, one where it is unclear who is playing with whom, God or man or neither. Endless re-plays seem possible, where winning is as mysterious as it is elusive. There is an experiential cast to the liturgical game, where the actors playing seem to be acted on in a phenomenological manner that transcends their understanding. This mysterious phenomenon acts on the social form of the rite from outside its boundaries, often where it is at its weakest and seems to have the least to say. Silence is an ambiguous phenomenon whose meaning changes subtly according to the social settings in which it arises. It denotes what is felt in the actions of the rite, and yet what is beyond language and human effort. Silence embodies a notion of limits, but in a way that seems to speak louder than words. It emerges in the gaps and pauses in a well-regulated rite, and gives its social form a phenomenological clothing that also awards it an indefinable, but distinctive content. In this chapter, I wish to explore the liminal aspects of rite, the numinous and mysterious qualities that endow its social form with a defining content, as distinctive as it is meaningful.

LITURGY AS RITUAL: FORMS OF HOLY OPENINGS

> Let no man beguile you of your reward in a
> voluntary humility and worshipping of angels,
> intruding into those things which he hath
> not seen, vainly puffed up by his fleshly mind.
>   (Col. 2:18)

In Catholicism, the mystery of a rite, such as a mass, has an objective element, one that is unaffected by subjective intention, disposition or sense of reception. An excess of emphasis on the mysterious aspects of rite might suggest some form of indexicality of liturgical 'success' that could be linked to the quality of ritual performance. This would be mistaken. A theological argument, on the other hand, could claim that the reasons why an informal rite, bare in symbol and slight in action, 'works' are also mysterious. There is also a pitfall in stressing the mysterious aspects of liturgy, that it might make too many of its parts unavailable for sociological understanding. Furthermore, an over-emphasis on the mysterious aspects of rite could be distorting. It could remove rite from public view, making it a cultic ritual. There is an ambiguous facet to the issue of how much, or how little mystery liturgy needs to have to 'work'. Of course, the mysterious nature of this content of liturgy could supply sociology with an alibi for not penetrating too far into a theological realm, where its insight might be deemed incredible.[6]

Actors operating in a ritual, whose basis and form are mysterious, do so with a strategy of advancing into implicit meanings and hidden understandings. A liturgical performance operates to effect an open-ing, one that facilitates the coming of a presence from outside the limits of rite, the form that gives it a ceremonial shape and order. It is what speaks in mystery beyond the boundaries of the purely obvious that generates a curiosity about liturgical enactments. This provides an incentive to look again, to understand what was thought to be understood in previous liturgical performances. Guardini expressed this point well when he noted that:

> the symbolising power of the liturgy becomes a school of measure and of spiritual restraint. The people who really live by the liturgy will come to learn that the bodily movements, the actions, and the material objects which it employs are all of the highest significance. It offers great opportunities of expression, of knowledge, and of spiritual experience; it is emancipating in its action, and capable of presenting a truth far more strongly and convincingly than can mere word of mouth.[7]

The need to give the mysterious some mode of expression through social means gives its issue a basis of sociological evaluation, but it also lends an opaque indeterminate cast to rite that has some distinctive theological functions. As I. H. Dalmais suggests,

> liturgical actions yield their intelligibility in their performance, and this performance takes place entirely at the level of sensible realities,

not as exclusively material but as vehicles of overtones capable of awakening the mind and heart to acceptance of realities belonging to a different order.[8]

Mystery is the mode of manifestation of the Divine in the world, and in an earlier work, Dalmais indicates we use phenomenological means to account for this in what we can describe.[9] Clearly, there is a contradiction involved in such an approach to the mysterious, which is often described in theological terms as being indescribable. But the mysterious effects of rite point to an availability. The incapacity to stipulate its effects, an indeterminacy that is as mysterious as it is elusive, gives rite an indefinite number of interpretations, a plurality of understandings difficult for sociology to contain. As Ratzinger observes 'in the liturgy, we are all given the freedom to appropriate, in our own personal way, the mystery which addresses us'.[10] The mystery in rite becomes available but in a mysterious way.

To gain sociological access to the mysterious basis of liturgical actions, a phenomenological approach is required. Edmund Husserl's phenomenological method involves a 'bracketing of the objective world'. Irving Zeitlin suggests this means that 'we recognize the claim to reality the object makes upon us but we temporarily suspend any judgement as to the validity of the claim. What remains is world as pure or mere phenomenon'.[11] Phenomenological approaches to religious belief stress sympathetic interpretations of the essence of their cultural forms, so that a fullness of meaning can be expressed.[12] An issue that has been unexplored is the 'intentional' structures of modes as they operate in the context of religious ritual.[13] My study tries to fill this sociological gap. Phenomenology points to the need to allow objects to reveal their essential qualities without premature judgements impeding what needs to be disclosed if a fullness of understanding is to be achieved. This bracketing of doubt or suspicion, to enable understanding to proceed, arises also in the context of hermeneutics, and will be explored more fully in the next two chapters.

As suggested earlier, anthropological approaches to ritual have moved from a concern with explanation and its functional nature in society. This reflected the view of Durkheim who regarded rituals as serving to express and to affirm social solidarity. The issue of the truth or falsity of these religious rituals was beside the point, for their 'real' function is social rather than spiritual. The god worshipped in ritual is 'only a figurative expression of the society'.[14] For Durkheim, a 'collective effervescence' gives rise to religious sensibilities that remove a man to a different world, but one where the social rather than a deity is magnified.[15] Social rather than spiritual enhancement is the effect of religious rituals.[16]

Emphasis in anthropological interpretations of ritual now stresses the distinctive meanings rituals open up, which point beyond the purely social. Rituals are deemed to have enhancing rather than reductionist tasks in handling meanings. This has led to an acceptance of what these rituals strive to represent. As Talal Asad has suggested, the idea that the ritual process is essentially symbolic and is concerned with communicating a message has become a central doctrine of British and American anthropology.[17] An American anthropologist, Clifford Geertz, who exercised an important influence on this change in emphasis, argued that, while religious rituals can be presented for scientific dissection, for believers they are

> in addition enactments, materializations, realizations of the religious perspective – not only models *of* what they believe, but also models *for* the believing of it. In these plastic dramas men attain their faith as they portray it.[18]

Earlier, he had indicated that religious symbols facilitate a convergence between a particular style of life and a specific metaphysic. More fundamentally, for our purposes, he suggested that 'each is sustained with the borrowed authority of the other'.[19] Contemporary approaches to ritual increasingly centre on the transformative effects their performance secures, an approach implicit in this work. This stress on the process of performance and the changes it accomplishes owe much to the American anthropologist Victor Turner, whose use of the term 'liminal' I consider in the next section. This change in anthropological attitudes to ritual has had profound implications for the comparative study of religion. It also facilitates a fuller sociological understanding of liturgy.[20]

Many examples of this change in anthropological approaches to ritual could be given. Perhaps the most persuasive is the study by Gilbert Lewis of initiation rites amongst the Gnau, a tribe in New Guinea. These painful rites involve bloodletting amongst the boys to be transformed into men, a process that strikes Western observers as cruel and unnecessary. The value of Lewis's analysis of these rituals is the way a suspension of judgement allows him to understand the symbolic value of blood amongst the Gnau. Blood is regarded as a sap that facilitates growth and maturation. Lewis has supplied a social account of its ritual use and transmission in terms other than those of physiology. It is the social circulation of blood between bodies in a ritual performance that interests. Blood is given its fullness of mystery, as a form of life – both social and physiological. The performance of the ritual provides access to aspects of the mystery of life in a way no other means would permit. Thus, Lewis suggests that

> by setting ordinary things within a ritual field, contrived and peculiar, asking for attention, the mind may attend to the thing as a sign or symbol which may yield up information about a mystery that seems to come within grasp when invested with perceptible form.[21]

Increasingly, there is a theological cast in the way anthropologists approach understandings of ritual. Oddly, reductionist accounts of religious ritual are more likely to come from liberal theologians than from sociologists and anthropologists, who seem to have developed a reverential awe of the sacred and the holy in ritely productions. Victor Turner produced an account of ritual and liturgy that was decidedly at odds with this liberal theological consensus in the early 1970s regarding the place of the mysterious in rite.

LIMINAL RITES: CASTING THE SOCIAL TO LIMBO

> The wilderness and the solitary place shall be
> glad for them; and the desert shall rejoice, and
> blossom as the rose.
>
> (Isaiah 35:1)

Liturgies operate as rites of passage that take the participants up to the limits of a limitless mystery. They are rites well geared to handle the marginal. Arnold van Gennep suggested that the ritual of the mass constitutes a rite of passage, one marked by separation, transition and incorporation.[22] This aspect of a rite of passage is apparent in the fourfold actions of the mass: taking gifts of bread and wine; prayer and thanksgiving; fraction; and communion.[23] Profane elements are placed apart, are separated and broken to admit access to a new order of existence. They are then returned to those who presented these gifts of human labour so that what has been reconstituted can effect a transformation in their lives.

Arnold van Gennep's notion of transition rites points to those that deal with the liminal or with thresholds. Liminal rites mark boundaries or doors that signify a union to be achieved on the other side. They operate between rites of separation and those of incorporation, servicing the needs of those deemed to be outsiders.[24] These rites refer to states of being between two opposites, such as adolescence. Liminality carries an antinomial quality, an element of standing before, but between elements such as the sacred and the profane. It denotes the idea of a boundary, one that also affirms something to be past it. The liminal operates on ritual frontiers, and, in our use, is a property that hovers between the form and the content of liturgy. An eschatological witness is supplied by the concept of liminality.

Victor Turner uses the term liminality to refer to a marginal state that bears a quality of ambiguity. Liminality also has an indeterminate aspect, one that is expressed through symbols and rituals. Monasticism institutionalises the state. In our account, the choirboy exemplifies the term in his liturgical act. When he sings solo, he seems to occupy a liminal state, one between boy and angel. Those endowed with liminality bear witness to that which is beyond structures of power, ambition, pride and worldly sagacity. They achieve a directness of communication in a way that seems unfettered by structural constraints and the social ties that bind the spirit. This achievement exemplifies Turner's notion of a communitas, a quality of holiness that transcends and breaks structures asunder. Communitas refers to a communion of equal individuals operating within a ritual. There is a quality of the holy and the sacred involved in its capacity to strip and to level institutions and structures. It signifies the power of the marginal to reverse worldly orders and forms of knowing. Communitas conveys the notion of the self standing against a structural order, but at the same time transcending it.

Liminality suggests what can be released out of a tension operating within a ritual form. The stripping away of the layers of structure involves a wrestling to admit that which lies outside to enter and to dominate the ritual form. Turner's account of liminality and communitas indicates a point made earlier, that the social is masked by ritual actors in a way that facilitates its disappearance into insignificance. But his idea of liminality has another important quality. By stressing the notion of a passage in between elements, he is indicating a means of coping with social attributes that are deemed antinomial. Communitas resolves the doubts of those who have to operate in a liminal state. Turner offers an account of ritual that complements our earlier approach to segments of liturgy, of appearance, role and gesture.

In his initial formulation, two important elements emerge. Firstly, liminality is related to conditions of structural inferiority. The social is domesticated before the holy and becomes its servant, not its master. Such an approach complements that of Simmel, which we discussed earlier. Secondly, the term liminal refers to an emergent property of binary oppositions. Liminality suggests the possibility of achieving a wholeness, a sense of belonging that emerges at the weakest point of the social base of the rite. By dealing with ambiguities, and the polyvalent outcomes of ritual endeavour, liminality and communitas both point to the prospect of deeper meanings emerging in enactment. Most importantly, for our purposes, both indicate the way cultural forms can effect the realisation of sacred or holy qualities that transgress or dissolve the social norms governing their reproduction. As their use involves an element of stripping or levelling, it must be assumed that rites employ a social apparatus sufficiently thick to make its dismemberment worthwhile.[25] In a point I will develop in the next chapter, Ronald Grimes indicates that Turner's concern with the liminal in ritual draws out its ludic qualities.[26]

Although Turner used the term widely to apply to pilgrimages, fiestas, hippies and Franciscans, he had a particular interest in its application to liturgy. Turner argued that rituals *'ought to* have a pervasive archaic, repetitive, formal quality' to stand against the self-centred values of modernity. Liminality was deemed the 'unconscious' of cultural man. Turner saw a sacred quality in the liminal in its representation of a stripping and levelling of man before the transcendental. His account suggests that actors seek the sacred at its point of structural weakness, not at the point of its capacity to dominate, where it is at its greatest collective strength, as Durkheim would argue.[27] The liminal refers to a sense of what is missing, or absent, an incompleteness that emerges when the structure of the ritual seems to fail. At this point, the issue of the numinous enters as a compensatory response to this weakness.[28] It comes as a sense of communitas, at the point where the structure of rite starts to fracture.

The liminal operates as an emergent property of a 'successful' rite, giving witness to what is hidden in the social, but also to that which is beyond it. Urban Holmes has suggested that liminality generates that sense of oneness which religions strive to possess.[29] Turner's use of the term liminal expanded its application from a concern with the marking of transitions in life cycles, to an emphasis on the way the ritual process communicates qualities of the sacred.[30] His use of the term communitas refers to the bonding achieved by the weak, those who occupy a margin. Despite their social slightness, they seem to have great spiritual power. The weak and the slight invert proper orders as discussed in Chapter 4. This stress on the liminal is not intended to suggest that it represents a guaranteed area of theological 'success' that overrides conventional ecclesiastical criteria of efficacy. Instead, it points to the significance of the margins and the dangers of over-looking the importance of ritual boundaries, which the liturgical actors police in areas where matters are most ambiguous. The communitas these rites accomplish is not always predictable, and little attention has been given to the experiences that constitute its basis.[31] Part of the purpose of this chapter is to explore one characterising facet of communitas – silence.

There is a link between Turner's interest in liturgy and theatre, one that also emerges in the case of von Balthasar. Good liturgical performances have a dramatic and engaging quality. They bear an aura that draws the curious to inspect their messages so solemnly presented. Liturgical enactments seem to 'flow' in performance in a way that converts that which is purely ceremonial into an occasion for the inspection of the holiness presented and realised. Through the use of restricted cultural patterns that characterise a ritual structure, actors strive to convert these resources into a sense of communitas. This sense becomes implicated in the 'flow' of the rite and becomes 'fused' to its stated purpose – to worship God.[32] The liminal generates a sense of self-forgetfulness, an inattention on the part of the actor to his former civil status. This arises in a ritual moment where awareness and action merge. A similar point has been made by Guardini.[33] The idea of a 'liturgical mistake' also bears on the production of a sense of the liminal. It points to what is best left unsignified, lest it interfere with the 'flow' of the rite, as it attempts to move away from its enabling, but confining structure, into a felt sense of communitas. 'Liturgical mistakes' subtract from that effort and what it serves to accomplish.

Efforts to operate liturgies require an ability to invert the mechanism, so that what is visible is kept insignificant and in its place. As Turner has suggested 'liminality is a temporal interface whose properties partially invert those of the already consolidated order which constitutes any specific cultural "cosmos"'.[34] Liturgies serve to invert the social in a recasting of otherwise disparate elements, and to render these in a coherent performance where the incredible is naturalised in a credible 'flow', one that attracts and invites an investment of belief in what it proclaims. The ambiguous is no longer perplexing; the capacity of the mechanism to lie becomes unsignified; and the sense of threshold the rite realises, makes the social mechanism redundant. Hamnett has argued that Durkheim's opposition between the sacred and the profane can be expressed in two forms of interconnection. One is a direct link, giving the sacred an ideal function removed from its profane rival. But the other involves an inverse relationship, where the sacred is cast down in a ritual order of reversal that affirms what ought to be distant from the profane.[35] It is the latter approach that governs our approach to liturgy and points to what 'liturgical mistakes' strive to regulate.

In a discussion of the idolatrous risks of liturgical images, George Pattison notes the way that 'the divine cannot be identified with any particular appearance or form but is to be found in the spiritual freedom which can only be recognized and grasped in the inwardness of faith'.[36] Even if one did affirm belief in a particular liturgical form or appearance, there is the risk that it can take on literal qualities that border on the idolatrous. The social form of rite represents more than the obvious, but also less than it. Its ambiguous properties also bear a phenomenological quality that supplies an added layer of ambiguity to rite. The phenomenon has to be believed if it is to be heard and to be fully understood. There is an arbitrary quality attached to this capacity to hear and to discern, that reflects a point in the Gospels. When Christ was asked why He spoke in parables, He said

> Because it is given unto you to know the mysteries of
> the kingdom of heaven, but to them it is not given. For
> whosoever hath, to him shall be given, and he shall have
> more abundance: but whosoever hath not, from him shall
> be taken away even that he hath. Therefore speak I to
> them in parables: because they seeing see not; and
> hearing they hear not, neither do they understand.
>
> (Matt. 13:11–13)

This capacity to discern and to be moved by the mysterious in rite represents a gift of grace. It is an enlightenment that comes from spiritual resources rather than those of reason. A sense of being is unfolded that wraps the inner sense of the actor in a sensibility of the holy, where the difference between appearance and the invisible no longer matters. The gap has been breached in a way that is mysteriously beyond sociological grasp. Something fuller than what is present speaks through an absence, a point I wish to pursue in the final chapter on the link between negative theology and the limitations of sociological understandings of liturgical performance.

Otto's approach to the numinous has all the hallmarks of an apophatic theology. He points to the mysterious sense of awe that acts from without on liturgical form, witnessing to what is beyond human manufacture and rational conceptualisation. The numinous forms a defining characteristic of what the liturgical form strives to petition, that gives sense to actions that would be otherwise senseless. Otto was concerned with the feeling of the numinous and its outward manifestation. The numinous refers to a 'creature feeling', an awakening to the august majesty, to the awe and power of God, that manifests itself in a manner beyond rational categorisation. It expresses a 'moment' in solemn worship that moves 'the spirit in the heart' to feel a submergence, a nothingness before the transcendent. It evokes a call, but also fulfils it. A sense of the numinous is conveyed in the decision, 'as for me, I will come into thy house in the multitude of thy mercy: and in thy fear will I worship toward thy holy temple' (Psalms 5:7). This feeling of the 'wholly other' arises at the weakest points of the rite, when the social seems to fade into insignificance. The numen is a response to that failure. As Turner has suggested, rituals mediate between the formed and indeterminate. But, he argues, this quality of indeterminacy 'should not be regarded as the absence of social being; it is not negation, emptiness, privation. Rather it is the potentiality, the possibility of becoming'.[37] It is the redemptive possibilities out of the paradoxical failures of the rite that facilitate the expression of the numen.

The actor is faced with a demand to become subordinated to the point of self-extinction, to encounter a nothingness, so that he can find a deeper meaning abiding in a holy void. For Otto, the religious feeling of longing to find what cannot be uttered, arises at a moment of 'solemnity', of gathered concentration and humble submergence in a private devotion that enables the mind to be exalted to the holy.[38] This moment of contact with the holy comes apart from what can be manipulated, arriving from above, and transcending what is below. Turner makes a similar point when he suggests that the sense of communitas, of a bonding into freedom, comes as a matter of 'grace'. He suggests that it 'cannot be legislated for or normalized, since it is the *exception* not the *law*, the *miracle*, not the *regularity* . . .'.[39] Going before the holy requires a certain reining back before the uncertain, a discipline in handling the social and the seen to confront the holy and the unseen.

Going before the holy requires a humility, a cleansing that marks a self-depreciation, a covering that acts as a shield against the numen. Such a cleansing and covering bears on the petition, mentioned earlier, of the choirboy, when he dons his clean white surplice to go to sing before his God. As Otto notes 'such a "covering" is then a "consecration", i.e. a procedure that renders the approacher himself "numinous", frees him from his "profane" being and fits him for intercourse with the numen'.[40] This point complements the arguments in Chapter 4, on the link between holiness and appearance. Unworthiness mixes with atonement, and in the concealing, the basis of revealing emerges. This is a fundamental antinomial property of liturgy. But Otto is looking for more than a preparation and an availability to discern the mysterious. He is examining the direct and indirect expressions of the numinous in relation to what is done in rite that bears on a sense of its manifestation.

The numinous is associated with absences, voids in buildings, music and action. Silence, emptiness and darkness are the habitats of the numinous. In the hallowed holiness of a Cathedral in an autumn gloom, when choral Evensong is being sung to a tiny congregation, the sound goes off into the darkening recesses of the roof, and the empty spaces resonate with a response, all the more powerful for coming down from the absent.

The regulation of actions within the performance of the rite intensifies a sense of the numinous, by marking an expectation of its possible presence, especially at points in the liturgy when movements cease and sound has abated. Otto suggested that a number of liturgical forms had a particular, if not privileged relationship to the numinous. Quaker assemblies and Lutheran Eucharists were very much in his mind. His bias was towards more elaborate and formal rituals. He suggested that the numinous was transmitted often through 'reverent attitude and gesture, in tone and voice and demeanour, expressing its momentousness, and in the solemn devotional assembly of a congregation at prayer . . .'.[41] The Book of Common Prayer seemed to have formed a model for Otto of an instrument that could most fruitfully generate religiosity. The presence or absence of the numinous seems to be implicated in the style and manner of worship.

Otto did not relate the details of how the performance of a rite could be linked to a manifestation of the numinous. It is, however, not difficult to imagine what liturgical forms are *unlikely* to realise the numinous. Rites with little discipline, much light and noise, that claim to have direct links with the production of the numinous, would seem to stand a slim chance in Otto's estimation. Those associated with humble and indirect petition of the holy, who strive to keep the social subservient, and which proceed in a solemn, formal manner, seem more likely to have success. He felt the most effective means of representing the numinous was in the 'sublime' enactments of rite. Consciousness of the numinous may be stirred by feelings analogous to it, and Otto argues that half intelligible or wholly unintelligible forms of devotion generate a real enhancement of awe in the worshipper.[42] Thus, the numinous is likely to arise in social conditions that imitate the qualities they strive to possess. A liturgical form with a mysterious cast is most likely to be related to a sense of the numinous. Using his favourite analogy of the interweaving of warp and woof in a fabric, similar interconnections are suggested for the mutual implication operating between form and content, which a liturgy with a mysterious cast can suggest.[43] The fabric of the rite, what is obvious and discernible in its 'use', becomes bound into a sensitive awareness of the need to listen for the numinous. There is a paradoxical cast to the means through which the numinous becomes available. It is surprising that a social resource, so useless for any other purpose, could be so dramatically transcended. The issue of silence exemplifies this point.

AWFUL SILENCE: THE REAL ABSENCE IN SACRED RITE

> Then a spirit passed before my face; the hair
> of my flesh stood up:
> It stood still, but I could not discern the form
> thereof: an image was before mine eyes, there was
> silence . . .

> (Job 4:15–16)

Silence is an attribute of the numinous, and is a phenomenon which Otto felt had a sacramental quality. It involves a waiting on God to respond to a limit of speech. A sense of presence is marked by an absence of movement, of sound or speech. In the stillness a resonance can be felt of varying degrees of intensity. Despite its slightness, its apparent insignificance, silence is a dangerous topic, one laden with metaphysical overtones, that penetrates the social and reaches a part of the self speech cannot touch. It is both an interior and exterior expression of the numinous. It can be elusive, yet all too apparent; distant, yet brooding; including but with the power to exclude. It is a paradoxical phenomenon that seems to escape categorisation. To speak of silence means reaching for an adjective to complete its meaning. Some silences are benign, or fragile, deep and frightening, or slight, including or excluding. It is a phenomenon that embodies a moral quality, a sense of healing goodness. But it can also convey a deep sense of evil, a foreboding of destruction. This ambiguous quality of silence imposes a choice. The relationship of silence to social forms is equally ambiguous. Commenting on social forms of secrecy, Simmel observed that 'if human sociation is *conditioned* by the capacity to speak, it is *shaped* by the capacity to be silent'.[44] It is this ability to shape implications in social forms that gives silence a sociological significance which can be used to understand liturgical performances.

There is an indeterminate or a determinate quality to the issue of silence, a slightness or a definiteness, whose variable qualities are puzzling. Despite its capacity to shape social forms, silence conveys an ability to act independently of them. It is this autonomous quality that gives silence a mysterious quality. In theological terms, it embodies a mystery but it also expresses a realisation of its presence, paradoxically through a felt sense of absence. Silence is a crucial aspect of the theological content of rite, but it is also one that has an effect on its regulation at the level of social form. It is a characterising backcloth to liturgical activity, a phenomenon inlaid in the ritual mosaic, that marks its potential capacity to speak of the holy. It binds paradox and ambiguity into a harmonious completion, all the more curious for emerging from an absence. By providing a significant contrast to a ritual activity, to music and to speech, it manages, as David Martin remarks, 'to signify what cannot be said, to indicate the limits on the potentiality, and the potentiality incarnate in the limit'.[45] It draws attention to the ambiguity of the limits of ritual, the borders of the definition of the rite, where the social affirms but cannot pass forward beyond what it marks.

The issue of silence marks a negative witness in the 'flow' of a ritual activity. A liturgical performance that hits a pool of silence, allows what is past the limits of the activity to be heard. A drawing back, a regulating of the social, to allow a sensibility to emerge, requires a sense of tact, a sensitivity to a response from the absent. At a recording of choral Evensong, those present exercise an awesome guard on their actions, to preclude disruptive sounds emerging. The microphones become the gods guarding the rights of the unseen audience. But in other times and places, the same choral Evensong moves before the presence of the real God, and comes to work with the language of absence that haunts a Cathedral. It is the signals of the transcendent that are cultivated, not those for transmission.

The elusive nature of silence is also shown in the number of disciplines that participate in its study. At all levels of knowing, it presents difficulties. In metaphysical terms, it marks a limit to the aesthetic, but in a way that is ambiguous. The same phenomenon can be used to endorse the honesty of a nihilistic approach, but it can also give rise to apophatic considerations, those embodied in a negative theology. The former persuades us of the meaningless nature of beauty and artistic endeavour, whereas the latter points to a redemptive meaning emerging from an absence. The ends of the struggle to understand the demands of silence are polyvalent, for they point to an affirmation of a theological imperative to believe, but also to a metaphysical process that could destroy it.

In silence, we find a phenomenon that has metaphysical overtones, that can complete what is incomplete in social forms, and to that degree admits a partial understanding. Silence hovers at a level that facilitates sociological access. It is an emergent and characterising facet of institutional arrangements, but again it is polyvalent in effect. In one form of life, it can serve to punish and to destroy the self. But in another institutional context it provides a space for spiritual growth, for the self to engage with transcendent possibilities. It is an instrument of great power in social intercourse, operating as a lethal moral tool. Used as a sanction, it can put an actor to a civil death, but it also can effect virtue, through guarding the tongue, and servicing the need for a kindly tact. The issue of silence goes further into the self. It can act as a contemplative resource, a means of fostering an inward culture. In so doing, silence supplies a power to the self to resist the pressures of social forces that might otherwise engulf. Impregnating the self with a sensibility towards meanings that lie at the outer rim of the rite, involves an element of grace and faith, an habitual inward listening to the silence that flows from without, coming in from the social form. Silence serves to bind the inward culture of the actor into its external expression in the social in a way that admits no division, that harmonises as it heals and releases as it binds.

This redemptive harmonisation conveys a sense of contact with the holy. It is expressed in a form of communitas, one that arrives in an instant, and which could easily pass unnoticed. Once noticed, silence generates a craving to retrieve an essence that speaks from beyond words. It acts as an unexpectedly slight witness to a freedom from the constraints of rite, an eschatological promise of a future which eye has not seen nor has ear heard. Silence signifies a plenitude, an offer of escape from the tyranny of form. As Susan Sontag observes, 'silence is the artist's ultimate other-worldly gesture: by silence, he frees himself from servile bondage to the world, which appears as patron, client, consumer, antagonist, arbiter and distorter of his work'.[46] It offers an independence from dependence, an access to a power of knowing that transcends the means of its accomplishment. By offering a release from the restrictions of form, an interest in silence generates a concern to keep the social means of its expression in a state of insignificance.

The relationship between liturgical form and silence bears on earlier points, on the need for tact, and a constraint in enactment to preclude unfruitful meanings being spelt out. The limits of liturgical form need to be marked to allow a content to be noticed, a phenomenon that might pass unsignified and unheard. The proper management of the social conditions in which silence emerges facilitates access to something greater than the purely communal. Silence acts as the phenomenological sense of the liminal, affirming what can emerge as a felt experience. It is a witness to the limits of social form, but also, and more importantly, to the content that lies beyond it. Silence provides a gratuitous gift of grace, that redeems the failures and limits of the social form.

Music has a particular capacity to convey these properties. Choral music, where four male parts combine, mobilises a heavenly power, not so much through the beauty of the sound, but in the echoes it stumbles into, and in the cavities where silence hides shyly. Music has a long tradition of liturgical use. It summons up deeper responses and understandings of the Incarnation. As Joseph Cardinal Ratzinger suggests, music integrates the actor into a faith in its existence.[47] Music enhances a sense of the holy, but as Otto notes, it reaches its greatest effect when it slowly ceases, and sound sinks into a stillness. In the end one, can 'hear the silence'. He goes on to add that the mysterium is most powerfully expressed through intimation rather than in forthright utterance.[48] This bears on a point of Sontag, that 'silence is only "reticence" stepped up to the nth degree'.[49]

In its institutional manifestation, silence becomes embedded in a way of life. It is a constraint on speech and is often a rule of a 'total institution'. It is also a means of securing virtue. In the case of an elected monastic silence, the stillness so embedded serves to effect and to sustain virtue. Silence realises qualities of humility, obedience, reverence, gravity, gentleness, charity and peace.[50] It serves to cultivate a spiritual career for the dedicated and the practised, who listen to God in a life of total availability. Silence has a fundamental purpose, 'to free the soul, to give it strength and leisure to adhere to God'.[51] It safeguards the monk against sins arising from misuse of the tongue, and from distracting frivolity and scandal.[52] Monastic silence serves to bind men, who might be otherwise fractious in their celibacy, into a life of harmony, holiness and inner peace. It also serves to establish a distance in which the self can survive potential engulfment by the communal demands of monastic life. Used properly, monastic silence helps to maintain a spiritual and social proportion in a life that can easily lurch into a disedifying disproportion.

The polyvalence of silence is illustrated in another form of 'total institution' where the self is there to be crushed. In Victorian prisons in England, prisoners were put to the silence, and had a dumbness inflicted on them that often destroyed sanity. Enforcement of silence was a denial of a fundamental civil right to speak. Social bonds were unsecured that would otherwise have given a sense of support in a dank life of institutional misery.[53]

In itself, silence cannot secure virtue, for its endurance can lead the self into moral dangers that are absent in a life of easy utterance. Silence penetrates into the divisions of the self, especially in the monastery. For instance, a sulky silence, riddled with pride, in a life apart from a corrupting world, can falsify a vocation. Even absolute monastic silence generates its own distinctive perils. It can lead to misunderstandings and jealousy being transferred to signs and symbols, to the realm of the unspoken.[54] Silence expresses antinomial qualities within the self and in its social life while at the same time offering a means of transcending these contradictions. The notion that silence lies within antinomies, but also acts above them in allowing a passage out of the dilemmas these generate, points to a theological mystery. Ranging from the metaphysical to its social expression, to its relationship to self, silence carries a penetrating and inescapable element of ambiguity. Despite its hesitant, tentative, adjectival quality, silence possesses profoundly dangerous qualities, that are all too easy to underestimate.

In the Old Testament, silence is related to destruction, to abandonment in the darkness (Isaiah 47:5). This sense of being cast off to a hopeless oblivion is captured in Shusaku Endo's novel *Silence*. The sea is represented as having a deep, brooding darkness, an uncanny

stillness that kills in its relentless tides. In this work, it comes to signify
a silent witness to apostasy and to martyrdom in seventeenth-century
Japan. Silence embodied an absence of a response, a depth of
emptiness, a void devoid of meaning, that seemed unaffected by
torture and death. Such emptiness can lead to a sense of terror, a
feeling of abandonment in which the ultimate produces nothing.[55]
Those facing death confront a silence, one where the wager is not a
matter of idle bourgeois speculation, but one loaded with fear of
damnation or the hope of redemption. The gentle layers of silence that
settle over the choir stalls seem far away from these stark options, yet
both settings, of singing or dying, flow into the same phenomenon, the
same puzzling presence, absent, but not sufficiently removed to be
discarded. The noise and bustle of cosmopolitan life places silence on
the edge, out in the suburbs of metaphysics, where few sociologists
tread and those who do, walk warily.

In a telling essay, Dupré regards secular society as a form of
wasteland, one peculiarly barren of a sense of God, where traditional
distinctions between the sacred and profane do not seem to operate.
He concludes that 'our age has created an emptiness that for the
serious God-seeker attains a religious significance. The mysticism of
negation provides him with an ideal model'.[56] Silence in rite comes to
signify the spiritual desert of contemporary society. For believers, it
comes to represent God's particular form of response to a rational
culture that claims to be too wise to see or to hear. Advanced
industrialised societies within which liturgy has to operate have a
certain blindness. Berger has noted the day and night-side of life, and a
past where there have been 'rituals to assuage, but at the same time to
represent the terror of the margins'. The silence lodged in contemporary life is hidden in the 'day-side', where reasons for living become
obscured and the threat of death is lightly borne. Berger goes on to
suggest that 'all questions that do not correspond to this reality are
ruled to be inadmissible. The denial of metaphysics may here be
identified with the triumph of triviality'.[57] Because silence cannot
speak as its own witness, its presence can easily be deemed absent. It
evokes no terror and demands no need of something more than a
rumour of angels to give comfort. Little worry is occasioned by the
saying: 'the dead praise not the Lord, neither any that go down into
silence' (Ps. 115:17).

This deafness to silence impairs the capacity to grasp the mysterious
tacit content of rite, as it processes from the obvious into the
unobvious. The behaviour discerned in liturgical enactment operates

in a context that makes it useless for any other purpose. The actors walk before what they cannot see, and hear what they cannot say, and know what they cannot understand, and to that degree they are blind, deaf and dumb for wholly sociological purposes. To describe is to stumble into the indescribable, to impute is to deny, and all presented in the Cathedral seems above and below sociological language. Yet following Simmel, although silence is part of sociology, the discipline seems to be largely silent about its existence. As Thomas Carlyle observed

> silence is the element in which great things fashion themselves together; that at length they may emerge, full-formed and majestic, into the daylight of Life, which they are thenceforth to rule.[58]

Silence points to an element of dialogue with speech, with action and its cessation. There is an attending and anticipating quality about its manifestation. An interdependence between word and silence is suggested. As Max Picard observed 'silence can exist without speech, but speech cannot exist without silence. The word would be without depth if the background of silence were missing'.[59] Silence is an utterance from the absent that often speaks louder than words. The issue of the Word made present and the responding resonance posed by its absence has implications for the link between hermeneutics and a negative theology, which I explore in the final chapters. If sociology is to say anything about liturgy, it must speak of silence. This represents another area of theological hazard for the sociologist. George Steiner speaks of the 'miraculous outrage of human speech' regarding it as the 'core of man's mutinous relations to the gods'.[60] Speech relates to the limits of human existence, a point where the issue of transcendence emerges. Steiner expresses this well, when he suggests that

> it is decisively the fact that language does have its frontiers, that it borders on three other modes of statement – light, music, and silence – that gives proof of a transcendent presence in the fabric of the world. It is just because we can go no further, because speech so marvellously fails us, that we experience the certitude of a divine meaning surpassing and enfolding ours.[61]

In our context, speech is a metaphor for the social act, employed to trespass on a limit, and to petition to be redeemed for its presumption. There is an eschatological aspect to the interconnection between the social act and the silence with which it is received in a liturgical context. A phenomenon becomes embedded in a ritual order that speaks of a future, where speech will no longer be unnecessary, and acts of worship no more will be riddled with ambiguities and antinomies.

Silence seems more 'real' than speech, for as Picard notes 'real speech is in fact nothing but the resonance of silence'.[62] Fully understood, silence gives point to a liturgical transaction. It supplies a paradoxical and ambiguous quality that exemplifies the procedures that characterise its social basis. Without reference to it, the social purpose of this particular form of ritual performance would be misunderstood. Silence can communicate sentiments denied to speech. It also endows the social with qualities utterance finds unstatable.

Nancy Jay Crumbine argues that silence accentuates background, by allowing a glimpse or intuition of the hidden and concealed. Thus, she states 'silence is the revelation of concealment, the "saying" of mystery. It is a bearing witness to what of the world cannot be taught'.[63] Innocence, simplicity and originality are gifts silence endows language with, that enable utterance to return to its mysterious origins.[64] Silence makes present a sensibility of what is eternal and mysterious, that which pre-exists a word said, but which also transcends its utterance. Confronting silence, is to encounter a phenomenon that characterises the liminal, yet in some way communicates more about it than speech can. A certain degree of reticence is required, a holding back to listen, but also to make a wager – for the absence might produce nothing of significance. Although silence is a distinctly 'useless' phenomenon as Picard notes, its unexploitable and weak nature is also the basis of its strength. An uncompanionable silence demands speech to fill in the gap, to complete what is dangerously left unsaid. In the case of liturgy, the 'holy uselessness' of silence demands a response that makes a worshipping gesture seem natural and instinctive. Picard suggests that 'where silence is, man is observed by silence. Silence looks at man more than man looks at silence. Man does not put silence to the test; silence puts man to the test'.[65]

Earlier, we noted the way the 'vital test' of Job arose in a way that gave access to a sociological consideration about the adequacies or inadequacies of social forms and their limits in relation to God. Misuse of the social form, giving it a literal purpose, led to misguided efforts to exhaust that which was of its nature inexhaustible. A failure in the testing led to abandonment, a casting off signified in the fate of Job. The test of the social form missed the point: its truth came down from above it. In a point that complements our approach to liturgy, Picard warns that 'when the layer of silence is missing, the extraordinary easily becomes connected with the ordinary, with the routine flow of things, and man reduces the extraordinary to a mere part of the ordinary, a mere part of the mechanical routine'.[66] There is an enhancing task involved in liturgical performance, and silence exemplifies this distinctive endeavour.

This testing that comes from without, that bears on a choice over a particular sequence of actions, often makes a demand of faith, a belief in what is unseen which overrides what can be seen. This testing arises in Søren Kierkegaard's *Fear and Trembling*. The call from a hidden God to Abraham to sacrifice his only son Isaac, to make of him a burnt offering, involves a silent assent on the part of the father, one that forms a test of his fear of the Lord. In her account of the test, Crumbine notes that the darkness surrounding Isaac mirrors the silence of God. Any interpretation requires reference to the mystery of hiddenness from which the divine and human emerges.[67] In his silent assent, the total faith of Abraham emerges, the fruit of something more powerful than speech or pure reason. As David Wren observes, his inexplicable silence bears witness to the capacity of faith to transcend the absurd and to venture into a breach of reason.[68]

Silence generates the need for some act of faith, for the emptiness it unfolds can be filled with the unholy, the uncontainable and the dangerous. Evelyn Underhill, who spoke warmly of the benefits of a corporate silence, qualified its use in worship by noting that it was appropriate only to the 'spiritually mature' and that furthermore in lifting the 'mind and heart to God – it leaves too much of our human nature behind'.[69] Prayer is a means through which faith is realised and understood. Picard writes of it as 'a pouring of the word into silence'.[70] It is an act of will, a desire to contemplate, to see more than what a social world presents. The presentation of the Word re-presents a means of re-defining self before its message, a process hermeneutics throws much light on. Silence complements this form of reception. As Picard comments, 'in the human mind silence is merely knowledge of the *Deus absconditus*, the hidden God'.[71] Every rite carries a felt sense of the holy – which might not come. Even assemblies ordered to wait on the holy, such as a Quaker gathering, can end up attending on a 'dead silence' produced in 'petrified meeting'.[72] There is a peculiarly gripping quality to a silence once present that makes it immune to disruption. On some occasions a sudden noisy disruption can have little effect, such as a person dropping pound coins in the collection box during the consecration at mass.

Liturgical silence cannot be manufactured, but an expectation can be marked at particular passages in the mass. In the General Instruction on the Roman Missal, the need for silence is noted, especially during the penitential act, the pause before the Collect, after the readings and reception of communion by all.[73] This instruction reflects a significant change in Catholic practice since Vatican II. In the Tridentine rite, there were no instructions given on silence, simply because they were unnecessary. Parts of the mass, marked as secret, were said silently by the priest. The altar server gave the responses on behalf of the congregation, who silently participated in an interior assent, following in their missals the unfolding sacred drama of the mass. Silence was given an objective status that was tied into the hallowed and unchanging form of the rite. The rubrics made little allowance for the 'pacing' of the mass. The newer instructions, that recognise the role of the laity in the mass, stipulate a need to enhance a sense of active participation in the rite. To that degree, a subjective element has been inserted, one that requires consideration of the interior needs of those present. Silence becomes a collective endeavour, a phenomenon that requires a joint waiting on God, between those on the sanctuary or in the choirstalls, and those present at the rite in the nave.

The idea of a congregational silence as a form of worship appears in Otto's essay on liturgical reform, though his comments apply to a Lutheran tradition. He sought a sense of the 'real presence' of God in divine service, when the prayer of the congregation led to an act of 'lofty composure in a holy silence' where the word 'is fulfilled in a special sense and in a higher degree'.[74] In this sense, the issue of silence relates less to a moment in the rite, than to an element that is intended to characterise the form of the rite as a whole. Some liturgies have a quality of 'hierophany', where the sacred shows itself to those present. It achieves a concentrated form in the issue of silence.[75] The order of the rite becomes gathered into a petition to be acted on from outside the form.

I wish to follow Bernard Dauenhauer in linking the issue of silence to an activating performance that 'paces' the unfolding of a holy message. There is an intersubjective collaboration involved in the task of maintaining an opening to the holy, a yielding that binds and joins in an awesome manner to a phenomenon that surpasses the actor's limits in active performance.[76] For this reason, all intervals and gaps in the 'flow' of the rite have to be rendered to account. Attention to the issue of silence gives a phenomenal dimension to the earlier discussion of 'liturgical mistakes'. If gaps arise, that are a function of carelessness or uncertainty, they subtract from the mechanism's task of regulating access to the absent, a felt sense of silence. An embarrassed silence has a contagious effect, and generates an uncertainty before a phenomenon. It is an uncomfortable response that becomes confused with the certainty that ought to characterise an authentic visitation of the Holy. There are enough ambiguities in the rite, without unproductive ones entering to confuse believers and non-believers alike.

Choral Evensong uses polyphonic music, where cadences and intervals are marked in the scores. These supply a discipline to the 'pacing' which binds all present into a sense of communion. These solemn surpliced songsters who deck the choirstalls play in attendance at a holy game. They embody an appearance of holiness that resonates with a holy sounding in the music they sing. In fleeting moments, a 'thick' sense of silence becomes attached to the condensed symbols and actions that characterise this liturgical event. Through habituated re-enactment of the rite, the actors can learn to listen, to be subtle, and to hear resonances of the holy becoming attached to their collective endeavours. Understanding this tacit phenomenon that hovers over a rite requires a particular sociological approach, one that will enhance what is already understood, and not discard what is evidently grasped by the actors involved in the production of this autonomous form of rite.

10 Action, Symbol, Text: Hermeneutics and Sociology

> Every one that is of the truth heareth my voice.
> Pilate saith unto him, What is truth?
>
> (John 18:37–38)

The fragments of rite, that formed the basis of the preceding analysis, present a small part of a mosaic whose reading represents an awkward transaction for the sociological gaze to decipher and to understand. Throughout the study, liturgy has been presented as a problem for sociologists, rather than for liturgists and theologians who conventionally deal with its interpretation. In more innocent times, a positivist glance at liturgical activities preserved the sociologist at a methodological distance, in a state of scientific anonymity, marking the objective contours of the surface of the rite. But the new fashion for engagement, moral commitment and involvement in the reflexive transactions of the actor, and the subjective meanings he produces in everyday life, have established a whole new agenda for sociological inquiry. Critical engagement gives an authenticity to the struggle to yield deeper insights.

There is, however, a lop-sided aspect to this new sociological demand to engage with life in all its hues. Much is known about the actor, but not so much is known about the sociologist who struggles to share the burden of his understandings. Sociologists are a reticent breed, spare on their biographies, private in their angsts, who roll out reproductions of cultural little worlds, in monographs that take on a life of their own, on the conference circuit, and in articles and books. Little is known about why they select particular areas to study. The printed word disguises a reason to struggle that seems best left unsaid. The self of the sociologist lies at a distance, masked and mute, well removed from any accountabliity for the questions targeted so critically at particular cultural and ideological constituencies. Placing accounts of liturgical life into debates on post-modernism and culture might seem an odd biographical throw, yet one no less odd when its neglect is considered. If liturgy is given a sociological place, it does raise some odd implications that have a bearing on the contemporary debate on culture and post-modernism. It gives sociological questions an unexpected cast, as they try to reflect that which has never been considered before as a topic of inquiry.

The innocent anthropologist studying exotic practices of non-Western societies, can puzzle happily over their odd rites. Somehow, different issues arise should he venture across the quad to study an equally odd ritual transaction: the chapel rites of an Oxford College, choral Evensong at sunset. Anthropological images of life suggest travel in another direction. Yet, with the issues that have arisen in debates on rationality and relativism, a journey home at some point seems unexpectedly likely to happen.

Studies of magical practices in primitive societies, that breach conventional Western scientific wisdom, have excited much philosophical interest. These ritual procedures beg a number of philosophical questions about translations between contexts of question and answer, that have unsettled many. Deferring to the internal rules of the context of enactment of an odd magical or healing practice enhances the authenticity of the account, by awarding victory to the actor's presuppositions, but at a price of admitting a relativism into the study. To do otherwise, and to defend a Western criterion of scientific understanding, is to defend a rationality that denies the actor's account and translates the ritual to an alien context. It is to denude the ritual of the puzzle that generated the initial anthropological interest.

The issue of relativism, that legitimises the autonomy of a context of enactment, points to conventions governing modes of artistic understanding in Western culture. The integrity of the style of the performance is affirmed in canons of aesthetic taste. For instance, an opera might seem a fussy, foppish way of presenting a play, whose dramatic quality might be obscured in musical elaboration of what is best left said. But to judge an opera such as *Macbeth* by the standards of the play would be considered to be ill-educated and misguided. Cultural and aesthetic judgement grants a common-sense status to ceremonies, accepting their distinctive style of representation in a way that might perplex philosophers.

Debate on relativism has been conducted on rather clean lines up to recently. Bizarre practices can be studied with philosophical impunity. The odd medical or oracular practices of distant tribes usually give rise to little metaphysical injury. Rather more complex issues arise when the question of bizarre practices is raised *within* the cultural context of inquiry of the anthropologist or the philosopher.

Christian rituals make a complete claim on the truth in a way that transcends the narrow issue of sociological method, the relativism it might encounter in studying their practice. Whereas a study of tribal ritual practices might lead to philosophical issues that perplex, Christian rites embody them, and the actors have varying degrees of awareness of this point. Liturgical enactments, however puzzling and perplexing, cannot be studied in isolation, much in the manner of a tribe, with its own peculiar belief system. Christian rites seen as particular events are instances in a complex belief system that can draw the sociologist away from playing games with the weak and unsophisticated, into deeper philosophical and theological waters that could drown the discipline. It is the implications the study of liturgy can be drawn into that unsettle any sociologist trying to understand its performative basis. Any effort to contain and to control these is likely to be an artificial exercise that can only achieve a partial success.

There is an ironic cast to sociology caught in post-modernist dilemmas struggling to understand a form of ritual that is so profoundly pre-modern. At this stage, one might be tempted to abandon the struggle and to argue that liturgy should *not* be subject to sociological study as the risks of metaphysical injury for the discipline are too high. The purpose of the last part of the study is to explore a way out for sociology through hermeneutics, so that its integrity and that of its object of inquiry can be preserved. Another and longer book would be required to cover adequately the theological turn of recent debate on post-modernism, and the degree to which contemporary discussions on symbols are greatly shaping cultural understandings in a way that has a beneficial effect on the study of liturgy as a religious ritual. A decade ago, this study of liturgy would have stood in glorious sociological and philosophical isolation. Debates on relativism, hermeneutics and post-modernism suggest that the cultural ground of understanding has greatly changed, and that the study of liturgy can be grounded centrally in sociology, where it always should have belonged. It should be said that theologians cannot sit back and gaze at the holy antics of the *flâneur*, seeing relativism as the sin of too much philosophical speculation. Berger's point still stands, that sociology is the specifically contemporary challenge to theology, the 'fiery brook' it has to pass.[1] Of course, the trouble with many liberal theologians is that they are too damp to notice the heat.

To use hermeneutics to understand the social basis of a Christian ritual is less of a distortion of the writings of Gadamer and Ricoeur than one might think. Gadamer devotes a considerable amount of attention to the issue of understanding the Word in *Truth and Method*. This incarnational stress is complemented in an essay on aesthetics and religious experience that indicates a sympathy for Christian rites in a post-Enlightenment era.[2] Ricoeur has declared himself to be a Christian and there are many theological aspects to his approach to hermeneutics, especially in the area of symbols.[3]

In this chapter, I wish to explore further the way debates on translation of incommensurable meanings have had a profound effect on sociological theory. Difficulties over translation and arbitration of meanings within debates on rationality and relativism have led to efforts to link hermeneutics to sociology, to provide a means of deciphering social transactions, whose interpretation can give rise to understandings and misunderstandings. In the final section of the chapter, we try to enlarge on Ricoeur's notion of text as action and apply this to the idea of liturgical form as an icon, a mirror of what can only be discerned unclearly. If it is seen too clearly, it has been misunderstood. This chapter draws on a point made in the introduction, that liturgies, combining text, symbol and action in performance, offer an unusually valuable ground to link hermeneutics to sociology. In the final chapter, the distinctive role of hermeneutics in assessing wagers, or forms of play in games, draws sociology into understandings that can be sent spinning in a theological direction that marks the end of the book.

HERMENEUTICS AND SOCIOLOGY: HORIZONS OF INTEREST

Hatchjaw remarks (unconfirmed, however, by Bassett) that throughout the whole ten years that went to the writing of *The Country Album* de Selby was obsessed with mirrors and had resource to them so frequently that he claimed to have two left hands and to be living in a world arbitrarily bounded by a wooden frame.
(Flann O'Brien, *The Third Policeman*)

The reasons why sociological debate has become entrapped in the question of relativism are complex. The issue has emerged from the study of belief systems in primitive societies and the status of their non-rational practices in Western rational thought. The crisis the rationality debate has generated for sociology has aroused much philosophical speculation. It has also contributed to a crisis within philosophy itself about the purpose of its reflections in modern thought. A disbelief in objective forms of scientific knowing that effects a dehumanisation has led to the pursuit of a philosophy that seeks to engage the spirit and to open the mind to dialogue. In an effort to link hermeneutics to the need to maintain conversation, and to supply a means of coping rather than explaining, Richard Rorty places the issue of relativism in the context of what he terms an edifying philosophy. He regards this as consisting of the

> 'poetic' activity of thinking up such new aims, new words, or new disciplines, followed by, so to speak, the inverse of hermeneutics: the attempt to reinterpret our familiar surroundings in the unfamiliar terms of our new inventions.[4]

In these terms, edification refers to an opening to dialogue in a process of creative development. It denotes an uncertainty where claims to absolute truth have collapsed. As Georgia Warnke indicates, 'to be edified is to be aware that our views do not derive from "the" truth or "the" moral law, they rather represent simply the best way of coping that *we* can thus far imagine'.[5] Rorty is criticising a misconceived notion of a scientific mirror as reflecting the essences of nature and social reality. A softer more hermeneutic orientation is required to refract social reality more subtly. His concern is with opening out a spirit of engagement, a conversational dialogue that seeks new forms of self-understanding. This represents a movement away from an exactitude that kills the 'spirit' and the imagination. We need not follow the philosophical means through which he arrives at a hermeneutic consideration that seeks to maintain a dialogue that humanises in a quest for solidarity in self-understanding.[6] The admission of such a consideration within philosophical debate has significant sociological implications for the way hermeneutics can approach the understanding of a ritual transaction such as liturgy. This new turn in methodological debate about the nature of the cultural sciences marks a return to an older insight of Wilhelm Dilthey which Michael Ermarth notes as suggesting that 'the tacit "sense of life" embodied in everyday understanding is the beginning but not the end for the methical understanding of the human sciences'.[7]

The reasons for this return to a hermeneutic dimension to socio-logical speculation form part of a complex cultural movement in the history of the discipline. One can only speculate briefly about the nature of the change in theoretical orientation, which is still very much in progress. This increased use of hermeneutics within sociology belongs to three distinct constituencies that have a degree of overlap. The first constituency relates to difficulties which have arisen over subjective understandings that emerge in common sense in modern society. The second emerges in efforts to understand primitive societies, whose non-rational belief systems operate with assumptions that violate Western notions of rational common sense. The third constituency relates to the problems generated by incommensurate meanings.

Phenomenology provided a philosophical backcloth for a movement of considerable importance in sociology in the sixties, which we have mentioned earlier. Ethnomethodology expressed a need to engage sympathetically with the 'real world' of common sense, and to characterise the indices or stocks of knowledge used by actors to negotiate a passage of survival through everyday life. Harold Garfinkel and Aaron Cicourel are associated with this school, which has had a significant impact on criminology and on forms of passing in a variety of social settings, whose tacit elements can be tested. Goffman hovers on the fringe of this school, but is too idiosyncratic to be part of it. There is a subjective cast to this sociological form of reporting, that might seem a new term for old practices of *verstehen* and the use of a traditional method – observer participation.[8] As a critique of positiv-ism, ethnomethodology has emphasised the process through which a definition of a situation is secured. An excellent example of this approach is a study of the explicit and implicit rules governing a verdict of suicide at a coroner's court.[9] The stress of ethnomethodolo-gists on the inter-subjective nature of social life draws out the accounting practices used to organise and to construct events that order everyday life.[10] This concern with tracing the accounting procedures through which social arrangements are monitored and rendered to account by the actors involved, links ethnomethodology to the writings of Evans Pritchard, whose study of the Azande has had such a profound effect on philosophy of social science.[11]

Ethnomethodology tries to operate as a pure form of reflection of everyday life. Every effort is made to minimise analytical interventions that might distort an understanding of the actor's own mode of self-accounting for his social actions. Josef Bleicher, who has tried to link

ethnomethodology to hermeneutics, conceives the task of the sociologist as a *primus inter pares*, a Socratic 'midwife' rather than an
absolute authority or expert.[12] Hermeneutics is concerned with understanding in the distinctive circumstances of a text whose hidden
message needs to be deciphered. Empirical accounts of actions are
limited to what is disclosed, what can be seen and what can be
observed; they neglect those elements which lie hidden, but which
have an important effect on what is to be understood. Ethnomethodology seeks to redress this situation. As Zygmunt Bauman notes, 'the
realization that all meaning and understanding is essentially "inside"'
has linked ethnomethodology to hermeneutics.[13]

Ethnomethodology came to sociology through phenomenology, and
the need to bracket a typical form of everyday behaviour to grasp its
essence. A reticence is imposed on sociology to allow a fuller basis of
understanding to be revealed about what the actor intends. This self-
limiting to maximise understanding has crucial implications for linking
hermeneutics to a sociological effort to understand the social basis of
rite. In this constituency, there is a sociological effort to connect to a
world deemed more complex than positivism can admit to understanding. Acceptance of what is hidden and is provisional in terms of
knowing generates a theoretical climate in sociology that enhances the
possibility of it understanding liturgical performance.

Magical practices and belief systems have always had an alien
quality that has aroused a sociological curiosity. Anthropological
tradition tended to treat these as primitive practices, as illusions that
could be explained in scientific terms, where the gifts of the Enlightenment could be used to convert those caught in non-rational forms of
thought and place them on the path of progress.[14] For nineteenth
century writers, the issue of primitive practices of magic and religion
was largely one of classification. Later anthropological efforts, in the
mid-twentieth century, have tried to understand religion in terms of
myth, structure and function. A more significant shift in approaches to
the beliefs and practices of primitive societies, was to see them as
handling a mode of thought that was different from, but by no means
unequal to that operating in Western society. This important change in
the early seventies, established a notion of equivalence between
Western and non-Western belief systems. It also led to an uncertainty
as to what terms to use to connect these contrasting belief systems. The
incapacity of scientific reasoning to verify or to falsify these practices
of primitive society pointed to a scientific limit to understanding, one
that evolved into a major concern with the implications of relativism.[15]

The bizarre nature of some of these practices, such as witchcraft, or healing rites, related to principles of belief at odds with those in the West. Notions of spells, and the idea of a metaphysical contagion involved in the use of witchcraft, pointed to properties of meaning that had to be understood rather than explained in some causal rational account. A language of symbols gave a fuller account than could be provided by the medical model.[16]

In Chapter 6, we examined the way rules and mistakes have an internal relationship that contextualises any account of ritual. Meaning and intended purpose delimit any sociological account, and this limitation not only constrains what can be understood but also what can be asked without avoidable misunderstandings arising. In making this point, one has a heavy debt to Peter Winch's *The Idea of a Social Science*, which marked a breakthrough of critical importance for developing the links between sociology and philosophy.[17]

The alien and inexplicable nature of the practices of some primitive societies exposed problems of translation between rational assumptions and non-rational criteria for actions. The need for some transcending bridgehead between the two belief systems became apparent. The debate on rationality had commenced with the question of the limits of what could be explained and has evolved into an agnosticism about what can be understood. An understanding has emerged amongst those with a relativist position, that bizarre behaviour was often misunderstood through category mistakes. Sociological failures stemmed from the concepts used to understand these odd practices. Problems of understanding lay with the sociologist rather than with the actor whose actions were deemed to be 'puzzling'.[18] The issue of relativism suggested that categories could distort and explain away that which was to be understood. The 'strong programme' of relativism in the study of beliefs has been made convincingly by Barry Barnes and David Bloor. The idea that there is some rational bridgehead that supplies a privileged non-contextual basis can be regarded as an act of scientific faith.

Barnes and Bloor made a significant advance in the debate on relativism. They argued that beliefs have an equivalence in terms of the causes of their local credibility. Specifying their social basis draws on the strengths of sociology of knowledge. Concern is with their social construction rather than whether they are true or false. The reward for abandoning an untenable absolute rationality is access to a context in which the belief is deemed possible by those who enact its basis. Recognition of an epistemological limit facilitates a distinctive sociological contribution to the shaping of knowledge – uncovering the indispensable social means to express its manifestation and its discernment.[19] Belief has to be grounded in a context of disclosure and, by examining the social conditions that make it credible, sociology enhances an understanding of what is already understood by the subject matter, the actor enacting. It is his relationship to the social circumstances of its manifestation that count, not an imputed notion of what he ought to think that might misconceive his intended purpose. This capacity to discern and to understand what is already known exasperates the relativism nascent within sociology and increases its dependency on the actor's account. Stress is now placed on the degree to which social actions are skilled accomplishments of the actor, which sociology has to understand. Many of these points are implicit in what has been analysed before in this study of liturgical praxis.

The debate on rationality has followed some odd paths, some of which Joanna Overing has summarised. She argues that in the early seventies, a conviction existed that the West was a highly rational place, while 'more "traditional" people lived a more poetic, mystical, less rational and more restricted world of thought'. The crisis of faith in science had not yet left its mark. Debate was focused on the alien practices of distant cultures and a link between the two had not been established. As anthropology confronts these philosophical issues from within its own interests of knowledge situated in Western thought, Overing suggests that the unexamined role of paradox and faith in social thought and practice will emerge as a crucial issue.[20] This point has formed a central theme of our study. Our concern has been to pursue an issue she raises regarding the status of incommensurable world views as they operate *within* a belief system, where equivocal meanings have to be used to express its domain assumptions.

In debates on rationality, there is often an assumption that the basis of the practices under study are clear cut and are comprehensible to the actor. The person who does not understand is assumed to be the Western scientific observer. The value of Overing's work is to suggest that some practices are *not* well understood by the actor, who finds a negotiation of their meaning problematic. The concern is now with how the actor minimises misunderstandings. This admits a distinctive hermeneutic consideration, one that echoes some of the dilemmas we have uncovered in efforts to understand the antinomies affecting liturgical reproduction.

In her collection, the complex and often bizarre practices and beliefs of primitive societies seem to suggest a natural abode for questions of relativity and issues of incommensurability. But as we have suggested earlier, rational and non-rational elements are also bound into Western liturgical practices and religious beliefs. These Christian rites operate with apparent 'success' for their followers and present non-rational elements for sceptical scrutiny in a society claimed to be dominated by rational considerations. For many, Christian rites can be equally bizarre and alienating to ritual practices found in non-Western societies.

Raymond Firth suggested that what is now sought as a result of the rationality debate, is the pursuit of intelligibility. This involves 'the imputation of a relationship between authors of mental process, in its behavioural manifestations'.[21] This notion of intelligibility puts rationality in its place. It suggests that making sense of a practice is what is to count in sociological efforts to understand. The notion of making sense points to a quality of persuasion in a sociological account, a sympathy for what the actor is trying to understand, that is non-judgemental. In our context, it refers to an acceptance of the dilemmas of the actor, as he operates to make sense of these in social practice. Even if one cannot fully make sense of what he is striving to understand, one can at least avoid making a category mistake in stipulating what he should comprehend.

In an innovative essay on 'witchcraft as insanity', Paul Hirst and Penny Woolley point to the problem of a category mistake, one that arises over a failure to accept the internal logic of a theological mind operating in the Renaissance period. Problems of categorisation of the phenomenon of witchcraft abound: whether it is to be understood in Freudian terms, or if it is to be regarded as a form of collective hysteria. There is an interconnection between thought and action, and Hirst and Woolley express it well, when they suggest that:

> conduct and organization cannot be separated from categories of morality and metaphysics, equally those categories are not merely matters of personal choice or intellectual conviction – they are part of social relations.[22]

In a creative attempt to link Mannheim's sociology of knowledge to Gadamer's hermeneutics, Susan Hekman tries to relate thought to the purpose of existence and to give this an analytical focus. Implicit in her analysis is an assumption, that Gadamer's hermeneutics can be given a concrete form of application in a manner of sociological expression that achieves an enhanced understanding, without resource to a method that embodies the prejudices of the Enlightenment.[23] There is a prescriptive aspect to her effort to link hermeneutics to sociology, yet her analysis lacks a focus on the treatment of a definite object of sociological inquiry.

There is a lot of philosophical baggage attached to hermeneutics that a sociologist might seem to be required to address, but which lies beyond the strict sphere of his competence. Yet these philosophical elements have had a profound effect on sociological theory. Ordinary language philosophy, of Austin and Wittgenstein, phenomenology, and some aspects of the Frankfurt School have made sociology more aware of the possibilities opened up by hermeneutics. It has been argued that there is a conservative bias in Gadamer's approach to hermeneutics, where tradition is affirmed in a way that seems to deny the possibility of emancipation such as advanced in Critical Theory.[24] Such criticisms are beside the point in this study. Issues of emancipation that stem from spiritual practices are rather different from those which emerge as gifts of the Enlightenment. Liturgical forms derive their legitimacy from a tradition they are established to conserve and to represent in ritual engagements with the holy. Hermeneutics facilitates an understanding of this social process.

Richard Bernstein has provided the best account to date of how issues of relativism and incommensurability are linked in a way that connects hermeneutics to praxis.[25] His effort to link Gadamer's approach to hermeneutics to contemporary sociological debate complements the tasks of John Thompson, in dealing with the writings of Paul Ricoeur.[26] It is unfortunate that both writers provide secularised accounts that diminish the theological resonances in both Gadamer and Ricoeur. This has the effect of masking religious aspects of hermeneutics and of making its application to an understanding of liturgy more artificial and unexpected than it ought to be.

Bernstein is concerned with the ontological implications of moving beyond objectivism and relativism to find a basis for dialogue and communication that lies at the root of collective existence. In relativism, he sees the dangers of an easy acceptance of a subjectivity that could descend into a nihilism, that precludes the possibility of dialogue and progress to understanding. A post-empiricism has led to the recovery of a hermeneutic dimension in science, and a renewed interest in issues of understanding and interpretation. Bernstein argues that theory choice in science is based less on determinate rules of logic, than on implicit subjective forms of judgement, such as Thomas Kuhn suggests in his account of paradigm shifts, which rest on social forms of persuasion and conversion.[27] Faith seems to effect movement between scientific mountains of certainty. There is a tacit, subjective element in the social and natural sciences that suggests a hermeneutic dimension to their efforts to understand especially when dealing with puzzles, with elements that contain seeds of indeterminacy and uncertainty, that do not 'fit' a consensus as to how to proceed.

At this point, we need to consider the issue of incommensurability, a term that is central to our interpretation of liturgical management. The term refers to disjunctions, incompatibilities, or elements that will not fit together, as they belong to belief systems that are deemed to be asymmetrical. Failure to generate a fit leads to a puzzle and perhaps the need to change scientific paradigms. Implicit in our analysis, is the notion that issues of incommensurability have a potential application to *all* aspects of rite, its form, the symbols used and the actions performed. Antinomial elements of rite have a quality of incommensurability. As we have suggested throughout the study, there is an element of rescued truth involved in liturgical operations. Actors in the rite face the risk of corrupted messages escaping unintentionally. This need to be guarded in treating incommensurable aspects of rite requires a degree of agency in handling its performance. It is this notion of agency that forms a focus for sociological understandings of the re-presentation of the holy.

The concept of incommensurability has been subject to dispute. The term has been used much by Kuhn and Paul Feyerabend. Bernstein argues that its rationale emerges in efforts to clarify native and rival scientific paradigms. Failure to make compatible disparate elements bears on an issue of anthropological method, one that is at the centre of the debate on relativism and rationality. Bernstein suggests that the truth conditions disclosed by incommensurability represent an opening, one that is amplified when the beliefs and categories of the inquirer are not imposed on the transactions of the subject-matter. It is the restraint of the observer that admits disclosure. To that degree his argument rests on a recognition of limits, but also an acceptance of wider, more indeterminate elements being disclosed for philosophical scrutiny.[28] Some of these points arose earlier in my discussion of the interpretation of ambiguities, where the limits of rational explanation were also considered.

By linking the issue of incommensurability to hermeneutics, Bernstein provides a fruitful means of connecting the arguments of ordinary language philosophy to the understanding of autonomous but alien social practices. In his use of Clifford Geertz, Bernstein draws out the degree to which a hermeneutic circle, of a dialectic between part and whole, already operates in anthropology. Geertz and Winch do not use the term incommensurate, and as Bernstein admits, the latter explicitly denies that he is a relativist.[29] Winch's concern, as Bernstein persuasively argues, is with the categories governing a comparison between alien beliefs and the principles of understanding of Western culture. Bernstein's interest lies in finding the most fruitful categories to be employed to read a belief in its fullness of meanings.[30] This has formed a central task in this sociological study of liturgy. There are hermeneutic elements involved in this approach of trying to be proximate to that which could be considered alien, but which on closer inspection might be understandable.

The link between the sacred and the secular carries qualities of incommensurability. The religious rituals of Christianity have always displayed signs of contradictions to the surrounding cultural land-scape. The improbable mysteries they display, the ambiguous and indeterminate qualities of their styles of enactment, all suggest they do not fit easily into the modern mind operating in advanced industria-lised societies. This problem of incompatibility has been at the heart of efforts of liberal theologians to make religion consonant with the assumptions of contemporary culture.

Liturgical enactments are instances in a belief system. They present an ambiguous front, of significance or insignificance, to an outsider shopping around, perhaps curious or not, at what he sees in their obvious facets. The outsider can elect to explore further, to look below the social surface, or he can walk away. He can decide to engage with the message the liturgy presents or he can disengage from it. This quality of musing over an odd and alien ritual, wondering whether to invest a belief in its enactment, bears a similarity to browsing in a bookshop, and deciding whether to purchase a title or not. Many covers are presented, and the phrase, not to judge a book by its cover, will be obvious to the discerning browser. Some titles will bear further exploration, while others can be easily discarded.

The objective, formalised cast of a liturgy gives it a similarity to a book, a text presented for inspection. A reading below the surface is called for, and as every text has its grammar, so too does every ritual have its own terms for discerning inspection. Hermeneutics draws attention to the interpretative dialogue that occurs in reading a ritual like a text.

HOLY UNDERSTANDINGS: HERMENEUTICS AND THE DISCOVERY OF THE SACRED

And Phillip ran thither to him, and heard him read
the prophet Esaias and said, Understandest thou what
thou readest?
And he said, How can I, except some man should guide me?

(Acts 8: 30–31)

One might think that the climate of agnosticism that enjoins sociology to study *any* belief system sympathetically would have positive benefits for Catholicism. This has not yet been the case. Its existence as a religion is treated with studied indifference, if not suspicion. E. E. Evans-Pritchard's point still prevails that many anthropologists regard religion as absurd, and belief as an illusion. He suggested that there was an atheistic or agnostic bias in the anthropological study of religion. Furthermore he noted that anthropologists 'found in primitive religions a weapon which could, they thought, be used with deadly effect against Christianity'. More significantly for our purposes, he went on to comment on the oddity of pioneering anthropologists, who had established themselves as authorities on primitive religion, but who had only 'a superficial understanding of the historical religions and of what the ordinary worshipper in them believes' a point that applies with particular force to Christian liturgies.[31] As I suggested earlier, there is a long sociological history of treating religion as a form of error.

Such a bias has been expressed by Ricoeur in terms of a hermeneutic of suspicion. In his pursuit of a critique of critique (that resembles Berger's efforts to relativise the relativisers) Ricoeur establishes a hermeneutics of affirmation or appropriation. This involves overcoming a sense of alienation and taking what is presented in the text or action as one's own. The self is enlarged by apprehending those worlds of meaning which genuine interpretation achieves.[32] There is a dilemma in understanding that faces the sociologist.

The more the sociologist believes and is sympathetic to what he examines, the more it will be held against him that his account of an action is subjective, private, and, in some ill-defined way, is unavailable to scientific scrutiny. But it could be argued that the more the sociologist is estranged from the belief a social phenomenon under study embodies, and the more suspicious he is of its basis, the more he is likely to misunderstand and fail to grasp its point from the perspective of the subjective intentions of the actors he examines. His scepticism makes him an outsider on the transaction and precludes him from entering fully into its meaningful basis.

In theology and biblical studies, hermeneutics has become associated with a liberal Protestant interpretation that has stressed a reductionist, demythologising approach to belief. In its most radical form it has affirmed a distance between the cultural context of the construction of the New Testament and the contemporary scientific thought that receives it. Suspicion rather than affirmation seem the hallmarks of this approach. In many respects, this is a theological version of the rationality debate within sociology. Writers such as Rudolf Bultmann, and later liberal Anglicans, have tried to release biblical truths from a mythology of angels, demons, and heavenly images, to provide an existential basis of choice more suited to the sophisticated demands of the age.[33] Berger has supplied a stringent sociological critique of these movements within contemporary theology.[34] Hermeneutics has become lodged in theological issues of text, in a way that has disguised its liturgical and sacramental possibilities. Because Protestants tend to have a lurking suspicion about ritual, and an ill-disguised view that this represents a Catholic prejudice, little attention has been given to the obvious issue of how hermeneutics can be applied to understanding liturgy.

Hermeneutics is concerned with problems of understanding that arise over the interpretation of a text. It stresses the process of reconciliation between author and reader that is involved in deciphering and translating the meaning of a text so that it reflects the intentions of both parties. The conditions of creation of a text embody the sentiments of an author which are inscribed in an objective text. The reader comes to the discernment of these recessed meanings in the text from a differing set of presuppositions. It would be unusual for a text to be read by a reader with the author present. Since he is usually absent, misapprehensions and misunderstandings arise for the reader. These cannot be resolved or negotiated directly, so that meanings have to be inferred. From his own circumstances, the reader reconstructs what he conceives to be the message of the text. His reading is a form of journeying into its hidden passages of meaning and rendering them explicit for his own purposes. A successful reading involves converting doubt into trust that the message of the book bears an investment of the self. Hermeneutics stresses the process of opening out of the self to the fullest meanings of the text, from an initial inquiry, into an acceptance of the potential for a fullness of understanding a reading offers.

Implicit in a hermeneutic approach to understanding is the notion of dialogue, and an availability to possibilities of interpretation which the text might seem to veil. The text conceals a message which an engaged reading allows to be revealed. Hermeneutic understanding stresses a notion of enlargement before the message of the text and to that degree there is a concern with future possibilities of meaning. It reflects a movement from the particular to the general; the re-shaping and enlargement of initial queries as they are redefined by entry into a dialogue of understanding; and a growth of a relationship between the absent author and the reader present before the text. This can be described in terms of a hermeneutic circle. Heremeneutics involves a wresting of understanding from an estranging text or action, and standing before it to allow a fullness of understanding to emerge and to develop.

In his approach to understanding a text, Ricoeur stresses the dialectic nature of appropriation and distanciation involved in its interpretation. The term appropriation refers to an interpretative task of making one's own what was hitherto alien. It is a surmounting of a cultural distance, to enclose a message and to make it part of the interpreter's capacity to understand more fully. Appropriation refers to an understanding that makes proximate that which existed at a remove or a distance in a way that releases and amplifies a message. This dialectic between appropriation and distanciation forms the corner-stone of hermeneutics for Ricoeur, who uses it to refer to the unfolding of a revelatory power that lies in a text, one that moves beyond the limits of the existential situation of the author. This capacity to transform and to enlarge is linked to Gadamer's discussion of play, and metamorphosis, a point developed in the next chapter.[35] In hermeneutics, there is an element of volition before the message, that involves a selective affinity with its basis to realise as much understanding as it can bear. The necessary tension between appropriation and distanciation facilitates an existential force. This dialectic has crucial implications for understanding the social basis of liturgy.

It is not difficult to feel that a liturgical performance has an alienating dimension, one that generates suspicion that the act is in some way deceiving and void of meaning. Nor is it difficult to argue that it might elicit a sympathetic response, so that the observer loosens his inhibitions, and brackets his suspicions. The act of reading more into the ritual action facilitates a task of appropriation, that allows the meanings so presented to resonate in a way that enlarges his self-understanding. Appropriation allows the interpreter to overcome an initially alienating distance, and possibly to accept the 'remedy' the rite offers. It facilitates the intended basis of the ritual, to present and to allow an indeterminate message to be received, to be shared and to be understood. Distanciation enables the enlargement of what is being presented in the text, or the ritual act; appropriation makes possible the grasping of its intended basis. Thus Ricoeur argues

> interpretation is completed as appropriation when reading yields something like an event, an event of discourse, which is an event in the present moment. As appropriation, interpretation becomes an event.[36]

Ricoeur's approach to hermeneutic understanding stresses the double nature of symbols, whose ambiguity and surplus of meaning require deciphering. His emphasis on appropriation as the aim of all hermeneutics has important implications for understanding the enlargement of religious sensibilities, such as those produced in the passage of liturgical performance.[37] There is a quality of mutual implication between the subject and object that enhances the possibility of a truth being found. Ricoeur manages to transform a hermeneutics of suspicion into one of affirmation, one that involves a letting go to enable what is concealed to be revealed. This stress on the 'opening out' nature of understanding, draws attention to the theological nature of what is to be understood. Something more than a perpetuation of conversation is suggested in his approach to hermeneutic understanding.

Symbols reflect the first stage of his interest in hermeneutics.[38] Understanding symbols is linked to the realisation of the sacred. There are very definite theological overtones in Ricoeur's use of hermeneutics. His discussion of evil, the myth of Adam, and the redemptive nature of the resurrection give Ricoeur's interest in hermeneutics an unapologetic Christian interest. He suggests that hermeneutic understanding reveals a definite eschatological consideration.[39]

It is perhaps true to say that Gadamer's *Truth and Method* has had a greater impact on sociological attitudes to hermeneutics than Ricoeur's writings, highly significant as they are. In a letter to Bernstein, Gadamer denied that he was a sociologist, but showed a sympathetic interest in sociological efforts to understand how hermeneutics could be used in its practice.[40] Hermeneutics forms part of a wider interest in aesthetics, epistemology and self-understanding. Poetic imagination was important to Gadamer. It is not difficult to find religious overtones in his work and resonances of theology that are seldom acknowledged by most sociologists. In a reflection on philosophical hermeneutics, he noted that he had become increasingly concerned with its application to 'different forms of religious speech, such as proclaiming, praying, preaching, blessing'.[41] Some of these elements relating to aesthetics and play will be pursued later.

Gadamer's interest in understanding develops from a notion of hermeneutics as facilitating dialogue, and as offering a basis for mediation between contrasting positions. A reaction against scientism and a tyranny of method that would foreclose communication lies behind his interest in hermeneutics, which is geared to sustain openings to understandings mutually achieved between author and interpreter. There is a provisional cast in his work that complements the uncertainty relativism has induced into sociology. In Gadamer, there is a stress on the future nature of understanding and this movement forward has been expressed in terms of a 'fusion of horizons'. Hermeneutics offers a means of turning a methodological liability into an interpretative asset, one that is open to new ideas and understandings. His interest in tradition relates to an awareness of philosophy of history. This has a wider significance in hermeneutics, of binding the interpreter into what Bernstein terms a 'belongingness', an affinity that makes the historian part of a past he strives to interpret.[42]

The situational nature of understanding has led Gadamer to stress the need for pre-judgement or prejudices, and these constrain the nature of the dialogue. Rehabilitation of prejudice has led to a famous comment of his that the Enlightenment bias against prejudice was one itself. There is a certain opacity in his complex and difficult *Truth and Method*, a work geared to study understanding which has led to numerous misunderstandings. The implications of this work have not fully percolated into sociological theory.

His concern with tradition being bound into the task of under-standing has led to criticisms. As indicated above, it has been argued that he fails to take into account forms of authority and domination. Critical theorists, such as Jurgen Habermas, argue that understanding involves dealing with systematically distorted communications. These ideological expressions need to be confronted through forms of rational enlightenment, such as psychoanalysis offers. Only this can emancipate and sustain the opening, the unfreeing, that a humanist dialogue seeks.[43] But, following Gadamer, it could be argued that psychoanalysis is a form of prejudice itself, whose claims to absolute truth are situated and context bound in a way that sustains Gadamer's justification of hermeneutics. Anyhow, psychoanalysis has its own prejudices about the need to keep aspects of its tradition hidden.[44]

Hermeneutics has its own tradition of handling resonances of meaning, of using inference to understand, and of reading between the lines. Gadamer suggests that this interest in tacit meanings, a concern of Friedrich Schleiermacher, reflects a hermeneutic tradition of deciphering elements which appear alien and unintelligible.[45] There is a quality of negotiation in hermeneutics, a wish to share a common understanding, that makes it a tradition well suited to handling the antinomies, ambiguities and tacit meanings embedded in liturgical performance. The idea of a total form of knowing is unpersuasive to Gadamer, for as Warnke notes, such absolute claims for him 'come straight out of a medieval theory of intelligence represented by the angel "who has the advantage of seeing God in his essence"'.[46] Accepting that total efforts to resolve indeterminate and indefinite qualities of knowing are a prejudice, a bias towards rationality, the question now emerges of how to cope with these when they are endemic in a form of ritual practice, where they pose inescapable dilemmas to actors who might seek to look closely at the social basis of their performance. This returns us to the inductive cast of this account of liturgical praxis so far, the emergent properties of performance, that represent hazards whose dilemmas admit a degree of sociological understanding. All the time, we have stressed the functional properties of ambiguities, and the need to avoid using any precluding rationalising account that would foreclose meanings. Hermeneutics has the advantage of being partly embedded in sociology, but in a way that draws attention to the need to be sensitive to the theological resonances that can emerge from these initially alien ritual acts. There are, however, risks involved in using hermeneutics for holy purposes.

Because hermeneutics is tolerant of doubt and the need to struggle with meanings, it can effect a descent into the more vicious aspects of relativism. The hermeneutic circle provides its own traps. In his discussion of *Truth and Method*, Joel Weinsheimer places Gadamer's use of the concept of *Bildung* in the context of the parable of the Prodigal son. *Bildung* is a complex philosophical term that refers to a mode of reflection that increases a sense of self. The parable points to the process of departure and return, and the enhanced understanding the son encounters on his return home from exile, where he had been a servant. This is an account of a man who became a stranger and returned to the familiar to gain an enhanced understanding of his self. His temporary career of being a servant had permitted him to come to master that which was hitherto alien.[47] Following Georg Hegel, Gadamer argues that, 'to seek one's own in the alien, to become at home in it, is the basic movement of spirit, whose being is only return to itself from what is other'. A sense of going beyond, to find, in order to return to the familiar, lies in this approach.[48] This dialectic of journeying and returning is reflected in approaches to liturgy, where the actors and audience re-do what has already been done before, but with a newness and a freshness that tries to capture what was already understood. Aspects of this point emerge in Ricoeur's approach to hermeneutics.

Ricoeur endeavours to attach a phenomenological dimension to his hermeneutics, especially in his approach to symbol, action and text. This effort has crucial implications for the use of hermeneutics in understanding the social basis of liturgical performance, how it sensitises, enhances and edifies. For Ricoeur, symbols give rise to thoughts and these admit a theological consideration. Symbols require a sensitive and particular form of understanding if their meanings are to be disclosed. This is apparent in the distinction he makes between a first and second form of naïveté. The first form has a regressive quality, one that embodies a pre-critical interest that admits an unquestioning acceptance of the surplus of meanings symbols present.[49] This form bears on the liturgical role of childhood innocence, which I have discussed in terms of the choirboy. A critical awareness expressed in a subjective form gives rise to a hermeneutics of suspicion, a distrust before a multitude of options that emerge in the light of experience. The loss of innocence in handling symbols suggests that we cannot return to that world lost in critical experience. This sense of contact and loss is well expressed in Alain-Fournier's *Le Grand Meaulnes*.[50] Ricoeur tries to resolve this plight when he suggests that

> if we can no longer live the great symbolisms of the sacred in accordance with the original belief in them, we can, we modern man, aim at a second naiveté in and through criticism. In short, it is by *interpreting* that we can *hear* again. Thus it is in hermeneutics that the symbol's gift of meaning and the endeavour to understand by deciphering are knotted together.[51]

It is along these lines we wish to use hermeneutics to understand the social basis of liturgical performance and the dilemmas its enactment routinely handles. Representations of the holy in visible images demand re-interpretation to grasp again, to re-present that which is lost, but now found in the act of realising through social means a need to make contact with the sacred.

MIRRORING THE HOLY IN RITE: THE BEGINNING OF A HERMENEUTIC UNDERSTANDING

> Gwendolen (*glibly*) Ah! that is clearly a metaphysical speculation, and like most metaphysical speculations has very little reference at all to the actual facts of real life, as we know them.
>
> (Oscar Wilde, *The Importance of Being Earnest*)

Many aspects of sociology involve a laborious reinvention of the wheel. Its painfully obvious rendition of life as lived by others seems to make the sociologist the perpetual voyeur on other people's disasters. Somehow, the sociologist seems outside life as lived, but desperately seeking a ticket to enter the sweatshop of cosmopolitan existence. This urge to belong, yet to be apart for analytical purposes, the antinomy of the sociological trade, gives its practitioners their own special angst. They seem outside humanity, but ultimately belong very much within it.

Stress on the need for empathy, for critical engagement and a moral integrity are distinctive traits of sociology as a discipline. These reflect an effort to give a humanist substance to sociological insights. Enlightenment with a humane purpose is the hallmark of the reasonable sociologist. The compass points for reading humanity with compassion are more likely to come from philosophy than from theology. Sociology has its own conceptual currency, but it follows a different exchange rate from that which governs theology. Yet despite their obvious differences, there are similarities in the coins they spend in the market-place of life. 'Empathy' is near to 'sympathy' and claims to moral integrity can come nearer to apologetics than one might think. Faith that permits conversion between paradigms that fail to satisfy puzzles, can move ideological mountains, when set in a theological context.

Since the early sixties, there has been a crisis in the humanities, one that has been expressed in the romantic efforts to find Arcadia in the late sixties, to affirm ecological values, animal rights, all in a galaxy of ideological effort spent over the past two decades. In the rush down the road, various bootmarks have been left on the sociological body by those seeking ideological straws in the winds of change. Somehow the vision of these times is running out in the 1990s. In a perverse way, theology seems to be about to replace ideology as the governing belief system of the academy in the nineties. It has not yet become that obvious in cultural studies, but it is clear the times are changing, and not in an ideological direction.

The collapse of Marxism in Eastern Europe has exposed to view a rich terrain of religious belief; Islamic religious fundamentalism has welled up in a level of zeal all too real for those who believed modernity would win; and alternative religions slake a spiritual thirst in taverns few Catholics would license. Increasingly, a theological agenda is entering sociology at its horizons of theoretical interests. There are seeds of a nascent theology buried in the problems of post-modernity. Cultural studies have come to know too much, to see so many permutations, so that choice is increasingly seen as an illusion.

This need to cope with a diversity of belief systems in a plurality of cultural circumstances, all packaged and fashioned in a market-place, has given rise to post-modernism. The artificial nature of what is so easily constructed and sold gives the illusion of satisfaction in a way that excites dissatisfaction. Illusion is married to disillusion. There is great interest in cultural studies in the packaging, styling and selling of artificial images through the mass media and the fashion industry. Post-modernism captures the flux and uncertainty of the contemporary human condition as it deals with fragmented and fragmenting culture shapes.[52] The movement points to a crisis of belief, one that has emerged from the secularisation of progress, and the death of God. Gianni Vattimo has argued that the theological crisis over belief has now passed into considerations of humanity itself, and has given rise to an interest in nihilism.[53] As sociology becomes implicated in debate on the nature of modern culture, the issue of metaphysics hovers nearer to 'real' life than one might think. At some point, the purpose of meaning, and the end of interpretation have to be questioned. Modernity cannot be believed to operate in a philosophical vacuum. Seeking ends to interpretation beg philosophical questions that also lead to inescapable theological queries. Denying that it is in this game can lead sociology into nihilism by default of making a wager. The price of doubt has led Steiner to wonder over the options available in contemporary thought. He characterises the dilemmas well in a passage worth citing in full. Steiner asks of our culture

> whether a secular, in essence positivist, model of understanding and of the experience of meaningful form (the aesthetic) is tenable in the light or, if you will, in the dark of the nihilistic alternative. I want to ask whether a hermeneutics and a reflex of valuation – the encounter with meaning in the verbal sign, in the painting, in the musical composition, and the assessment of the quality of such meaning in respect of form – can be made intelligible, can be made answerable to the existential facts, if they do not imply, if they do not contain, a postulate of transcendence.[54]

This need to fill out meanings rather than empty them of significance takes us back to earlier themes, of the ambiguities the inspection of liturgy imposes on its beholder. Steiner suggests we are moving in the realm of embarrassments in the failures of language. We have to settle for inference to understand what is beyond words. For some, he has unexpectedly argued that thought now takes us to thresholds where the presence or absence of God does matter, and does have a profound effect on aesthetics. His stress on the tentative, on understandings that fall short, gives him a basis to plea for a sociology of marginality.[55] This echoes some aspects of our approach to understanding liturgy.

In another point that bears on some of our themes, he suggests the sense of the overwhelming reaches a point of density in the child, who has the facility of keen interest in things apparently trivial.[56] This draws us back to the terrain of innocence and experience, and the exercise of a second naïveté. Things trivial and useless belong to the childhood of life, where the deepest of its meanings are handled with impunity. The choirboy sings and embodies a theological truth in an almost playful manner. His act relates to aspects of Charles Baudelaire's essay, 'A Philosophy of Toys', where the child dominates the object with an awesome facility. Baudelaire notes 'this ease in gratifying the imagination is evidence of the spirituality of childhood in its artistic conceptions'.[57] This playful dimension to rite generates a link with hermeneutic considerations, which I explore in the final chapter.

Following Ricoeur, one can suggest that hermeneutics is a creature of modernity that in some ways manages to transcend its weaknesses.

It defends openings to meanings, whose incompleteness require dialogue. Such a failure to complete can be complemented by the negative theology that forms the end of the study. It is clear that sociology cannot give a blank gaze at liturgical enactments. There is a need to go deeper. Sociology cannot stare at rites through opera glasses without seeing the oddity of its gaze mirrored back. If it wants to see more, hermeneutics can assist in this task.

Hermeneutics can make many contributions to sociological under-standings of liturgy. Symbols, the public presentation of text, or the sermon, are some areas that come to mind that could be explored elsewhere. Implicit in our use of hermeneutics is the notion that it involves a reading afresh, an understanding of what was thought to be understood. This forms a crucial means of linking the fine distinction between representation and re-presentation. Admittedly this might marry sociology to theology in a relationship that is as unexpected as it is perplexing. There is, one must acknowledge, a narrow passage between understanding and believing to understand. This account started from within a sociological ambit, and it is no great disaster if it goes off in a theological direction. Given that its subject-matter is the issue of liturgical enactment, such a pious fate might seem excusable. I wish to comment on two distinctive facets of hermeneutics which sociology can exploit to achieve a deeper understanding of liturgical enactments. The first bears on the relationship between actions and text, and the degree to which this points to a distinctive means of reading liturgical enactments. The second relates to a facet of Gadamer's approach to hermeneutics which has been insufficiently explored. This is his exploration of play and games, which have obvious implications for sociological efforts to use hermeneutics to understand liturgical performances better. I pursue this facet of hermeneutics in the final chapter.

Ricoeur has tried to establish text as a paradigm for interpretation for the social sciences and for action in particular. His essay is most persuasive and has been of considerable influence. Discourse is the temporal means of actualising language, which achieves an objective form through writing made available in a text. This form of fixation enables a wide audience to be addressed and a meaning to be amplified. Action has a similar objectifying and amplifying facility as written discourse or text. Social actions present a 'delineated pattern which has to be interpreted according to its inner connections'.[58] There is a dialectic involved in deciphering an action filled event, whose tacit elements qualify what is available to be understood. This leads Ricoeur to suggest that 'a meaningful action is an action the *importance* of which goes "beyond" its *relevance* to its initial situation'.[59] Ricoeur goes on to make a crucial point, that text bears detachment from its author, and in like manner an action takes on consequences of its own. Detachment facilitates amplification. Bracketing the degree to which this complicates issues of volition and intention, the point has considerable importance. It indicates the way an action becomes part of public discourse, so that the meanings presented are to be shared. Actions leave a 'trace' and by making marks become the documents of human meaningful activity. For Ricoeur, actions 'speak' of more than their agents might perceive or understand. Thus, in the case of the meaning of an important event, action 'exceeds, overcomes, transcends, the social conditions of its production and may be re-enacted in new social contexts'. This point has obvious implications for understanding the repetitious nature of liturgical enactments. As an event, liturgy makes a mark in a way that exceeds the stature of the actors involved in its production. Another point of similarity between text and human action is that the meaning of the latter 'is also something which is *addressed* to an indefinite range of possible readers'.[60] This capacity to amplify and to bear a possible range of meanings accentuates the problems of ambiguities emerging in performance of actions such as in liturgies.

Deciphering the basis of a text or action involves an element of guesswork. Guessing is a synonym for *verstehen*. Ricoeur introduces the notion of validation as a means of testing guesses. This establishes the idea of a dialectic between reader and author. Validation refers less to verification than to a form of argument, similar to the juridical procedures of legal interpretation. Acceptance of an argument operates on the basis of indicating 'what can defeat a claim'. Ricoeur presents this in a non-binding way. Guessing and its validation also complement the dialectic between explanation and understanding so characteristic of the social sciences. But this dialectic is believed to operate in the context of a hermeneutic circle, one less vicious, especially when the exchange is considering social actions that have the power of disclosing a world to be understood. Ricoeur concludes his essay by emphasising the role of personal commitment in understanding human phenomena. The emancipatory thrust of his interest in hermeneutics is expressed in his stress on the use of judgement, of probability, as a means of understanding social actions. With symbols, these point to a surplus of meaning that goes beyond their immediate and empirical use. In this sense, the hermeneutic circle moves the interpreter into an issue of faith and personal commitment, a suitably sympathetic frame for approaching the understanding of liturgical transactions.[61]

How does one apply one's effort to link action and text to an understanding of liturgy? In one sense, the link is already made in the rite, for a text of the mass is followed that gives order, validity and accountability to liturgical praxis. In this context, there is a pleasingly ambiguous quality to the notion of playing the rite by the book. A metaphor is suggested, of the enactment proceeding in a way which permits it to be read like a book. By following the contours laid down in a book of rules, it establishes a social form whose shape has an exactitude that mirrors the directions in text it follows. The liturgical enactment fulfils that which the text stipulates it should express. An exact order is reproduced that elicits a reappraisal of what has already been seen, but which has not been fully understood. There is a discipline in the layout of a text, which follows a grammar, which embodies stylistic conventions that regulate what lies on the page, and which gives it a predictable quality. Far from being a liability that imprisons the author's message, the formalised layout of the text facilitates an amplification of the message in a way that minimises unnecessary misunderstandings arising over its form of presentation. It frees the message. To endeavour to understand the order of a rite purely at the level of its formalised disciplined surface, in its obvious facets, would be to misread and to deny the means through which it is to be understood.

Like a text, the enactment of a liturgy operates with the assumption that deeper meanings will be read into the form of the rite, so that its domain properties can be extracted, received and understood. These tacit, yet open and mysterious qualities permit an almost endless re-play, similar to the way that a book can be endlessly re-read, especially if it is ambiguous and resonates with an infinity of meanings.

The more difficult it is to attach one interpretation to a book, the more likely it is to be re-read and to be discussed. A similar point applies in the case of a social transaction, such as a liturgical performance, that generates a plurality of meanings and interpretations. This capacity of rite to produce openings to meanings that exceed its immediate relevance and use, forms the basis of considering text as a paradigm for understanding social actions. The capacity to make a meaningful mark, to leave a record of an event through a social action, indicates an ability to yield meanings that can be detached from the actor as they can be separated from the author in a text. A message is released that manages to go beyond the significance of the actor. The message is no longer the total possession of the actor, and being presented for public gaze, it takes on an autonomous existence similar to that of the text. By so arguing, Ricoeur manages to place text and action in the common concerns of hermeneutics to achieve a fuller understanding of the message that both seek to amplify through artificial means.

Some social transactions take on a binding characteristic, as in the case of those making a promise, or exchanging gifts. The event becomes objective to the degree to which the actors involved make the act public and agree to its being considered binding and irreversible, without some form of re-negotiation. In Chapter 6, I noted this quality of social actions being binding in Rappaport's effort to resolve the capacity of liturgy to deceive. Such public actions do not permit a retreat from accountability without the actor being regarded as untrustworthy.

The need to decipher that which is artificially amplified through the means of a text links its conditions of understanding with those governing the basis of liturgical transactions. Part of the purpose of this study has been to draw attention to the sociological implications of amplifying holy messages through antinomial social means, where the actor is not fully in control of what he discloses in the liturgical act. There is another link between conditions of meaning the text discloses and those which can be applied to understanding actions involved in a ritual such as liturgy. They both refract and mirror properties that exceed their immediate relevance and that which can be understood. This point has been explored in Lucien Dällenbach's understanding of recessed meanings in the text, where a quality of mirroring is discerned.

He makes a subtle and interesting point that has some application to an understanding of liturgical enactments. In his work, he is concerned with a phrase of André Gide, *mise en abyme* and goes into literary details that do not concern us. He defines the term as '*any internal mirror that reflects the whole of the narrative by simple, repeated or "specious" (or paradoxical) duplication*'.[62] An example of its use would be the play within the play in Hamlet, or a design within a shield that reflects the whole pattern. The concept only applies to particular types of novels, and is not given a specific sociological application in his analysis. Its use has a specific function of revealing an aspect of the text in a way that transcends it.[63] There is another use of the term, where in a text the narrative is undertaken by a sponsor for the author, somebody marginal, not integral to the plot, who has a privileged access to the truth. The innocent fulfil this role and mirror the wider properties of the text or the action. They represent greater issues than their minute status might initially indicate.[64] The value of his contribution is that he alerts us to the possible significance of points of detail, and the degree to which they can embody disproportionate aspects of meaning in texts, but also in ritual transactions. The notion of *mise en abyme* draws attention to the degree to which detail within a rite is a microcosm of a far greater, but invisible image that is believed to transcend the purely social, which so imperfectly refracts its existence. In a pattern that bears investment to yield interpretation, detail does matter. One needs to look closely to decipher that which might count. Actors involved in liturgical productions need to monitor the patterns they present, lest a corrupting and distorting shape emerges, that could yield unnecessary misunderstandings.

Literary critics often speak of the corruption of a text, interpolations added to 'improve' the original, or to rectify printer's errors that manifestly disimprove what the author wrote originally. These distortions are believed to warp the original ideas of the writer and so necessitate the need to purify the text. The means through which social forms of rite are purified of corrupting tendencies is more complex. Infelicities and impurities can be deemed to be endemic in particular liturgical forms, as was discussed in Chapter 6. But such a deterministic reading neglects the contribution of the actors to shaping what is presented in liturgical enactments. This marks a crucial difference between text and action. The shape of a book is usually uncontentious enough to be so defined for the purpose of reading, but the social form governing an event, such as a liturgy, has a subjective strand that belies what is presented as an objective accomplishment. The definition of the rite is less secured and actions have to be adjusted to rectify failures in shape. Credibility in transmission is an accomplishment peculiar to actions that point to procedures for delivery of a message that are different from those governing the use of a text. Understanding this point admits sociological considerations that might easily be overlooked.

The shape of a rite reflects a capacity to order and to represent in an objective manner that which has a subjective and indeterminate basis. There is an element of hazard in this operation so geared to handling uncertain outcomes. This need to marshal the shape of the social form, to secure its holy ends, lends a quality of wager in the reading of rite, that it might be misread in what it accomplishes. Liturgy is like a holy game replayed daily or weekly. Regulation of a social form to pursue an uncertain outcome characterises football matches. Teams get knocked out of shape by their opponents but regroup to achieve a result best not known in advance. This capacity to cope with uncertainty is a distinctive characteristic of the game and, indeed, justifies its basis as a social transaction.

Liturgies face peculiar problems that complicate efforts to secure a credible shape, a form to be deciphered in contemporary culture. They have no means of achieving a monopoly either over their form, or over their resources. Other groups, sects and cultures play the same game, at least in a similar form. They also compete in a market-place replete with images, groupings, and attractions presented in advertising, in consumer items and in the mass media. Liturgies are a means of presenting one objective amongst many. Whereas in the medieval world, paintings and objects of consumption were rare and access was limited to the few, the contemporary democratisation of use and purchase of commodities points to an opposite problem, of a plenitude that gives rise to a cultural indigestion. Liturgies are vulnerable in modern culture, as a result of having to compete with so many imitators. Securing their distinctive message is a peculiar sociological *and* theological accomplishment. Contemporary modern circumstances conspire to make liturgical acts more incredible than their theological message might justify. Modernity embodies a particular plight, a blindness that disables an appreciation of liturgical transactions. Liberal theologians have sought to adjust Christian forms and styles of belief to the fashions of modernity, but in so doing, they simply assimilate its ills into liturgical enactments. With the growth of post-modernism, they find themselves orphans of the times, plodding up a road to see sociologists coming running down in the opposite direction seeking 'signals of transcendence' elsewhere.

In his essay 'The Painter of Modern Life', Baudelaire spoke of the restless search of the *flâneur*, 'the painter of the passing moment and of all the suggestions of eternity that it contains'. This cosmopolitan and passionate spectator sees freshly like the child, and never for a moment without its genius. The *flâneur* is caught in the search 'to distil the eternal from the transitory' from the clothing and fashion of the age. Baudelaire notes it is easier to reproduce past costumes and to parade these as fashion in a way that avoids seeking the pursuit of the mysterious in present circumstances. This ease of appropriation, of making an instant mark, relates to his innovative notion of modernity. Baudelaire uses the term to refer to 'the ephemeral, the fugitive, the contingent, the half of art whose other half is the eternal and the immutable'. There is a moral aspect to his critique of modernity, where he points to the dangers of settling for the superficial and the immediate, that which is easy to appropriate and to reproduce as authentic, but in a way which betrays no search, no struggle, to find its own mysterious beauty. This easeful dalliance with life disables. It becomes a disincentive to search, when purchase will satisfy. Failure to explore below the surface of social exchange embodies an incapacity to view the 'fantastic reality of life' and to take one's fill. The correlation between the 'body' and the 'soul', explains for Baudelaire, 'quite clearly how everything that is "material", or in other words an emanation of the "spiritual", mirrors and will always mirror, the spiritual reality from which it derives'.[65] Modernity impairs the capacity to view, to stop sufficiently long to allow the material object to mirror the spiritual. In an age where fame lasts fifteen minutes, and the attention span for a television programme is thirty seconds, the incapacity of those who promenade around the Cathedrals, to stay and sit for the fifty minutes for choral Evensong becomes understandable, if not still perplexing. The cancer of modernity blunts sensibilities of the holy, eating into the need to attend to view that which lies below the social surface of rite. The graceless purchase grace in a way that blinds them to the value of seeking that which lies beyond price.

11 Apophatic Liturgy: Re-presenting the Absent in Rite

And he dreamed, and behold a ladder set up on
the earth, and the top of it reached to heaven;
and behold the angels of God ascending and descending on it.

(Genesis 28: 12)

Elementary forms of liturgical life convey a sense of unction in the function. Where it exists, the actors play in a way that suggests the heavenly born on earthly leave of absence. There is a balming quality in their act. The liturgical actors seem well filled with grace in their parts. Unctuousness conveys dissimilar, more worldly sentiments. It is a quality of the fawning classes seeking to entice the unwary into sticky relationships. Their oiliness feigns interest to entrap the unwary in a gush of flattery that should warn the wise. Both qualities, so near yet so far apart in meanings, suggest a need for subtle discrimination. Each has a seductive quality that can lead or mislead. Whereas unction conveys qualities beyond calculation, unctuousness embodies its use.

In a liturgical performance, unction suggests a sense of being acted on with a grace that descends from on high. An aura becomes attached to the actions of the pious that lubricates what is being unfolded. To look closely at an actor so endowed generates the risk of being enticed into gazing at heavenly highways, invisible, but clearly marked. Unctuousness has a pejorative overtone that matches its deceiving, ingratiating art. Both qualities signify trust or distrust. A fine judgement is required to preserve the integrity of self before the allures of each.

Sociology might find a happier hunting ground in stalking and entrapping unctuous practitioners. There is plenty of theoretical ammunition to fire at their smooth veneers. Unction is a rather more puzzling quality for a sociologist to handle, who is unused to heavenly dealings. It eludes analytical grasp and takes sociology away from its more proper and orthodox concerns. Yet this sense of analytical failure has its own purpose. Karl Jaspers has suggested that a boundary awareness is developed as the limits of knowledge are approached.

Ambiguities emerge that cannot be understood through the generation of further information. They demand choices between options that can lead from the philosophical to the theological. Failure to resolve these ambiguities can give rise to madness or to escapism into an everyday cynicism. But, as Jaspers has indicated, they can also lead to an authentic conversion, a form of awakening that leads to 'transcendence arising upon its ruins'.[1] The need to choose in the face of options liturgical transactions present is inescapable, for the denial of choice can lead to the occupation of a reductionist position by default.

This point bears on some aspects of the philosophy of Maurice Blondel. He was concerned with pursuing the implications of actions into a supernatural realm. His point that the denial of meaning in action, a form of nihilism is itself a positive statement, led him to affirm the need to choose between a negative and a positive solution that involves a wager. By opening to the supernatural out of sheer necessity of choice the actor accepts a relationship to what is otherwise inaccessible.[2] This need to act, to engage with God, has been expressed in terms of play by the Swiss Catholic theologian, Hans Urs von Balthasar in *Theodramatik*. His notion of participation in the ultimate sacred drama facilitates a link between theology and sociology which he has explored through the writings of Simmel and Goffman. An important sociological school is placed in the context of theological debate and is used to develop an aesthetics of the holy.

The strength of hermeneutics lies in its capacity to go deeper into what is recessed in meanings, to converse about what is tacit in a human life and in a culture that manifests a 'relentless tension between illumination and concealment'.[3] This tension can be expressed in an antinomial form and is exemplified in liturgical productions where revelation operates in a dialectic manner with the hidden. Hermeneutics claims to operate in a way that opens out understanding so that a fullness of meaning can be achieved. It sheds light on elements that impair or hinder understanding, even in theological and liturgical matters.

Gadamer has argued that since the Reformation there is no longer

> unambiguous evidence of a unity of worship and religious behaviour. We are faced with the precarious and intricate question as to how far we can fulfil and sustain the whole work of cult, prayer and benediction, since the sincerity of faith is at stake.[4]

He notes that this disassociation has happened since the inception of Christianity. But awareness of this disjunction generates new problems of understanding and relates to Ricoeur's notion of a second naïveté. Because we cannot live with sacred symbols in their original form, but only through the medium of modern consciousness, hermeneutics suggests a means of interpretation that allows us to rehear what has been lost. A disposition towards understanding is required which hermeneutics cultivates. This re-emphasises the importance of a second naïveté in approaching and deciphering symbols. For Ricoeur 'this second naïveté aims to be the postcritical equivalent of the precritical hierophany'.[5] In his analysis, symbols give rise to thoughts, but as I have suggested repeatedly, in liturgical use, these are manifest in a divided form as antinomies, whose interpretative procedures have a social basis. A sociological stress on the divisions symbols generate places the actor more centrally in a position of agency over their use and interpretation. It enhances the notion of wager, which Ricoeur regards as the means of going beyond the hermeneutic circle.

This notion of recovery complements Gadamer's approach to narrative as referring to what happened 'once upon a time'. Narration is a characteristic form of religious speaking. It deals in representation 'where one "makes something visible" through the use of an illustrating figure'. Something is re-presented so that it is present. For instance a flag paraded embodies the notion of nationhood, and so commands respect.[6] Gadamer feels hermeneutics acquires 'a profound religious character since it no longer has to do with a method or with the skill of our rational faculty'. In a point that refers to the New Testament, but that also applies to the understanding of liturgical enactments, Gadamer suggests that hermeneutics 'has the special task of making acceptable what seems to be fundamentally incomprehensible: that faith is not the product of a believer's merit but an act of grace'.[7]

There is a tensive quality in liturgical transactions that relates to Philip Wheelwright's notion of a striving for adequacy. Religious gestures have an aura and for the authentic worshipper have the power to elict awe. These gestures have an ambiguous quality that gives rise to a tension as the liturgical actors strive to achieve a transcendence of their antinomial instruments of worship.[8] In a theological sense, adequacy can never be achieved from within the social resources of the rite, hence the struggle to grasp what they cannot fully understand and to believe in a truth that cannot be possessed in all its completeness. Alan Olson suggests that there is a particular philosophical language responsive 'to the limits and the boundaries of human experience and knowledge'.[9] As indicated before, to move beyond social limits of enquiry means entering an arena of metaphysical choice. Some have taken the option of nihilism as that which affirms what is beyond the limits of modernity, but others have used a negative theology with some ingenuity.

Dupré has argued that anti-religious stances have been abandoned in a humanist era where the sacred has lost its social power. Religious belief has returned to the margins of society and is increasingly a subjective quest of the individual, often expressed in a concern with mysticism. But his most telling point is that the absence of the sacred in the social marks a means of finding God's transcendence in the world. By linking the social to the apophatic, Dupré opens up a possible connection between sociology and negative theology. Vitalising this negative experience, this sense of God's absence, draws man back to the spirituality of the desert, except this time the void operates in the centre of social relations, in the fulcrum of modernity – the city. Dupré suggests that 'our age has created an emptiness that for the serious God-seeker attains a religious significance. The mysticism of negation provides him with an ideal model'.[10] It should be said that Dupré is not establishing a notion of a retreat into a social void, but rather is indicating that a negative mysticism opens out the possibility of a return to a religious community. There are a number of reasons why a negative theology best fits sociological forms of analysis. It lurks already in aspects of Critical Theory and in some of the early writings of the Frankfurt School. But it has other attractions.

A negative theology belongs to Patristic traditions of piety and mysticism. It offers a deep spiritual understanding that can be set at a distance from social issues. This enables analytical distinctions between sociology and theology to be more easily marked and understood. As Simon Tugwell observes, 'negative theology is the shield which protects us from idolatry, which reminds us that any conceivable encounter with God in this life is always an encounter veiled in creatures'.[11] It is a theology that establishes a limit to the social, for it underlines the degree to which concepts are inadequate as a means of comprehending God, who cannot be known in such terms. A negative theology seems well suited to a post-Enlightenment era. It marries a 'mysticism of gloom' to 'a sociology of pessimism' to produce the sort of theology Weber might have liked.[12] It has a particular attraction for our analysis with its stress on paradox, ambiguity and the transcendence of antinomies. It deals in dazzling darknesses and clouds of unknowing. Because it represents a theology of failure that succeeds, it

seems particularly well suited to complement sociological efforts to
understand liturgical enactments. It is a theology that stresses the
notion of emptying as a means through which a filling becomes
possible. This bears on a point in Corinthians where Paul writes 'we
have this treasure in earthen vessels, that the excellency of the power
may be of God, and not of us' (2 Cor. 4:7).

In this chapter, liturgical forms are treated as playful means of
handling the holy. This approach draws out the degree to which these
are ritualised games dealing in wagers, in hopes, that the players and
their audience will find what they seek in the enactment of liturgy.
Ambiguities and antinomies are preserved, but are understood in a
way that gives them a transcendent purpose. The writings of von
Balthasar form the next section, where the sociological themes of the
book are given a theological gloss, one that takes into account the
limits of social form, but in a way that permits access to a theology of
aesthetics. The final section reconsiders most of the elements of the
book in terms of a negative theology, one that concentrates on the
Pseudo-Dionysius. This apocryphal fifth- or sixth-century writer
specialised in handling liturgical forms in terms of images of ascent
and descent in a way that has a circular connotation. Reference to his
writings supplies an edifying approach to the hermeneutic circle and
through an emphasis on transcendence offers a means of escape from
its viciousness. Because he was also concerned with the symbolic
aspects of liturgy, with angelic presences and with antinomial
elements in forms of knowing (presented in a paradoxical manner)
he supplies a fitting theological end to this tentative sociological effort
to understand the social basis of liturgical enactments.

HOLY GAMES: UNDERSTANDING INFINITE RE-PLAYS

Praise this world to the Angel, not the untellable: you
can't impress him with the splendour you've felt; in the cosmos
where he more feelingly feels you're only a novice. So show him
some simple thing, refashioned by age after age,
till it lives in our hands and eyes as a part of ourselves.
            (Rainer Maria Rilke, 'Duino Elegies. The Ninth Elegy')

Sunday sung Evensong somewhere in the North of England proceeded
solemnly through the psalms and canticles to the sermon – on the
responsibilities of giving to Christian Aid. Suddenly, the sonorously

cast sermon was interrupted. Out of the vestry door clad in his white surplice, ruff and cassock came a choirboy on a bicycle. Pedalling furiously, he shot down the south aisle, and up the central nave, flinging tracts on facts on poverty out to a transfixed congregation. Vanishing through an opened door, he departed as mysteriously as he came, having deposited the congregation on to the horns of a liturgical dilemma.

For some, choral Evensong could be deemed a form of play with the holy, but for others it was hardly a game to be played with in this manner. An ambiguous question had been posed for the congregation. Clearly, solemn assemblies ought to be kept in proper ceremonial repair, but then, prophecy could be argued to override ritual proprieties, even if such an announcement came via a treble on a bicycle. Anyhow, the issue was resolved with a shoal of letters of complaint to the vicar, who had instigated the event to illustrate his sermon.[13] Still a puzzle arises: was choral Evensong a game, a 'mere' form of play, whose 'real' social basis had been inadvertently revealed by the choirboy?

Liturgical events have qualities of a game, with their own peculiar rules for holy winners and unholy losers. This staging of a sacred drama involves a sense of play that is faintly ludicrous. Antics on the altar, the bows and scrapes in fancy clothing, with props such as thuribles and candles held, convey a sense of oddness, all the more felt, when it is remembered that this ritual is performed weekly, or in some cases, daily. Despite this slighting aspect, these rites are believed to offer redemptive possibilities and to be capable of bearing a more serious and holy purpose. It is a game played often, and somehow bears repeating. If it is a game, it is an odd one, for it is not clear who wins or loses, or indeed who has played with whom.

In what follows, I wish to explore how liturgies can be considered as forms of play. Huizinga's point still stands that sacred activities that appear as forms of play have been given little attention in anthropology and sociology.[14] The issue of play embodies many of the ambiguities and paradoxes that characterise the social basis of rite. Unfortunately, play is not an easy concept to define.[15] Following Huizinga, play can be regarded as a meaningful form of activity, one that transcends the normal antithesis of wisdom and folly. It carries an element of contradiction in its activities, yet at the same time manages to break free. There is an element of tension management, not only in handling these contradictions (of realising a quality of seriousness through trivial means) but also risks of trivialising what is after all a supposedly serious endeavour to find God in a public place. There is also the chance of producing an event that is meaningless and is truly without purpose. This poses a challenge to the spiritual capacities of the actor. It involves a testing in the handling of a number of contradictions, which, if faced, can enhance meanings and might allow doubt to be suspended. As Hugo Rahner has noted 'to play is to yield oneself to a kind of magic, to enact to oneself the absolutely other, to pre-empt the future, to give the lie to the inconvenient world of fact'. As a sacral form of play, liturgy bears an element of hope 'for another life taking visible form in gesture'.[16]

Play has a limiting property that enables it to open up the limitless. It encloses a segment of the world, but in so restricting opens out an order with its own complex rules. By limiting 'real life', it actualises a means of identification with an order of belief that represents more than life. This capacity to actualise through representation enables forms of play to make 'real' that which would be otherwise considered unreal. The rules of play restrict, but in an arbitrary way that is precarious, for the rules presented can easily be broken. One has to accept the bounds of the game to play. If one breaks the rules, and disbelieves in their basis, then the illusion becomes shattered, and one is denied access to what is enhanced and made actual in the game. There is an arbitrary but vulnerable quality to play. It offers a peculiar and particular means of representing the intangible, but in so manifesting this quality, play renders itself a form of activity useless for any other purpose.[17] It is a precarious form of engagement with a world of illusions, and to that degree it can entrap the unwary into believing in activities that are less than serious. Play could represent an act of folly intended to mislead and to deceive the wise into finding a significance in something that is insignificant in the end. Liturgical transactions can easily be dismissed as 'mere' forms of play. But, as Kurt Riezler has suggested, the terms 'merely' or 'not merely' give play a profoundly ambiguous relationship to ordinary life. He indicates that 'whenever an ultimate horizon grips the whole of our being our playing is no longer "merely" playing, ordinary life is bound to be serious, and our concern with whatever it is is really real concern'.[18]

The dilemmas of understanding play are similar to those confronted by the experienced in interpreting the actions of the innocent. It relates to qualities that are near the childlike, but which in Ricoeur's terms invite a second naïveté to understand more fully. The act of playing suggests access to elements that have a quality of the sacred, an entry that arises from conditions of dependence and innocence that comes most naturally from the child. Play elicits a sense of deference before the slight to yield the weighty. As Guardini has noted, the child plays in an aimless way. Not having a language of purpose represents an apparent deficiency, yet one, paradoxically, that seems to give him privileged access to the unapparent and the imaginative in a way that enables him to defy the limits of the wise. He handles the useless without embarrassment or a self consciousness that his actions could be other than what they appear. For him their ambiguous quality is not a question. This is what play means: 'it is life, pouring itself forth without an aim, seizing upon riches from its own abundant store, significant through the fact of its existence'.[19] Guardini goes on to add that it is 'in the imaginary sphere of representation, that man tries to reconcile the contradiction between that which he wishes to be and that which he is'.[20]

There is a liminality implied in the notion of play as an activity that moves between contradictions. Thus, Turner suggests that the 'solemn' and the 'ludic' are polarities similar to those of the sacred and the profane. The 'flow' of the rite, which we noted earlier, binds disparate elements together in a way that embodies a liminality for those involved in the social construction of the performance.[21] This sense of 'flow' reflects Roger Caillois's approach to play, where free separate elements recombine in a manner, whose basis is uncertain, to provide an engagement with the make-believe. Elements, otherwise unproductive, are harnessed to rules or conventions in a way that appears to suspend ordinary laws. The effect is an awareness of 'a free unreality, as against real life'.[22] This freeing becomes possible despite a clutter of detail that might otherwise hinder and bind. As Guardini has noted, 'the fact that the liturgy gives a thousand strict and careful directions on the quality of the language, gestures, colours, garments and instruments which it employs, can only be understood by those who are able to take play seriously'.[23] A sense of grave rule combines with a freeing that allows the participants to let go and to fashion an entry into the holy. Play pre-supposes a degree of agency, and a capacity to be selective about what is being presented. Without this selectivity, it could trespass into what it might fear: meaningless activities dealing only with the trivial.

This capacity to discard elements of the ordinary, to release the extraordinary, relates to a point of Goffman's. He suggested that focused gatherings require rules of irrelevance to operate in an effective manner. In games, factors are precluded in a selective order of in-attention, whose basis is arbitrary and not available for re-negotiation

without redefining what is being played. Thus, he argues, the character
of an encounter is based in part

> upon rulings as to properties of the situation that should be
> considered irrelevant, out of frame, or not happening. To adhere
> to these rules is to play fair. Irrelevant visible events will be
> disattended; irrelevant private concerns will be kept out of mind.
> An effortless unawareness will be involved, and if this is not possible
> then an active turning-away or suppression will occur.[24]

This need for a ritual tact to preserve the hidden and to avoid the
undesirable being spelt out, relates to the notion of virtuous dissimulation in liturgical engagements. Inconsistencies in games need not be
fatal as long as they are kept intact. Indeed, one can agree with
Richard Grathoff that 'games are structured by a system of "pre-
defined" inconsistencies'.[25] Ritual rules regulate these inconsistencies
and provide a selective means of minimising their unproductive use.
The reward for this selective affinity with the phenomenon so
presented is a stratum of feeling that yields a sense of wanting to
possess what has been disclosed. This point arises in dealing with
music.

As Thomas Clifton notes, a belief in the presence of the phenomenon of music occurs at the same time as a neutralising of any belief
about its factual existence. He goes on to add that 'the certainty of
belief seems to be contemporaneous with the act of possessing'.[26]
Games reflect forms of imitation or mimesis. Re-plays of games are
attempts to grasp that elusive entity that can be merely represented and
imitated. As Steiner has indicated aptly 'mimesis is repossession'.[27]

There is a long philosophical tradition of regarding play as
providing a means of access to artistic imagination.[28] At this point
we wish to draw on Gadamer's *Truth and Method* to provide some
hermeneutic insights into the nature of the game, and what its
performance realises. In a point that echoes Ricoeur's notion of a
second naïveté, Gadamer notes that 'we have lost that naïve innocence
with which traditional concepts were made to support one's own
thinking' and this fragmentation of belief requires a rediscovery of the
traditions that shaped contemporary consciousness.[29] It is against this
background, that his approach to play needs to be understood.

Gadamer's approach to play and games is suggestive rather than
conclusive. His interests are directed to artistic representation and to a
lesser degree religious rites. He regards play as the clue to ontological

explanation. It involves a seriousness of purpose for it bears a mode of being in what it represents. Repetition is a forming of re-seeing what is being enacted in the play. Because a game, such as a liturgy, bears an inexhaustible ambiguity, there is no limit to the number of times it can be re-played and re-interpreted. The actions of a play are not random, but are implicated in a structure that gives order to what is re-presented. Recalling a phrase he has used earlier, of 'the transformation into a structure' (as relating to a perfection in artistic representation), Gadamer suggests that

> play is structure – this means that despite its dependence on being played it is a meaningful whole which can be repeatedly represented as such and the significance of which can be understood. But the structure is also play, because – despite this theoretical unity – it achieves its full being only each time it is played.[30]

Play acts to transform into structure what is believed to be true. In a religious act, or a sermon, a 'contemporaneity' is found. Thus, 'the sense of being present is here the genuine sharing in the redemptive action itself'. It involves a fullness of presence. As Gadamer suggests, 'that which detaches him from everything also gives him back the whole of his being'. Many of Gadamer's illustrations at this point are drawn from liturgy.[31] Playing in a ritual facilitates participation in what is affirmed as true. Gadamer notes that 'in the representation of play, what is emerges. In it is produced and brought to light what otherwise is constantly hidden and withdrawn'.[32] This relates to an earlier concern of Gadamer with the need for tact as a means of handling the inexplicit and the inexpressible. Tact represents to Gadamer a mode of knowing and being. It facilitates access to what would be otherwise unavailable. Gadamer suggests that 'tact helps one to preserve distance, it avoids the offensive, the intrusive, the violation of the intimate sphere of the person'.[33] Tact involves an acceptance, a yielding before what is believed to be hidden. This acceptance involves a degree of deference to an order, one that will dominate and change the reader or spectator. It facilitates the transformation of what might be merely repetitious into an act that transforms and brings forth the means of recognition of an essence, one embodied in the social construction of a liturgy, but which transcends its apparent basis.

There is an element of contradiction in Gadamer's approach to play. Play binds as well as frees the actor in an antinomial manner that does not hurt. As Warnke notes, Gadamer's understanding of play involves a normative authority being imposed on player and audience alike, that regulates their participation in what is being represented. This element of domination governs the dialogue which play enables. It operates in a paradoxical manner, much in the way Simmel approached the question of fashion. A degree of autonomy is made possible, but at a price of demanding dependence on the game, which starts to play the player.[34] This subservience to play has a distinctive effect on the player. It fulfils 'its purpose only if the player loses himself in his play'.[35] Giving in to the 'flow' of play and going along with its movements draws the player into what it represents. Absorption into the play of the ritual process makes the player subservient before the game, but in so limiting, a loosening is effected into an autonomy of being unavailable by other means. In soaking up the player, play 'takes from him the burden of the initiative which constitutes the actual strain of existence'.[36] The passage of play and the absorption it effects relates to an increased unawareness of the means of reproduction of the game. It seems to pass out of awareness as the actor grasps further the self representation and transformation the act of play realises, and which he shares with the audience. The game absorbs in a way that seems to indicate it has engulfed the player. This leads Gadamer to suggest that 'understanding is possible only if one forgets oneself'.[37] Redemption requires a yielding to enter the realm effected by a transformation of structure. This task links the actor to his audience in a mutual effort to open out and to achieve an understanding.

Earlier the tendency of form to be dominated by content was noted in Simmel's analysis. Social forms only become significant when they approach conditions of their own insignificance, where their incomplete and indeterminate basis can be recognised. Forms fulfil their functions when they are kept subordinate to the content they are established to yield. They are useful to the degree to which they reach limits and thresholds inexhaustible in meaning. The ambiguous interdependence between form and content has a fuller meaning when it is understood in terms of play, where the infinite is represented through finite means. Play suggests a representation in something larger than the purely social can convey. It permits a detachment of the self from the immediate and generates the possibility of understanding through interpretation. Thus, Weinsheimer notes 'true interpretation is not just true to the play; it is interpretation of the play's truth. It is not only the play that comes to exist in the interpretation but the thing that the play represents. What Gadamer is describing is the process by which worlds come to be, an event of being and truth'.[38]

One crucial aspect of Gadamer's interest in understanding lies in the area of symbols. These have a duality, a tension that is necessary between the coincidence of sensible appearance and supra-sensible meanings. The more disproportionate and obscure the relationship is, the more likely the symbol is to stand for deeper meanings.[39] A symbol has to be instituted to secure its representative character. It manifests a presence and in some way participates in what it re-presents. Aspects of this were noted in the sections dealing with religious clothing in Chapter 4. Gadamer suggests that a work of art signifies an increase in being. Each work has an element of mimesis which 'implies that something is represented in such a way that it is actually present in sensuous abundance'.[40] This overabundance, or excess, is also attached to play. The notion of mimesis, or imitation through play, acts to effect a representation of an entity otherwise unavailable. 'All true imitation', Gadamer argues 'is a transformed reality because it brings before us intensified possibilities never seen before. Every imitation is an exploration, an intensification of extremes'.[41] Gadamer suggests that 'in our relationship to the world, and in all our creative labours – forming or co-operating in the play of form as the case may be – our accomplishment lies in retaining what threatens to pass away'.[42] 'Liturgical mistakes' come to represent that which might subtract from an excess, an abundance of meaning central to the performance, but so precarious in its coming.

Gadamer argues that an indeterminacy or ambiguity of meaning gives rise to interpretation. This is 'not a reading in of some meaning but clearly a revealing of what the thing itself already points to'.[43] In this context a symbol can be understood to facilitate recognition. This point has implications for understanding gesture and relates to our earlier discussion of sacred bows. Gadamer suggests that 'every gesture is also opaque in an enigmatic fashion. It is a mystery that holds back as much as it reveals. For what the gesture reveals is the being of meaning rather than the knowledge of meaning'.[44]

In an important essay that enables a link to be explored between the theology of von Balthasar and his approach to hermeneutics, Gadamer examines the problem of deciphering aesthetic and religious experience. He sees 'the real task of hermeneutics here is to overcome the fundamental strangeness and alien quality that lies in the Christian message itself . . . .'[45] A crucial means of overcoming these alien conditions are the social resources of rite. For Gadamer, 'all the other forms of Christian worship, the whole life of the Church, in the last analysis represent aids to faith: hymns, prayers, blessings, the eucharist and all the other aspects of the liturgy'.[46] This emphasis on believing through sharing in what is communally recognised bears on the issue of truth manifest in the Word, and the distinctive understanding achieved by the sermon in the Lutheran tradition that seems to form the basis of Gadamer's interest in Christianity.[47] The radical nature of Christianity is shown in what we cannot achieve through our own resources and for that reason the notion of a sign in religious belief has a certain and necessary indeterminacy. Gadamer indicates that 'it is not something that everyone has been able to see, not something to which one can refer, and yet, if it is taken as a sign, there is something incontestably certain about it'.[48] This point moves into a consideration of wider theological issues, that affect and effect sociological understandings of rite. The next stage of the study is to give these insights a theological location in the writings of the Catholic Swiss theologian, Hans Urs von Balthasar.

BEAUTY AND HOLINESS: EXCEEDING SOCIOLOGICAL LIMITS

> Howbeit we speak wisdom among them that
> are perfect: yet not the wisdom of this world, nor
> of the princes of this world, that come to nought:
> But we speak the wisdom of God in a mystery,
> even the hidden wisdom, which God ordained
> before the world unto our glory.
>
> (1 Cor. 2:6–7)

There are a number of reasons why von Balthasar presents difficulties for a sociological reading of his work. He wrote over fifty books and numerous articles, many of which are untranslated. The depth of his scholarship and the width of his cultural and theological interests present an awesome array of material to handle. In his writings he had an uncommon mastery of Greek philosophy, patristics, and French, German and English literature, which, combined with a massive theological erudition and knowledge of philosophy, gave him a breadth of cultural interest that is difficult to match. For many, he is the most important and creative Catholic theologian of the twentieth century and one whose theological vision of the cultural is likely to have a profound effect on what sociologists can think and say about the holy. The scale of his productivity and the absence of translations of many of his key works has limited his impact. A further reason for his marginalisation was his opposition to the ordination of women and married clergy, his scepticism about the role of lay theologians and his deeply hostile attitude to the liberal interpretations of theology which followed Vatican II. Indeed, he was never consulted during the Council. The spiritual and romantic cast of his theology places him at odds with the more ideological and rational styles favoured by theologians who tend to dominate higher education.[49]

There is a traditional quality in his Catholicism that makes him deeply critical of the efforts of liberal theologians to repackage belief to meet the expectations of modern man. To some extent and in a way that needs to be explored further, von Balthasar is an apt theologian for the post-modernist condition. Many of his writings were directed against the fragmenting effects of modernity. He felt that undue deference to modern rational thought led to a reductionism and a dilution of the mysteries of the Church.[50] In his writings, he showed much sympathy for the autonomy of the cultural sciences as a means of affirming the humanities in general and theology in particular.[51] Many of his insights have a significant bearing on the links sociology can make with theology. Unfortunately, only two volumes of *Theodramatik*, which has a central importance for our approach to liturgy, have been translated. This section of his work, dealing with action in a theatrical context, uses a dramatic metaphor for theological purposes, unlike Goffman's, where it was used to coin sociological insights. From commentaries on the five volumes, it is possible to construct a tentative sketch of his arguments. His use of play to characterise relationships between God and man has a bearing on hermeneutic understanding, which we wish to explore. The idea of form is a central part of his theological approach to beauty and this can be related to sociological approaches to the same concept. Unfortunately, it has not been used in a systematic way in his writings.

In a suggestive essay on von Balthasar, Rowan Williams notes the implicit community of interest between his writings and the whole post-Heidegger approach to hermeneutics. Williams also draws attention to the parallels between von Balthasar and Ricoeur.[52] These have been briefly explored by Jeffrey Kay, who draws attention to a shared concern with a contemporary forgetfulness of signs of the sacred, and a tendency amongst liberal theologians to offer reduction-ist interpretations of symbols. Kay observes that Balthasar's approach to biblical texts has a naïve, childlike quality that echoes Ricoeur's notion of a second naïveté.[53] There is a quality of innocence in von Balthasar's approach, an imaginative quality of enhancement that presents a theology that seeks to move through metaphor and literary sources to beyond the finite. His concern with the transcendent and the spiritual gives meaning to paradox, which, in religious enactment, would otherwise be meaningless. These elements of contradiction, double meanings and antinomies are linked to an apophatic theology. The daunting effects of this theology are offset by his abiding concern with the way the actor plays in an eschatological image, where paradox is harmonised and sealed in a form of beauty that expresses truth.

Throughout his writings, Hans Urs von Balthasar noted a theological need to link aesthetics, which was concerned with light, image and vision, to deed, event and to drama. His theology was concerned with styles of engagement with God that operate through forms of the beautiful. He tried to connect a theological dramatics, where the poignancy of play was most evident, to the idea of roles conceived at the social and individual level. Sociological and psychological aspects of roles were explored in the first volume of *Theodramatik*. Published in German in 1973, the short section dealing with sociology is remarkably thorough, comprehensive and insightful. Much use is made of Simmel, Goffman and Berger, in a sophisticated reading that is most unusual for a major Catholic theologian. His central question is 'who am I' and this quest for understanding takes him in a sociological direction, but one whose limits are well recognised. The idea of dramatic representation, through roles and play, as a way of accounting for man's relationship before God, admits a sociological facet but in a manner that enhances theological efforts to understand more fully the plight of the human condition. Von Balthasar insisted that all facets of dramatic action, as an event, involving author, actor, producer and audience, had to be explored. This study of liturgy has tried to take these elements further in a sociological reading that aims to be compatible with his theological writings.[54]

For von Balthasar, acting in theological terms means participating in the ultimate drama. One of the sociological attractions of his writing is that he seeks to express 'this in a form in which all the dimensions and tensions of life remain present instead of being sublimated in the abstractions of a "systematic" theology'.[55] Grounding the realisation of beauty and glory in issues of praxis and performance gives sociology access to a theological question. The emergent ambiguities and paradoxes of liturgical enactments can be focused on play, a concept he shares with Gadamer. The variability of meaning and the ambiguous play on relationship presented in the theatre generates a curiosity. It involves a mutual interplay on a variety of meanings between the audience and author, which hermeneutics strives to decipher and to understand. Von Balthasar uses this mutual interplay as a metaphor for understanding the relationship between man acting out before God.[56] As Waldstein notes, theatre represents for von Balthasar a means of representing the dramatic tensions of existence clearly. Theatre transforms expressive images into action, and does so through words.[57]

In his summary of von Balthasar's *Theodramatik*, O'Meara notes that the human personality is considered to be free but finite, so affirming the capacity to choose to accept what God reveals through play. He suggests also that in his works von Balthasar 'draws on the apophatic tradition of dark faith and a hidden God to find in human existence a dramatic theater, at times lyric, at other times epic or tragic'. Elements of drama find their ultimate departure in the notion of Apocalypse, and these follow a passage through contradictory forces within which the Church has to operate to arrive at the final act.[58] Tragedy implicates us in an account of fall. Theatre represents

the inner social world and activity of people. In theater we will try to perceive a kind of transcendence which through a transformation – the dialectic of mask and costume as hiding and disclosing – can come into a pure openness where it allows revelation to come towards it. Then, in metaphor, a door to the truth of real revelation opens.[59]

Masks establish a distance, a disguise that allows the actor to rise above the particular. A tension is generated between the visual and verbal that draws the audience into dealing with the implications of what has been staged.[60]

The endless ambiguities, ploys and tacit meanings the actor encounters during his performance of rite, which seem to confound sociological intervention, can lead to deeper meaning when they are channelled into the central focus of the activity – God. The more sociological analysis amplifies these dilemmas, the more it exposes a critical dimension of the human condition. The analytical limits it confronts draw attention to the limitless questions of infinity, which an apophatic tradition can receive and contain. Aspects of this were touched on in the earlier account of the relationship between a phenomenon such as silence, and the distinctive capacity of liturgical form to domesticate and to contain its more dangerous and ambiguous qualities in a meaningful harmony that permits repeated examination. The apophatic tradition represents a limitless ultimate that permits an indefinite range of sociological permutations to be mapped and marked out within the confines of a ritual. In such an approach, the relativist and ambiguous qualities of liturgical action can be given a redemptive twist. Instead of being presented as paradoxes that can be grounded into meaningless and contradictory conditions, these qualities can be given an emancipatory dimension. A sense of the eschatological permits him to escape from contradictions that would otherwise engulf him.

Only a fuller study of *Theodramatik* and his other untranslated work would show how von Balthasar connected his notion of play, as staged, to the issue of liturgical performance. In view of his stress on praxis, it would be odd if his theological aesthetics could not be applied to liturgy. As with Gadamer, Goffman and Simmel, there is an opacity in von Balthasar's work that is both an asset and a liability. Many terms, such as 'form' 'aesthetics' and 'the actor' need to be refined in a way that lies outside the compass of this book. The analysis which follows is tentative.

There are some pointers in his writings that indicate his views on liturgy. In understanding von Balthasar, it is essential not to underestimate his concern with the spiritual dimensions of theology. For him, a great work of art has a mysterious and inexhaustible quality, that gives it a self-explanatory quality. Its meaning is never obvious or immediately intelligible. Some of these points related to his views on liturgy. He laid much emphasis on the dangers of the social becoming an end in itself, where the form of rite is tailored to secure an unambiguous response, so exhausting the mystery it is there to represent. The social in rite is an instrument, a means of expressing a hallowed end, and within liturgy it has no intrinsic value. Von Balthasar continually warned against self-edification and self-celebration in liturgical communities.[61]

There is an admitted ambiguity involved in the celebration of rite where the 'vitality' of the social self can become confused with that of the spirit. This is reflected in Durkheim's confusion of collective effervescence with the spiritual enhancement a disciplined, richly-cast ceremonial produces. The social needs to be harnessed and to be directed to preclude it dominating liturgical performance. It has to be marked off and unsignified to admit an opening, a space for the holy to come down. Liturgies are not about the social, but the phenomenon that surpasses it and confirms its insignificant status. Some method of casting off from the social into the transcendent is required in the management of rite, if it is to secure its desired and intended effects. This reflects a point von Balthasar argues repeatedly.

For instance, he notes that the sermon should be aimed exclusively at directing 'the attention of everyone (including even the preacher) to the mystery celebrated in its inexhaustibly manifold aspects and, in so doing, allowing no reflection from the divine brilliance to fall back upon the speaker and the spoken word'.[62] This form of tactful casting off from the social has been a central consideration in our approach to understanding the 'successful' performance of liturgy. The corrupting possibilities of the aesthetic, of worshipping the intrinsic qualities of beauty in an objectively cast form, can lead to subjective feelings that are deceptive. Fake religious experiences can arise from ignoring the need to attend to the task of worship, and von Balthasar is only too well aware of the possibilities of corruption in the use of the beautiful to find the holy. The need to spiritualise the aesthetic and to preserve it as a form of revelation of God's Glory is an abiding theme in his writings. For von Balthasar, the social resources of rite are to be exclusively domesticated to keep the individual in the service of the mysterium. He was rather frigid about the convivial qualities of the new rite, which diluted a sense of the mystery it was there to service. Dignity, grandeur and beauty were his central considerations. An interesting example of where beauty and glory combine in a liturgical form to effect an inner transformation of the self arises in the case of Paul Claudel. It also bears on the themes of this study in a way that connects to von Balthasar's approach to theology and liturgy.

Hans Urs von Balthasar had a deep interest in French poets and writers, including Péguy and Claudel, many of whose works he translated into German.[63] Both were laity who found deep contradictions between Catholicism and the world as they found it. Claudel's account of his conversion exemplifies the power of liturgy to effect unexpected changes. Having attended high mass on Christmas Day in 1886, 'without any great pleasure' and having little else to do, he returned for Vespers. He noticed 'the choir-boys in white surplices, and the pupils of the Petit Seminaire of Saint-Nicolas-du-Chardonnet who were helping them, were singing what I afterwards found out was the *Magnificat*'. An event happened there that changed his life. He found himself believing totally in the love of God. His experience left a mark, for he notes 'I had suddenly had the excruciating sense of the

Innocence, of the eternal Childhood of God, – an ineffable revelation'. Long afterwards Claudel gratefully remembered those choirboys 'who enunciated one after the other the divine affirmations of the *Magnificat*'. This was an important conversion, whose centenary was marked in France by the publication of a collection of essays and an exhibition at Notre Dame, Paris. It is unusual for all the central elements of von Balthasar's theology to mix so well within a liturgical event. Beauty was combined in a form that allowed Claudel to be acted on, and to be embraced in a revelatory response that showed forth God's glory and love. Plain chant and choral music had a profound effect on Huymans, Claudel and Simone Weil, who had a conversion experience at Easter ceremonies at Solesmes.[64] Acts and responses only proceed from something enacted, and these require some form, or means of expression, that is both theological and sociological.

Form is a central aspect of von Balthasar's theology. It has a facilitating function, offering and shaping a discernible means of assimilating and understanding what is revealed by God. A seeing through appearing allows an essence to be grasped in the form. Elements of the glory of God are made manifest in an image of beauty that mirrors a purity of truth available to those who seek and wish to find. The display form facilitates and allows man to realise his sense of participation in the glory of God through action and play. Hans Urs von Balthasar's theology has a phenomenological dimension.[65] This admits a particular type of sociology, one that deals in forms in the way Simmel has used them. Von Balthasar's use of the term 'form' is complicated.[66]

It is used to refer to that which bears, shapes and radiates a truth. The beautiful operates in a form and the light of truth it conveys breaks forth from its interior. A beauty of integrity is mixed with an aesthetics to produce a uniquely potent definition that has sociological *and* theological implications. There is a long passage in Volume One of *The Glory of the Lord* that encapsulates his ideas on form, and has a particular relevance for our interests. He writes:

> Visible form not only 'points' to an invisible, unfathomable mystery; form is the apparition of this mystery, and reveals it while, naturally, at the same time protecting and veiling it. Both natural and artistic form has an exterior which appears and an interior depth, both of which, however, are not separable in the form itself. The content (*Gehalt*) does not lie behind the form (*Gestalt*) but within it.

Whoever is not capable of seeing and 'reading' the form will, by the same token, fail to perceive the content. Whoever is not illumined by the form will see no light in the content either.[67]

Form and content are mutually implicated, the latter completing the meanings of the former by supplying it with a truth revealed from outside that which is shaped in the social. There are similarities between the sociological use of the term, and von Balthasar's theological use. Following Simmel and Goffman, form is an enabling device. It is a stable, artificial means of clothing a content, that could be theological or aesthetic. Working through social means, forms supply a frame for identifying and characterising an event as a happening, whose significance exceeds the crucible used to contain and bear it. Form has a subservient facilitating use that makes it disposable but not dispensable. In liturgical enactments, form is simply the social frame that refracts an image. It serves a similar purpose to the frame surrounding an icon. It provides a focus for what is within the boundaries of the picture frame.

To grasp the hidden properties of meaning, 'the radiance of holiness' it is necessary to possess a 'spiritual eye capable of perceiving (*wahrnehmen*) the forms of existence with awe'.[68] The ordering and dissolving of sound which governs music is an example he uses frequently to indicate truth is symphonic and is played in a harmony that yields holy echoes.[69] To be understood, one has to be able to 'hear' its tune. Using a term that complements the process of deciphering in hermeneutics, von Balthasar sees 'erudition' as the process through which a person extracts spiritual and divine life from hidden material. Thus, man becomes filled with meaning through repeated engagement with the unmanifest. Habitual coping in a career of appropriation makes contact with liturgy less unintelligible than it might initially appear to the casual observer.[70] Thus, 'faith is the light of God becoming luminous in man'.[71] Forms only have an intelligibility in terms of the interior they express.

There is a holistic element in von Balthasar's use of form that precludes it being broken down into its constituent parts. Contemplation is the means of entry into their fuller, invisible transcendent elements. Beauty and form operate to effect a movement to what is beyond contradiction and concealment. They lead to greater things, and as von Balthasar notes, 'the appearance of the form, as revelation of the depths, is an indissoluble union of two things. It is the real presence of the depths, of the whole of reality, *and* it is a real pointing beyond itself to these depths'.[72] Form betokens what cannot be seen but nevertheless is a representation of it, a point noted in Chapter 4 in the discussion on the relationship between the choirboy and the angel.

In the medieval world, their images got mixed up, so that the angel was often represented clad as a subminister attending on an eternal mass. This practice of clothing angels in albs stemmed from the late fourteenth century and was apparent in the visual arts, in glass and paintings. Medieval liturgical dramas supplied the basis for these artistic models, where boys or young men were dressed in mass vestments to perform angelic functions in the plays.[73] It is important not to confuse the two, who complement each other in liturgical activities. This bears on a useful point of von Balthasar: 'an image, thus, has significance only in so far as it succeeds in making present the forms and proportions of the original, which it never tends to replace with its own standards'.[74]

Forms make an opening to faith for man. They present a manifestation of God, who allows himself to be expressed in a tangible shape, through the sensory and the social as used in rite and sacrament. For von Balthasar the sensory is touched with the spiritual and becomes contagious through the social as expressed in the activities of the Church.[75] Revelation through aesthetic symbols and ostensive images of the world is accepted by von Balthasar. These elements are incomplete manifestations, for as he notes when dealing with an essentially symbolic reality, the thing itself lies in a veiled form that reveals it. Liturgical resources, such as vestments and gestures manifest a harmony, an effort to enhance the correspondence believed to exist between the material and the spiritual, when used for ecclesiastical purposes.[76] The dialectic between concealment and revelation generates a possibility of growth into a God who becomes more non-manifest and incomprehensible. Again, this draws us to the issue of the apophatic, but it also accounts for the curiosity that shapes repeated use of liturgical resources. Repeated use generates a passage of growth into understanding the implications of what cannot be grasped, and at the same time fuels a wish to have more revealed from what is concealed. This is a fundamental aspect of the capacity of liturgy to bear repeated use. The actors involved in the playing of rite have to effect a passage through these double meanings that lend a tension to the performance. Because the rite is dealing with inexhaustible means, the scope for repetition is endless.

There is a necessary failure to fully grasp the total meaning of a liturgical enactment, which has been expressed by von Balthasar in the following way:

> The inspiration of a great work of art is impenetrable and the result it achieves is not fully analysable. Inspiration resists analysis in the sense that while the latter can indeed point out the proportion and harmony of the parts, it can never synthesise the whole given simply the parts, and it is this whole which remains ungraspable in its patent beauty.[77]

A similar infirmity afflicts sociology in its effort to understand religion. It has no analytical means, other than a fragmenting and reductionist perspective, for interpreting a ritual believed by its practitioners to be capable of realising a distinctive harmonious whole, whose totality can be discerned by believers. The spiritual is believed to operate in some indeterminate manner through the social means. Our concern throughout has been to show how a mishandling of the social in liturgy could subtract from a sense of the Divine if the meaningful implications which arise in enactment are not directly confronted. This draws us back to an earlier point, on the need in Ricoeur's phrase to cultivate a second naïveté. This involves finding the social conditions within which symbols can be enhanced and rituals can be harnessed to secure a fuller contact with the holy. It involves a quest for a more secure form of petition by mobilising the social to a more focused end. Von Balthasar observes that

> in his understanding of the world, modern man shows himself to be at least as naïve as the man with a mythical image of the world: what the latter at least holds on to through his intuition and imagistic representations the former has lost as a result of his all-destructive rationalisms.[78]

In his final comments on the attestation of the form, von Balthasar writes

> and so, in the end, what is involved is a reciprocal vicarious vision: just as the angels of the little ones on earth always behold the face of the Father for them in heaven (Mt 18.10), so, too, men on earth behold for the angels the beauty of the God who has concealed himself in flesh.[79]

If sociological understanding ventures into limits beyond which a truth speaks louder than words, the theology it requires should complement that which lies beyond its powers to conceptualise. It would provide a theological endorsement for what sociology cannot complete, and would allow a means of living with limits that are limitless. For this reason a negative theology that operates in paradox, that has an apophatic cast, fits most closely the interpretative sociological approach taken in this work. The apophatic redresses the areas of analytical failure of sociology, the dilemmas it highlights but cannot resolve. It speaks for what sociology cannot say. It relates to a quest to find what is beyond utterance and paradox. In the final section we try to understand how this notion of the apophatic can be applied to a sociological interpretation of a 'successful' performance of liturgy.

SURPASSING SOCIAL LIMITS: NEGATIVE THEOLOGY AND SOCIOLOGICAL UNDERSTANDINGS

> So long thy power hath blest me, sure it still
> Will lead me on
> O'er moor and fen, o'er crag and torrent, till
> The night is gone,
> And with the morn those Angel faces smile,
> Which I have loved long since, and lost a while.
> (John Henry Newman, 'Lead Kindly Light')

Apophatic theology represents a classical tradition of thought, that stresses the transcendent, the mystical and the spiritual. The theologian most associated with this school, the Pseudo-Dionysius, has defied a vast scholarly enquiry to find his identity. The dating of his writings and the question of whether they are forgeries or not, seem characteristic issues for a man who wrote so eloquently on the unknowability of God.[80] There are many reasons why the writings of the Pseudo-Dionysius are a suitable theology upon which to end this sociological analysis. He was deeply concerned with the role of the angels in a liturgical theology that had a strong emphasis on the spiritual implications of movement of actions, a stress that has obvious sociological attractions. There are also unexpected sociological resonances in his emphases on the tacit, the symbolic and imaginative aspects of liturgy. His description of angelic hierarchies is complemented by his account of their earthly manifestations in liturgical orders. The influence of the Pseudo-Dionysius on the development of medieval Gothic architecture, his stress on vestments and sacramentals, give him added attractions as the writer to conclude this study. Throughout his work there is an emphasis on redemption from failures of meaning, on paradox and antinomies and a play on double meanings that mark the limits of understanding through social means. A negative theology is able to handle and to contain antinomies that arise in symbols and in actions which can give rise to misunderstandings in performance. His theology draws together all the pitfalls of analysis of understanding displayed in this work and offers a theological means for their redemption from meaninglessness.

The problem of knowing God through negative means is the particular characteristic of apophatic theology. It argues that God exists in a Being beyond categorisation and who lives in a way that is unavailable to human logic. This emphasis on the incomprehensibility of God, of placing him beyond human knowing, operates in a paradox, that despite His absence, He chooses to make himself present in acts of revelation. Man comes to know God through a dialectic between that which is apophatic, negative, and missing, and a cataphatic theology, that operates with positive affirmations that can be understood through revelation. These contradictory strands are united in paradoxical terms such as 'dazzling darkness' and the 'manifestation of the unmanifest'. This emphasis on God being transcendent and beyond rational categorisation accounts for the strong imaginative and mystical cast that operates in this theology. It makes a contemplative demand that moves man to think of life beyond human categories. For Vladimir Lossky, it effects a passage from within knowledge to what is beyond it, so 'proceeding by negations one ascends from the inferior degrees of being to the highest, by progressively setting aside all that can be known, in order to draw near to the Unknown in the darkness of absolute ignorance'.[81]

The term 'apophatic' refers to that which is beyond speech, what is to be understood through casting off past words. I wish to develop a related term that bears on how liturgical actions are to be understood, both in a sociological sense and in what they strive to achieve in theological terms. 'Apopraxis' refers to that which is meaningfully secured in actions that have a self denying quality, where an element of concealment is involved in the act of revealing.[82] It is a variation on the other term I used earlier, virtuous dissimulation. Liturgical actions operate best when they manifest Godlike qualities in performance, signifying what is past understanding.

There is an element of abandonment and separation involved in acts of denial that enable an otherwise unavailable essence to be revealed. This involves working through a transcending way on the part of the seeker after God. The seeker has to deny in order to affirm, to abandon in order to find, and, in handling paradoxes to trust that all will be revealed in holy awe. There is a filtering and selective approach involved in constructing belief. The Pseudo-Dionysius wrote that believers should be like

> sculptors who set out to carve a statue. They remove every obstacle to the pure view of the hidden image, and simply by this act of clearing aside they show up the beauty which is hidden.[83]

Again, this returns us to the element of mystery in what is so revealed. There is an element of ambiguity in the mystery that emerges from a clearing and cutting away of extraneous material. Mystery relates to that which is concealed in symbols, embodying the secrecy of God, but it also relates to the eschatological, to what is to be revealed in the future.[84] The notion of going beyond the concealed and the veiled to find what is above and beyond paradox appears in the account of Moses on Mount Sinai. Having been purified and been separated from the unpurified, Moses hears 'many voiced trumpets' and sees pure lights. He moves ahead to the summit of God, not to meet Him, but to contemplate where he dwells, and then he plunges into

> the truly mysterious darkness of unknowing. Here, renouncing all that the mind may conceive, wrapped entirely in the intangible and the invisible, he belongs completely to him who is beyond everything. Here, being neither oneself nor someone else, one is supremely united by a completely unknowing inactivity of all knowledge, and knows beyond the mind by knowing nothing.[85]

Successful enactments of rite involve a realisation that something had been effected that speaks from beyond the limit of the rite. This relates to a point of John Wright's, regarding Israel praying to a hidden God. The cult, the ark, the tent of meeting and the temple were 'an attempt to encapsulate the presence of God through the "veil of his seeming absence"'. The notion of God hiding relates to the idea that it would be impossible to remain human and to see him for 'a God comprehended is no God'.[86] There is an element of the apophatic involved in Otto's notion of *mysterium tremendum*, of which silence is a crucial aspect. As Wright notes, the incomprehensibility of God so stressed by Otto represents a negative experience that is positive in its effects and so relates to the central concerns of an apophatic theology.[87]

There is an abstract, ephemeral dimension in negative theology, that generates a worry that the emptiness so affirmed could be conducive to a form of nihilism. It makes belief a wager that could end up trusting in what might not exist beyond the capacity to categorise. An element of folly is attached to negative theology which is bound to the scandal it provokes that wordly wisdom might not matter.[88] Negative theology seems oddly well suited to the contemporary crisis in the humanities where relativism indicates 'something is missing' in our forms of knowing, and somehow rationality will not supply us with the means to tell the truth. Theodor Adorno and Walter Benjamin became fascinated with the idea of a negative theology in the context of Judaism. For the former, it became equated with the pursuit of aesthetic experience and for the latter, it was part of an interest in mysticism.[89]

The sociological significance of liturgical actions lies less in their description than in achieving a degree of understanding, however limited, of the hidden properties they realise routinely. Deciphering, reading and understanding reflect a capacity to grasp that which is manifest in the opaque, to discern what resonates in the sounding, and to see what lies in the invisible. The Pseudo-Dionysius was deeply concerned with the practice of liturgy as it related to the transcendent and the invisible. He had a particular concern with the symbolic representation of angels in the enactment of rite, linking the invisible to the visible in a way that complements the approach in Chapter 4. His theology is one of use, of encountering the double meanings, negations and concealments that effect a passage into the transcendent. In his assessment of the Pseudo-Dionysius, von Balthasar noted that

> to the extent that liturgy is a human, ecclesial act which, as a response of praise and thanksgiving, seeks to echo the form of the divine revelation, the categories of the aesthetic and art will play a decisive role in it, and there has hardly been a theology so deeply informed by aesthetic categories as the liturgical theology of the Areopagite.[90]

Gothic settings and assumptions of beauty govern the shape of liturgy used in this analysis. The Pseudo-Dionysius offers a bridge between the early Church and medieval practices, not only in the expected area of mysticism, but also in the development of Gothic architecture. He was an important influence on Abbot Suger's Church in Paris. Built in the twelfth century, this church represented a notable architectural advance in Gothic style. Paul Rorem notes that the primary authority for the uplifting effect of the building came from the Pseudo-Dionysius. The soaring arches and windows of Gothic architecture, and its style of pointing up from the visible to the invisible had the aim of elevating and uplifting. The style served to edify.[91] The Pseudo-Dionysius had a notable impact on Cistercian monastic thought in the medieval period, and on later Benedictine liturgical practices.[92] There is an implicit sociology in his approach to the understanding of liturgy that is as remarkable as it is unexpected. He provides sociology with a theological means of uplift out of the quagmire of antinomy and doubt into which its analysis might otherwise sink.

This emphasis on uplift forms a central aspect of his writings, where liturgical acts are interconnected with heavenly effects. There is a dialectical quality to the Pseudo-Dionysius expressed in his notion of procession and return, which, as we have suggested before, renders it a holy version of the hermeneutic circle, one that decants man into heavenly knowing rather than hellish unknowing. The notion of 'procession' refers to the antecedent movement of God, His descent and revelation to man. 'Return' is the means of uplift and connection made by man in response. It involves an ascent, a rising

> from what is below up to the transcendent, and the more it climbs, the more language falters, and when it has passed up and beyond the ascent, it will turn silent completely, since it will finally be at one with him who is indescribable.[93]

The notion of response, of working through symbols, images and actions to enter a realm that lies beyond the categorisable involves an inescapable passage through the social that cannot be given a theological bypass. The necessity of working through the social to a divine end, admits qualified sociological comment about the mode of entry to the passage. The social is important in this form of theology to the degree to which it can be discarded. The process of uplift involved in the notion of return effects an abandonment of liturgical props as the passage of affirmation moves beyond that which is accessible to conceptualisation to enter a deeper and fuller relationship with the unknowable. In his commentary, Rorem suggests that this pattern of procession and return is the interpretative method of the Pseudo-Dionysian biblical hermeneutics and liturgical theology.[94]

Negative theology transcends the issue of specification, and to that degree its relationship to the 'scandal of particularity' is weak. The Pseudo-Dionysius partly resolves this problem in his notion of ascent and return, by regarding the former as embodying a unifying simplicity that contains the plural and the complex. He expresses the solution in this way:

> the divine sacrament of synaxis remains what it is, unique, simple, and indivisible and yet, out of love for humanity, it is pluralized in a sacred variegation of symbols. It extends itself so as to include all the hierarchical imagery. Then it draws all these varied symbols together into a unity, returns to its own inherent oneness, and confers unity on all those sacredly uplifted to it.[95]

Movement from complexity to simplicity has crucial implications for understanding his use of symbols. Procession effects a movement through the symbolic that uplifts. Censing of the altar is a form of liturgical movement that embodies this principle. Symbols have an unexpectedly central place in his theology, where negation is an instrument of movement, a case of an analytical liability being converted into a spiritual asset. In his approach, God reveals Himself in a manner of concealment in earthly symbols, so that their use allows him to be revealed.[96] From a sociological viewpoint, it is noteworthy that he pays little attention to the symbolic nature of the architecture of a church building or the sacramental substances, but as Rorem indicates, he concentrates on liturgical movements and actions.[97] This binds an apophatic theology into social elements available to sociological scrutiny. It gives social actions an enhancing and uplifting capacity and a crucial focus towards a theological end. Even though social actions operate in a way that sows the seeds of their extinction and ultimate abandonment, they are given a crucial facilitating role.

Any sociological effort to elaborate and to amplify a plurality of meanings in the use of symbols can operate in theological safety in the scheme of the Pseudo-Dionynsius, for it confirms their use to the degree to which they can be unsignified and cast off. Good liturgical manners are linked to their mysterious effect in the exercise of tact. An exaggerated sociological emphasis on the variability of symbols and the plurality of meanings attached to perceptible forms of worship could be corrosive of belief. Accepting the arguments of the Pseudo-Dionysius gives sociology considerable latitude in amplifying the double meanings embedded in liturgical actions, without doing much theological damage. Indeed, the further sociology forces liturgical symbols and actions to descend into the ambiguous, the more it enhances a theological possibility of ascent. The polyvalent and concealing nature of liturgical actions is a condition that facilitates access to that which transcends such a disability. Their use invites a dependence on a procession down to uplift them from chaos into harmony.

Symbols in liturgy are presented for use and interpretative response. But, as Rorem suggests, 'uplifting does not occur by virtue of the rites or symbols themselves but rather in their interpretation, in the upward movement through the perceptible to the intelligible'.[98] Symbols are forms of analogy used to speak of the things of God. They are a means of naming what is nameless and of placing within sense perception what is beyond the senses. They invoke a sense of yearning and embody a notion of acting in order to be acted on in a process of negation and affirmation that can permit access to a mystical sensibility. Sacred symbols are 'the manifest images of unspeakable and marvellous sights'.[99] They are not to be used haphazardly, but in whatever way is appropriate to causes, powers and orders of which they are revealing signs. His approach to symbols has some important sociological implications for understanding liturgical practices.

Symbols operate in two forms in his writings. The similar refers to objects which have a plausible affinity to the invisible which they betoken. Oil used in anointing has a fragrance that is suggestive of what it is supposed to effect sacramentally. It gives form to that which of its nature is without form. In the second version, dissimilar symbols have an element of incongruity that generates a curiosity before that which is so unexpectedly proclaimed. They speak of connections that seem incredible. This point particularly arises in the case of angels, who are given a bewildering variety of forms in scripture and come to symbolise many things.[100] It might be argued, however, that the dissimilarity of symbols as applied to angels relates more to the Old than to the New Testament.

Because the Divine transcends what can only be known in a paired fashion, through double but interdependent meanings, the Pseudo-Dionysius has leeway to lay stress on their merger into one, however paradoxical the outcome. The like-mannered combined with the incongruous serve to produce heavenly representations, such as the fiery river, the channel through which grace flows.[101] Sacramental symbols tend to have a more exact quality, being similar and closer to perceptible images. This need for a close fit operates in areas where misinterpretations might have fatal spiritual effects. For instance in baptism, triple immersions are used to imitate the three days in the tomb, and the bright clothes conferred mark a re-birth. He suggests that 'sacred symbols are actually the perceptible tokens of the conceptual things'.[102]

Particular stress is laid on the hidden nature of sacred knowledge and the need to protect it from profanations. Divine beauties 'reveal themselves solely to minds capable of grasping them'.[103] The Pseudo-Dionysius comments on the way the great variety of sacred symbols mentioned in scriptures, when observed from the outside, 'seem filled with incredible and contrived fantasy'.[104] His approach to beauty bears on the comments of von Balthasar, pointing to the light that is revealed from the form that has a matchless integrity of truth. Counterfeit forms and empty appearances are to be left to the mob and to foolish despisers. A need to guard sacred knowledge, as it is expressed in the sacraments, is often noted.

Dissimilar symbols have a particular function of attracting the curious and the unwary, rather in the manner of the Holy Fool. They have a negating function, one that is initial and is dispensable, for they attract attention to the beauty hidden in the images. He goes on to argue,

> let us not suppose that the outward face of these contrived symbols exists for its own sake. Rather, it is the protective garb of the under-standing of what is ineffable and invisible to the common multitude. This is so in order that the most sacred things are not easily handled by the profane but are revealed instead to the real lovers of holiness. Only these latter know how to pack away the workings of childish imagination regarding the sacred symbols. They alone have the simplicity of mind and the receptive, contemplative power to cross over to the simple, marvelous, transcendent truth of the symbols.[105]

This need to guard a hidden and sacred order points to the necessity of some form of regulation. It admits a notion of agency that invites a comment on the use of social ingredients to achieve a holy 'success'.

In his work there is a particular concern to mark out the link between angelic hierarchies and their earthly manifestations in sacerdotal orders. Forms of appearing are related to a capacity to inspire belief. Fire is regarded as having a purifying intense quality, one associated with God. It is a quality of purity attributed to 'the intelligent beings of heaven' and is associated with earthly manif-estations of angels . This relates to the discussion on the link between a white surplice and the wearer being endowed with angelic qualities which was discussed in Chapter 4. The Pseudo-Dionysius claimed that the 'shining and fiery robe symbolizes the Divine form' and accords with the imagery of fire. He goes on to add that 'the priestly vestment signifies the capacity to guide spiritually to the divine and mysterious sights, and to consecrate one's whole life'.[106]

Angels have a central importance for the Pseudo-Dionysius, both in terms of a relationship to God, and also of presenting an image in liturgy that inspires the actors involved to strive towards the angelic life.[107] Angels provide an image for emulation and the appropriation of their qualities into earthly manifestations by all too human actors. It has been argued that the 'scandal of particularity' poses particular problems for the *via negativa*.[108] Yet, there are sections of his writings where detail is matched to angelic issues. Hierarchs are the highest of his three earthly orders, and their liturgical duties are very closely specified in a way that has heavenly implications. These are designated as 'angels'. Although the choirboy and later the monk have been used, in the liturgical parts in this analysis, the comments made about the link between the hierarch and the angel apply also to our actors. The Pseudo-Dionysius wrote

> I see nothing wrong in the fact that the Word of God calls even our hierarch an 'angel', for it is characteristic of him that like the angels he is, to the extent of which he is capable, a messenger and that he is raised up to imitate, so far as a man may, the angelic power to bring revelation.[109]

This notion of revelation through imitation suggests a plausibility of fit between the actor and the image so incarnated, a point that applies to the choirboy who sounds like an angel in the sanctuary. Discerning the image and accepting its plausibility is perhaps a matter of revelation, but it also bears on a wider issue of accepting what one wants to believe. As the Pseudo-Dionysius notes, 'those who are stone deaf to what the sacred sacraments teach also have no eye for the imagery'.[110] Incongruous symbols demand interpretation, and to that degree enable the blind to think about seeing. Both text and liturgy have an inscrutable quality. As Rorem notes 'although the arena of ceremonial symbolism requires a more discerning and experienced interpreter, since it does not jolt the beginner with obvious dissimilarities, the basic process of interpretation is nevertheless identical'. He has noted also that liturgical symbols are never presented as dissimilar and at one point, he calls for the use of 'precise images'.[111] Believers see the hidden in what is manifest, and faith places ambiguity and detail in a meaningful order of account.

The wider theological assumptions of liturgy force any sociological account into confronting inconvenient elements of belief that sit uneasily amidst the alien prose. The notion of affirming a risen Christ at a sociology conference would exceed the bounds of ideological taste. It would seem scandalous for a sociologist to affirm such a belief under the shadow of the forefathers of the discipline who prophesied otherwise. But the study of liturgy generates for sociology its own version of the 'scandal of particularity'. Usually the term refers to the peculiar time and place in which a saving event occurred, and points to a discomfort over the specific having such general consequences. It relates to a foolishness embedded in the Christian message. St Paul wrote

> For the Jews require a sign, and the Greeks
> seek after wisdom:
> But we preach Christ crucified, unto the Jews
> a stumblingblock, and unto the Greeks foolishness.
>   (1 Cor. 1:22–23)

The 'scandal of particularity' in its sociological setting refers to the affront of having to understand a repetitious social act, which can only be fully understood in terms that lie outside the rhetoric of the discipline. The notion of God present in a particular Church, to liturgical actors, who believe in acting before Him represents a hard demand for a soft discipline such as sociology to fully understand. Yet a sociologist who believes cannot really present an inhibited and incomplete vision of what he understands. As Flannery O'Connor noted,

> we forget that what is to us an extension of sight is to the rest of the world a peculiar and arrogant blindness, and that no one today is prepared to recognize the truth of what we show unless our purely individual vision is in full operation.[112]

In his assessment of the Pseudo-Dionysius, von Balthasar notes the way liturgical actions involve entry into a movement, where the cataphatic and the apophatic are interlinked. They have a mutual implication and the movement they suggest has a circular quality that echoes the problems of question and answer that arise in the hermeneutic circle. Whereas the latter has a vicious nihilistic aspect to it, where relativism denies a secure place to know, the former offers a redemptive possibility, an uplifting that suggests a fulfilling form of enlargement.[113] Sociology has no means of making a choice. That is an issue for theology. But if a choice is made to go below the social surface of rite, then a sociological account can be pushed in a particular theological direction to effect the fullest of meanings and understandings, without generating misunderstandings about the re-presentation of the holy in everyday modern life.

Conclusion

Pereant, inquit, qui ante nos nostra dixerunt.
(Aelius Donatus)

The end of a book provides a basis for reflection on a theme that came to pass through a text. Some conclusions go out with a sociological bang; others end in a series of wholesome philosophical platitudes on the need to keep the conversation going; and others terminate with a theological whimper, as in this work. What started as great visions in the night have ended as the sociologist's tale from the pew, mimical mutterings about what was seen in the unseen and what was heard about the unspoken. The end product of this sociological effort to understand seems modest, to say the least, a plethora of perplexed little insights about an elusive subject, where any definite conclusion would be a distortion. If nothing else, one begins to understand why sociologists seem to have elected to neglect the study of liturgy. One has found a topic that seems to defy the disciplinary remit to cover all facets of the social. An endless series of ambiguities and irresolvable antinomies have been encountered in a form of ritual determined to deal with the indeterminate in a way that peculiarly resists sociological efforts to understand. Liturgies contain endless series of paradoxes that play tricks on the sociological imagination. What started as a study of the obvious sank into the unobvious, but in an ambiguous manner that came to characterise the passage of the account as a whole. Were the ambiguities that have arisen figments of a sociological mind cast on rite, or were they theological truths a humbled sociology had uncovered? Did sociology add anything to the understanding of liturgy or did such an effort make sociology seem pale and less virile? If anything, the status of sociology as the clone ranger of the social sciences seems to have been re-affirmed.

To defend the study by saying these are the dilemmas of the liturgical actor that bear sociological understandings hardly helps. The more these are highlighted, the more sociology seems incapable of resolving them. Perhaps one can rejoice in the analytical paradox that has emerged: the more a sociological account of liturgy 'succeeds' the more it 'fails'. At best sociology can mirror that which it can discern dimly in the looking glass self of the actor as he plays in a representation of the holy in a public performance. But at worst, it does not seem to say very much that was not already understood in a theological context. That which eludes the sociological grasp lies hidden in the liturgical mosaic, somewhere between its obvious and its unobvious facets, an area of analytical liminality where sociology ought to say the most, but somehow ends up saying the least.

It is easy to supply an endless chronicle of the opaque and indeterminate qualities of rite, thus confirming suspicions of the *flâneur* that this represents the holy game of a club not worth joining. One can gamble with a lot of interpretations that permit detachment or attachment, that play along the surface of the rite, or risk going deeper into meanings that are concealed in what is being revealed. The sociologist might start with the obvious aspects of the liturgical performance, but it is its unobvious aspects that lead away beyond the sociological pale.

Sociology itself seems to become involved in the wager the rites present. It takes on the ambiguous qualities it sees in the social form which it strives to represent to the discipline as a whole. In affirming its insights into the limits of rite, sociology comes to exercise a Janus faced guardianship over its social form, which is represented as indispensable but best kept invisible in the transaction. A completeness of meaning and understanding is denied to the cultural fabric of rite, but in a way that points to the concerns of a negative theology. Sociology supplies a negative witness to the transcendent basis of rite. That is its tragedy in a post-modernist era. It exemplifies the quest of the *flâneur* lurking and listening, labouring on the edge, looking to find, but not staying long enough to notice.

All liturgical enactments have a front, a mask that conceals and disguises matters of great mystery and imagination. This study has been geared to get behind the social façade of liturgy, the presenting image that governs its ritual staging. Given a façade to scrutinise, most sociologists will reach for some acid stripping comments to gain access to the rear to reveal the 'real' purpose of the transaction. The tacit elements of performance, such as Goffman explored, give a secular witness to the significance of the unobvious. It could not be said that Goffman's accounts were objective. They were idiosyncratic, peculiar, and unprovable, but they were also remarkably persuasive, making him the sociologist of post-modernism, who adorned with insight that which he despised.

The need to go below the social surface to find the truth was given a place in the sociological sun in this account of liturgical life. A dialectic between distrust and trust became the basis of conversation with the liturgical actor as he strove to find an accommodation between the demands of appearing and the necessity of disappearing into the self to survive. A moral dimension was added to description and the need to make sociological judgements beyond the obvious was affirmed. After all, it was what was *not* manifest in the performance that interested Goffman. But the bias towards scepticism and cynicism, which his work exemplifies in dealing with the unmanifest is not written in stone. Innocence and virtue might also lurk in what is concealed, qualities of the humble that flourish in their own shadow land. Vice and virtue are two sides of the same coin, an antinomy buried in the unmanifest that requires a subtle sociological excavation to get the fullest exchange rate on the cultural market.

Focusing on the unobvious aspects of liturgy, that which its impression management serves to conceal, could reveal the triumph of folly, where vanity reigns as the actors bask in unholy stratagems to deceive the weak in mind. Cynicism might be confirmed in the liturgical actor's account that affirms the bad faith of the sociologist in such holy transactions. But equally, the actors could have a deadly purpose in their guardianship of the holy, using guile to conceal vanity and exercising a tact to secure a purity of purpose, one that produces an innocence in the act that deceives the experienced. As these actors move, as if before holy mirrors, the impressions they convey about the unobvious aspects of rite could transmit a witness to the truth of the obvious rather than its capacity to lie. It would be an arbitrary reading to suggest that the unobvious aspects of liturgical performance could reveal only a set of meanings that would discount the belief system embodied in the ritual under scrutiny. Another reading of the unobvious could accept the religious truth of what it strives to signify, if for no other reason than to gain access to the properties of meaning the actors engaged in a liturgy believe lie meaningfully below the social surface. In the last analysis, the actor's account counts, as sociological credence is given to his meanings and understandings, in a compensatory response to the imperialising claims of structuralism in the early 1980s.[1]

This analysis has tried to work from within the liturgical actor's self-understanding in a way that gives it a sociological focus. For theologians, grace secures the operation of rite in a way that places it above human weakness. In a bleaker sociological account, one cannot assume the presence of grace, but can only work on the basis of its absence. Fear, mistrust, worry and scruple can mark the actor engaged in liturgy, where carelessness presumes, idolatry is near at hand, vanity is proximate and corruption in enactment seems only too possible.

Our concern has been with the relationship between the actor and the social form of the rite, the procedures and actions he has to use to effect that which he believes it might realise and the responsibilities he has to exercise if the willed intentions are to become 'real' in their theological consequences. Making the holy manifest presupposes a qualified degree of agency, the need to act to effect. Liturgies express an imperative to act, to do, to use and to make manifest a message, a warrant that is both biblical and social. The truth proclaimed in the Gospel has to be enacted in some manner, so that its properties can be known and understood. It is this knowing and understanding, based on a need to harness cultural elements in a selective manner that admits a sociological consideration, a capacity to comment on matters that might seem purely theological. Part of the purpose of this study has been to draw attention to the infelicities and distortions that achieve an antinomial expression when the actors engaged in a ritual fulfil this imperative to do in memory.

Too much of the theology and liturgy that came after Vatican II in the mid-sixties endorsed the wisdom of the world in a naïve manner that is increasingly seen as unproductive and irrelevant to the changing circumstances of the 1990s, where religious rather than ideological fundamentalism is changing the terms of the debate on culture. The modernity the Council seemed to endorse has been converted into a crisis of post-modernity. At present, there are growing efforts to re-weigh Catholic forms of worship with a sacerdotal significance, which the preceding two decades had deemed to be incredible. Efforts to make Catholicism relevant to the modern world had the unintended effect of leading to a loss of images of heaven and hell. Fear of fate in this life and the next became diluted. This decline in the need to service the after-life occurred at the same time as a New Puritanism arose over the place of beauty and art in liturgy.

It cannot be said that these liturgical reforms have stemmed the tide of secularisation, or that they have reversed the decline in Church attendance over the past two decades. None of the constituencies the reforms were established to satisfy seem to feel their problems have been resolved; youth still claims to be 'bored', students are alienated, the middle classes remain divided and the working class is indifferent.[2] There is a crisis in liturgy, because its sociological basis in a modern culture has never been properly examined or understood. Second thoughts have not yet cohered into a reconsideration of what has gone wrong. Rites no longer grip, symbols seem thin rather than thick and an unproductive uncertainty mixes with a disillusion at the outcome of the liturgical reforms. Too much got cast away in the decade following Vatican II.

Religious enthusiasms are dangerous; those in liturgy can be fatal. Somehow the glue holding rites together has come unstuck and the workmen seeking to repair the damage have never left the building. The process of renewal seems to have generated a profound indifference to debate on liturgical matters. The implications of the political changes in Eastern Europe and Russia have yet to be fully understood. It is clear that the Christian Churches were of considerable importance as mobilising forces for the revolution in 1989. Religion rather than ideology gripped the masses in a way that provides a remarkable contrast to the malaise of post-modernism that afflicts Western cultural thought. Some liberal Western theologians and liturgists are likely to find little comfort in the strengths conveyed by the deeply felt formal and traditional rituals that mark styles of Christianity in Eastern Europe. These achieved an effect, a populism, a capacity to bind that have been lost in efforts at liturgical renewal in the West in the past two decades. Formal traditional forms of rite cannot be dismissed as being inherently culturally incredible. The belief that they cannot 'work' in the West is questionable. These rites only become incredible when they are deemed to be so and when their language of purpose is arbitrarily denied.

Liturgical renewal achieved its closest proximity to sociology in its period of inception in mid-nineteenth century France. In some of his recent writings, R. W. Franklin suggests that the generation of a sense of community was considered a central social function of liturgical enactments. Although he touches on the issue only indirectly, the liturgical renewal movement drew from similar moral concerns to those leading to the foundation of sociology. A heightened worry about individualism, combined with fears of the fragmenting and alienating effects of urbanisation and industrialisation, were part of the cultural agenda of the liturgical movement. This common set of worries gave liturgy an unexpected link with sociology. It is the earlier and innovative interests of Guéranger in liturgical renewal that form the interests of this study, and not its later twentieth century interpretation where the idea of community became synonymous with suburban middle-class values of meeting and joining. Guéranger's concerns were monastic and Benedictine. Franklin indicates that

Guéranger was also interested in preserving an awe of the transcendent in liturgy. His interest in the Gothic style of liturgy reflected an awareness of the need to represent the sacredness of mystery in Christianity.[3] One of the aims of this study has been to provide a sociological account of liturgy that could be connected back to the origins of the renewal movement.

It is very unlikely that Guéranger had sociological arguments in mind in his quest for liturgical renewal. Despite many important innovations, such as the translation of the Daily Office for use by the laity, the liturgical renewal movement as it came to fruition after Vatican II has made many unfortunate detours from its original purposes. These are partly due to the failure to find an adequate means of 'reading' and understanding the cultural facets of rite that are used in its social construction and enactment as a form of ritual. Debate on liturgy has become too concerned with its external cultural image and credibility in a way that has distracted attention from the internal means through which it reproduces its form in a credible manner that marks it as a holy event worth noting. For sociologists, the crucial questions about rites centre on how they secure their plausibility, and not their pliability. There is a fascinating sociological question buried in liturgy that has never been pursued: how do the actors involved in its production render that which is implausible plausible?

Mysterious aspects of rite could be regarded as excluding, but they also could effect a sense of inclusion in a collective search for understanding. A common and habitual search for fuller meanings binds all participants in liturgy into a deeper sense and appreciation of the richness of its actions. This study is a sociological affirmation of that point. It has tried to explore those facets of rite that cannot be spelt out in liturgical performance in an analytical manner that protects what is distinctive about these mysterious social transactions. The best form of protection of the mysterious qualities of rite was to use a sociological analysis that stressed its ambiguous and antinomial qualities. This accounts for the way proximities were paired together to establish their differences, as in the case of the altar server and the waiter. Part of the purpose of the study has been to give sociological expression to the autonomous social means through which liturgies are reproduced, regulated and understood by actors who strive to convey, sometimes 'successfully', a plausible impression of management of contact with holy, a sense of which might, or might not be realised.

In a superficial way, this account of liturgy could be understood as the romantic retreat of a sociologist into the cloister or the Cathedral, where concern has centred on a rite rarely performed. The insights derived might seem to represent a collection of rumours, the product of what Underhill has termed 'the folly of the sacristy'.[4] There has been a worry displayed about detail in this study, that is magnified into a sociological concoction of insights liturgists and theologians might seem safely dispensed from knowing about. In defence it should be said that trivia or minute details *can* matter. In theological terms, these are incarnational facets of rite that cannot be arbitrarily discarded. They form part of the mosaic of rite that gives it shape. Liturgical details are aspects of the 'scandal of particularity' that give rite its distinctive theological basis. As liturgical detail is ambiguous and its effects are indeterminate, maybe trivial, possibly serious, sociology has no authority to arbitrate on these matters. One is reminded of the lines in William Blake's prophetic book, *Jerusalem*:

He who would do good to another must do it in Minute
    Particulars.
General Good is the plea of the scoundrel, hypocrite & flatterer:
For Art & Science cannot exist but in minutely organized
    Particulars,
and not in generalizing Demonstrations of the Rational Power.[5]

As those who engage habitually in the social construction of stable forms of rite become more self-conscious and more aware of the mechanism used, considerations of detail are bound to emerge. Attention wanders and finds a detail to decipher and to ponder on. Liturgical details are part of human frailty. They draw the actor back from a sense of bonding with the heavenly to find the clutter of an earthly lot. Detail in the ritual form enables access to the holy, but it can also disable unproductively if its subservience is not maintained. For sociological purposes, detail in rite presents a basis upon which to confront a dilemma the actor might face. The issues selected for consideration in this study might have seemed arbitrary and odd, but the detailed facets of another form of rite could seem equally selective and implausible.

Our list of detail, minor liturgical roles, clothing, gestures and forms of rite all draw attention to facets of the social basis of rite, but with a price. A holistic sense of the liturgical process is missing, where all elements, symbols, sights and sounds merge in a harmonised movement that gathers all present into a sense of transcendence. The sound of a choir singing a descant, as they process off the sanctuary with the other actors, down to the vast congregation of a Cathedral who join in the hymn, marks in a totality, a collective sense of worship that evades sociological encapsulation. Sociology has to operate with partial aspects of rite to gain access to its whole, a methodological necessity that echoes the comment of Proclus that 'affirmations cut off realities in slices'.[6] There are a number of costs in sociological efforts to understand rite and these we have tried to minimise.

At some point liturgical forms will have be considered in sociology, if for no other reason than religious rituals have been studied in so many other contexts that the absence of such an account will be noticed as a gap in the literature. The detail and the quality of the sociological accounts of rituals in primitive societies, in comparative religion and within modern secular cultures, beg questions as to why equivalent studies of similar depth have not been made of Christian liturgies. The reason for the neglect of these rites that do operate with varying degrees of 'success' in advanced industrialised societies forms part of a wider blindness to the study of religion in contemporary sociology. Beckford has argued that sociology displays a wilful disregard of religion as it affects the cultural contours of these societies. Debates on secularisation and the disproportionate interest of sociology of religion in sects, have meant that the wider issue of the viability of Christian belief has been ignored in the mainstream of the discipline. Its study has been condemned to the margins. Ironically, he argues that critical theorists are displaying an increased awareness of the implications of religiosity in their accounts of late capitalism.[7] It can be argued that an implicit theology is increasingly entering sociological considerations in a post-modernist era [8] and some of these aspects have been noted earlier in comments on Steiner's recent book *Real Presences*.[9] This development of an implicit theology within sociology forms the background and intended direction of this analysis. It also accounts for the reason why this study is less directed to liturgists than to sociologists and to a lesser extent theologians.

The links between sociology and theology are remarkably inchoate. Failure to develop a fruitful dialogue between the two disciplines has generated acute complications for this study. The ground rules for advancing a link between sociology and theology have not been formulated and this has made principles of methodological advance difficult. The sociological means through which liturgy is to be studied raise acute problems that are unresolved in this study. A methodological atheism precludes access to the subject matter, liturgical enactments and their distinctive concerns; an avowedly confessional position renders the account unavailable save to the most deeply committed believers. There are antinomial elements buried in the sociological gaze as it tries to catch sight of what fleetingly emerges in liturgical productions. An effort has been made to minimise the difficulties these might generate for sociological efforts to understand liturgical enactments. By using Gadamer's notion of hermeneutics, the issue of method has been marginalised if not avoided. Relativism has been presented as a wager and the doubts it has sown in the sociological mind have been connected to the agnosticism ethnomethodology inspires about the truth or falsity of the actor's account. Through these means, one has tried to steer an uneasy, if not idiosyncratic, passage into the study of a religious ritual which seems to have defied sociological comment. One cannot wait indefinitely for links to grow between theology and sociology so that methodological procedures and a mutual understanding of presuppositions can emerge between the two disciplines. Debate on these matters is only beginning. At some point a more direct intervention is required.

There are a number of domestic reasons why sociology has so neglected the study of liturgy, some of which were mentioned in the introduction. Although a Catholic high mass lasts about eighty minutes and its sequence is easy to describe, its sociological and theological implications are enormously difficult to interpret and to understand. Sociological neglect of liturgies suggests a backhanded compliment to their complexity. Liturgy is not just an ordinary religious ritual. Almost all the humanities can be used to understand liturgical enactments. These range from philosophy, aesthetics and music to psychology, anthropology and, of course, sociology. All these disciplines compete to understand the differing strands of liturgy that bear on their expertise. Allowing for these elements generates a paradox for sociological accounts of liturgy. Despite so many aspects of the humanities achieving a condensed place in this ritual, it only achieves 'success' in the eyes of the actors when it is uneventful, when little goes wrong, and a smoothness in operation prevails. Such a criteria of 'success' conspires against sociology getting a grip on the obvious facets of rite that present themselves for understanding. This reflects the comments of C. S. Lewis on the need for the social base of rite to disappear, for it to be unnoticed, and in such social unawareness, awareness of God can emerge.[10] When the social is domesticated and kept invisible, then the rite 'works' best. A sociological affirmation of this point might seem paradoxical, for it seems to remove liturgy from the possibility of sociological scrutiny. Part of the purpose of this study has been to resolve this apparent paradox and to supply a means of understanding why the social has to be domesticated in monitoring procedures that enable the holy to be re-presented in a routinised manner. We have tried to argue that when the social base of rite becomes precarious and intrusive, it subtracts from the transcendent qualities the actors strive to achieve in their liturgical performance. When the social is presented in an ambiguous and antinomial form to the actor, some form of negotiation is required if an impression of the holy is to be plausibly realised. It is this need for choice that admits a sociological consideration that can enhance an understanding of liturgical praxis.

In our account, antinomial aspects of liturgy achieve a representative form in the contrast between innocence and experience. These qualities carry an aura that puzzles, that elicits a testing, a wanting to know the authentic truth of what is proclaimed. Unfortunately, the possibilities of lying and deception in innocence and experience are legion. The issue of innocence is believed to be embodied in the child in a manner that has given rise to considerable philosophical puzzle. Hegel, Rousseau and Nietzsche have all been perplexed by the innocence of the child and his proximity to issues of truth. The triumph or tragedy of this proximity to the essences of meaning has a long literary lineage. In the past two decades there has been a strong growth of interest in the sociology of the child, his image, attributes and philosophical significance. Many French writers in the middle and later nineteenth century were fascinated by this theme. Rogers indicates that Huysmans, Baudelaire, Rimbaud and Barbey D'Aurevilly were all concerned with innocence and childhood.[11] Péguy also shared this wonder and like the others came to the issue from a world of experience. All these writers had strong links to Catholicism and were only too well aware of decadence (and in some cases Satanism), yet they all came to need to believe in the innocence of the child. It was the imaginative capacities of the child and his proximity to the transcendent that fired their curiosity, if not awe.

Since liturgical forms service heavenly activities, the issue of the visible realisation of invisible realities emerged as a central concern in the study. Qualities of innocence and the angelic are embodied in the role of the choirboy. Of all the liturgical actors, he is perhaps the most visible in the English mass media, especially at Christmas. Clad in his cassock, ruff and long white surplice, he reminds many of what the angels sang in a way that has a disproportionately devastating impact on the artificial commercialised efforts to bring seasonal joy to all – at a price. Somehow, the artifice of modernity, the degree to which it disguises spiritual needs by giving glittering prizes in lieu, is shown in a stark light by the choirboy in his liturgical act. If he is 'successful' there is an aura attached to his act that casts a long shadow on contemporary culture. He seems to express qualities that are exemplified in the liturgical performance as a whole, elements modernity seems to have corrupted. The fragility of aura in modern culture and the degree to which it is a quality at risk emerges in the writings of Walter Benjamin. He is perhaps an unexpected figure to cite to affirm this point.

Although he was a Marxist, whose writings on culture have had a profound influence, and was Jewish, with little sympathy or interest in Catholic liturgy, Walter Benjamin used theology as a means of making philosophical arguments and many of these have resonances for this study, not least his interest in the account of the fall.[12] Benjamin's interest in Baudelaire led him to produce a biography that has had considerable influence. In the section dealing with some motifs in Baudelaire, the issue of aura is discussed. In his effort to reconstruct Benjamin's childhood, David Frisby notes the way Benjamin was armed with what Baudelaire had termed 'the naïve gaze of childhood' to rediscover the roots of modernity in Paris.[13] There is an aspect of Ricoeur's second naïveté in dealing with issues of aura. It requires a subtle interpretation for its intangible qualities to emerge. Conditions of modernity can conspire to blind one to the implications of its presence. If rites suffer from an incredibility in modern cultural conditions, it could be that they effect in a peculiar manner a misunderstanding of what can be understood in liturgical enactments. If sociology is a creature of modernity producing the analytical circumstances that enable it to flourish, it is also perhaps the best instrument to show its shortcomings. It can show the price of what is concealed in culture. Aura is one of the hidden casualties of modernity.

A quality of aura usually denotes a subtle emanation that can be heard or is noticed. For Benjamin, it refers to the associations clustering around an object. These have an inexact quality, providing a sense of attachment often represented in an image. A central aspect of this sociological account of liturgy has emphasised the degree to which the social resources of rite are delicate antinomial instruments that require careful handling if properties of the holy are to be represented in a routine and credible manner.

There is an inexact, intangible quality to this claim to mirror these qualities of the invisible, which some discern, others realise, and most fail to see. These indeterminate elements can be considered as having qualities of aura. It refers to the enhancing and enchanting elements that surround the 'successful' staging of rite, its halo effect that gives it a holy surround. Aura is invaluable in rite because it points to its intangible products of grace and favour. It relates to the elements in liturgical performance that attract, that generate a curiosity and a wish to pursue that manages also to disarm suspicion.

The means and context of reproduction of an image can be the enemy of aura. Benjamin noted the possibilities of reductionism in the aura attached to the image, when he commented on Baudelaire's worries about photography. Benjamin argued that photography can grasp an image and reproduce it with an endless ease that can lead to a 'decline of the aura'. Victorian forms of photography required the subject to be still. But the effect was inhuman since 'the camera records our likeness without returning our gaze'. It is the absence of attention from the subject, the lack of a reciprocal glance that reduces aura and eventually dehumanises the image. Thus, Benjamin argues that 'to perceive the aura of an object we look at means to invest it with the ability to look at us in return'. This point gives us an unexpected insight into the disabling conditions of modernity liturgy has to operate within.

The tragedy of modernity is that it confers the right to gaze but in a way that frees the *flâneur* from responsibilities to the object seen. He sees attachments in a manner that always seems detached. Gazing does not commit and objects are offered to the spectator for disinterested view. This capacity to gaze freely gives rise to a restless moving around in a quest to find an image that will fill the self with meaning and belonging. Modernity presents the *flâneur* with a gift of the right to view with impunity, but at a price of denuding the object found of its capacity to impose responsibilities. There is a right to remove objects from their frame of reference. Icons are moved from Church to gallery and music once the sole province of the choirstall is played in the concert hall. Sacred objects are plundered and sold in a culture that values their intrinsic beauty but denies the message they were established to convey.

Liturgical images compete with many others in the post-modern market-place. The Church no longer has custody of its images nor has it a monopoly of control over their reproduction. In the medieval world, where paintings were rare, sacred music had to be heard within the liturgy and holy images had pride of place. There was no technology to reproduce holy messages in another context, to convert them for profane use in alien settings. Now the technology of reproduction squeezes with ease the aura out of holy images. We have become too experienced to hear them innocently, and because we can play them again through the miracle of technology, the awe their aura presents vanishes. No longer does one have to wait to hear a Haydn mass. One can play it with ease, instantly and anywhere, on a CD player, or on a video, in a way that makes no demands that might unsettle with a reciprocal gaze. We do not permit the sacred object to ask a question. The CD player asks little except to be switched on. It respects privacy without staring back in a way that makes uncomfortable obligations. A gin and tonic can be had while stretched out on the sofa, giving the Sanctus an uplifting effect. One can recline secure in the knowledge that no manners are violated in this civil right to private listening to sacred music with no holy strings attached.

Technology ruptures the relationships liturgies can make by civilising that which is sacerdotal. The demands of modern aesthetics profane the sacred with impunity. They convert ecclesiastical obligations into those of commerce and piety is reduced to a question of uncivil manners. Perhaps the oddest aspect of sacred music in the past two decades has been the way liturgists have marked it as irrelevant and have deposited it on to the market-place, where the more worldly and more astute have grasped its capacity to give comfort to the afflicted. Now, Allegri's *Miserere* receives profound applause in the concert hall. The only investment demanded is that of the box office and the only obligation is to observe the mores of the bourgeois aesthetics, to applaud, and not to give expression to any discomforting religious sentiments. The audience is a spectator on piety, gazing at penitential demands in secular awe, secure in the knowing that the ticket price does not confer obligations to go and do likewise. Any notion that a profound Christian witness had been made would be received with total embarrassment by these *flâneurs*. For them, penitential pronouncements convey pleasure not the pain of pious yearning. The secular appropriation of sacred music, where it is converted into a commodity amongst others, disables the capacity to hear anew its message when heard in a holy place.

Aura also relates to the manifestation of distance. Earlier we noted the degree to which distanciation and appropriation were interlinked, an insight gained from Ricoeur's approach to hermeneutics. Text and objects have a distancing quality, initially, before they can be appropriated to internal meaning and use. They present their message best in a dialectic of interpretation, one that leads to a relationship between the author and the reader. The deeper the reading the more intimate the relationship becomes, as alienating distance is dissolved and the message is appropriated.

Earlier, we noted Flannery O'Connor's comment, that the prophet is the realist of distance and that he makes his own without reference to human expectations of scale. Somehow, he manages to defy and to transcend the expected constraints of distance. To Benjamin, aura comprises the 'unique manifestation of a distance'. By linking aura and distance, he argues that this 'designation has the advantage of clarifying the ceremonial character of the phenomenon. The essentially distant is the inapproachable: inapproachability is in fact a primary quality of the ceremonial image'. Benjamin notes the way Baudelaire insisted on the magic of distance. Aura is a quality of that sense of distance. In speaking of aura, Benjamin refers to Baudelaire's famous lines:

> Man wends his way through forests of symbols
> Which look at him with their familiar glances.

These lines capture the ordinary, expected quality of gazing at the familiar which can take on qualities of the unfamiliar in a passage into deeper meanings. It is unlikely that Benjamin had in mind icons, when he made the following comment on these verses, although they could well apply to their stereotyped, unoriginal nature. They present themselves in a predictable way that can yield unpredictable results. Benjamin wrote:

> The deeper the remoteness which a glance has to overcome, the stronger will be the spell that is apt to emanate from the gaze. In eyes that look at us with a mirrorlike blankness the remoteness remains complete. It is precisely for this reason that such eyes know nothing of distance.[14]

In our account of liturgical enactments, the social form of the rite itself was given a sacramental character. Sacraments transmit grace through their forms, visible means for invisible ends. But the act itself has a quality of grace, a sacramental character of aura for the actors who realise its basis. Although liturgical actions bear antinomial divisions, enabling and disabling, their grace laden qualities offer redemptive possibilities to the confused and worried, caught in the divisions of the act. Given proper use, these actions bear and confirm sensibilities of holiness in use. They affirm holiness, but also have a potential to realise it. In endeavouring to 'make' holiness manifest, the actors in a rite come to mirror this quality themselves. The reflection presents itself in an availability to see in a way that reveals an element of aura in the liturgical actor, one that can be spotted at a distance, being emitted almost accidentally. It is a rare and peculiar sight, one given largely to those with a grace to see, a point that hardly helps sociological efforts to fully understand what has been re-presented in the rite.

When a liturgical actor displays to an observer a form remembered and makes present a sensibility of what was dimly recollected elsewhere, the effect can be surprising. For instance, some late medieval paintings showed angels in flowing white robes kneeling before the throne of God, set high at a heavenly remove. The picture conveys an image of an aura seemingly above and beyond the human condition. One views and admires that which is transmitted from within the frame of the painting. The image heightens sensibilities of heavenly labour. But seeing a similar image at a mass, if noticed, draws one to attend to an aura transmitted from within a social frame, from actors who live in the world, yet convey properties of what lies beyond it. Aura generates a relationship with the implications of what is seen from a tactful distance. Two altar servers might be noticed deep in prayer after communion at the side of the sanctuary (it does happen!). Clad in their white albs, their heels hidden and their hands clasped, one might get a glimpse of the image of angels passing across their faces as they ponder inward, innocent in peace with their lowly lot in life with God. One cannot 'prove' this realisation of an image, that springs from the social frame, blurring reality with unreality. The boys are trained to represent the angels in earth-bound liturgical tasks and so it strikes as an odd gift of grace when these actors come to incarnate the qualities they represent. There is a light of grace on their faces as they mirror what they cannot see, being blind to what they cannot know. All one can note is a quality of aura attached to the fleeting image that signifies qualities different from, but similar to those caught by glancing at a painting that enshrines the same ethereal aspect. One cannot force the pace of interpretation to demonstrate that which is seen, or give sight to the blind, who cannot see what might have been so movingly noticed. All religious examples of liturgical aura are subjective and arbitrary.

There has been a fashionable emphasis in liturgical renewal over recent decades on proximity and closeness. I wish to suggest that since these rites, so cast for relevance, do not service a sense of distance, they deny the people a means of appropriation and cripple them at the point of a leap into religious imagination. Liturgies operate with a dialectic between appropriation and distanciation, dealing in deep meanings difficult to decipher and to grasp. They demand more than a glance, but cannot stipulate what is to be understood in the gaze. The unpredictable nature of the effects of liturgy on the observer, the degree to which manufacture of religiosity is precluded for the actors, combine to produce a sense of uncertainty. This risk of uncertainty corrupting the mechanism of reproduction has to be guarded against by the actors if the performance is to 'succeed' in realising its purpose of making a sense of the holy manifest through ambiguous and antinomial social means. There is a hidden and disguised quality to rite that generates endless prospects for simulation and dissimulation in the parts.

This quality of playful disguise, suggested in the above example of the altar servers at prayer, begs questions. The description of their oblivious prayerfulness could be read as a pious fantasy, a wistful thinking, or it could very accurately capture the holiness which was transmitted and which could be deemed a characterising instance that denotes the tenor of a 'successful' rite. Liturgical actions can be 'read' in so many ways that can give rise to worries over what is to be interpreted in rite and on what secure basis. The trouble with liturgical transactions is that they admit all manner of responses, friendly and unfriendly. They transmit an endless variety of religious experiences, which can be known ultimately in private subjective terms, ones that are difficult to articulate. Because liturgical actions release multi-layers of meaning, these can generate conflicting understandings and judgements even amongst the most sincere of believers.

For instance, in a well known Benedictine monastery in Northern Europe, the Abbot felt the need to remonstrate with his community in Chapter over the quality of abasements during Vespers the preceding evening. Some monks, he noted, did not bow at all, one lowered himself so much he nearly fell over, and another seemed collapsed in a state of despair on his misericord. The Abbot felt that this failure to keep custody of their abasements could give rise to scandal for any laity who might have been present at that office. Furthermore it could generate irretrievable misunderstandings about the nature of their vocation. All the monks trooped off feeling like chided schoolboys. As it happened, a retreat for university students was going on at this time. In a spiritual consultation with one of the young women present, a monk was told that the retreat had been empty and boring until the previous night at Vespers, when she felt everything started to make sense. She noticed that the monks at Vespers did not bow very well. Some did not bow at all, one seemed to be sunk in despair on his seat throughout, and another abased very deeply and precariously. This unevenness of witness indicated to her that monks were human, and if this was compatible with their spirituality, then she had found a link that gave meaning to her life.

Holiness has a selective quality in what it transmits. The random nature of its appreciation points to a gift of grace given to some, but denied to others. This point is reflected in the statement in the New Testament, 'For judgement I am come into this world, that they which see not might see; and that they which see might be made blind' (John 10.39). There is an elusive, intangible quality of aura attached to the social issue of virtue and to its 'successful' realisation that involves a very subjective capacity to discern and to discriminate. Often there is an antinomial quality to the distinctions made that involve the recognition of authentic virtue, one that involves the recognition of possible deception. J.-K. Huysmans, whose own vices were completely heterosexual, commenting in a letter on the degeneracy of a male underworld of vice he had known before his return to Catholicism, noted that

> chastity seems to have an undeniable grandeur, and to be the only decent thing that exists. I know young men with souls of perfect whiteness, as are their bodies; these children have an aura, have something exquisite about them that those who 'know' a woman or a man will never have. One really needs to have lived in these opposing worlds to have any notion that such people belong to the same race. Clothing can be misleading. Yet their bodies are the same, but that is where the soul, so much denigrated, emerges. It completely transforms everything.[15]

Huysmans was no fool either as a writer or an art critic. His gifts of spiritual discernment mark an erudition, a capacity to see below the social surface qualities of holiness and worth. His ability to see that which transforms the social into the spiritual marks a quality deeply difficult to understand that has plagued this study. Perhaps it accounts for the inconclusive nature of its conclusion. Reading rites involves access to a grammar of assent or dissent from the message proclaimed and this greatly affects what is believed to have been understood in and by liturgical actions. Writers, such as the French sociologist, Pierre Bourdieu, have pointed to the peculiar nature of sociology and the degree to which it has a reflexive quality difficult for outsiders to understand. It cannot be said that this reflexive quality has yet evolved in a spiritual direction. Yet, when sociology has its interests directed towards the spiritual and theological, the insights revealed are perhaps as unexpected as they are surprising. They come from an unexpected source, a discipline of the outsider, schooled to perceive that which lies undervalued at the edge of society, its borderland, where much goes unsignified.

Sociology does not seem to have caught the great dramatic quality of liturgical enactments, at least in this account. The aims have been more modest, of leaving the metaphysic to Hamlet, and the coining of sociological insights to fit lowly figures, such as Rosencrantz and Guildenstern. After all, this study has come from the fringe of theology, has settled on the boundaries of liturgical form, and has been presented by a discipline that operates best as the classical outsider.

At the end of this work, one is only too conscious that if it has worked, it simply marks a beginning, a direction for future study of other forms and aspects of Catholic and, perhaps, Anglican liturgy. Other methods and other forms of rite could have been studied. For instance, one could follow further Mary Neitz's study of charisma and community and apply its methodology to the study of other liturgical forms.[16] Doubtless some will wonder why this study concentrated so heavily on traditional Benedictine Cathedral-style rites.

Without repeating what was said earlier, a puzzle ran through this study, at the disjunction between the vast numbers of tourists who visit English Cathedrals and monasteries, and the small, if not tiny, number, who attend the rites routinely performed within. There are exceptions, such as the very large number who attend choral Evensong at King's College, Cambridge during the summer. In English society, there is a deep and abiding fascination with Cathedrals, and to a lesser extent monasteries. It could reflect a deep-seated historical sense of guilt at the rupture by the Reformation of a settled Catholic order where beauty and holiness marked the land. The reason for this attachment to these Cathedrals, perhaps, also reflects a sense of loss of spiritual beauty and a depth of meaning. The liberal theologians and liturgists of the 1970s greatly assisted in this task of demolition, making many strangers in the house of God. A theology was supplied to the flâneur that affirmed him in his modernist plight in a way that denied relief at the Cathedral door. The liberal theology of Honest to God, and the debate surrounding it, bought a cheap and easy victory for its proclaimers in the 1970s. Interest in the arguments presented was less about their efficacy, than the proclamation of doubt by those paid to uphold the faith. An extraordinary realisation emerged that political morality, where doubt led to resignation, was far higher than that current in Anglicanism. A sociological density about the nature of liturgy reached a realm of thickness few would have expected, in the recent report of the Liturgical Commission of the General Synod of the Church of England. It is scarcely surprising that one liturgist complained about the bad press surrounding their activities which seemed to bring a kiss of death to their subject. One despairs of Anglican liturgists and theologians taking the subject of liturgy seriously.

If the Liturgical Commission of the Church of England is stuck in a groove that dates back to 1975, matters in Catholicism are showing a distinct sign of improvement and a parting of the way from the agreements with Anglicans formulated in the 1960s. There is a realisation of a need to re-sacralise rites in a way that shows an increasing degree of awareness of their sociological significance. This work has been written to try to push this task further in the Catholic Church. There are signs of a sense of recovery of the sacred in English society amongst Catholics, especially in relation to the choral tradition. Choirs of men and boys now operate in most English Catholic Cathedrals and a Benedictine witness to the beauty of choral music flourishes.

The study of liturgy and music both share a common neglect of the study of performance and its history. Authenticity, tradition and the cultural context of enactment pose acute problems for understanding in music and in the study of liturgy.[17] There are also similarities between music and liturgy in the way objective constraints enable subjective appreciation to occur. Something out of time is made present in a way that transcends its immediate circumstances of construction and delivery. Both also involve a veiling of techniques, so that the event just seems to unfold and to happen in a way that seems independent of human agency.

Is there a sociological future for the study of liturgy? The purpose of this study is to suggest that there is, but not along the lines which liberal theologians and liturgists have pursued with such recent and damaging effect. As debate on the nature of culture expands in sociology, the context in which liturgical enactments *can* be understood will also change. Issues of the limits of modernity and the nature of post-modernity are engaging increased sociological attention. There is, as has already been suggested, an implicit theology operating within sociology that seems about to come to the surface in sociology in the next decade. As theology becomes married to sociological insights, reflections are likely to move in some unexpected directions. The translation into English of von Balthasar's *Theodramatik* will provide sociology with a unique ticket of entry into theology in a way that can be linked to the study of liturgy. This study has been conceived as a prelude to that examination and to a debate in which the links between theology and sociology are likely to become stronger and more fruitful.

Notes and References

Introduction

1. Marcel Proust, *Marcel Proust. A selection from his miscellaneous writings*, trans. Gerard Hopkins, London: Allan Wingate, 1948, pp. 97–98.
2. Margaret Mead, *Twentieth Century Faith, Hope and Survival*, London: Harper & Row, 1972, p. 126.
3. Frank Parkin, *Max Weber*, London: Tavistock, 1982, p. 23.
4. Oscar Wilde, *The Works of Oscar Wilde*, London: Galley Press, 1987, p. 17.
5. See preface to special issue, 'Hell: what it means not to be saved', *New Blackfriars*, vol. 69, no. 821, November 1988, pp. 467–471. For an interesting reflection on the disappearance of heaven in the modern world, see Colleen McDannell and Bernhard Lang, *Heaven. A History*, London: Yale University Press, 1988.
6. See Bernarr Rainbow, *The Choral Revival in the Anglican Church (1839–1872)*, London: Barrie & Jenkins, 1970, Chapter 2, 'The Image confused: John Jebb', pp. 26–42.
7. R. G. Collingwood, *An Autobiography*, Oxford: Oxford University Press, 1970, 'Question and Answer' , pp. 29–43.
8. Barbara Beaumont, ed. and trans., *The Road from Decadence. From Brothel to Cloister. Selected Letters of J. K. Huysmans*, London: The Athlone Press, 1989, p. 131.

1 Sociology and Theology: A Career in Misunderstanding

1. Michael Ermarth, *Wilhelm Dilthey: The Critique of Historical Reason*, Chicago: The University of Chicago Press, 1978, Chapter 5, pp. 241–276.
2. W. G. Runciman, ed., *Max Weber. Selections in translation*, trans. E. Matthews, Cambridge: Cambridge University Press, 1978, pp. 7–32.
3. Robert S. Lynd, *Knowledge for what? The Place of Social Science in American Culture*, Princeton: Princeton University Press, 1970. See also Jack D. Douglas, ed., *The Relevance of Sociology*, New York: Appleton-Century-Crofts, 1970.
4. Wolf Lepenies, *Between Literature and Science: the Rise of Sociology*, trans. R. J. Hollingdale, Cambridge: Cambridge University Press, 1988.
5. Georg Simmel, *Essays on Interpretation in Social Science*, trans. and ed. Guy Oakes, Manchester: Manchester University Press, 1980, pp. 27–46.
6. Arthur Mitzman, *The Iron Cage. An Historical Interpretation of Max Weber*, New Brunswick: Transaction Books, 1985.
7. Geoffrey Hawthorn, *Enlightenment & Despair. A history of sociology*, Cambridge: Cambridge University Press, 1976.

8. See Wolf Lepenies, *Between Literature and Science: the Rise of Sociology op. cit.*, pp. 19–46.
9. Alfred Schutz, 'Concept and Theory Formation in the Social Sciences' in Dorothy Emmet and Alasdair MacIntyre, eds, *Sociological Theory and Philosophical Analysis*, London: Macmillan, 1970, pp. 1–19.
10. Robin Horton and Ruth Finnegan, eds, *Modes of Thought. Essays on Thinking in Western and non-Western Societies*, London: Faber & Faber, 1973.
11. Anthony Giddens, 'The social sciences and philosophy – trends in recent social theory' in *Social Theory and Modern Sociology*, Cambridge: Polity Press, 1987, pp. 52–72.
12. Kenneth Thompson, 'How Religious are the British?' in Terence Thomas, ed., *The British. Their Religious Beliefs and Practices 1800–1986*, London: Routledge, 1988, pp. 211–239.
13. David Martin, *A General Theory of Secularization*, Oxford: Basil Blackwell, 1978. From an early period in his writings Peter Berger has linked pluralism of theology to secularisation. See for example: 'A Sociological view of the Secularization of Theology', *Journal for the Scientific Study of Religion*, vol. 6, no. 3, 1967, pp. 3–16; and Peter L. Berger and Thomas Luckmann, 'Secularisation and Pluralism', *International Yearbook for the Sociology of Religion*, vol. 2, 1966, pp. 73–84. See also Peter L. Berger, 'From the Crisis of Religion to the Crisis of Secularity', in Mary Douglas and Steven Tipton, eds, *Religion and America. Spiritual Life in a Secular Age*, Boston: Beacon Press, 1983, pp. 14–24.
14. Rex Davies, 'Bibliography: New Religious Movements', *The Modern Churchman*, n.s., vol. XXVII, no. 4, 1985, pp. 41–46. See also Dorothee Sölle, 'The Repression of the Existential Element, or Why so many People become Conservative' in Gregory Baum, ed., *Neo-Conservatism: Social and Religious Phenomenon*, Concilium, Edinburgh: T. & T. Clark Ltd., 1981, pp. 69–75.
15. Thomas Robbins, 'The Transformative Impact of the Study of New Religions on the Sociology of Religion', *Journal for the Scientific Study of Religion*, vol. 27, no. 1, 1988, pp. 12–27.
16. Kieran Flanagan, 'Theological Pluralism: a sociological critique', in Ian Hamnett, ed., *Religious Pluralism and Unbelief: Studies Critical and Comparative*, London: Routledge, 1990, pp. 81–113.
17. Quoted in Thomas Robbins, 'The Transformative Impact of the Study of New Religions on the Sociology of Religion', *op. cit.*, p. 23.
18. Alison Lurie, *Imaginary Friends*, London: Heinemann, 1967.
19. Richard Fenn, 'The Sociology of Religion: A Critical Survey', in Tom Bottomore, Stefan Nowak, and Magdalena Sokolowska, eds, *Sociology: The State of the Art*, London: Sage Publications, 1982, pp. 101–127. See also Peter L. Berger, 'Some Second Thoughts on Substantive versus Functional Definitions of Religion', *Journal for the Scientific Study of Religion*, vol. 13, no., 2, June 1974, pp. 125–133.
20. James Beckford, 'The Insulation and Isolation of the Sociology of Religion', *Sociological Analysis*, vol. 46, no. 4, 1985, pp. 347–354.

21. Arnold S. Nash, 'Some Reflections upon the Sociological Approach to Theology', *International Yearbook for the Sociology of Religion*, vol. 2, 1966, pp. 185–197.
22. Ian Hamnett, 'Sociology of Religion and Sociology of Error', *Religion*, vol. 3, Spring 1973, pp. 1–12.
23. Ian Hamnett, 'A Mistake about Error', *New Blackfriars*, vol. 67, no. 788, February 1986, p. 77.
24. Daniel Bell, 'The Return of the Sacred? The Argument on the Future of Religion', in *Sociological Journeys. Essays 1960–1980*, London: Heinemann, 1980, p. 348.
25. Paul Webster, 'Victim of a broken mind', *The Guardian*, 8th October 1988, p. 19.
26. Louis Dupré, 'Spiritual Life in a Secular Age' in Mary Douglas and Steven Tipton, eds, *Religion and America. Spiritual Life in a Secular Age, op. cit.*, pp. 3–13.
27. Ronald J. McAllister, 'Theology Lessons for Sociology' in William H. Swatos, ed., *Religious Sociology. Interfaces and Boundaries*, New York: Greenwood Press, 1987, p. 28.
28. John Habgood, *Church and Nation in a Secular Age*, London: Darton, Longman & Todd, 1983, p. 173.
29. Peter L. Berger, *The Social Reality of Religion*, London: Penguin, 1973, pp. 54–60.
30. *Ibid.*, pp. 155–158.
31. Peter L. Berger, *The Heretical Imperative. Contemporary Possibilities of Religious Affirmation*, London: Collins, 1980, p. 47.
32. Peter L. Berger, *A Rumour of Angels. Modern Society and the Rediscovery of the Supernatural*, London: Penguin Books, 1971.
33. Peter L. Berger, *The Heretical Imperative, op. cit.*, p. 49.
34. Peter L. Berger, 'For a World with Windows', in Peter L. Berger and Richard John Neuhaus, eds, *Against the World. For the World. The Hartford Appeal and the Future of American Religion*, New York: The Seabury Press, 1976, pp. 8–9.
35. Peter L. Berger, *The Social Reality of Religion, op. cit.*, p. 56.

2 Liturgical Theology: Some Sociological Implications

1. I. H. Dalmais, 'The Liturgy as Celebration of the Mystery of Salvation' in Aimé Georges Martimort, ed., *The Church at Prayer*. vol. 1, *Principles of the Liturgy*, trans. Matthew J. O'Connell, London: Geoffrey Chapman, 1987, p. 259.
2. John Orme Mills, 'God, Man and Media: on a problem arising when theologians speak of the modern world' in David Martin, John Orme Mills and W. S. F. Pickering, eds, *Sociology and Theology: Alliance and Conflict*, Brighton: The Harvester Press, 1980, p. 136. See also Robin Gill, ed., *Theology and Sociology. A Reader*, London: Geoffrey Chapman, 1987 and also his earlier book, *The Social Context of Theology*, London: Mowbrays, 1975.

3. Alexander Schmemann, *Introduction to Liturgical Theology*, London: The Faith Press, 1966, p. 9.
4. Stephen Sykes, *The Identity of Christianity*, London: SPCK, 1984, p. 267.
5. Austin Flannery, ed., *Vatican II. The Conciliar and Post Conciliar Documents*, Dublin: Dominican Publications, 1975.
6. Urban T. Holmes, 'Liminality and Liturgy', *Worship*, vol. 47, no. 7, 1973, pp. 386–387.
7. See for example: Bruce Kapferer, 'Ritual Process and the Transformation of Context', *Social Analysis*, no. 1, February 1979, pp. 3–19; and Catherine Bell, 'Discourse and Dichotomies: the structure of ritual theory', *Religion*, vol. 17, April 1987, pp. 95–118.
8. Luis Maldonado, 'The Church's Liturgy: Present and Future' in David Tracy, Hans Kung, and Johann B. Metz, eds, *Toward Vatican III. The work that needs to be done*, Dublin: Gill & Macmillan, 1978, pp. 228–229.
9. Austin Flannery, ed., *Vatican II. The Conciliar and Post Conciliar Documents*, *op. cit.*, p. 967.
10. See for example: James D. Shaughnessy, ed., *The Roots of Ritual*, Grand Rapids, Michigan: William B. Eerdmans Publishing Company, 1973; and Kevin Seasoltz, 'Anthropology and Liturgical Theology: Searching for a Compatible Methodology', in David Power and Luis Maldonado, eds, *Liturgy and Human Passage*, New York: The Seabury Press, 1979, pp. 3–13.
11. Liturgists in North America tended to use anthropology in the mid-seventies to justify liberal positions, and produced an odd fragmented reading of 'rite'. For an insightful sociological account of the way in which liturgy renewal was shaped to reflect liberal American assumptions see Kenneth Smits, 'Liturgical Reform in Cultural Perspective', *Worship*, vol. 50, no. 2, March 1976, pp. 98–110. The issue of feminism started to creep into the question of methodology, making suggestions on the wider cultural implications of rite suspect and insular. See Mary Collins, 'Liturgical Methodology and the Cultural Evolution of Worship in the United States', *Worship*, vol. 49, no. 2, March 1975, pp. 85–102. For a more subtle and sociologically acceptable use of similar types of material, put to good critical use, see James Hitchcock, *The Recovery of the Sacred*, New York: The Seabury Press, 1974.
12. See George A. De Napoli, 'Inculturation as Communication', in Arij A. Roest Crollius, ed., *Effective Inculturation and Ethnic Identity*, Rome: Pontifical Gregorian University, 1987, pp. 71–98.
13. Kieran Flanagan, 'Theological Pluralism: a sociological critique', *op. cit.*, pp. 81–113. For some apt critical reservations about the processes of acculturation see David N. Power, 'Unripe Grapes: The Critical Function of Liturgical Theology', *Worship*, vol. 52, no. 5, September 1978, pp. 386–399.
14. Anscar J. Chupungco, *Cultural Adaptation of the Liturgy*, New York: Paulist Press, 1982, pp. 74–76.
15. See for example: Joseph A. Jungmann, *The Mass of the Roman Rite*, trans. Francis A. Brunner, London: Burns & Oates, 1959; A.G.

Martimort, ed., *Introduction to the Liturgy*, trans. Roger Capel, New York: Desclée Company, 1968; and Johannes H. Emminghaus, *The Eucharist. Essence, Form, Celebration*, trans. Matthew O'Connell, Collegeville, Minnesota: The Liturgical Press, 1978. For a work that represents Catholic, Anglican and Free Church traditions, see Cheslyn Jones, Geoffrey Wainwright, and Edward Yarnold, eds, *The Study of Liturgy*, London: SPCK, 1978. Two Anglican works which have achieved wide circulation are: Dom Gregory Dix, *The Shape of the Liturgy*, London: A. and C. Black Ltd., 1945; and Percy Dearmer, *The Parson's Handbook*, London: Humphrey Milford, 1932.

16. It would be odd not to mention the pioneering work of Stark, which covers a vast range of material in an interpretative order that has few sociological equivalents. See Werner Stark, *The Sociology of Religion. A study of Christendom*, London: Routledge & Kegan Paul, 1972, pp. 63–222.

17. Charles Davis, 'Ghetto or Desert: Liturgy in a Cultural Dilemma', *Studia Liturgica*. vol. 7, no. 2–3, 1970, pp. 10–27.

18. Quoted in Carl A. Last, ed., *Remembering the Future. Vatican II and Tomorrow's Liturgical Agenda*, New York: Paulist Press, 1983, p. 45.

19. For an appropriately acid account of short lived American enthusiasm for liturgical experiments, innocent of the issue of how far one can go, see James Hitchcock, *The Decline and Fall of Radical Catholicism*, New York: Image Books, 1972.

20. Simone Weil, *Waiting on God*, trans. Emma Craufurd, London: Fontana, 1959, p. 140.

21. Dietrich von Hildebrand, *Liturgy and Personality*, New York: Longmans, Green and Co., 1943, p. 59.

22. Alasdair MacIntyre, *After Virtue. A Study in Moral Theory*, London: Duckworth, 1981, pp. 244–245.

23. James Laver, *The First Decadent. Being the Strange Life of J.K. Huysmans*, London: Faber & Faber, 1954.

24. Robert Baldick, *The Life of J.-K. Huysmans*, Oxford: Clarendon Press, 1955, p. 229.

25. J.-K. Huysmans, *The Cathedral*, trans. Clara Bell, London: Kegan Paul, Trench, Trubner & Co., Ltd., 1898, p. 80.

26. *Ibid.*, p. 330.

27. J.-K. Huysmans, *En Route*, trans. C. Kegan Paul, London: Kegan Paul, Trench, Trubner & Co., Ltd., 1918, p. 235.

28. George Every, *The Mass*, Dublin: Gill and Macmillan, 1978, Chapters 9–10, pp. 143–172.

29. Louis Bouyer, *Life and Liturgy*, London: Sheed and Ward, 1956, Chapters 4–5, pp. 38–69.

30. Theodor Klauser, *A Short History of the Western Liturgy. An account and some reflections*, 2nd edn, trans. John Halliburton, Oxford: Oxford University Press, 1979, pp. 117–123.

31. R.W. Franklin, 'The Nineteenth Century Liturgical Movement', *Worship*, vol. 53, no. 1, January 1979, p. 39.

32. R.W. Franklin, 'Guéranger: A View on the Centenary of His Death', *Worship*, vol. 49, no. 6, November 1975, pp. 324–326.

33. Robert A. Nisbet, *The Sociological Tradition*, London: Heinemann, 1967, Chapter 3, pp. 47–106. See also his later work, *The Quest for Community*, Oxford: Oxford University Press, 1969.
34. R. W. Franklin, 'Guéranger: A View on the Centenary of His Death', *op. cit.*, pp. 327–328.
35. R. W. Franklin, 'Guéranger and Variety in Unity', *Worship*, vol. 51, no. 5, September 1977, p. 399.
36. R. W. Franklin, 'Guéranger and Pastoral Liturgy: A Nineteenth Century Context', *Worship*, vol. 50, no. 2, March 1976, pp. 152–155.
37. Ernest Benjamin Koenker, *The Liturgical Renaissance in the Roman Catholic Church*, Chicago: University of Chicago Press, 1954, pp. 116–117 and pp. 132–134.
38. Garry Wills, *Bare ruined choirs: doubt, prophecy, and radical religion*, New York: Delta Books, 1972.
39. Anthony Archer, *The Two Catholic Churches. A Study in Oppression*, London: SCM Press Ltd., 1986.
40. 'Class and Church. After Ghetto Catholicism. Facing the issues raised by Anthony Archer's The two Catholic Churches', *New Blackfriars*, vol. 68, no. 802, February 1987.
41. Anthony Archer, *The Two Catholic Churches*, Chapter 7, 'Vatican II and the Passing of the Simple Faithful', *op. cit.*, pp. 126–146. See also Kieran Flanagan, 'Resacralising the Liturgy', in 'Class and Church', *op. cit.*, pp. 64–75.
42. Anton Baumstark, *Comparative Liturgy*, English Edition, F. L. Cross, London: A. R. Mowbray, 1958.
43. Austin Flannery, O. P., ed., *Vatican II. The Conciliar and Post Conciliar Documents*, *op. cit.*, p. 146.
44. *Ibid.*, p. 105.
45. Odo Casel, *The Mystery of Christian Worship and other writings*, London: Darton, Longman & Todd, 1962, p. 103.
46. *Ibid.*, p. 201.
47. *Ibid.*, pp. 48–49.
48. Joseph Cardinal Ratzinger, with Vittorio Messori, *The Ratzinger Report. An Exclusive Interview on the State of the Church*, trans. Salvator Attanasio and Graham Harrison, Leominster, Herefordshire: Fowler Wright Books Limited, 1985, pp. 126–127. For a thorough discussion of the nature of active participation, see A.-M. Rouget, 'Participation in the Mass: the theological principles', in Vincent Ryan, ed., *Studies in Pastoral Liturgy*, vol. 2, Dublin: Gill and Son, 1963, pp. 120–137.
49. See for example, Patrick Collins, *More than meets the eye. Ritual and Parish Liturgy*, New York: Paulist Press, 1983 and also Regis A. Duffy, ed. *Alternative Futures for Worship*. vol. I, *General Introduction*, Collegeville, Minnesota: The Liturgical Press, 1987.
50. Avery Dulles, 'Catholic Ecclesiology since Vatican II' in Giuseppe Albergio and James Provost, eds, *Synod 1985 – an Evaluation*, Edinburgh: T. & T. Clark Ltd., 1986, p. 12.
51. For a perceptive account of changing attitudes to contemporary monasticism, see Richard North, *Fools for God*, London: Collins, 1987.

52. Hermann Pottmeyer, 'The Church as Mysterium and as Institution', in Guiseppe Albergio and James Provost, eds, *Synod 1985 – an Evaluation, op. cit.*, pp. 100–101. This worry about the loss of the sacred in the new rites was apparent in the mid-seventies. See Rembert G. Weakland, 'The "Sacred" and Liturgical Renewal', *Worship*, vol. 49, no. 9, 1975, pp. 512–529.

53. Quoted from G. Duncan Mitchell, ed., *A Dictionary of Sociology*, Chicago: Aldine Publishing Company, 1968, p. 47.

54. Margaret S. Archer, *Culture and Agency: The Place of Culture in Social Theory*, Cambridge: Cambridge University Press 1988.

55. Friedrich H. Tenbruck, 'The Cultural Foundations of Society' in Hans Haferkamp, ed., *Social Structure and Culture*, New York: Walter de Gruyter, 1989, pp. 15–35.

3 Sociological Understandings of Liturgy: Some Aspects

1. J.-K. Huysmans, *The Cathedral, op. cit.*, pp. 62–63.

2. *Ibid.*, pp. 77–79.

3. Robert Baldick, *The Life of J.-K. Huysmans, op. cit.*, p. 180.

4. Quoted in Flannery O'Connor, *Mystery and Manners*, London: Faber and Faber, 1972, p. 176.

5. Robert Baldick, *The Life of J.-K. Huysmans, op. cit.*, pp. 82–83. See also Claude Pichois, *Baudelaire*, trans. Graham Robb, London: Hamish Hamilton, 1989, pp. 365–366.

6. David Frisby, *Fragments of Modernity. Theories of Modernity in the Work of Simmel, Kracauer and Benjamin*, Cambridge: Polity Press, 1985, p. 17.

7. Hans Urs von Balthasar, *The Glory of the Lord. A Theological Aesthetics*. vol. 3, *Studies in Theological Style: Lay Styles*, John Riches, ed., trans. Andrew Louth, John Saward, Martin Simon, and Rowan Williams, Edinburgh: T. & T. Clark, 1986, p. 504.

8. Charles Péguy, *Basic Verities. Prose and Poetry*, trans. Ann and Julian Green, London: Kegan Paul, 1943, 'Innocence and Experience', pp. 223–231.

9. Hans Urs von Balthasar, *The Glory of the Lord*, vol. 3, *op. cit.*, pp. 511.

10. Friedrich von Schiller, *Naive and Sentimental Poetry and On the Sublime*. trans. Julius A. Elias, New York: Frederick Ungar Publishing Co., 1966.

11. Flannery O'Connor, *Mystery and Manners, op. cit.*, p. 109.

12. Kieran Flanagan, 'To be a Sociologist and a Catholic: A Reflection' *New Blackfriars*, vol. 67, no. 792, June 1986, pp. 256–270.

13. For a commentary on her works see Frederick Asals, *Flannery O'Connor. The Imagination of Extremity*, Athens, Georgia: The University of Georgia Press, 1982. See also Flannery O'Connor, *The Habit of Being*, ed. Sally Fitzgerald, New York: Farrar, Straus, Giroux, 1979.

14. Flannery O'Connor, *Mystery and Manners, op. cit.*, p. 153.

15. *Ibid.*, p. 179.

16. *Ibid.*, p. 204.

17. Frank Parkin, *Max Weber, op. cit.*, pp. 27–30.

18. See Colin Buchanan, Trevor Lloyd and Harold Miller, eds, *Anglican Worship Today*, London: Collins, 1980; and Michael Perham, *Liturgy Pastoral and Parochial*, London: SPCK, 1984.

19. Garry Hesser and Andrew J. Weigert, 'Comparative Dimensions of Liturgy: A Conceptual Framework and Feasibility Application', *Sociological Analysis*, vol. 41, no. 3, Fall 1980, pp. 215–229.

20. Andrew W. Bryant, 'Lay Communicants' attitudes to the Eucharist in relation to Liturgical Change in the Church of England', in Denise Newton, ed., *Liturgy and Change*, University of Birmingham: Institute for the Study of Worship and Religious Architecture, 1983, pp. 75–97.

21. O. Schreuder, 'Religious Attitudes, Group Consciousness, Liturgy and education', *Social Compass*, vol. 10, 1963, pp. 29–52. Doubtless many German and French sociological studies of liturgy have been undertaken since 1963.

22. George Manly, 'Experiments in a Group Mass', *Studia Liturgica*, vol. 8, no. 4, 1971–72, pp. 244–253.

23. See Jocelyn Cornwell, *Hard-Earned Lives. Accounts of Health and Illness from East London*, London: Tavistock, 1984, and Michael Calnan, *Health & Illness*, London: Tavistock, 1987.

24. Peter E. Fink, 'Towards a Liturgical Theology', *Worship*, vol. 47, no. 10, 1973, p. 602.

25. Robin Williams, 'Understanding Goffman's Methods' in Paul Drew and Anthony Wotton, eds, *Erving Goffman. Exploring the Interaction Order*, Cambridge: Polity Press, 1988, p. 73.

26. A. E. Carter, *Charles Baudelaire*, Boston: Twayne Publishers, 1977, pp. 80–82.

27. Paul Ricoeur, *The Symbolism of Evil*, trans. Emerson Buchanan, Boston: Beacon Press, 1969.

28. See special edition of *30 Days*, January 1989, which was devoted to Satanism.

29. Paul Ricoeur, 'The model of the text: meaningful action considered as a text' in John B. Thompson, ed. and trans. Paul Ricoeur. *Hermeneutics and the Human Sciences*, Cambridge: Cambridge University Press, 1981, pp. 197–221.

30. For an account of the clothing of an oblate see anon. *The Benedictine Oblate Companion*, St. Meinrad Archabbey, St. Meinrad, Indiana, 1981, pp. 57–68. See also J.-K. Huysmans, *The Oblate*, trans. Edward Perceval, London: Kegan Paul, Trench, Trubner & Co. Ltd., 1924, pp. 176–179.

31. I. H. Dalmais, *Introduction to the Liturgy*, trans. Roger Capel, London: Geoffrey Chapman, 1961, pp. 86–87.

32. 'The Constitution on the Sacred Liturgy', in Austin Flannery, O. P., ed., *Vatican II. The Conciliar and Post Conciliar Documents, op. cit.*, p. 5.

33. See entry on sacramentals in *New Catholic Encyclopedia*, vol. 12, Washington D.C.: The Catholic University of America, 1967, p. 790–792.

34. I am grateful to Ian Hamnett for drawing my attention to this point.

35. Tony Holden, *Explaining Icons*, Welshpool, Powys: Stylite Publishing, Ltd., 1985.

36. Flannery O'Connor, *Everything that Rises Must Converge*, London: Faber and Faber, 1980, p. 239.
37. *Ibid.*, p. 244.
38. Gillian Rose, *The Melancholy Science. An Introduction to the Thought of Theodor W. Adorno*, London: Macmillan, 1978, see especially pp. 54–56 and pp. 149–150.
39. Gary Zabel, 'Adorno on music: a reconsideration', *The Musical Times*, vol. 130, no. 1754, April 1989, pp. 198–201.
40. Quoted in Hans Urs von Balthasar, *The Glory of the Lord. A Theological Aesthetics.* vol. 1, *Seeing the form*, Joseph Fessio and John Riches, eds, trans. Erasmo Leiva-Merikakis, Edinburgh: T. & T. Clark, 1982, p. 97.
41. Quoted *ibid.*, p. 265.
42. Quoted in Hans Urs von Balthasar, *The Glory of the Lord*, vol. 3, *op. cit.*, pp. 180–181.
43. G. A. Phalp, ed., *Management of Minor Illness*, London: King's Fund Publishing Office, 1979.
44. Claudine Herzlich, *Health and Illness. A Social Psychological Analysis*, trans. Douglas Graham, London: Academic Press, 1973, p. 53.
45. Alphonse D'Houtaud and Mark G. Field, 'New Research on the Image of Health' in Caroline Currer and Margaret Stacey, eds, *Concepts of Health, Illness and Disease. A Comparative Perspective*, Leamington Spa: Berg Publishers Ltd., 1986, pp. 235–255.
46. Claudine Herzlich and Janine Pierret, *Illness and Self in Society*, trans. Elborg Forster, Baltimore: The Johns Hopkins University Press, 1987.
47. Robert Baldick, *The Life of J.-K. Huysmans*, *op. cit.*, p. 229.
48. Henri J. M. Nouwen, *Behold the Beauty of the Lord. Praying with Icons*, Notre Dame, Indiana: Ave Maria Press, 1987, p. 14.
49. Aidan Nichols, *The Art of God Incarnate. Theology and Image in Christian Tradition*, London: Darton, Longman & Todd, 1980, p. 45.
50. *Ibid.*, p. 57.
51. *Ibid.*, p. 84.
52. Cyprian Vagaggini, *Theological Dimensions of the Liturgy*, trans. Leonard J. Doyle, vol. 1, Collegeville, Minnesota: The Liturgical Press, 1959, p. 20.
53. *Ibid.*, pp. 191–4.
54. J.-K. Huysmans, *En Route*, *op. cit.*, pp. 52–53.
55. Peter Brown, *The Body and Society. Men, Women and Sexual Renunciation in Early Christianity*, London: Faber and Faber, 1989, pp. 101–102.
56. Umberto Eco, *The Aesthetics of Thomas Aquinas*, trans. Hugh Bredin, London: Radius, 1988, pp. 130–137.
57. Emile Durkheim, *The Elementary Forms of the Religious Life*, trans. Joseph Ward Swain, London: George Allen & Unwin Ltd., 1915, p. 386.
58. Claudine Herzlich, *Health and Illness*, *op. cit.*, pp. 11–12.
59. Johan Huizinga, *Homo Ludens. A Study of the Play-Element in Culture*, London: Routledge & Kegan Paul, 1949, p. 14.
60. This discussion is drawn from Chapter 1, *Ibid.*, pp. 1–27.
61. *Ibid.*, p. 25.

62. George Steiner, *Real Presences*, London: Faber and Faber, 1989.
63. Richard J. Bernstein, *Beyond Objectivism and Relativism: Science, Hermeneutics and Praxis*, London: Basil Blackwell, 1983.
64. Hans Urs von Balthasar, *La Dramatique divine*, 1. *Prolegomenes*, trans. Andre Monchoux with Robert Givord and Jacques Servais, Paris: Editions Lethielleux, 1984.
65. Hans Urs von Balthasar, *The Glory of the Lord*, vol. 1, *op. cit.*, p. 99.

4 Angels and Surplices: Appearing As Holy Becoming

1. Auguste Comte, *The Catechism of Positive Religion*, trans. Richard Congreve, 3rd edn, London: Kegan Paul, Trench, Trubner, & Co. Ltd., 1891, pp. 84–86.
2. Peter L. Berger, *A Rumour of Angels*, *op. cit.*
3. Peter C. Hammond, *The Parson and the Victorian Parish*, London: Hodder and Stoughton, 1977, pp. 84–85.
4. Quoted in David Bearne, 'Mediaeval Choristers', *The Month*, vol. 82, September-December, 1894, p. 514. See also Nicholas Orme, 'The Medieval Clergy of Exeter Cathedral. II. The Secondaries and Choristers', *Devonshire Association for Advancement of Literary Science. Report and Transactions*, vol. 115, December 1983, pp. 79–100; Kathleen Edwards, *The English Secular Cathedrals in the Middle Ages*, 2nd edn, Manchester: Manchester University Press, 1967, Chapter 4, sections 3–4, pp. 303–317; and Craig Wright, *Music and Ceremony at Notre Dame of Paris, 500–1550*, Cambridge: Cambridge University Press, 1989, Chapter 5, 'The Choirboys', pp. 165–195.
5. Christian Bembridge, *The Choir Schools Review*, 1983, p. 26.
6. Quoted in Patrick Leigh Fermor, *A Time to Keep Silence*, London: Penguin, 1988, p. 34.
7. William Anderson, *The Rise of the Gothic*, London: Hutchinson, 1985, p. 125.
8. Peter Brown, *The Body and Society*, *op. cit.*, Chapter 16, '"These Are Our Angels": Syria', pp. 323–338.
9. Jean Leclercq, *The Love of Learning and the Desire for God. A Study of Monastic Culture*, trans. Catherine Misrahi, New York: Fordham University Press, 1961, pp. 71–72. See also Patricia A. Quinn, *Better than the Sons of Kings. Boys and Monks in the Middle Ages*, New York: Peter Lang, 1989, p. 141.
10. 'De Profundis' in Oscar Wilde, *The Complete Works of Oscar Wilde*, *op. cit.*, p. 869.
11. Eric Peterson, *The Angels and the Liturgy: the status and significance of the holy angels in worship*, trans. Ronald Walls, London: Darton, Longman & Todd, 1964, p. 42.
12. William I. and Dorothy Swaine Thomas, 'Situations Defined as Real Are Real in Their Consequences' in Gregory P. Stone and Harvey A. Farberman, eds, *Social Psychology through Symbolic Interaction*, Waltham, Massachusetts: Xerox College Publishing, 1970, pp. 154–155.
13. Rob van der Hart, *The Theology of Angels and Devils*, Cork: The Mercier Press, 1972, Chapter 1, 'Doubts about the Angels', pp. 9–25.

14. John A. T. Robinson, *But that I can't believe!*, London: Collins, 1967, p. 92.
15. Karl Rahner, *et al.*, eds, *Sacramentum Mundi*, vol. 1, London: Burns & Oates, 1968, p. 32.
16. Ladislaus Boros, *Angels and Men*, trans. John Maxwell, London: Search Press, 1976, pp. 17–22.
17. H. C. Moolenburgh, *A Handbook of Angels*, trans. Amina Marix-Evans, Saffron Walden: C. W. Daniel, 1984, p. 49.
18. Rob van der Hart, *The Theology of Angels and Devils*, *op. cit.*, p. 54.
19. Paul Glenn, *A Tour of the Summa*, Rockford, Illinois: Tan Books, 1978, pp. 45–46.
20. St Thomas Aquinas, *Summa Theologiae*, vol. 15, London: Blackfriars with Eyre & Spottiswoode, 1970, p. 21.
21. *Ibid.*, pp. 21–31.
22. St Thomas Aquinas, *Summa Theologiae*, vol. 9, Oxford: Blackfriars, 1967, p. 37.
23. *Ibid.*, p. 41.
24. Ladislaus Boros, *Angels and Men*, *op. cit.*, p. 51. See also John Saward, 'Towards an Apophatic Anthropology', *Irish Theological Quarterly*, vol. 41, 1974, pp. 228–231.
25. Quoted in Georges Huber, *My Angel will go before you*, trans. Michael Adams, Dublin: Four Courts, 1983, p. 47.
26. Eric Peterson, *The Angels and the Liturgy*, *op. cit.*, p. 25. See also Cyprian Vagaggini, *Theological Dimensions of the Liturgy*, *op. cit.*, pp. 189–199. For comment on the notion of offering in the Tridentine rite, that would also apply to the revised liturgy, see Joseph Jungmann, *The Mass of the Roman Rite*, *op. cit.*, pp. 437–439.
27. Pie-Raymond Régamey, *What is an Angel?* trans. Mark Pontifex, New York: Hawthorn Books, 1960, pp. 111–112.
28. Jean Danielou, *The Angels and their Mission*, trans. David Heimann, Westminster, Maryland: The Newman Press, 1956, Chapter 6, 'The Angels and the Sacraments', pp. 55–67.
29. Ladislaus Boros, *Angels and Men*, *op. cit.*, p. 37.
30. George Boas, *The Cult of Childhood*, London: The Warburg Institute, 1966, pp. 45–49.
31. Neil Postman, *The disappearance of childhood*, London: W. H. Allen, 1983. The child has had a precarious place in literature and this is an important part of his tradition. See Phillipe Ariès, *Centuries of Childhood. A Social History of Family Life*, trans. Robert Baldick, New York: Vintage Books, 1962; Robert Pattison, *The Child Figure in English Literature*, Athens: The University of Georgia Press, 1978; and Reinhard Kuhn, *Corruption in Paradise. The Child in Western Literature*, London: University Press of New England, 1982.
32. Robin Lane Fox, *Pagans and Christians*, London: Viking, 1986, p. 366.
33. Peter Brown, *The Body and Society*, *op. cit.*, pp. 213–240.
34. Quoted in Boniface Ramsey, *Beginning to read the Fathers*, London: Darton, Longman & Todd, 1986, pp. 145–146.
35. Peter Brown, *The Body and Society*, *op. cit.*, p. 331.

36. 'The Truth of Masks. A note on Illusion' in *The Complete Works of Oscar Wilde, op. cit.*, p. 1017.
37. Simon Callow, *Being an Actor*, London: Penguin, 1985, p. 184.
38. Gregory P. Stone, 'Appearance and the Self', in Gregory P. Stone and Harvey A. Farberman, eds *Social Psychology through Symbolic Interaction, op. cit.*, pp. 408–409. See also Mary Shaw Ryan, *Clothing. A Study in Human Behaviour*, New York: Holt, Rinehart & Winston, Inc., 1966.
39. Erving Goffman, *Asylums*, London: Pelican, 1968, pp. 28–30.
40. Nathan Joseph, *Uniforms and nonuniforms. communication through clothing*, London: Greenwood Press, 1987.
41. Andrew Travers, 'Ritual Power in interaction', *Symbolic Interaction*, vol. 5, no. 2, 1982, p. 281.
42. *Ibid.*, pp. 282–284.
43. For a discussion of properties of risk and their management see Mary Douglas, *Purity and Danger. An analysis of the concepts of pollution and taboo*, London: Ark Paperbacks, 1984.
44. Marcelle Bernstein, *Nuns*, London: Collins, 1976, pp. 198–199.
45. Georg Simmel, 'Fashion', *The American Journal of Sociology*, vol. 62, no. 6, May 1957, pp. 548–549.
46. *Ibid.*, pp. 552–553.
47. Peter Somerville-Large, *Cappaghglass*, London: Hamish Hamilton, 1985, p. 171.
48. Thorstein Veblen, *The Theory of the Leisure Class*, London: Unwin Books, 1970, Chapter 7, 'Dress as an Expression of the Pecuniary Culture', pp. 118–131.
49. Thomas Carlyle, *Sartor Resartus*, London: Dent, 1973, p. 162.
50. Ernest Crawley, 'Sacred Dress' in Mary Ellen Roach and Joanne Bubolz Eicher, eds, *Dress, Adornment, and the Social Order*, New York: John Wiley & Sons, Inc., 1965, p. 141.
51. Pseudo-Dionysius. *The Complete Works*, trans. Colm Luibheid with Paul Rorem, London: SPCK, 1987, p. 186.
52. James Elwin Millard, *Historical Notices of the office of Choristers*, London: James Masters, 1848, p. 71.
53. Henry Wace and Phillip Schaff, eds, *Nicene and Post-Nicene Fathers of the Christian Church*, vol. 2, Oxford: James Parker, 1894, p. 202.
54. Robert Lesage, *Vestments and Church Furniture*, London: Burns & Oates, 1960, pp. 100–101.
55. Rudolf Otto, *The Idea of the Holy*, trans. John W. Harvey, Oxford: Oxford University Press, 1958, pp. 54–57.
56. J. W. Goethe, *Italian Journey* [1786–1788], trans. W. H. Auden and Elizabeth Mayer, London: Penguin Books, 1970, p. 201.
57. Michel Fauque, *Petit Guide des Fonctions Liturgiques*, Paris: Tequi, 1983, p. 64.
58. T. H. Passmore, *Durandus on the Sacred Vestments*, London: Thomas Baker, 1899. For reference to comments in the surplice, see pp. 15–17 and on the girdle, see pp. 33–37. See also Janet Mayo, *A History of Ecclesiastical Dress*, London: B. T. Batsford Ltd., 1984, pp. 154–155. For a fuller account of the history of the surplice, see E. A. Roulin,

Vestments and Vesture. A Manual of Liturgical Art, trans. Justin McCann, London: Sands & Co., 1931, pp. 29–35.

59. James Bentley, *Ritualism and Politics in Victorian Britain*, Oxford: Oxford University Press, 1978, pp. 16–19.

60. For an account of the vestarian controversy, see entry in F. L. Cross and E. A. Livingstone, eds, *The Oxford Dictionary of the Christian Church*, 2nd edn, Oxford: Oxford University Press, 1983, p. 1434.

61. See E. G. Cuthbert F. Atchley, 'The Hood as an ornament of the minister at the time of his ministrations in Quire and elsewhere' in *Transactions of the St. Paul's Ecclesiological Society*, vol. 4, 1900, pp. 313–328. See also: Anon., 'The Gown or the Surplice' in *Christia Observer*, vol. 70, April 1871, pp. 291–301; J. T. Tomlinson, *The Craving for Mass Vestments*, London: Robert Scott, 1908. For a rather jaundiced view of the whole question see Anon., 'Thrilling views of the surplice question', *Eclectic Review*, vol. 125, 1867, pp. 236–252. For an account of the spread of the surpliced choir in the Anglican Church, see, Nicholas Temperley, *The Music of the English Parish Church*, vol. I, Cambridge: Cambridge University Press, 1983, pp. 278–283.

It is easy to mock these earnest Victorian Anglican deliberations and to forget that concern with detail in clothing is of widespread interest in sociology and anthropology. See for example, Justine M. Cordwell and Ronald A. Schwarz, eds, *The Fabrics of Culture. The Anthropology of Clothing and Adornment*, New York: Mouton Publishers, 1979; and Marilyn J. Horn, *The Second Skin: An Interdisciplinary Study of Clothing*, Boston: Houghton Mifflin, 1968.

62. Maria Boulding, 'Background to a theology of the monastic habit', *The Downside Review*, vol. 98, no. 331, April 1980, p. 123. See also Pseudo-Dionysius, *The Complete Works, op. cit.*, pp. 246–249.

63. Anon., 'Chorister Boys', *Tinsley's Magazine*, vol. 28, 1880, p. 84.

64. Friedrich von Schiller, *Naive and Sentimental Poetry and On the Sublime, op. cit.*, p. 87.

65. *Ibid.*, p. 103.

66. Rollo May, *Power and Innocence*, London: Collins, 1976, p. 199. See also Peter Johnson, *Politics, Innocence, and the Limits of Goodness*, London: Routledge, 1988.

67. See Kieran Flanagan, 'Innocence and folly; a sociology of misunderstanding', *Culture, Education & Society*, vol. 39, no. 4, Autumn 1985, pp. 338–358 and a related article 'The Experience of Innocence as a Social Construction', *Philosophical Studies*, vol. 28, 1981, pp. 104–139. Material in this section of the chapter is drawn from these two essays.

68. Leslie Fiedler, 'The Eye of Innocence', in *The Collected Essays of Leslie Fiedler*, vol. 1, New York: Stein and Day, 1971, p. 506.

69. R. W. Lewis, *The American Adam: Innocence, Tragedy and Tradition in the Nineteenth Century*, Chicago: The Chicago University Press, 1955, pp. 129–130.

70. Herman Melville, *Billy Budd, Sailor & Other Stories*, London: Penguin, 1970, p. 327.

71. *Ibid.*, p. 330.

72. Henry James, *The Turn of the Screw and Other Stories*, London: Penguin, 1969, p. 30.
73. *Ibid.*, p. 31.
74. *Ibid.*, p. 119.
75. Frank Parkin, *Max Weber, op. cit.*, Chapter 1, 'Methods and Procedures' pp. 17–39.
76. D. G. Gillham, *William Blake*, Cambridge: Cambridge University Press, 1973, p. 141.
77. Rollo May, *Power and Innocence, op. cit.*, p. 215.
78. Herbert Morris, *On Guilt and Innocence. Essays in Legal Philosophy and Moral Psychology*, Berkeley: University of California Press, 1976, p. 146.
79. See J. M. J. Fletcher, *The Boy Bishop of Salisbury and Elsewhere*, Salisbury: Brown, 1921; and Arthur F. Leach, 'The Schoolboy's Feast', *The Fortnightly Review*, vol. 59, n.s. January–June 1896, pp. 128–141.
80. See E. O. James, *Christian Myth and Ritual*, London: John Murray, 1933, Chapter 10, 'Seasonal Games and Burlesques', pp. 293–298.
81. E. K. Chambers, *The Mediaeval Stage*, vol. 1, Oxford: The Clarendon Press, 1903, Chapter XV, pp. 336–371.
82. Dora H. Robertson, *A History of the Life and Education of Cathedral Choristers for 700 years*, London: Jonathan Cape, 1938, p. 79.
83. Quoted in Clement A. Miles, *Christmas in Ritual and Tradition Christian and Pagan*, London: T. Fisher Unwin, 1912, p. 303.
84. Dora H. Robertson, *A History of the Life and Education of Cathedral Choristers for 700 years, op. cit.*, p. 83.
85. *a ryght exellent sermon and full of frute and edificacyon of the chylde Jesus*, Robert Redman, B. M. (C. 53. 15, imp.).
86. This sermon is reproduced in *The Camden Miscellany*, vol. 7, 1875.
87. *Ibid.*, p. 16.
88. *Ibid.*, p. 21.
89. *Ibid.*, pp. 22–23.
90. Pseudo-Dionysius. *The Complete Works, op. cit.*, p. 89.

5 Simulation and Dissimulation: Self-revealing Paradoxes

1. Romano Guardini, *The Spirit of the Liturgy*, trans. Ada Lane, London: Sheed & Ward, 1930, p. 22.
2. Richard Steele, *Tatler*, in A. Chalmers, ed., *The British Essayists*, vol. 4, London: C. and J. Rivington *et al.*, 1823, p. 133.
3. Roy Rappaport, 'Sanctity and Lies in Evolution', *Ecology, Meaning and Religion*, Richmond, California: North Atlantic Books, 1979, p. 226.
4. Francis Bacon, 'Of Simulation and Dissimulation' in Henry Lewis, ed., *Bacon's Essays*, London: W. Collins, 1873, p. 40.
5. Mr MacKenzie, *The Mirror*, in A. Chalmers, ed., *The British Essayists*, vol. 5, *op. cit.*, p. 206.

6. Arthur Miller, 'Death of a Salesman', *Collected Plays*, London: Secker & Warburg, 1967, p. 146.

7. George Gonos, 'The Class Position of Goffman's Sociology: Social Origins of an American Structuralism', Jason Ditton, ed., *The View from Goffman*, London: Macmillan, 1980, p. 153. For a general appreciation of Erving Goffman, see: Eliot Freidson, 'Celebrating Erving Goffman', *Contemporary Sociology*, vol. 12, no. 4, July 1983, pp. 359– 362; Robin Williams, 'Erving Goffman: An Appreciation', *Theory, Culture & Society*, vol. 2, no. 1, 1983, pp. 99–102; Simon Johnson Williams, 'Appraising Goffman', *The British Journal of Sociology*, vol. 37, no. 3, September 1986, pp. 348–369; Mark N. Wexler, 'The Enigma of Goffman's Sociology', *Quarterly Journal of Ideology*, vol. 8, no. 3, 1984, pp. 40–50; and Anthony Giddens, 'Erving Goffman as a systematic social theorist', in *Social Theory and Modern Sociology, op. cit.*, pp. 109–139.

8. Alvin W. Gouldner, *The Coming Crisis of Western Sociology*, London: Heinemann, 1971, p. 383.

9. Erving Goffman, *Asylums, op. cit.*, p. 280.

10. Erving Goffman, *Frame Analysis*, London: Penguin, 1975, pp. 43–44.

11. *Ibid.*, p. 58.

12. Alasdair MacIntyre, *After Virtue, op. cit.*, pp. 31–32.

13. Anselm Strauss, ed., *George Herbert Mead on Social Psychology*, Chicago: The University of Chicago Press, 1956, p. 205.

14. Mark L. Wardell and Stephen P. Turner, *Sociological Theory in Transition*, Boston: Allen & Unwin, 1986, p. 5.

15. Wes Sharrock and Bob Anderson, *The Ethnomethodologists*, London: Tavistock Publications, 1986, p. 14.

16. *Ibid.*, p. 36.

17. Alasdair MacIntyre, *After Virtue, op. cit.*, p. 109.

18. See C. Wright Mills, *White Collar*, New York: Oxford University Press, 1956 and William H. Whyte, Jr., *The Organization Man*, New York: Doubleday, 1957.

19. Arlie Russell Hochschild, *The Managed Heart. Commercialization of Human Feeling*, Berkeley: University of California Press, 1983, p. 7.

20. Nicky James, 'Emotional labour: skill and work in the social regulation of feelings', *The Sociological Review*, vol. 37, no. 1, February 1989, pp. 15–42.

21. Alvin Gouldner, *The Coming Crisis of Western Sociology, op. cit.*, p. 383.

22. Richard Sennett, 'Two on the Aisle', *New York Review of Books*, vol. 20, no. 17, 1st November, 1973, pp. 29–31.

23. John Lofland, 'Early Goffman: Style, Structure, Substance, Soul', in Jason Ditton, ed., *The View from Goffman, op. cit.*, pp. 39–45.

24. Erving Goffman, *Asylums, op. cit.*

25. Erving Goffman, *Stigma. Notes on the Management of Spoiled Identity*, London: Penguin Books, 1968.

26. See his presidential address to the American Sociological Association, entitled 'The Interaction Order', *American Sociological Review*, vol. 48, no. 1, February 1983, pp. 1–17.

356 Notes and References to pp. 128–39

27. Quoted in John Lofland, 'Erving Goffman's Sociological Legacies', *Urban Life*, vol. 13, no. 1, April 1984, p. 25 and p. 30.
28. Thomas G. Miller, 'Goffman, Positivism and the Self', *Philosophy of Social Science*, vol. 16, 1986, p. 188.
29. Claudine Herzlich, *Health and Illness*, *op. cit.*, p. 118.
30. Alan Dawe, 'The underworld-view of Erving Goffman', *The British Journal of Sociology*, vol. 24, no. 2, June 1973, p. 248.
31. Thomas G. Miller, 'Goffman, Social Acting, and Moral Behaviour', *Journal for the Theory of Social Behaviour*, vol. 14, no. 2, July 1984, p. 143.
32. *Ibid.*, pp. 159–162.
33. Don Mixon, 'A Theory of Actors', *Journal for the Theory of Social Behaviour*, vol. 13, 1983, p. 103.
34. Richard Sennett, *The Fall of Public Man*, Cambridge: Cambridge University Press, 1977, p. 117.
35. Quoted *ibid.*, p. 110.
36. *Ibid.*, p. 113.
37. Simon Callow, *Being an Actor*, *op. cit.*, p. 204.
38. Michael Schudson, 'Embarrassment and Erving Goffman's idea of human nature', *Theory and Society*, vol. 13, no. 5, September 1984, p. 637.
39. Paul Creelan, 'Vicissitudes of the Sacred. Erving Goffman and the Book of Job', *Theory and Society*, vol. 13, no. 5, September 1984, p. 694.
40. Ralf Dahrendorf, 'Homo Sociologicus', in *Essays in the Theory of Society*, London: Routledge & Kegan Paul, 1968, pp. 74–78.
41. See 'Sociology and Human Nature. A Postscript to Homo Sociologicus' *ibid.*, pp. 88–106.
42. Sissela Bok, *Secrets: On the Ethics of Concealment and Revelation*, Oxford: Oxford University Press, 1984, see especially Chapter 3, 'Coming to Experience Secrecy and Openness', pp. 29–44.
43. John Saward, *Perfect Fools. Folly for Christ's Sake in Catholic and Orthodox Sprituality*, Oxford: Oxford University Press, 1980.
44. Heribert Jone, *Moral Theology*, trans. Urban Adelman, Cork: The Mercier Press, 1948, p. 260.
45. Sissela Bok, *Lying. Moral Choice in Public and Private Life*, London: Quartet Books, 1980, p. 15.
46. Quoted in St Thomas Aquinas, *Summa Theologiae*, vol. 41, London: Eyre & Spottiswoode, 1971, p. 163.
47. This is well understood in studies of power. See Steven Lukes, *Power. A Radical View*, London: Macmillan, 1974.
48. St Thomas Aquinas, *Summa Theologiae*, vol. 16, *op. cit.*, p. 181.
49. Quoted *ibid.*, p. 177.
50. *Ibid.*, p. 175.
51. Paul Delatte, *The Rule of St Benedict. A Commentary*, trans. Justin McCann, London: Burns Oates & Washbourne, 1921, pp. 118–119.
52. Roger Grainger, *The Language of the Rite*, London: Darton, Longman & Todd, 1974, p. 53. He has some valuable comments on deception in rite. He regards neurotic and obsessional rites as expressions of a private anxiety. Because religious rites are public and shared, they

become a means of expressing and containing a private worry. See pp. 47–77.
53. Walter J. Ong, *Hopkins, the Self, and God*, Toronto: University of Toronto Press, 1986.
54. Patricia A. Quinn, *Better than the Sons of Kings, op. cit.*
55. Desiderius Erasmus, 'The Whole Duty of Youth', trans. Craig R. Thompson, *The Colloquies of Erasmus*, Chicago: The University of Chicago Press, 1965, p. 32.
56. William Golding, *Lord of the Flies*, London: Faber & Faber Ltd., 1954.
57. Ilham Dilman and D. Z. Phillips, *Sense and Delusion*, London: Routledge & Kegan Paul, 1971, p. 63.
58. St Thomas Aquinas, *Summa Theologiae*, vol. 41, *op. cit.*, p. 175.
59. Francis Bacon, 'Of Simulation and Dissimulation', *op. cit.*, p. 41.
60. (Possibly) Samuel Johnson, *The Rambler*, in A. Chalmers, ed., *The British Essayists*, vol. 17, *op. cit.*, pp. 42–43.
61. Herbert Fingarette, *Self-Deception*, London: Routledge & Kegan Paul, 1969 p. 29 and p. 47. The question of self deception has generated a vast philosophical literature. See for example: Mike W. Martin, *Self-Deception and Morality*, Lawrence: Kansas University Press, 1986; Roderick M. Chisholm and Thomas D. Feehan, 'The Intent to Deceive', *The Journal of Philosophy*, vol. 84, no. 3, March 1977, pp. 143–159; Kent Bach, 'An Analysis of Self-Deception', *Philosophy and Phenomenological Research*, vol. 41, September 1980 - June 1981, pp. 351–370; Mrinal, Miri, 'Self-Deception', *Philosophy and Phenomenological Research*, vol. 34, September 1973– June 1974, pp. 576–585; David Pears, 'Freud, Sartre and Self- Deception', in Richard Wollheim, ed., *Freud. A Collection of Critical Essays*, New York: Anchor Books, 1974, pp. 97–112; and Alan Paskow, 'Towards a theory of self-deception', *Man and World*, vol. 12, 1979, pp. 178–191.
62. Erving Goffman, *The Presentation of Self in Everyday Life*, New York: Doubleday & Company Ltd., 1959, pp. 234–237.
63. Herbert Fingarette, *Self-Deception, op. cit.*, p. 44.
64. David Kipp, 'Self-Deception, Inauthenticity, and Weakness of Will' in Mike Martin, ed., *Self-Deception and self-understanding*, Kansas: University Press of Kansas, 1985, p. 278.
65. Herbert Fingarette, *Self-Deception, op. cit.*, p. 67.
66. *Ibid.*, p. 140.
67. D. W. Hamlyn and H. O. Mounce, 'Self-Deception', *The Aristotelian Society*, vol. 45, 1971, pp. 50–51.
68. Anthony Palmer, 'Characterising Self-Deception', *Mind*, vol. 88, n.s., 1979, p. 52.
69. Ilham Dilman and D. Z. Phillips, *Sense and Delusion, op. cit.*, pp. 76–77.
70. M. R. Haight, *A Study of Self-Deception*, Sussex: The Harvester Press, 1980.
71. David Kipp, 'Self-Deception, Inauthenticity, and Weakness of Will', *op. cit.*, p. 267.
72. G. W. O. Addleshaw, *The High Church Tradition. A Study in the Liturgical Thought of the Seventeenth Century*, London: Faber & Faber, Ltd., 1941, p. 83.

6 Holy and Unholy Rites: Lies and Mistakes in Liturgy

1. These comments are taken from Garrett Green, 'The Sociology of Dogmatics: Niklas Luhmann's Challenge to Theology', *The Journal of the American Academy of Religion*, vol. 50, no. 1, 1982, pp. 23–24.
2. Peter L. Berger, *The Heretical Imperative*, *op. cit.*, pp. 17–31. See also *The Social Reality of Religion*, Chapter 6, 'Secularization and the Problem of Plausibility', *op. cit.*, pp. 131–156.
3. Robin Gill, *Competing Convictions*, London: SCM Press, 1989, pp. 143–145.
4. The Liturgical Commission of the General Synod of the Church of England, *Patterns for Worship*, Church House Publishing, 1989, p. 10.
5. David Cannadine and Simon Price, eds, *Rituals of Royalty. Power and Ceremonial in Traditional Societies*, Cambridge: Cambridge University Press, 1987.
6. Joseph Gelineau, *The Liturgy Today and Tomorrow*, trans. Dinah Livingstone, London: Darton: Longman & Todd, 1978, p. 16.
7. David Martin, 'Profane Habit and Sacred Usage', *Theology*, vol. 82, no. 686, March 1979, pp. 83–95.
8. Compton Mackenzie, *Sinister Street*, London: Penguin, 1960, p. 179.
9. Max Weber, *The Sociology of Religion*, trans. Ephraim Fischoff, London: Methuen, 1966, p. 7.
10. Kieran Flanagan, 'Competitive Assemblies of God: Lies and mistakes in liturgy', *Research Bulletin*, University of Birmingham: Institute for the study of worship and religious architecture, 1981, pp. 20–69.
11. Emile Durkheim, *The Elementary Forms of the Religious Life*, *op. cit.*, p. 382.
12. Anthony Giddens, *Central Problems in Social Theory. Action, Structure and Contradiction in Social Analysis*, London: Macmillan, 1979, Chapter 2, 'Agency, Structure', pp. 49–95.
13. Gilbert Lewis, *Day of Shining Red. An Essay on Understanding Ritual*, Cambridge: Cambridge University Press, 1980, p. 38.
14. Robert Merton, *Social Theory and Social Structure*, New York: The Free Press, 1968, p. 241.
15. Donald N. Levine, *The Flight from Ambiguity. Essays in Social and Cultural Theory*, Chicago: The University of Chicago Press, 1985.
16. *Ibid.*, Chapter 3, 'The Flexibility of Traditional Cultures', pp. 44–54.
17. Ian Hamnett, 'Ambiguity, classification and change: the function of riddles', *Man*, vol. 2, no. 3, September 1967, pp. 379–391.
18. Patricia S. Greenspan, 'A case of mixed feelings: ambivalence and the logic of emotion' in Amélie Rorty, ed., *Explaining Emotions*, Berkeley: University of California Press, 1980, p. 240.
19. Gilbert Lewis, *Day of Shining Red*, Chapter 2, 'Problems of ritual in general', *op. cit.*, pp. 6–38.
20. Alan Dawe, 'The Two Sociologies', *The British Journal of Sociology*, vol. 21, no. 2, June 1970, pp. 207–218.
21. Alan Dawe, 'Theories of Social Action', in Tom Bottomore and Robert Nisbet, eds, *A History of Sociological Analysis*, London: Heinemann, 1978, p. 414.

22. Anthony Giddens, *Studies in Social and Political Theory*, London: Hutchinson, 1977, Chapter 2, 'Functionalism: *aprés la lutte*', pp. 96–134.
23. Emile Durkheim, *The Elementary Forms of the Religious Life*, *op. cit.*, p. 386.
24. Gregory W. H. Smith, 'Snapshots "sub specie aeternitatis"': Simmel, Goffman and Formal Sociology', *Human Studies*, vol. 12, nos. 1–2, June 1989, pp. 19–57.
25. Georg Simmel, *Essays on Interpretation in Social Science*, *op. cit.*, pp. 8–46. See also: David Frisby, *Sociological Impressionism. A Reassessment of Georg Simmel's Social Theory*, London: Heinemann, 1981, pp. 61–67; and his book *Georg Simmel*, London: Tavistock, 1984, pp. 59–63.
26. Kurt H. Wolff, ed. and trans., *The Sociology of Georg Simmel*, New York: The Free Press, 1950, pp. 402–408.
27. Arnold van Gennep, *The Rites of Passage*, trans. Monika B. Vizedom and Gabrielle L. Caffee, London: Routledge and Kegan Paul, 1977, pp. 33–38.
28. Quoted in Donald N. Levine, *The Flight from Ambiguity, op. cit.*, p. 110.
29. Georg Simmel, 'Contribution to the Sociology of Religion', *The American Journal of Sociology*, vol. 60, no. 6, May 1955, p. 12. See also Georg Simmel, *Sociology of Religion*, trans. C. Rosenthal, New York: Philosophical Library, 1959, pp. 31–35.
30. Georg Simmel, *Essays on interpretation in social science, op. cit.*, pp. 18–25.
31. *Ibid.*, pp. 35–36.
32. F. H. Tenbruck, 'Formal Sociology' in Lewis Coser, ed., *Georg Simmel*, New Jersey: Prentice Hall, Inc., 1965, p. 94.
33. Kurt H. Wolff, trans. and ed., *The Sociology of Georg Simmel, op. cit.*, pp. 352–355.
34. C. Henry Phillips, *The Singing Church*, London: Faber & Faber, Ltd., 1945, p. 238.
35. Gareth Matthews, 'Ritual and the Religious Feelings' in Amélie Rorty ed., *Explaining Emotions, op. cit.*, 1980, p. 342.
36. Ian Hamnett, 'Idolatry and Docetism: Contrasting Styles of Proclamation' in Denise Newton, ed., *Liturgy and Change*, University of Birmingham: Institute for the Study of Worship and Religious Architecture, 1983, pp. 21–37.
37. Maurice Bloch, 'Symbols, Song, Dance and Features of Articulation. Is religion an extreme form of traditional authority?', *Archives Européens de Sociologie*, vol. 15, 1974, p. 77.
38. Roy Rappaport, 'The Obvious Aspects of Ritual', in *Ecology, Meaning and Religion, op. cit.*, p. 173.
39. *Ibid.*, p. 209.
40. Roy Rappaport, 'Sanctity and Lies in Evolution' in *Ecology, Meaning and Religion, op. cit.*, p. 229.
41. Roy Rappaport, 'The Obvious Aspects of Ritual', in *Ecology, Meaning and Religion, op. cit.*, p. 200.
42. John Skorupski, *Symbol and Theory. A Philosophical Study of Theories of Religion in Social Anthropology*, Cambridge: Cambridge University Press, 1976, Chapter 7, 'Operative Ceremonies', pp. 93–115.

43. S. J. Tambiah, *A Performative Approach to Ritual*, London: The British Academy, 1981, p. 140.
44. Roy Rappaport, 'The Obvious Aspects of Ritual', in *Ecology, Meaning and Religion, op. cit.*, p. 195.
45. Roy Rappaport, 'Sanctity and Lies in Evolution', in *Ecology, Meaning and Religion, op. cit.*, p. 231.
46. *Ibid.*, p. 233.
47. *Ibid.*, p. 234.
48. Hugh Vickers, *Great Operatic Disasters*, London: Macmillan, 1979.
49. Anthony Trollope, *Barchester Towers*, London: J. M. Dent & Sons, Ltd., 1975, p. 46.
50. Adrian Fortescue, *The Ceremonies of the Roman Rite Described*, London: Burns Oates & Washbourne Ltd., 1920, p. xviii.
51. Pierce Ahearne and Michael Lane, *Pontifical Ceremonies. A Study of the Episcopal Ceremonies*, London: Burns Oates & Washbourne Ltd., 1942, p. vi.
52. For suggestive comments on how ritual might be understood in terms of its use of rules see Paul Heelas, 'Semantic Anthropology and Rules', in Peter Collett, ed., *Social Rules and Social Behaviour*, Oxford: Basil Blackwell, 1977. Compare this analysis with Jean Ladrière, 'The Performativity of Liturgical Language' in Herman Schmidt and David Power, eds, *Liturgical Experience of Faith*, New York: Herder & Herder, 1973, pp. 50–62.
53. Peter Winch, *The Idea of a Social Science and its Relation to Philosophy*, London: Routledge & Kegan Paul, 1963, p. 32.
54. Emily Ahern, 'Rules in Oracles and Games', *Man*, n.s. vol. 17, 1982. pp. 302–312.
55. Rom Harré, 'Social rules and social rituals' in Henry Tajfel, ed., *The Social dimension. European developments in social psychology*, vol. 1, Cambridge: Cambridge University Press, 1984, p. 303. Harré bases most of his argument around observations on Oxford degree ceremonies.
56. David E. Babin, *The Celebration of Life: Our Changing Liturgy*, New York: Morehouse-Barlow, 1969, Chapter 4, 'A fourth element', pp. 40–52.
57. Victor Turner, 'Ritual, Tribal and Catholic', *Worship*, vol. 50, no. 6, November 1976, pp. 504–526.
58. P. Charles Augustine, *Liturgical Law. A handbook of the Roman Liturgy*, London: B. Herder, 1931, pp. 1–4.
59. J. B. O'Connell, *The Celebration of Mass*, Milwaukee: The Bruce Publishing Company, 1956, Chapter 11, 'Defects in the celebration of Mass', pp. 181–211.
60. John M. Huels, 'The Interpretation of Liturgical Law', *Worship*, vol. 55, no. 3, May 1981, p. 233.
61. J. B. O'Connell, *The Celebration of Mass, op. cit.*, pp. 679–680.
62. Erving Goffman, 'Embarrassment and Social Organization', *Interaction Ritual. Essays on Face-to-Face Behaviour*, London: Penguin, 1972, pp. 97–112.
63. Erving Goffman, 'On Face-Work. An Analysis of Ritual Elements in Social Interaction' *ibid.*, pp. 5–45.

64. Victor Turner, 'Ritual, Tribal and Catholic', *op. cit.*, pp. 520–524. See also his book *From Ritual to Theatre. The Human Seriousness of Play*, New York: Performing Arts Journal Publications, 1982, pp. 55–59.
65. Erving Goffman, *Frame Analysis, op. cit.*, Chapter 11, 'The Manufacture of Negative Experience', pp. 378–438.
66. *Ibid.*, pp. 1–4.
67. Andrew Travers, 'Social Beings as Hostages: Organizational and Societal Conduct Answering to a Siege Paradigm of Interaction' in I. L. Mangham, ed., *Organization Analysis and Development*, New York: John Wiley & Sons Ltd., 1987, pp. 223–253.
68. Erving Goffman, *Interaction Ritual, op. cit.*, p. 31.

7 Sacred and Profane Abasements: The Management of Esteem

1. Alec Guinness, *Blessings in Disguise*, London: Fontana/Collins, 1986, p. 67.
2. Charles Strachey, ed., *The Letters of the Earl of Chesterfield to his son*, 2nd edn, vol. 2, London: Methuen & Co. Ltd., 1924, p. 104.
3. *Ibid.*, vol. I, p. 116 and p. 145.
4. See Mary Ritchie Key, *Nonverbal communication: a research guide*, Metuchen, N.J.: The Scarecrow Press, 1977. See also Francis Hayes, 'Gestures: a working bibliography', *Southern Folklore Quarterly*, vol. 21, no. 4, 1957, pp. 218–317. For two useful articles on the interpretation of gestures, see Weston Labarre, 'The Cultural Basis of Emotions and Gestures', *Journal of Personality*, vol. 16, September 1947, pp. 49–68, and Raymond Firth, 'Verbal and bodily rituals of greeting and parting' in J. S. La Fontaine, ed., *The Interpretation of Ritual*, London: Tavistock, 1972, pp. 1–38.
5. Antoine Vergote, 'Symbolic Gestures and Actions in the Liturgy' in David Power, ed., *Liturgy in Transition*, London: Herder and Herder, 1971, p. 43. For a detailed account of stylised gesture in acting, see Dene Barnett (with assistance of Jeanette Massy-Westropp) *The Art of Gesture: The practices and principles of 18th century acting*, Heidelberg: Carl Winter. Universitätsverlag, 1987.
6. Charles Strachey, ed., *The Letters of the Earl of Chesterfield to his son*, vol. 2, *op. cit.*, p. 218.
7. Karen Halttunen, *Confidence Men and Painted Women. A Study of Middle-class Culture in America, 1830–1870*, New Haven: Yale University Press, 1982, pp. 115–116. She also notes that during the decades after the American Civil War many in the middle class had a 'deep conviction of the vulnerability of genteel performance' and the risk of the 'fragile mask of manners' being ripped away to reveal the vulgarity of the wearer. p. 116.
8. Quoted in Leonore Davidoff, *The Best Circles. Society Etiquette and the Season*, London: Croom Helm, 1973, pp. 45–46.
9. Norbert Elias, *The History of Manners*, trans. Edmund Jephcott, Oxford: Basil Blackwell, 1978.
10. John Henry Newman, *The Idea of a University*, New York: Image Books, 1959, p. 144.

11. Charles Strachey, ed., *The Letters of the Earl of Chesterfield to his son*, vol. 1 *op. cit.*, p. 238.
12. Judith Martin, *Miss Manners' Guide to Excruciatingly Correct Behaviour*, London: Penguin, 1984, p. 662.
13. Erving Goffman, 'The Nature of Deference and Demeanor', *Interaction Ritual*, *op. cit.*, p. 57.
14. Desiderius Erasmus, 'De Civilitate morum puerilium' ('On Good Manners for Boys'), trans. and annot. Brian McGregor, in J. K. Sowards, ed., *Collected Works of Erasmus*, Toronto: University of Toronto Press, 1985, p. 280. For his advice on the vagaries and misunderstandings that arise from different styles of civil bows, see p. 278.
15. Romano Guardini, *Sacred Signs*, trans. G. C. H. Pollen, London: Sheed & Ward, 1930, p. xi.
16. Cited in Boniface Ramsey, *Beginning to Read the Fathers*, *op. cit.*, p. 173.
17. J. D. Hilarius Dale, *Ceremonial according to the Roman Rite*, London: Charles Dolman, 1853, pp. 4–5.
18. Fyodor Dostoyevsky, *The Brothers Karamazov*, trans. David Magarshack, London: Folio Society, 1964, p. 51.
19. John Skorupski, *Symbol and Theory*, *op. cit.*, p. 101.
20. Erving Goffman, 'The Nature of Deference and Demeanour', *op. cit.*, pp. 56–57.
21. Charles Strachey, ed., *The Letters of the Earl of Chesterfield to his son*, vol. 1, *op. cit.*, p. 371.
22. Joan Wildeblood and Peter Brinson, *The Polite World: A Guide to English Manners and Deportment from the Thirteenth to the Nineteenth Century*, Oxford: Oxford University Press, 1965, Appendix 1, 'Salutations. Technical Descriptions', pp. 261–277. See also J. L. Styan, *Restoration Comedy in Performance*, Cambridge: Cambridge University Press, 1986, pp. 68–70.
23. Jean Baptiste Molière, 'The Would-be gentleman' , trans. John Wood, London: Penguin Books, 1953, p. 11.
24. J. L. Cranmer-Byng, ed., *An Embassy to China*, London: Longmans, 1962, pp. 32–34. See also Dun J. Li, ed., *China in Transition: 1517–1911*, New York: Van Nostrand Reinhold Company, 1969, pp. 46–49.
25. Joan Wildeblood and Peter Brinson, *The Polite World*, *op. cit.*, pp. 276–277. See also Raymond Firth, 'Postures and Gestures of Respect' in Jean Pouillon and Pierre Maranda, eds, *Echanges et Communications*, vol. 1, The Hague: Mouton, 1970, pp. 188–209.
26. H. R. Haweis, 'Bowing', *Belgravia*, vol. 4, 1881, pp. 185–87.
27. Erving Goffman, 'The Nature of Deference and Demeanour' in *Interaction Ritual* , *op. cit.*, p. 54.
28. *Ibid.*, p. 91.
29. V. G. L., *Manners at Mass. The Movements and Gestures of Public Worship*, London: Burns & Oates, 1955, p. 9.
30. Romano Guardini, *Sacred Signs*, *op. cit.*, p. 8.
31. Richard Whately, *Bacon's Essays: with Annotations*, 5th edn, London: John Parker, 1860, pp. 550–551.

32. Johannes H. Emminghaus, *The Eucharist. Essence, Form, Celebration*, *op. cit.*, pp. 108–109. See also the general instruction of the Roman Missal, nos. 84 and 234, *St. Luke's Daily Missal*, Alcester and Dublin: C. Goodcliffe Neale Ltd., 1975, p. xl and p. lviii.
33. J. B O'Connell, *The Celebration of Mass*, *op. cit.*, pp. 263–270. For further information on liturgical gestures and bows in the Catholic Church see: Aimé Georges Martimort, ed., *The Church at Prayer*, vol. 1, *op. cit.*, pp. 179–187. Anglican approaches to gestures and bows are more complex. See Vernon Staley, *The Ceremonial of the English Church*, London: A. R. Mowbray, 1899, Chapter IV, Section 1, pp. 193–198; Percy Dearmer, *The Parson's Handbook*, *op. cit.*, pp. 199–212; and Vernon Staley, ed., *Hierurgia Anglicana. The Ceremonial of the Anglican Church after the Reformation*, vol. 3, part II, New Edition, London: The De La More Press, 1903, 'Reverences', pp. 67–74.
34. Vernon Staley, ed., *Hierurgia Anglicana*, *op. cit.*, p. 80.
35. *Ibid.*, pp. 87–89.
36. *Ibid.*, p. 105.
37. Ignatius Brianchaninov, *The Arena. An offering to Contemporary Monasticism*, Madras: Diocesan Press, 1970, pp. 73–78.
38. *Ibid.*, p. 254.
39. Richard C. Trexler, 'Legitimating prayer gestures in the twelfth century. The *De Penitentia* of Peter the Chanter', *History and Anthropology*, vol. 1, 1984, p. 109 and p. 115. See also the introduction by Jean-Claude Schmitt, pp. 1–15 in *ibid.*
40. Jean-Claude Schmitt, 'Between text and image: the prayer gestures of Saint Dominic' , *History and Anthropology*, *op. cit.*, p. 128.
41. Geoffrey Moorhouse, *Against all Reason*, London: Weidenfeld & Nicolson, 1969, Appendix 2, p. 283.
42. Gareth Matthews, 'Ritual and the Religious Feelings' in Amélie Rorty, ed., *Explaining Emotions*, *op. cit.*, pp. 339–353.
43. Joanne Finkelstein, *Dining Out. A Sociology of Modern Manners*, Cambridge: Polity Press, 1989, p. 166.
44. *Ibid.*, p. 131.

8 Altar Servers and Waiters: Serving in Worlds Apart

1. Richard Sennett, *The Fall of Public Man*, *op. cit.*, pp. 38–41.
2. Michael Farrell, *Thy Tears Might Cease*, London: Arena Books, 1968, pp. 77–79.
3. Kathleen Edwards, *The English Secular Cathedrals in the Middle Ages*, *op. cit.*, pp. 303–307.
4. Joseph A. Jungmann, *The Mass of the Roman Rite*, *op. cit.*, p. 166. See also reference to the longstanding custom of having a server in attendance, pp. 154–156. Jungmann indicates that the active assistance of servers was prescribed for the first time in a liturgical document on the restored Easter Vigil, and later in the general reform of Holy Week in 1955.

5. There is no adequate history of the altar server. For an Anglican version see W. S. Williams, *The History of Acolytes and Servers and of what they have done for the Church down the Centuries*, Chatham: Parrett & Neves, Ltd., 1938.

6. *Ministeria Quaedam*, in Austin Flannery, ed., *Vatican Council II, op. cit.*, pp. 427–432. See also entry on the server in Gehard Podhradsky, *New Dictionary of the Liturgy*, London: Geoffrey Chapman, 1962, pp. 184–185.

7. For account of the serving procedures in the Sarum Rite, see Charles Walker, *The Server's Handbook: containing the manner of serving at simple and solemn celebrations of the Holy Eucharist: and at solemn Matins and Evensong, according to the Rubrical Directions of the Sarum and Roman Office-Books; with appropriate devotions*, London: C. J. Palmer, 1871.

8. Charles Walker, *The Liturgy of the Church of Sarum*, London: J. T. Hayes, 1866, pp. 44–48.

9. J. B. O'Connell, *The Celebration of Mass, op. cit.*, pp. 500–502.

10. Joseph König, 'Serving at the Altar' in Alfons Kirchgaessner, ed., *Unto the Altar. The Practice of Catholic Worship*, London: Nelson, 1963, pp. 138–146.

11. Highly detailed manuals for altar servers have been produced in Germany and France. Perhaps the best current work in English is Michael Kwatera, *The Ministry of Servers*, Collegeville, Minnesota: The Liturgical Press, 1982.

12. Morley Roberts, 'Waiters and Restaurants', *Murrays Magazine*, vol. 7, 1890, p. 534.

13. Gerald Mars and Michael Nicod, *The World of Waiters*, London: George Allen & Unwin, 1984, p. 35.

14. R. W. C. T. 'Waiters', *Dublin University Magazine*, vol. 75, May 1870, p. 583. See also Anon., 'Waiters', *All the Year Round*, vol. 59, 1887, pp. 813–816.

15. Jean Paul Sartre, *Being and Nothingness. An Essay on Phenomenological Ontology*, trans. Hazel E. Barnes, London: Methuen & Co. Ltd., 1957.

16. Gerald Mars and Michael Nicod, *The World of Waiters, op. cit.*, pp. 98–99.

17. Thorstein Veblen, *The Theory of the Leisure Class, op. cit.*, pp. 53–54.

18. Gerald Mars and Michael Nicod, *The World of Waiters, op. cit.*, Chapter 4, 'The Politics of Service: Who gets the jump', pp. 65–88.

19. William Foote Whyte, 'The Social Structure of the Restaurant', *The American Journal of Sociology*, vol. 54, November 1948, pp. 302–310.

20. Gerald Mars and Michael Nicod, *The World of Waiters, op. cit.*, p. 28.

21. George Orwell, *Down and Out in Paris and London*, London: Penguin, 1975, p. 61.

22. Erving Goffman, 'The Nature of Deference and Demeanour' in *Interaction Ritual, op. cit.*, p. 78.

23. Norbert Elias, *The History of Manners, op. cit.*, p. 121. For a marvellous account of the collapse of the veneer of civility and the embarrassing limits of 'good service' in a restaurant, see Tom Wolfe, *The Bonfire of the Vanities*, London: Picador, 1988, pp. 598–613.

24. Norbert Elias, *The History of Manners, op. cit.*, p. 115.
25. Gordon Marshall, 'The Workplace Culture of a Licensed Restaurant', *Theory, Culture & Society*, vol. 3, no 1, 1986, pp. 33–47.
26. Pierre Smith, 'Aspects of the Organization of Rites' in Michael Izard and Pierre Smith, eds, *Between Belief and Transgression. Structuralist Essays in Religion, History and Myth*, trans. John Leavitt, London: Chicago University Press, 1982, p. 103.
27. Richard Sennett, *The Fall of Public Man , op. cit.*, p. 111.
28. Erving Goffman, *The Presentation of Self in Everyday Life, op. cit.*, p. 112.
29. Richard Sennett, *The Fall of Public Man, op. cit.*, pp. 165–66.
30. Nicholas R. Curcione, 'Family Influence on Commitment to the Priesthood: A Study of Altar Boys', *Sociological Analysis*, vol. 34, 1973, pp. 265–280.
31. Michael Kwatera, *The Ministry of Servers, op. cit.*, p. 11.
32. Charles Walker, *The Server's Handbook, op. cit.*, p. 8.
33. Domenico Luigh Cesari, *Manual for Serving Boys at Low Mass*, trans., R. W. Brundrit, London: Burns, Oates, & Co., 1868, pp. 7–8.
34. Anon., *Servers' Manual of the Archconfraternity of Saint Stephen*, London: Burns and Oates, 1907, p. 35f.
35. Adrian Fortescue, *The Ceremonies of the Roman Rite described, op. cit.*, pp. 99–105.
36. Joseph William Kavanagh, *The Altar Boys' Ceremonial*, New York: Benziger Brothers, Inc., 1956, p. 248.
37. Michael Kwatera, *The Ministry of Servers, op. cit.*, p. 14.
38. Lester Yeo, *The Server's Handbook. The Alternative Service Book, 1980. Rite A*, Exeter: Religious and Moral Education Press, 1984. Compare the instructions in this with those in an earlier Anglican book. Denis E. Taylor, *Serving at the Altar. A Manual for Servers*, Exeter: The Religious Education Press Ltd., 1966.
39. Adrian Fortescue, *The Ceremonies of the Roman Rite described, op. cit.*, p. 31.
40. Gordon Marshall, 'The Workplace Culture of a Licensed Restaurant' *op. cit.*
41. Joanne Finkelstein, *Dining Out, op. cit.*, pp. 176–185.

9 Liturgy as Ritual: Playing On Social Limits

1. Odo Casel, *The Mystery of Christian Worship, op. cit.*, p. 100.
2. *Ibid.*, p. 158.
3. Hans-Georg Gadamer, 'The relevance of the beautiful. Art as play, symbol, and festival' in *The Relevance of the Beautiful and other Essays*, Robert Bernasconi, ed., trans. Nicholas Walker, Cambridge: Cambridge University Press, 1986, pp. 33–36.
4. Quoted in Marjorie Villiers, *Charles Péguy. A Study in Integrity*, London: Collins, 1965, p. 301.
5. G. K. A. Bell and D. Adolf Deissmann, eds, *Mysterium Christi. Christ-ological Studies by British and German Theologians*, London: Longmans, Green & Co., 1930, pp. 31–34.

6.   For an excellent overview of the main contours of contemporary theology, see David F. Ford, ed., *The Modern Theologians. An introduction to Christian theology in the twentieth century*, vols. 1–2, Oxford: Basil Blackwell, 1989.

7.   Romano Guardini, *The Spirit of the Liturgy*, op. cit., p. 84.

8.   I. H. Dalmais, 'The Liturgy as Celebration of the Mystery of Salvation', in Aimé Georges Martimort, ed., *The Church at Prayer*, vol. 1, op. cit., p. 259.

9.   I. H. Dalmais, *Introduction to the Liturgy*, op. cit., p. 68.

10. Joseph Cardinal Ratzinger, *Feast of Faith. Approaches to a Theology of the Liturgy*, trans. Graham Harrison, San Francisco: Ignatius Press, 1986, p. 67. See also Aidan Nichols, *The Theology of Joseph Ratzinger. An Introductory Study*, Edinburgh: T. & T. Clark, 1988, especially Chapter 10, pp. 207–224.

11. Irving M. Zeitlin, *Rethinking Sociology. A Critique of Contemporary Theory*, Englewood Cliffs, New Jersey: Prentice Hall, Inc., 1973, p. 145.

12. Joseph Dabney Bettis, ed., *Phenomenology of Religion*, New York: Harper & Row, 1969, pp. 1–4. See also Anthony J. Blasi, *A Phenomenological Transformation of the Social Scientific Study of Religion*, New York: Peter Lang, 1985.

13. Sanford Krolick, 'Through a Glass Darkly: What is the phenomenology of religion?' *International Journal for Philosophy of Religion*, vol. 17, 1985, pp. 197–198.

14. Emile Durkheim, *The Elementary Forms of the Religious Life*, op. cit., p. 227.

15. Steven Lukes, *Emile Durkheim. His Life and Work*, London: Allen Lane, The Penguin Press, 1973, p. 463.

16. For a discussion of critics and followers of Durkheim, see Ian Hamnett, 'Durkheim and the study of religion' in Steve Fenton, *Durkheim and Modern Sociology*, Cambridge: Cambridge University Press, 1984, pp. 202–218.

17. Talal Asad, 'On ritual and discipline in medieval Christian monasticism', *Economy and Society*, vol. 16, no. 2, May 1987, see especially pp. 161–167. See also Mark Kline Taylor, 'Symbolic Dimensions in Cultural Anthropology', *Current Anthropology*, vol. 26, no. 2, April 1985, pp. 167–185.

18. Clifford Geertz, 'Religion as a Cultural System', in Donald Culter, ed., *The Religious Situation: 1968*, Boston: Beacon Press, 1968, p. 670.

19. *Ibid.*, p. 642.

20. For an early assessment of his liturgical significance, see Mary Collins, 'Ritual Symbols and the Ritual Process: The Work of Victor W. Turner' and John H. McKenna, 'Ritual Activity', both in *Worship*, vol. 50, no. 4, July 1976, pp. 336–346 and pp. 347–352.

21. Gilbert Lewis, *Day of Shining Red*, op. cit., pp. 30–31.

22. Arnold van Gennep, *The Rites of Passage*, op. cit., p. 96.

23. Gregory Dix, *The Shape of the Liturgy*, Chapter IV, 'Eucharist and Lord's Supper', op. cit., pp. 48–102.

24. Arnold van Gennep, *The Rites of Passage*, op. cit., pp. 20–21.

25. Victor Turner, *The Ritual Process. Structure and Anti-Structure*, London: Routledge & Kegan Paul, 1969, Chapter 3, 'Liminality and Communitas', see especially pp. 128–129. Three differing forms of communitas are noted on p. 132.
26. Ronald Grimes, 'Ritual Studies: A Comparative Review of Theodor Gaster and Victor Turner', *Religious Studies Review*, vol. 2, no. 4, October 1976, p. 20.
27. Victor Turner, 'Passages, Margins, and Poverty: Religious Symbols of Communitas', Part 1, *Worship*, vol. 46, no. 7, 1972, pp. 390–392.
28. Victor Turner, 'Passages, Margins, and Poverty: Religious Symbols of Communitas', Part 2, *Worship*, vol. 46, no. 8, 1972, pp. 485–486.
29. Urban T. Holmes, 'Liminality and Liturgy', *Worship, op. cit.*, 393.
30. Victor Turner, ed., *Celebration. Studies in Festivity and Ritual*, Washington, D.C., Smithsonian Institution Press, 1982, pp. 204–205.
31. Barbara Myerhoff, 'Rites of Passage: Process and Paradox' *ibid.*, pp. 117–122.
32. Victor Turner, *From Ritual to Theatre, op. cit.*, pp. 79–81.
33. Romano Guardini, *The Spirit of the Liturgy, op. cit.*, pp. 46–50.
34. Victor Turner, *From Ritual to Theatre, op. cit.*, p. 41.
35. Ian Hamnett, 'Idolatry and Docetism' *op. cit.*, p. 30.
36. George Pattison, 'Idol or Icon? Some principles of an Aesthetic Christology', *Journal of Literature & Theology*, vol. 3, no. 1, March 1989, p. 5.
37. Victor Turner, *From Ritual to Theatre, op. cit.*, p. 77.
38. Rudolf Otto, *The Idea of the Holy, op. cit.*, p. 35.
39. Victor Turner, *From Ritual to Theatre, op. cit.*, p. 49.
40. Rudolf Otto, *The Idea of the Holy, op. cit.*, pp. 54–55.
41. *Ibid.*, p. 60.
42. *Ibid.*, pp. 64–65.
43. *Ibid.*, p. 46.
44. Kurt H. Wolff, trans. and ed., *The Sociology of Georg Simmel, op. cit.*, p. 349. Some of the material in this section is drawn from my essay 'Liturgy, ambiguity and silence: the ritual management of real absence', *The British Journal of Sociology*, vol. 36, no. 2, June 1985, pp. 193–223.
45. David Martin, *The Breaking of the Image. A Sociology of Christian Theory and Practice*, Oxford: Basil Blackwell, 1980, p. 148.
46. Susan Sontag, 'The Aesthetics of Silence' in *Styles of Radical Will*, New York: Farrar, Straus and Giroux, 1976, p. 6.
47. Joseph Cardinal Ratzinger, 'Liturgy and Sacred Music', *Communio*, vol. 13, no. 4, Winter 1986, pp. 381–385.
48. Rudolf Otto, *The Idea of the Holy, op. cit.*, pp. 70–71.
49. Susan Sontag, 'The Aesthetics of Silence', *op. cit.*, p. 32.
50. Ambrose G. Wathen, *Silence. The Meaning of Silence in the Rule of St Benedict*, Washington, D.C., Consortium Press, 1973, p. 85.
51. Paul Delatte, *Commentary on the Rule of St Benedict, op. cit.*, p. 99.
52. St Benedict, *The Rule of Saint Benedict*, trans. David Parry, London: Darton, Longman & Todd, 1984, p. 22.
53. Michael Ignatieff, *A Just Measure of Pain*, London: Macmillan, 1978, pp. 178–179 and pp. 194–195.

54. Paul Delatte, *Commentary on the Rule of St Benedict, op. cit.*, p. 92.
55. Shusaku Endo, *Silence*, trans. William Johnston, London: Quartet Books, 1978.
56. Louis Dupré, 'Spiritual Life in a Secular Age', in Mary Douglas and Steven Tipton, eds, *Religion and America. Spiritual Life in a Secular Age, op. cit.*, p. 10.
57. Peter Berger, *A Rumour of Angels, op. cit.*, pp. 95–96.
58. Thomas Carlyle, *Sartor Resartus, op. cit.*, p. 150.
59. Max Picard, *The World of Silence*, trans. Stanley Godman, South Bend, Indiana: Regnery/Gateway, Inc., 1952, p. 28.
60. George Steiner, *Language and Silence*, London: Faber & Faber, 1967, p. 55.
61. *Ibid.*, p. 58.
62. Max Picard, *The World of Silence, op. cit.*, p. 27.
63. Nancy Jay Crumbine, 'On Silence', *Humanitas*, May 1975, p. 148.
64. Max Picard, *The World of Silence, op. cit.*, pp. 39–40.
65. *Ibid.*, pp. 17–18.
66. *Ibid.*, pp. 227–228.
67. Nancy Jay Crumbine, 'On Silence', *op. cit.*, p. 151.
68. David Wren, 'Abraham's Silence and the Logic of Faith' in Robert L. Perkins, *Kierkegaard's* Fear and Trembling: *Critical Appraisals*, Alabama: The University of Alabama Press, 1981, p. 161. See also Ramona Cromier, 'Silence in Philosophy and Literature', *Philosophy To Day*, vol. 2, Winter, 1978, pp. 301–306.
69. Evelyn Underhill, *Worship*, New York: Crossroad, 1982, p. 96.
70. Max Picard, *The World of Silence, op. cit.*, p. 230.
71. *Ibid.*, p. 29.
72. L. Violet Hodgkin, *Silent Worship: The Way of Wonder*, London: Headley Bros. Publishers Ltd., 1919, p. 77. For issues raised about the management of silence in a slightly different form of liturgy, see Daniel N. Maltz, 'Joyful Noise and Reverent Silence: The Significance of Noise in Pentecostal Worship' in Deborah Tannen and Muriel Saville-Troike, eds, *Perspectives on Silence*, Norwood, New Jersey: Ablex Publishing Corporation, 1985, pp. 113–138.
73. General Instruction on the Roman Missal, *op. cit.*, section 23, p. xxiv.
74. Rudolf Otto, 'Towards a Liturgical Reform. 1. The Form of Divine Service' in *Religious Essays. A supplement to 'The Idea of the Holy'* trans. Brian Lunn, Oxford: Oxford University Press, 1931, p. 54.
75. Mircea Eliade, *The Sacred & the Profane. The Nature of Religion*, New York: Harcourt Brace Jovanovich, 1959, pp. 11–13.
76. Bernard P. Dauenhauer, *Silence. The Phenomenon and its Ontological Significance*, Bloomington: Indiana University Press, 1980, pp. 18–19.

10   Action, Symbol, Text: Hermeneutics and Sociology

1. Peter L. Berger, *A Rumour of Angels*, Chap. 2, 'The Perspective of Sociology: Relativizing the Relativizers', *op. cit.*, pp. 43–65.
2. Hans-Georg Gadamer, 'Aesthetic and religious experience' in *The Relevance of the Beautiful, op. cit.*, pp. 140–153.
3. See T. M. van Leeuwen, *The Surplus of Meaning. Ontology and*

Eschatology in the Philosophy of Paul Ricoeur, Amsterdam: Rodopi, 1981, Chapter V, 'The mutual promotion of reason and faith', pp. 179–189. For a useful account of the theological aspects of his writings, see David E. Klemm, *The Hermeneutical Theory of Paul Ricoeur. A Constructive Analysis*, London: Associated University Presses, 1983. Richard Kearney has some useful comments on this facet of Ricoeur. See his *Dialogues with contemporary Continental thinkers. The phenomenological heritage*, Manchester: Manchester University Press, 1984, pp. 33–46, and his essay, 'Religion and Ideology: Paul Ricoeur's hermeneutic conflict', *The Irish Philosophical Journal*, vol. 2, Spring 1985, pp. 37–52.

4. Richard Rorty, *Philosophy and the Mirror of Nature*, Oxford: Basil Blackwell, 1980, p. 360.
5. Georgia Warnke, *Gadamer: Hermeneutics, Tradition and Reason*, Cambridge: Polity Press, 1987, p. 157.
6. Richard Rorty, *Philosophy and the Mirror of Nature*, op. cit., pp. 357–394.
7. Michael Ermarth, *Wilhelm Dilthey: The Critique of Historical Reason*, op. cit., p. 259.
8. Bob Gidlow, 'Ethnomethodology – a new name for old practices' *The British Journal of Sociology*, vol. 23, no. 4, December 1972, pp. 395–405.
9. J. Maxwell Atkinson, *Discovering Suicide. Studies in the Social Organization of Sudden Death*, London: Macmillan, 1982.
10. Wes Sharrock and Bob Anderson, *The Ethnomethodologists*, op. cit., p. 57.
11. Mary Douglas, *Evans-Pritchard*, London: Fontana, 1980, Chapters 5–6, pp. 49–73.
12. Josef Bleicher, *The Hermeneutic Imagination. Outline of a Positive Critique of Scientism and Sociology*, London: Routledge & Kegan Paul, 1982, p. 151.
13. Zygmunt Bauman, *Hermeneutics and Social Science. Approaches to understanding*, London: Hutchinson, 1978, p. 21.
14. Brian Morris, *Anthropological Studies of Religion. An Introductory Text*, Cambridge: Cambridge University Press, 1987, Chapter 3, pp. 91–140.
15. Robin Horton and Ruth Finnegan, eds, *Modes of Thought. Essays on Thinking in Western and Non-Western Societies*, op. cit.
16. See for example, John Middleton, ed., *Magic, Witchcraft & Curing*, London: University of Texas Press, 1967; George M. Foster and Barbara Gallatin Anderson, *Medical Anthropology*, New York: John Wiley & Sons, Ltd., 1978; and Cecil Helman, *Culture, Health and Illness*, Bristol: Wright, 1985.
17. Peter Winch, *The Idea of a Social Science*, op. cit.
18. Bryan R. Wilson, ed., *Rationality*, Oxford: Basil Blackwell, 1970.
19. Barry Barnes and David Bloor, 'Relativism, Rationalism and the Sociology of Knowledge' in Martin Hollis and Steven Lukes, eds, *Rationality and Relativism*, Oxford: Basil Blackwell, 1982.
20. Joanna Overing, ed., *Reason and Morality*, London: Tavistock Publications, 1985, pp. 2–3.

21. *Ibid.*, p. 33.
22. Paul Hirst and Penny Woolley, *Social Relations and Human Attributes*, London: Tavistock Publications, 1982, p. 272.
23. Susan J. Hekman, *Hermeneutics & the Sociology of Knowledge*, Cambridge: Polity Press, 1986.
24. John B. Thompson, *Critical Hermeneutics. A study in the thought of Paul Ricoeur and Jurgen Habermas*, Cambridge: Cambridge University Press, 1981.
25. Richard J. Bernstein, *Beyond Objectivism and Relativism*, op. cit.
26. John B. Thompson, ed. and trans., *Paul Ricoeur. Hermeneutics and the human sciences*, op. cit.
27. Richard J. Bernstein, *Beyond Objectivism and Relativism*, op. cit., pp. 56–57.
28. *Ibid.*, see especially Part 2, 'Science, Rationality and Incommensurability', pp. 51–108.
29. *Ibid.*, pp. 98–99.
30. *Ibid.*, p. 108.
31. E. E. Evans-Pritchard, *Theories of Primitive Religion*, Oxford: Clarendon Press, 1966, pp. 14–17.
32. John B. Thompson, ed. and trans., *Paul Ricoeur. Hermeneutics and the human sciences*, op. cit., Chapter 7, 'Appopriation' pp. 182–193.
33. See the entry on hermeneutics in Alan Richardson and John Bowden, eds, *A New Dictionary of Christian Theology*, London: SCM, 1983, pp. 250–253. See also Anthony C. Thiselton, *The Two Horizons. New Testament Hermeneutics and Philosophical Description with Special Reference to Heidegger, Bultmann, Gadamer, and Wittgenstein*, Exeter: The Paternoster Press, 1980.
34. Peter L. Berger, *The Heretical Imperative*, op. cit.
35. John B. Thompson, ed. and trans., *Paul Ricoeur. Hermeneutics and the human sciences*, op. cit., pp. 185–187. See also William Schweiker, 'Beyond Imitation: Mimetic Praxis in Gadamer, Ricoeur and Derrida', *The Journal of Religion*, vol. 68, no. 1, January 1988, pp. 21–38.
36. Paul Ricoeur, *Interpretation theory: discourse and the surplus of meaning*, Fort Worth, Texas: The Texas Christian University Press, 1976, p. 92.
37. For further discussion of the theological implication of his writings see David E. Klemm, *The Hermeneutical Theory of Paul Ricoeur*, op. cit., and also Peter Joseph Albano, *Freedom, Truth and Hope. The Relationship of Philosophy and Religion in the Thought of Paul Ricoeur*, Lanham, Md.: University Press of America, 1987.
38. T. M. Van Leeuwen, *The Surplus of Meaning*, op. cit., pp. 110–126.
39. Paul Ricoeur, *The Symbolism of Evil*, op. cit.
40. See letter from Gadamer on his attitudes to critical sociology in Richard J. Bernstein, *Beyond Objectivism and Relativism*, op. cit., pp. 261–265. See also Hans-Georg Gadamer, 'Hermeneutics and Social Science' in *Cultural Hermeneutics*, vol. 2, 1975, pp. 307–316, and Roy Boyne, 'Interview with Hans-Georg Gadamer', *Theory, Culture & Society*, vol. 5, no. 1, February 1988, pp. 25–34.
41. Hans-Georg Gadamer, *Philosophical Apprenticeships*, trans. Robert S. Sullivan, London: The MIT Press, 1985, pp. 192–193.

42. Richard J. Bernstein, *Beyond Objectivism and Relativism, op. cit.*
43. Jurgen Habermas, 'A Review of Gadamer's *Truth and Method*' in Frederick Dallmayr and Thomas A. McCarthy, eds, *Understanding and Social Inquiry*, Notre Dame, Indiana: University of Notre Dame Press, 1977, pp. 335–363. See also Georgia Warnke, *Gadamer: Hermeneutics, Tradition and Reason, op. cit.*, pp. 107–138.
44. See Janet Malcolm, *In the Freud Archives*, London: Fontana, 1986.
45. Hans- Georg Gadamer, *The Relevance of the Beautiful, op. cit.*, pp. 141–45.
46. Quoted in Georgia Warnke, *Gadamer: Hermeneutics, Tradition and Reason, op. cit.*, p. 130.
47. Joel C. Weinsheimer, *Gadamer's Hermeneutics. A Reading of* Truth and Method, London: Yale University Press, 1985, pp. 66–71.
48. Hans-Georg Gadamer, *Truth and Method*, 2nd edn, John Cumming, and Garrett Barden, eds, trans. William Glen-Doepel, London: Sheed and Ward, 1979, p. 15.
49. For a useful exposition of this point, see David E. Klemm, *The Hermeneutical Theory of Paul Ricoeur, op. cit.*, pp. 69–73.
50. Alain-Fournier, *Le Grande Meaulnes*, trans. Frank Davison, London: Penguin, 1966.
51. Paul Ricoeur, *The Symbolism of Evil, op. cit.*, p. 351.
52. See for example Steven Connor, *Postmodernist Culture. An Introduction to Theories of the Contemporary*, Oxford: Basil Blackwell, 1989. See also the special edition on post-modernism, edited by Mike Featherstone, of *Theory, Culture & Society*, vol. 5, nos. 2–3, June 1988.
53. Gianni Vattimo, *The End of Modernity. Nihilism and Hermeneutics in Post-modern Culture*, trans. Jon R. Snyder, Cambridge: Polity Press, 1988.
54. George Steiner, *Real Presences, op. cit.*, p. 134.
55. *Ibid.*, p. 168.
56. *Ibid.*, pp. 190–191.
57. Charles Baudelaire, *The Painter of Modern Life and other Essays*, ed. and trans. Jonathan Mayne, London: Phaidon Press, 1964, p. 199.
58. Paul Ricoeur, 'The model of the text: meaningful action considered as a text' in John B. Thompson, ed. and trans., *Paul Ricoeur. Hermeneutics and the human sciences, op. cit.*, p. 204.
59. *Ibid.*, p. 207.
60. *Ibid.*, p. 208. See also G. B. Madison, 'Text and Action: The Hermeneutics of Existence', *University of Ottawa Quarterly*, vol. 55, no. 4, 1985, pp. 135–145, and Mark A. Schneider, 'Culture-as-text in the work of Clifford Geertz', *Theory and Society*, vol. 16, pp. 809–839.
61. Paul Ricoeur, 'The model of the text' in John B. Thompson, ed. and trans., *Paul Ricoeur. Hermeneutics and the Human Sciences, op. cit.*, pp. 214–215. See also Susan Hekman, 'Action as a Text: Gadamer's Hermeneutics and the Social Scientific Analysis of Action', *Journal for the Theory of Social Behaviour*, vol. 14, no. 3, October 1984, pp. 333–354.
62. Lucien Dällenbach, *The Mirror in the Text*, trans. Jeremy Whiteley with Emma Hughes, Cambridge: Polity Press, 1989, p. 36.

63. *Ibid.*, pp. 101–106.
64. *Ibid.*, pp. 52–53.
65. Charles Baudelaire, *The Painter of Modern Life and other Essays, op. cit.*, pp. 12–15.

11 Apophatic Liturgy: Re-presenting the Absent in Rite

1. Quoted in Alan M. Olson, 'Myth, Symbol and Metaphorical Truth' in Alan M. Olson, ed., *Myth, Symbol and Reality*, Notre Dame, Indiana: University of Notre Dame Press, 1980, p. 111.
2. For a useful summary of his writings, see René Latourelle, *Man and his problems in the light of Jesus Christ*, New York: Alba House, 1983, Chapter 4, 'Maurice Blondel. The Christian Hypothesis or the Awaited Response', pp. 159–194. Unfortunately little of his writings has been translated into English. For another detailed account of his life and work, see Maurice Blondel, *The Letter on Apologetics and History and Dogma*, trans. and introduction by Alexander Dru and Illtyd Trethowan, London: Harvill Press, 1964, especially pp. 13–116.
3. Georgia Warnke, *Gadamer: Hermeneutics, Tradition and Reason, op. cit.*, p. 123.
4. Hans-Georg Gadamer, 'Religious and Poetical Speaking' in Alan M. Olson, ed., *Myth, Symbol and Reality, op. cit.*, p. 89. See also Robert Hollinger, ed., *Hermeneutics and Praxis*, Notre Dame, Indiana: University of Notre Dame Press, 1985; Hans-Georg Gadamer, 'The Religious Dimension in Heidegger' in Alan M. Olson and Leroy S. Rouner, eds, *Transcendence and the Sacred*, Notre Dame, Indiana: University of Notre Dame Press, 1981, pp. 193–207.
5. Paul Ricoeur, *The Symbolism of Evil, op. cit.*, p. 352.
6. Hans-Georg Gadamer, 'Religious and Poetical Speaking', in Alan M. Olson, ed., *Myth, Symbol and Reality, op. cit.*, p. 93.
7. *Ibid.*, p. 97.
8. Phillip Wheelwright, *Metaphor & Reality*, Bloomington: Indiana University Press, 1962, pp. 45–47.
9. Alan M. Olson, 'Myth, Symbol and Metaphorical Truth' in Alan M. Olson, ed., *Myth, Symbol and Reality, op. cit.*, p. 107.
10. Louis Dupré, 'Spiritual Life in a Secular Age', in Mary Douglas and Steven Tipton, eds, *Religion and America. Spiritual Life in a Secular Age, op. cit.*, p. 11. See also Kenneth Surin, '*Contemptus Mundi* and the Disenchanted World: Bonhoeffer's "Discipline of the Secret" and Adorno's "Strategy of Hibernation"', in *Journal of the American Academy of Religion*, vol. 53, 1985, p. 395.
11. Simon Tugwell, 'Spirituality and Negative Theology', *New Blackfriars*, vol. 68, no. 805, May 1987, p. 260.
12. John F. Teahan, 'A Dark and Empty Way: Thomas Merton and the Apophatic Tradition' *The Journal of Religion*, vol. 58, 1978, p. 269.
13. Much of the material in this section is drawn from my essay, 'Liturgy as Play: A Hermeneutics of Ritual Re-Presentation', *Modern Theology*, vol. 4., no. 4, July 1988, pp. 345–372.

14. J. Huizinga, *Homo Ludens*, op. cit., p. 20.
15. See Richard Burke, '"Work" and "Play"', *Ethics*, vol. 82, 1971–72, pp. 33–47. See also Robert K. Johnston, *The Christian at Play*, Grand Rapids, Michigan: William Eerdmans, 1983, Chapter 2, pp. 31–52; Michael Salter, ed., *Play: Anthropological Perspectives*, New York: Leisure Press, 1978; and Drew A. Hyland, *The Question of Play*, Lanham, Md.: University Press of America, 1984.
16. Hugo Rahner, *Man at Play*, trans. Brian Battershaw and Edward Quinn, London: Burns & Oates, 1965, p. 65.
17. This discussion is drawn from J. Huizinga, *Homo Ludens*, op. cit., Chapters 1–2, pp. 1–45.
18. Kurt Riezler, 'Play and Seriousness', *The Journal of Philosophy*, vol. 38, no. 19, September 1941, p. 517.
19. Romano Guardini, *The Spirit of the Liturgy*, op. cit., p. 99.
20. *Ibid.*, p. 100.
21. Victor Turner, 'Frame, Flow and Reflection: Ritual and Drama as Public Liminality', in Michel Benamou and Charles Caramello, eds, *Performance in postmodern culture*, Milwaukee: University of Wisconsin Center for twentieth century studies, 1977, pp. 33–55.
22. Roger Caillois, *Man, Play, and Games*, trans. Meyer Barash, London: Thames and Hudson, 1962, p. 10. See also his *Man and the Sacred*, trans. Meyer Barash, Illinois: Free Press, 1959, Appendix II, pp. 152–162.
23. Romano Guardini, *The Spirit of the Liturgy*, op. cit., p. 103.
24. Erving Goffman, 'Fun in Games', in *Encounters*, London: Penguin, 1972, p. 24.
25. Richard H. Grathoff, *The Structure of social inconsistencies. A contribution to a unified theory of play, game, and social action*, The Hague: Martinus Nijhoff, 1970, pp. 144–148.
26. Thomas Clifton, *Music as Heard. A Study in Applied Phenomenology*, New Haven: Yale University Press, 1983, pp. 274–275.
27. George Steiner, *Real Presences*, op. cit., p. 206.
28. See entry by Julius A. Elias, on 'Art and Play' in Phillip Wiener, ed., *A Dictionary of the History of Ideas*, vol. 1, New York: Charles Scribner, 1973, pp. 99–107.
29. Hans-Georg Gadamer, *Truth and Method*, op. cit., pp. xiv–xv. See also James S. Hans, 'Hermeneutics, Play, Deconstruction', *Philosophy Today*, vol. 24, Winter 1980, pp. 299–317 and Lawrence M. Hinman, 'Quid Facti or Quid Juris? The Fundamental Ambiguity of Gadamer's Understanding of Hermeneutics', *Philosophy and Phenomenological Research*, vol. 40, June 1980, pp. 512–535.
30. Hans-Georg Gadamer, *Truth and Method*, op. cit., p. 105.
31. *Ibid.*, pp. 112–114.
32. *Ibid.*, 101.
33. *Ibid.*, p. 17.
34. Georgia Warnke, *Gadamer: Hermeneutics, Tradition and Reason*, op. cit., pp. 60–63. See also Giuliano Di Bernardo, 'Sense, Hermeneutic Interpretations, Actions', *Noûs*, vol. 18, 1984, pp. 479–503.
35. Hans-Georg Gadamer, *Truth and Method*, op. cit., p. 92.

36. *Ibid.*, pp. 94–95.
37. *Ibid.*, p. 299.
38. Joel C. Weinsheimer, *Gadamer's Hermeneutics, op. cit.*, p. 113.
39. Hans-Georg Gadamer, *Truth and Method, op. cit.*, pp. 69–71.
40. Hans-Georg Gadamer, 'The relevance of the beautiful' in collection of essays, same title, *op. cit.*, pp. 35–36.
41. 'The festive character of theater' *ibid.*, p. 64.
42. 'The relevance of the beautiful' *ibid.*, p. 46.
43. 'Composition and intepretation' *ibid.*, p. 68.
44. 'Image and gesture' *ibid.*, p. 79.
45. 'Aesthetic and religious experience' in *ibid.*, p. 149.
46. *Ibid.*, pp. 149–150.
47. See especially Hans-Georg Gadamer, *Truth and Method, op. cit.*, pp. 378–387.
48. 'Aesthetics and religious experience' in Hans Georg-Gadamer, *The relevance of the beautiful* , *op. cit.*, p. 152.
49. For some comments on his life and work see: Aidan Nichols, 'Balthasar and his Christology', *New Blackfriars*, vol. 66, nos. 781–82, July–August 1985; Louis Roberts, *The Theological Aesthetics of Hans Urs von Balthasar*, Washington: The Catholic University of America Press, 1987, Chapter 1, 'The Man and His Work', pp. 6–26; Medard Kehl and Werner Loser, eds, *The von Balthasar Reader*, trans. Robert J. Daly and Fred Lawrence, Edinburgh: T. & T. Clark, 1982, introduction by Medard Kehl, pp. 1–54; Michael Waldstein, 'An introduction to von Balthasar's *The Glory of the Lord'*, *Communio*, vol. 14, Spring 1987, pp. 12–33; and John Riches, 'Hans Urs von Balthasar' in David Ford, ed., *The Modern Theologians*, vol. 1., *op. cit.*, pp. 237–254.
50. Hans Urs von Balthasar, *Truth is Symphonic. Aspects of Christian Pluralism*, trans. Graham Harrison, San Francisco: Ignatius Press, 1987. See also his collection of short essays, whose title exemplifies his position in relation to contemporary Catholicism: *A Short Primer for Unsettled Laymen*, trans. Mary Theresilde Skerry, San Francisco: Ignatius Press, 1985.
51. Medard Kehl and Werner Loser, eds, *The von Balthasar Reader*, 'Theology – a Science?' , *op. cit.*, pp. 359–362.
52. Rowan Williams, 'Balthasar and Rahner' in John Riches, ed., *The Analogy of Beauty. The Theology of Hans Urs von Balthasar*, Edinburgh, T. & T. Clark, 1986, pp. 26–29.
53. Jeffrey Kay, 'Hans Urs von Balthasar, a Post-critical Theologian?' in Gregory Baum, ed., *Neo-Conservatism: social and religious phenomenon*, Concilium, Edinburgh: T. & T. Clark, 1981, pp. 84–86. This concern with the childlike appears at a number of points in von Balthasar's writings.
54. Hans Urs von Balthasar, *La Dramatique Divine, op. cit.*, pp. 451–462. There seems to have been a shift in von Balthasar's attitude to sociology. He makes a number of passing critical comments of a scientific sociology that is reductionist in intent, and which does not observe theological limits. In Medard Kehl and Werner Loser, eds, *The von Balthasar Reader, op. cit.*, p. 5 his unsympathetic attitude to

sociology is noted, though this can be understood to refer to its abuses rather than its uses.

55. John Riches, ed., *The Analogy of Beauty*, *op. cit.*, pp. 224–226.
56. Medard Kehl and Werner Loser, eds, *The von Balthasar Reader*, *op. cit.*, pp. 48–49.
57. Michael Waldstein, unpublished manuscript, p. 2.
58. T. F. O'Meara, 'Notes of Art and Theology: Hans Urs von Balthasar's Systems', in *Theological Studies*, vol. 42, 1981, pp. 273–276.
59. Quoted *ibid.*, p. 274.
60. Louis Roberts, *The Theological Aesthetics of Hans Urs von Balthasar*, *op. cit.*, pp. 75–76.
61. See Hans Urs von Balthasar, 'The grandeur of the liturgy', *Communio*, vol. 5, no. 4, Winter 1978, pp. 344–351. The dangers of a misuse of community as a criterion for liturgical celebration had been noted earlier by sociologists. See Andrew Greeley, 'Religious Symbolism, Liturgy and Community' in Herman Schmidt, ed., *Liturgy in Transition*, New York: Herder and Herder, 1971, especially pp. 66–69.
62. Medard Kehl and Werner Loser, eds, *The von Balthasar Reader*, *op. cit.*, p. 331. Style of preaching and celebration of sacrament have definite similarities. See Joseph Fessio and John Riches, eds, *The Glory of the Lord*, vol. 1, *op. cit.*, pp. 593–596.
63. For a useful discussion of these two French writers, see Joy Nachod Humes, *Two Against Time. A Study of the very present worlds of Paul Claudel and Charles Péguy*, Chapel Hill: University of North Carolina, 1978.
64. Mary Ryan, *Introduction to Paul Claudel*, Cork: Cork University Press, 1951, pp. 6–7. See also David McLellan, *Simone Weil. Utopian Pessimist*, London: Macmillan, 1989, pp. 135–138.
65. Louis Roberts, *The Theological Aesthetics of Hans Urs von Balthasar*, *op. cit.*, pp. 34–35.
66. For some useful comments on his idea of form, see *ibid.*, pp. 188–194 and 224–229. If a fruitful link is to be established between his theology and sociology, further refinement of this term will be required.
67. Hans Urs von Balthasar, *The Glory of the Lord*, vol. 1, *op. cit.*, p. 151.
68. *Ibid.*, p. 24.
69. Hans Urs von Balthasar, *Truth is Symphonic*, *op. cit.*
70. Hans Urs von Balthasar, *The Glory of the Lord*, vol. 1, *op. cit.*, p. 99. Later he develops the notion of beholding as taking to oneself, a term that has similarities to appropriation as used in Ricoeur's hermeneutics, discussed above. see pp. 120–121 in *ibid.*
71. *Ibid.*, p. 156.
72. *Ibid.*, p. 118.
73. See Emile Mâle, *Religious Art in France. The Late Middle Ages. A Study of Medieval Iconography and Its Sources*, trans. Marthiel Mathews, Princeton: Princeton University Press, 1986, pp. 62–63 and footnote 121, pp. 464–465.
74. Hans Urs von Balthasar, *The Glory of the Lord*, vol. 1, *op. cit.*, p. 546.
75. *Ibid.*, pp. 355–359.
76. *Ibid.*, pp. 422–423.

77. *Ibid.*, p. 488.
78. *Ibid.*, p. 661.
79. *Ibid.*, p. 677.
80. For a useful introduction to his writings, see Paul Rorem, 'The Uplifting Spirituality of Pseudo-Dionysius', in Bernard McGinn and John Meyendorff, eds, *Christian Spirituality. Origins to the Twelfth Century*, London: Routledge & Kegan Paul, 1986, pp. 132–151. See also: Hans Urs von Balthasar, *The Glory of the Lord. A Theological Aesthetics*. vol. 2: *Studies in Theological Style: Clerical Styles*, John Riches, ed., trans. Andrew Louth, Francis McDonagh and Brian McNeil, Edinburgh: T. & T. Clark, 1984, pp. 144–154; and Andrew Louth, *Denys the Areopagite*, London: Geoffrey Chapman, 1989.
81. Vladimir Lossky, *The Mystical Theology of the Eastern Church*, London: James Clarke , 1957, p. 25. See also R. G. Williams, 'The Via Negativa and the Foundations of Theology: an introduction to the thought of V. N. Lossky' in Stephen Sykes and Derek Holmes, eds, *New Studies in Theology* I, London: Duckworth, 1980, pp. 95–117 and Michael Casey, '"Emotionally Hollow, Esthetically Meaningless and Spiritually Empty". An Inquiry into Theological Discourse', *Colloquium*, 1981, vol. 14, 1981, pp. 54–61.
82. I am very grateful to my colleague Ian Hamnett for coining this phrase.
83. Pseudo-Dionysius *The Complete Works*, op. cit., p. 138.
84. John Wright, 'The concept of mystery in the Hebrew Bible: an example of the via negativa' in Raoul Mortley and David Dockrill, eds, *Prudentia. The Via Negativa*, University of Auckland, Supplementary number 1981, pp. 18–19.
85. Pseudo-Dionysius, *The Complete Works*, op. cit., pp. 136–137. For a useful commentary on this passage see Paul Rorem, *Biblical and Liturgical Symbols within the Pseudo-Dionysian Synthesis*, Toronto: Pontifical Institute of Mediaeval Studies, 1984, pp. 140–142.
86. John Wright, 'The concept of mystery in the Hebrew Bible' in Raoul Mortley and David Dockrill, eds, *Prudentia. The Via Negativa*, op. cit., p. 21 and p. 27.
87. *Ibid.*, pp. 30–33.
88. K. J. Walsh, 'Northern Humanists and the Negative Way' in Raoul Mortley and David Dockrill, eds, *Prudentia. The Via Negativa*, op. cit., p. 83.
89. Susan Buck-Morss, *The Origin of Negative Dialectics. Theodor W. Adorno, Walter Benjamin, and The Frankfurt Institute*, Brighton: The Harvester Press, 1977.
90. Hans Urs von Balthasar, *The Glory of the Lord*, vol. 2, op. cit., pp. 153–154.
91. Paul Rorem, *Biblical and Liturgical Symbols within the Pseudo-Dionysian Synthesis*, op. cit., p. 145.
92. Jean Leclercq, 'Influence and noninfluence of Dionysius in the Western Middle Ages' in Pseudo-Dionysius, *The Complete Works*, op. cit., pp. 25–32.
93. *Ibid.*, p. 139.

94. Paul Rorem, *Biblical and Liturgical Symbols within the Pseudo-Dionysian Synthesis, op. cit.*, p. 63.
95. Pseudo-Dionysius, *The Complete Works, op. cit.*, pp. 212–213.
96. Paul Rorem, 'The Uplifting Spirituality of Pseudo-Dionysius', in Bernard McGinn and John Meyendorff, eds, *Christian Spirituality, op. cit.*, pp. 135–137.
97. *Ibid.*, p. 138.
98. Paul Rorem, *Biblical and Liturgical Symbols within the Pseudo-Dionysian Synthesis, op. cit.*, p. 116.
99. Pseudo-Dionysius, *The Complete Works, op. cit.*, pp. 284–285.
100. *Ibid.*, pp. 147–153 and 182–191.
101. *Ibid.*, pp. 189–190.
102. *Ibid.*, pp. 204–208.
103. *Ibid.*, p. 225.
104. *Ibid.*, p. 281.
105. *Ibid.*, p. 283.
106. *Ibid.* p. 186. See also p. 247 for an account of the clothing ceremony of a monk.
107. *Ibid.*, pp. 72–73.
108. Jaroslav Pelikan, 'Negative Theology and Positive Religion. A Study of Nicholas Cusanus *De pace fidei*' in Raoul Mortley and David Dockrill, eds, *Prudentia. The Via Negativa, op. cit.*, pp. 69–72.
109. Pseudo-Dionysius, *The Complete Works, op. cit.*, p. 176.
110. *Ibid.*, p. 215.
111. Paul Rorem, *Biblical and Liturgical Symbols within the Pseudo-Dionysian Synthesis, op. cit.*, pp. 118–121.
112. Flannery O'Connor, *Mystery and Manners, op. cit.*, p. 180. There is a strong apophatic element in O'Connor's writings. See David Williams, 'Flannery O'Connor and the *via negativa*', *Studies in Religion*, vol. 8, no. 3, 1979, pp. 303–312.
113. Hans Urs von Balthasar, *The Glory of the Lord*, vol. 2, *op. cit.*, pp. 165–170.

Conclusion

1. Alain Touraine, *Return of the Actor. Social Theory in Postindustrial Society*, trans. Myrna Godzich, Minneapolis: University of Minnesota Press, 1988.
2. For an honest Anglican account of second thoughts on the outcome of liturgical renewal since the mid-sixties see T. G. A. Baker, 'Is Liturgy in Good Shape?' in Eric James, ed., *God's Truth. Essays to celebrate the twenty-fifth anniversary of* Honest to God, London: SCM, 1988, pp. 1–14.
3. R. W. Franklin, 'Response: Humanism and Transcendence in the Nineteenth Century Liturgical Movement', *Worship*, vol. 59, 1985, pp. 342–353.
4. Evelyn Underhill, *Worship, op. cit.*, p. 35.

5. William Blake, *The Prophetic Books of William Blake Jerusalem*, E. R. D. Maclagan and A. G. B. Russell, eds, London: A. H. Bullen, 1904, p. 65.
6. Quoted in A. H. Armstrong, 'The Escape of the One. An investigation of some possibilities of apophatic theology imperfectly realised in the West' , *Studia Patristica*, vol. 13, 1975, p. 81.
7. James A. Beckford, 'The Sociology of Religion 1945–1989', *Social Compass*, vol. 37, no. 1, March 1990, pp. 45–64.
8. Kieran Flanagan, 'J.-K. Huysmans: The first post-modernist saint', *New Blackfriars*, vol. 71, no. 838, May 1990, pp. 217–229. For a reflection on the degree to which post-modernism has had an influence on theological reflection, see David F. Ford, 'Epilogue: Postmodernism and postscript', in his edited work, *The Modern Theologians*. vol. 2, *op. cit.*, pp. 291–297.
9. George Steiner, *Real Presences, op. cit.* The critical reception this work received, suggested a resonance had been hit by its plea for the recognition of transcendent elements in culture and art. It is, perhaps, in the field of cultural studies that most of the future advances in theology are likely to be made.
10. C. S. Lewis, *Prayer: Letters to Malcolm*, London: Collins, 1977, pp. 5–6.
11. B. G. Rogers, *The Novels and Stories of Barbey D'Aurevilly*, Genéve: Libraire Droz, 1967, pp. 247–248.
12. See Julian Roberts, *Walter Benjamin*, London: Macmillan, 1982 and also Andrew Benjamin, ed., *The Problems of Modernity. Adorno and Benjamin*, London: Routledge, 1989.
13. David Frisby, *Fragments of Modernity, op. cit.*, p. 269.
14. Walter Benjamin, *Charles Baudelaire. A Lyric Poet in the Era of High Capitalism*, trans. Harry Zohn, London: Verso, 1983, pp. 147–150.
15. Barbara Beaumont, ed. and trans., *The Road from Decadence, op. cit.*, p. 157.
16. Mary Jo Neitz, *Charisma and Community. A Study of Religious Commitment within the Charasmatic Renewal*, New Brunswick, U. S. A.: Transaction Books, 1987.
17. Joseph Kerman, *Musicology*, London: Collins, 1985. See also Thrasybulos Georgiade, *Music and Language. The Rise of Western Music as exemplified in settings of the mass*, trans. Marie Louise Gollner, Cambridge: Cambridge University Press, 1982.

Bibliography

Addleshaw, G. W. O., *The High Church Tradition. A Study in the Liturgical Thought of the Seventeenth Century*, London: Faber & Faber Ltd, 1941.

Ahearne, Pierce and Lane, Michael, *Pontifical Ceremonies. A Study of the Episcopal Ceremonies*, London: Burns Oates & Washbourne Ltd, 1942.

Ahern, Emily, 'Rules in Oracles and Games', *Man*, n.s. vol. 17, 1982, pp. 302–312.

Alain-Fournier, *Le Grand Meaulnes*, trans. Frank Davison, London: Penguin, 1966.

Albano, Peter Joseph, *Freedom, Truth and Hope. The Relationship of Philosophy and Religion in the Thought of Paul Ricoeur*, Lanham, Md.: University Press of America, 1987.

Anderson, William, *The Rise of the Gothic*, London: Hutchinson, 1985.

Anon., 'Thrilling views of the surplice question', *Eclectic Review*, vol. 125, 1867, pp. 236–252.

Anon., 'The Gown or the Surplice', *Christia Observer*, vol. 70, April 1871, pp. 291–301.

Anon., 'Chorister Boys', *Tinsley's Magazine*, vol. 28, 1880, pp. 83–88.

Anon., 'Waiters', *All the Year Round*, vol. 59, 1887, pp. 813–816.

Anon., *Servers' Manual of the Archconfraternity of St Stephen*, London: Burns and Oates, 1907.

Anon., *The Benedictine Oblate Companion*, St Meinrad Archabbey, St Meinrad, Indiana, 1981.

Aquinas, St Thomas, *Summa Theologiae*, vol. 9, Oxford, Blackfriars, 1967.

Aquinas, St Thomas, *Summa Theologiae*, vol. 15, London: Blackfriars with Eyre & Spottiswoode, 1970.

Aquinas, St Thomas, *Summa Theologiae*, vol. 41, London: Blackfriars with Eyre & Spottiswoode, 1971.

Archer, Anthony, *The Two Catholic Churches. A Study in Oppression*, London: SCM Press, Ltd, 1986.

Archer, Margaret S., *Culture and Agency: The Place of Culture in Social Theory*, Cambridge: Cambridge University Press, 1988.

Ariès, Phillipe, *Centuries of Childhood. A Social History of Family Life*, trans. Robert Baldick, New York: Vintage Books, 1962.

Armstrong, A. H., 'The Escape of the One. An investigation of some possibilities of apophatic theology imperfectly realised in the West', *Studia Patristica*, vol. 13, 1975, pp. 77–89.

Asad, Talal, 'On ritual and discipline in medieval Christian monasticism', *Economy and Society*, vol. 16, no. 2, May 1987, pp. 159–203.

Asals, Frederick, *Flannery O'Connor. The Imagination of Extremity*, Athens, Georgia: The University of Georgia Press, 1982.

Atchley, E. G. Cuthbert F., 'The Hood as an ornament of the minister at the time of his ministrations in Quire and elsewhere', *Transactions of the St Paul's Ecclesiological Society*, vol. 4, 1900, pp. 313–328.

Atkinson, J. Maxwell, *Discovering Suicide. Studies in the Social Organization of Sudden Death*, London: Macmillan, 1982.

Augustine, P. Charles, *Liturgical Law. A handbook of the Roman Liturgy*, London: B. Herder, 1931.

Babin, David E., *The Celebration of Life. Our Changing Liturgy*, New York: Morehouse-Barlow, 1969.

Bach, Kent, 'An Analysis of Self-Deception', *Philosophy and Phenomenological Research*, vol. 41, September 1980– June 1981, pp. 351–370.

Bacon, Francis, 'Of Simulation and Dissimulation' in Henry Lewis, ed., *Bacon's Essays*, London: W. Collins, 1873, pp. 39–45.

Baker, T. G. A., 'Is Liturgy in Good Shape?' in Eric James, ed., *God's Truth. Essays to celebrate the twenty-fifth anniversary of* Honest to God, London: SCM, 1988, pp. 1–14.

Baldick, Robert, *The Life of J.-K. Huysmans*, Oxford: Clarendon Press, 1955.

Balthasar, Hans Urs von, 'The grandeur of the liturgy', *Communio*, vol. 5, Winter 1978, pp. 344–351.

Balthasar, Hans Urs von, *The Glory of the Lord. A Theological Aesthetics*, vol. 1, *Seeing the form*, Joseph Fessio and John Riches, eds, trans. Erasmo Leiva-Merikakis, Edinburgh: T. & T. Clark, 1982.

Balthasar, Hans Urs von, *La Dramatique divine*, I. *Prolegomenes*, trans. André Monchoux with Robert Givord and Jacques Servais, Paris: Editions Lethielleux, 1984.

Balthasar, Hans Urs von, *The Glory of the Lord. A Theological Aesthetics*. vol. 2, *Studies in Theological Style: Clerical Styles*, John Riches, ed., trans. Andrew Louth, Francis McDonagh and Brian McNeil, Edinburgh: T. & T. Clark, 1984.

Balthasar, Hans Urs von, *A Short Primer for Unsettled Laymen*, trans. Mary Theresilde Skerry, San Francisco: Ignatius Press, 1985.

Balthasar, Hans Urs von, *The Glory of the Lord. A Theological Aesthetics*. vol. 3, *Studies in Theological Style: Lay Styles*, John Riches, ed., trans. Andrew Louth, John Saward, Martin Simon and Rowan Williams, Edinburgh: T. & T. Clark, 1986.

Balthasar, Hans Urs von, *Truth is Symphonic. Aspects of Christian Pluralism*, trans. Graham Harrison, San Francisco: Ignatius Press, 1987.

Barnes, Barry and Bloor, David, 'Relativism, Rationalism and the Sociology of Knowledge' in Martin Hollis and Steven Lukes, eds, *Rationality and Relativism*, Oxford: Basil Blackwell, 1982, pp. 21–47.

Barnett, Dene (with assistance of Massy-Westropp, Jeanette) *The Art of Gesture: The practices and principles of 18th century acting*, Heidelberg: Carl Winter, Universitätsverlag, 1987.

Baudelaire, Charles, *The Painter of Modern Life and other Essays*, ed. and trans. Jonathan Mayne, London: Phaidon Press, 1964.

Bauman, Zygmunt, *Hermeneutics and Social Science. Approaches to understanding*, London: Hutchinson, 1978.

Baumstark, Anton, *Comparative Liturgy*, English Edition, F. L. Cross, London: A. R. Mowbray, 1958.

Bearne, David, 'Mediaeval Choristers', *The Month*, vol. 82, September–December, 1894, pp. 503–516.

Beaumont, Barbara, ed. and trans., *The Road from Decadence. From Brothel to*

Cloister. Selected Letters of J.K. Huysmans, London: The Athlone Press, 1989.

Beckford, James, 'The Insulation and Isolation of the Sociology of Religion', *Sociological Analysis*, vol. 46, no. 4, 1985, pp. 347–354.

Beckford, James A., 'The Sociology of Religion 1945–1989', *Social Compass*, vol. 37, no. 1, March 1990, pp. 45–64.

Bell, Catherine, 'Discourse and Dichotomies: the structure of ritual theory', *Religion*, vol. 17, April 1987, pp. 95–118.

Bell, Daniel, 'The Return of the Sacred? The Argument on the Future of Religion' in *Sociological Journeys. Essays 1960–1980*, London: Heinemann, 1980, pp. 324–354.

Bell, G. K. A. and Deissmann, D. Adolf, eds, *Mysterium Christi. Christological Studies by British and German Theologians*, London: Longmans, Green and Co., 1930.

Bembridge, Christian, *The Choir Schools Review*, 1983.

Benedict, St, *The Rule of Saint Benedict*, trans. David Parry, London: Darton, Longman & Todd, 1984.

Benjamin, Andrew, ed., *The Problems of Modernity. Adorno and Benjamin*, London: Routledge, 1989.

Benjamin, Walter, *Charles Baudelaire. A Lyric Poet in the Era of High Capitalism*, trans. Harry Zohn, London: Verso, 1983.

Bentley, James, *Ritualism and Politics in Victorian Britain*, Oxford: Oxford University Press, 1978.

Berger, Peter L. and Luckmann, Thomas, 'Secularisation and Pluralism', *International Yearbook for the Sociology of Religion*, vol. 2, 1966, pp. 73–84.

Berger, Peter L., 'A Sociological view of the Secularization of Theology', *Journal for the Scientific Study of Religion*, vol. 6, no 3, 1967, pp. 3–16.

Berger, Peter L., *A Rumour of Angels. Modern Society and the Rediscovery of the Supernatural*, London: Penguin Books, 1971.

Berger, Peter L., *The Social Reality of Religion*, London: Penguin, 1973.

Berger, Peter L., 'Some Second Thoughts on Substantive versus Functional Definitions of Religion', *Journal for the Scientific Study of Religion*, vol. 13, no. 2, 1974, pp. 125–133.

Berger, Peter L., 'For a World with Windows' in Peter L. Berger and Richard John Neuhaus, eds, *Against the World. For the World. The Hartford Appeal and the Future of American Religion*, New York: The Seabury Press, 1976, pp. 8–19.

Berger, Peter L., *The Heretical Imperative. Contemporary Possibilities of Religious Affirmation*, London: Collins, 1980.

Berger, Peter L., 'From the Crisis of Religion to the Crisis of Secularity' in Mary Douglas and Steven Tipton, eds, *Religion and America. Spiritual Life in a Secular Age*, Boston: Beacon Press, 1983, pp. 14–24.

Bernardo, Giuliano Di, 'Sense, Hermeneutic Interpretations, Actions', *Noûs*, vol. 18, 1984, pp. 479–503.

Bernstein, Marcelle, *Nuns*, London: Collins, 1976.

Bernstein, Richard J., *Beyond Objectivism and Relativism: Science, Hermeneutics and Praxis*, London: Basil Blackwell, 1983.

Bettis, Joseph Dabney, ed., *Phenomenology of Religion*, New York: Harper & Row, 1969.

Blake, William, *The Prophetic Books of William Blake Jerusalem*, E. R. D. Maclagan and A. G. B. Russell, eds, London: A. H. Bullen, 1904.

Blasi, Anthony J., *A Phenomenological Transformation of the Social Scientific Study of Religion*, New York: Peter Lang, 1985.

Bleicher, Josef, *The Hermeneutic Imagination. Outline of a Positive Critique of Scientism and Sociology*, London: Routledge & Kegan Paul, 1982.

Bloch, Maurice, 'Symbols, Song, Dance and Features of Articulation. Is religion an extreme form of traditional authority?', *Archives Européens de Sociologie*, vol. 15, 1974, pp. 55–81.

Blondel, Maurice, *The Letter on Apologetics and History and Dogma*, trans. and introduction by Alexander Dru and Illtyd Trethowan, London: Harvill Press, 1964.

Boas, George, *The Cult of Childhood*, London: The Warburg Institute, 1966.

Bok, Sissela, *Lying. Moral Choice in Public and Private Life*, London: Quartet Books, 1980.

Bok, Sissela, *Secrets. On the Ethics of Concealment and Revelation*, Oxford: Oxford University Press, 1984.

Boros, Ladislaus, *Angels and Men*, trans. John Maxwell, London: Search Press, 1976.

Boulding, Maria, 'Background to a theology of the monastic habit', *The Downside Review*, vol. 98, no. 331, April 1980, pp. 110–123.

Bouyer, Louis, *Life and Liturgy*, London: Sheed and Ward, 1954.

Boyne, Roy, 'Interview with Hans-Georg Gadamer', *Theory, Culture & Society*, vol. 5, no. 1, 1988, pp. 25–34.

Brianchaninov, Ignatius, *The Arena. An offering to Contemporary Monasticism*, Madras: Diocesan Press, 1970.

Brown, Peter, *The Body and Society. Men, Women and Sexual Renunciation in Early Christianity*, London: Faber & Faber, 1989.

Browning, Robert, *Robert Browning: The Poems*, vol. 1, John Pettigrew, ed., New Haven: Yale University Press, 1981.

Bryant, Andrew W., 'Lay Communicants' attitudes to the Eucharist in relation to Liturgical Change in the Church of England' in Denise Newton, ed., *Liturgy and Change*, University of Birmingham: Institute for the Study of Worship and Religious Architecture, 1983, pp. 75–97.

Buchanan, Colin, Lloyd, Trevor and Miller, Harold, eds, *Anglican Worship Today*, London: Collins, 1980.

Buck-Morss, Susan, *The Origin of Negative Dialectics. Theodor W. Adorno, Walter Benjamin, and The Frankfurt Institute*, Brighton: The Harvester Press, 1977.

Burke, Richard, '"Work" and "Play"', *Ethics*, vol. 82, 1971–72, pp. 33–47.

Caillois, Roger, *Man and the Sacred*, trans. Meyer Barash, Illinois: Free Press, 1959.

Caillois, Roger, *Man, Play, and Games*, trans. Meyer Barash, London: Thames and Hudson, 1962.

Callow, Simon, *Being an Actor*, London: Penguin, 1985.

Calnan, Michael, *Health & Illness*, London: Tavistock, 1987.

Cannadine, David and Price, Simon, eds, *Rituals of Royalty. Power and Ceremonial in Traditional Societies*, Cambridge: Cambridge University Press, 1987.

Carlyle, Thomas, *Sartor Resartus*, London: Dent, 1973.

Carter, A. E., *Charles Baudelaire*, Boston: Twayne Publishers, 1977.

Casel, Odo, *The Mystery of Christian Worship and other writings*, London: Darton, Longman & Todd, 1962.

Casey, Michael, '"Emotionally Hollow, Esthetically Meaningless and Spiritually Empty". An Inquiry into Theological Discourse'. *Colloquium*, vol. 14, 1981, pp. 54–61.

Cesari, Domenico Luigh, *Manual for Serving Boys at Low Mass*, trans. R. W. Brundrit, London: Burns, Oates & Co., 1868.

Chambers, E. K., *The Medieval Stage*, vol. 1, Oxford: The Clarendon Press, 1903.

Chisholm, Roderick and Feehan, Thomas D., 'The Intent to Deceive', *The Journal of Philosophy*, vol. 84, no. 3, March 1977, pp. 143–159.

Chupungco, Anscar J., *Cultural Adaptation of the Liturgy*, New York: Paulist Press, 1982.

'Class and Church. After Ghetto Catholicism. Facing the issues raised by Anthony Archer's The two Catholic Churches', *New Blackfriars*, vol. 68, no. 802, February 1987.

Clifton, Thomas, *Music as Heard. A Study in Applied Phenomenology*, New Haven: Yale University Press, 1983.

Collins, Mary, 'Liturgical Methodology and the Cultural Evolution of Worship in the United States', *Worship*, vol. 49, no. 2, March 1975, pp. 85–102.

Collins, Mary, 'Ritual Symbols and the Ritual Process: The Work of Victor Turner', *Worship*, vol. 50, no. 4, July 1976, pp. 336–346.

Collins, Patrick, *More than meets the eye. Ritual and Parish Liturgy*, New York: Paulist Press, 1983.

Collingwood, R. G., *An Autobiography*, Oxford: Oxford University Press, 1970.

Comte, Auguste, *The Catechism of Positive Religion*, trans. Richard Congreve, 3rd edn, London: Kegan Paul, Trench, Trubner & Co. Ltd, 1891.

Connor, Steven, *Postmodernist Culture. An Introduction to Theories of the Contemporary*, Oxford: Basil Blackwell, 1989.

Cordwell, Justine M. and Schwarz, Ronald A., eds, *The Fabrics of Culture. The Anthropology of Clothing and Adornment*, New York: Mouton Publishers, 1979.

Cornwell, Jocelyn, *Hard-Earned Lives. Accounts of Health and Illness from East London*, London: Tavistock, 1984.

Cowper, William, *Cowper Poetical Works*, H. S. Milford, ed., London: Oxford University Press, 1967.

Cranmer-Byng, J. L., ed., *An Embassy to China*, London: Longmans, 1962.

Crawley, Ernest, 'Sacred Dress' in Mary Ellen Roach and Joanne Bubolz Eicher, eds, *Dress, Adornment, and the Social Order*, New York: John Wiley & Sons, Inc., 1965, pp. 138–141.

Creelan, Paul, 'Vicissitudes of the Sacred. Erving Goffman and the Book of Job', *Theory and Society*, vol. 13, no. 5, September 1984, pp. 663–695.

Cromier, Ramona, 'Silence in Philosophy and Literature', *Philosophy To Day*, vol. 2, Winter 1978, pp. 301–306.

Cross, F. L. and Livingstone, E. A., eds, *The Oxford Dictionary of the Christian Church*, 2nd edn, Oxford: Oxford University Press, 1983.

Crumbine, Nancy Jay, 'On Silence', *Humanitas*, May 1975, pp. 147–165.

Curcione, Nicholas, 'Family Influence on Commitment to the Priesthood: A Study of Altar Boys', *Sociological Analysis*, vol. 34, 1973, pp. 265–280.

Dahrendorf, Ralf, 'Homo Sociologicus' in *Essays in the Theory of Society*, London: Routledge & Kegan Paul, 1968, pp. 19–87.

Dahrendorf, Ralf, 'Sociology and Human Nature. A Postscript to Homo Sociologicus' in *Essays in the Theory of Society*, London: Routledge & Kegan Paul, 1968, pp. 88–106.

Dale, J. D. Hilarius, *Ceremonial according to the Roman Rite*, London: Charles Dolman, 1853.

Dällenbach, Lucien, *The Mirror in the Text*, trans. Jeremy Whiteley with Emma Hughes, Cambridge: Polity Press, 1989.

Dalmais, I. H., *Introduction to the Liturgy*, trans. Roger Capel, London: Geoffrey Chapman, 1961.

Dalmais, I. H., 'The Liturgy as Celebration of the Mystery of Salvation' in Aimé Georges Martimort, ed., *The Church at Prayer*. vol. 1, *Principles of the Liturgy*, trans. Matthew J. O'Connell, London: Geoffrey Chapman, 1987, pp. 253–272.

Danielou, Jean, *The Angels and their Mission*, trans. David Heimann, Westminster, Maryland: The Newman Press, 1956.

Dauenhauer, Bernard P., *Silence. The Phenomenon and its Ontological Significance*, Bloomington: Indiana University Press, 1980.

Davidoff, Leonore, *The Best Circles. Society Etiquette and the Season*, London: Croom Helm, 1973.

Davies, Rex, 'Bibliography: New Religious Movements', *The Modern Churchman*, n.s., vol. 27, no. 4, 1985, pp. 41–45.

Davis, Charles, 'Ghetto or Desert: Liturgy in a Cultural Dilemma', *Studia Liturgica*, vol. 7, no. 2–3, 1970, pp. 10–27.

Dawe, Alan, 'The Two Sociologies', *The British Journal of Sociology*, vol. 21, no. 2, June 1970, pp. 207–218.

Dawe, Alan, 'The underworld-view of Erving Goffman', *The British Journal of Sociology*, vol. 24, no. 2, June 1973, pp. 246–253.

Dawe, Alan, 'Theories of Social Action' in Tom Bottomore and Robert Nisbet, eds, *A History of Sociological Analysis*, London: Heinemann, 1978, pp. 362–417.

Dearmer, Percy, *The Parson's Handbook*, London: Humphrey Milford, 1932.

Delatte, Paul, *The Rule of St Benedict. A Commentary*, trans. Justin McCann, London: Burns Oates & Washbourne, 1921.

D'Houtaud, Alphonse and Field, Mark G., 'New Research on the Image of Health' in Caroline Currer and Margaret Stacey, eds, *Concepts of Health, Illness and Disease. A Comparative Perspective*, Leamington Spa: Berg Publishers Ltd, 1986, pp. 235–255.

Dilman, Ilham and Phillips, D. Z., *Sense and Delusion*, London: Routledge & Kegan Paul, 1971.

Dix, Gregory, *The Shape of the Liturgy*, London: A. and C. Black Ltd, 1945.

Dostoyevsky, Fydor, *The Brothers Karamazov*, trans. David Magarshack, London: Folio Society, 1964.

Douglas, Jack D., ed., *The Relevance of Sociology*, New York: Appleton-Century-Crofts, 1970.

Douglas, Mary, *Evans-Pritchard*, London: Fontana, 1980.

Douglas, Mary, *Purity and Danger. An analysis of the concepts of pollution and taboo*, London: Ark Paperbacks, 1984.

Duffy, Regis A., *Alternative Futures for Worship*, vol. 1, *General Introduction*, Collegeville, Minnesota: The Liturgical Press, 1987.

Dulles, Avery, 'Catholic Ecclesiology since Vatican II' in Giuseppe Albergio and James Provost, eds, *Synod 1985 – an Evaluation*, Edinburgh: T. & T. Clark, Ltd, 1986, pp. 3–13.

Dupré, Louis, 'Spiritual Life in a Secular Age' in Mary Douglas and Steven Tipton, eds, *Religion and America. Spiritual Life in a Secular Age*, Boston: Beacon Press, 1983, pp. 3–13.

Durkheim, Emile, *The Elementary Forms of the Religious Life*, trans. Joseph Ward Swain, London: George Allen & Unwin Ltd, 1915.

Eco, Umberto, *The Aesthetics of Thomas Aquinas*, trans. Hugh Bredin, London: Radius, 1988.

Edwards, Kathleen, *The English Secular Cathedrals in the Middle Ages*, 2nd edn, Manchester: Manchester University Press, 1967.

Eliade, Mircea, *The Sacred & the Profane. The Nature of Religion*, New York: Harcourt Brace Jovanovich, 1959.

Elias, Julius A., 'Art and Play' in Phillip Wiener, ed., *A Dictionary of the History of Ideas*, vol. 1, New York: Charles Scribner, 1973, pp. 99–107.

Elias, Norbert, *The History of Manners*, trans. Edmund Jephcott, Oxford: Basil Blackwell, 1978.

Emminghaus, Johannes H., *The Eucharist. Essence, Form, Celebration*, trans. Matthew O'Connell, Collegeville, Minnesota: The Liturgical Press, 1978.

Endo, Shusaku, *Silence*, trans. William Johnston, London: Quartet Books, 1978.

Erasmus, Desiderius, 'The Whole Duty of Youth', trans. Craig R. Thompson, *The Colloquies of Erasmus*, Chicago: The University of Chicago Press, 1965, pp. 30–41.

Erasmus, Desiderius, 'De Civilitate morum puerilium' ('On Good Manners for Boys'), trans. and annot. Brian McGregor, in J. K. Sowards, ed., *Collected Works of Erasmus*, Toronto: University of Toronto Press, 1985, pp. 273–289.

Ermarth, Michael, *Wilhelm Dilthey: The Critique of Historical Reason*, Chicago: The University of Chicago Press, 1978.

Evans-Pritchard, E. E., *Theories of Primitive Religion*, Oxford: Clarendon Press, 1966.

Every, George, *The Mass*, Dublin: Gill and Macmillan, 1978.

Farrell, Michael, *Thy Tears Might Cease*, London: Arena Books, 1968.

Fauque, Michel, *Petit Guide des Fonctions Liturgiques*, Paris: Tequi, 1983.

Featherstone, Mike, ed., Special issue on postmodernism, *Theory, Culture & Society*, vol. 5, nos. 2–3, June 1988.

Fenn, Richard, 'The Sociology of Religion: A Critical Survey' in Tom Bottomore, Stefan Nowak and Magdalena Sokolowska, eds, *Sociology: The State of the Art*, London: Sage Publications, 1982, pp. 101–127.

Fermor, Patrick Leigh, *A Time to Keep Silence*, London: Penguin, 1988.

Fiedler, Leslie, 'The Eye of Innocence' in *The Collected Essays of Leslie Fiedler*, vol. 1, New York: Stein and Day, 1971, pp. 471–511.

Fingarette, Herbert, *Self-Deception*, London: Routledge & Kegan Paul, 1969.

Fink, Peter E., 'Towards a Liturgical Theology', *Worship*, vol. 47, no. 10, 1973, pp. 601–609.

Finkelstein, Joanne, *Dining Out. A Sociology of Modern Manners*, Cambridge: Polity Press, 1989.

Firth, Raymond, 'Postures and Gestures of Respect' in Jean Pouillon and Pierre Maranda, eds, *Echanges et Communications*, vol. 1, The Hague: Mouton, 1970, pp. 188–209.

Firth, Raymond, 'Verbal and bodily rituals of greeting and parting' in J. S. La Fontaine, ed., *The Interpretation of Ritual*, London: Tavistock, 1972, pp. 1–38.

Flanagan, Kieran, 'The Experience of Innocence as a Social Construction', *Philosophical Studies*, vol. 28, 1981, pp. 104–139.

Flanagan, Kieran, 'Competitive Assemblies of God: Lies and mistakes in liturgy', *Research Bulletin*, University of Birmingham: Institute for the study of worship and religious architecture, 1981, pp. 20–69.

Flanagan, Kieran, 'Liturgy, ambiguity and silence: the ritual management of real absence', *The British Journal of Sociology*, vol. 36, no. 2, June 1985, pp. 193–223.

Flanagan, Kieran, 'Innocence and folly: a sociology of misunderstanding', *Culture, Education & Society*, vol. 39, no. 4, Autumn 1985, pp. 338–358.

Flanagan, Kieran, 'To be a Sociologist and a Catholic: a Reflection', *New Blackfriars*, vol. 67, no. 792, June 1986, pp. 256–270.

Flanagan, Kieran, 'Resacralising the Liturgy' in 'Class and Church. After Ghetto Catholicism. Facing the issues raised by Anthony Archer's the two Catholic Churches', *New Blackfriars*, vol. 68, no. 802, February 1987, pp. 64–75.

Flanagan, Kieran, 'Liturgy as Play: A Hermeneutics of Ritual Re-Presentation', *Modern Theology*, vol. 4, no. 4, July 1988, pp. 345–372.

Flanagan, Kieran, 'J.-K. Huysmans: the first post-modernist saint', *New Blackfriars*, vol. 71, no. 838, May 1990, pp. 217–229.

Flanagan, Kieran, 'Theological Pluralism: a sociological critique' in Ian Hamnett, ed., *Religious Pluralism and Unbelief: Studies Critical and Comparative*, London: Routledge, 1990, pp. 81–113.

Flannery, Austin, ed., *Vatican II, The Conciliar and Post Conciliar Documents*, Dublin: Dominican Publications, 1975.

Fletcher, J. M. J., *The Boy Bishop of Salisbury and Elsewhere*, Salisbury: Brown, 1921.

Ford, David F., ed., *The Modern Theologians. An introduction to Christian theology in the twentieth century*, vols. 1–2, Oxford: Basil Blackwell, 1989.

Ford, David F., 'Epilogue: Postmodernism and postscript' in *The Modern Theologians. An introduction to Christian theology in the twentieth century*, vol. 2, Oxford: Basil Blackwell, 1989, pp. 291–297.

Fortescue, Adrian, *The Ceremonies of the Roman Rite Described*, London: Burns Oates & Washbourne Ltd, 1920.

Foster, George M. and Anderson, Barbara Gallatin, *Medical Anthropology*, New York: John Wiley & Sons, Ltd, 1978.

Fox, Robin Lane, *Pagans and Christians*, London: Viking, 1986.

Franklin, R. W., 'Guéranger: a View on the Centenary of His Death', *Worship*, vol. 49, no. 6, November 1975, pp. 318–328.

Franklin, R. W., 'Guéranger and Pastoral Liturgy: A Nineteenth Century Context', *Worship*, vol. 50, no. 2, March 1976, pp. 146–162.

Franklin, R. W., 'Guéranger and Variety in Unity', *Worship*, vol. 51, no. 5, September 1977, pp. 378–399.

Franklin, R. W., 'The Nineteenth Century Liturgical Movement', *Worship*, vol. 53, no. 1, January 1979, pp. 12–39.

Franklin, R. W., 'Response: Humanism and Transcendence in the Nineteenth Century Liturgical Movement', *Worship*, vol. 59, 1985, pp. 342–353.

Freidson, Eliot, 'Celebrating Erving Goffman', *Contemporary Sociology*, vol. 12, no. 4, July 1983, pp. 359–362.

Frisby, David, *Sociological Impressionism. A Reassessment of Georg Simmel's Social Theory*, London: Heinemann, 1981.

Frisby, David, *Georg Simmel*, London: Tavistock, 1984.

Frisby, David, *Fragments of Modernity. Theories of Modernity in the Work of Simmel, Kracauer and Benjamin*, Cambridge: Polity Press, 1985.

Gadamer, Hans-Georg, 'Hermeneutics and Social Science', *Cultural Hermeneutics*, vol. 2, 1975, pp. 307–316.

Gadamer, Hans-Georg, *Truth and Method*, 2nd edn, John Cumming and Garrett Barden, eds, trans. William Glen-Doepel, London: Sheed and Ward, 1979.

Gadamer, Hans-Georg, 'Religious and Poetical Speaking' in Alan M. Olson, ed., *Myth, Symbol and Reality*, Notre Dame, Indiana: University of Notre Dame Press, 1980, pp. 86–98.

Gadamer, Hans-Georg, 'The Religious Dimension in Heidegger' in Alan M. Olson and Leroy S. Rouner, eds, *Transcendence and the Sacred*, Notre Dame, Indiana: University of Notre Dame Press, 1981, pp. 193–207.

Gadamer, Hans-Georg, *Philosophical Apprenticeships*, trans. Robert S. Sullivan, London: The MIT Press, 1985.

Gadamer, Hans-Georg, 'The relevance of the beautiful. Art as play, symbol and festival' in *The Relevance of the Beautiful and other Essays*, Robert Bernasconi, ed., trans. Nicholas Walker, Cambridge: Cambridge University Press, 1986, pp. 3–53.

Gadamer, Hans-Georg, 'The festive character of theater' in *The Relevance of the Beautiful and other Essays*, Robert Bernasconi, ed., trans. Nicholas Walker, Cambridge: Cambridge University Press, 1986, pp. 57–65.

Gadamer, Hans-Georg, 'Composition and intepretation' in *The Relevance of the Beautiful and other Essays*, Robert Bernasconi, ed., trans. Nicholas Walker, Cambridge: Cambridge University Press, 1986, pp. 66–73.

Gadamer, Hans-Georg, 'Image and gesture' in *The Relevance of the Beautiful and other Essays*, Robert Bernasconi, ed., trans. Nicholas Walker, Cambridge: Cambridge University Press, 1986, pp. 74–82.

Gadamer, Hans-Georg, 'Aesthetic and religious experience' in *The Relevance of the Beautiful and other Essays*, Robert Bernasconi, ed., trans. Nicholas Walker, Cambridge: Cambridge University Press, 1986, pp. 140–153.

Geertz, Clifford, 'Religion as a Cultural System' in Donald Culter, ed., *The Religious Situation: 1968*, Boston: Beacon Press, 1968, pp. 639–688.

Gelineau, Joseph, *The Liturgy Today and Tomorrow*, trans. Dinah Livingstone, London: Darton, Longman & Todd, 1978.

388   *Bibliography*

The General Instruction on the Roman Missal in *St. Luke's Daily Missal*, Alcester and Dublin: C. Goodcliffe Neale Ltd, 1975.

Gennep, Arnold van, *The Rites of Passage*, trans. Monika B. Vizedom and Gabrielle L. Caffee, London: Routledge and Kegan Paul, 1977.

Georgiade, Thrasybulos, *Music and Language. The Rise of Western Music as exemplified in settings of the mass*, trans. Marie Louise Gollner, Cambridge: Cambridge University Press, 1982.

Giddens, Anthony, 'Functionalism: après la lutte' in *Studies in Social and Political Theory*, London: Hutchinson, 1977, pp. 96–134.

Giddens, Anthony, *Central Problems in Social Theory. Action, Structure and Contradiction in Social Analysis*, London: Macmillan, 1979.

Giddens, Anthony, 'The social sciences and philosophy – trends in recent social theory' in *Social Theory and Modern Sociology*, Cambridge: Polity Press, 1987, pp. 52–72.

Giddens, Anthony, 'Erving Goffman as a systematic social theorist' in *Social Theory and Modern Sociology*, Cambridge: Polity Press, 1987, pp. 109–139.

Gidlow, Bob, 'Ethnomethodology – a new name for old practices', *The British Journal of Sociology*, vol. 23, no. 4, December 1972, pp. 395–405.

Gill, Robin, *The Social Context of Theology*, London: Mowbrays, 1975.

Gill, Robin, ed., *Theology and Sociology: A Reader*, London: Geoffrey Chapman, 1987.

Gill, Robin, *Competing Convictions*, London: SCM Press, 1989.

Gillham, D. G., *William Blake*, Cambridge: Cambridge University Press, 1973.

Glenn, Paul, *A Tour of the Summa*, Rockford, Illinois: Tan Books, 1978.

Goethe, J. W., *Italian Journey [1786–1788]*, trans. W. H. Auden and Elizabeth Mayer, London: Penguin Books, 1970.

Goffman, Erving, *The Presentation of Self in Everyday Life*, New York: Doubleday & Company Ltd, 1959.

Goffman, Erving, *Stigma. Notes on the Management of Spoiled Identity*, London: Penguin Books, 1968.

Goffman, Erving, *Asylums*, London: Pelican, 1968.

Goffman, Erving, 'Fun in Games' in *Encounters*, London: Penguin, 1972, pp. 17–72.

Goffman, Erving, 'On Face-Work. An Analysis of Ritual Elements in Social Interaction' in *Interaction Ritual. Essays on Face-to-Face Behaviour*, London: Penguin, 1972, pp. 5–45.

Goffman, Erving, 'The Nature of Deference and Demeanor' in *Interaction Ritual. Essays on Face-to-Face Behaviour*, London: Penguin, 1972, pp. 47–95.

Goffman, Erving, 'Embarrassment and Social Organization' in *Interaction Ritual. Essays on Face-to-Face Behaviour*, London: Penguin, 1972, pp. 97–112.

Goffman, Erving, *Frame Analysis* , London: Penguin, 1975.

Goffman, Erving, 'The Interaction Order', *American Sociological Review*, vol. 48, no. 1, February 1983, pp. 1–17.

Golding, William, *Lord of the Flies*, London: Faber & Faber Ltd, 1954.

Gonos, George, 'The Class Position of Goffman's Sociology: Social Origins of an American Structuralism' in Jason Ditton, ed., *The View from Goffman*, London: Macmillan, 1980, pp. 134–169.

Bibliography

Gouldner, Alvin W., *The Coming Crisis of Western Sociology*, London: Heinemann, 1971.

Grainger, Roger, *The Language of the Rite*, London: Darton, Longman & Todd, 1974.

Grathoff, Richard H., *The Structure of social inconsistencies. A contribution to a unified theory of play, game and social action*, The Hague: Martinus Nijhoff, 1970.

Greeley, Andrew, 'Religious Symbolism, Liturgy and Community' in Herman Schmidt, ed., *Liturgy in Transition*, New York: Herder and Herder, 1971, pp. 59–69.

Green, Garrett, 'The Sociology of Dogmatics: Niklas Luhmann's Challenge to Theology', *The Journal of the American Academy of Religion*, vol. 50, no. 1, 1982, pp. 19–34.

Greenspan, Patricia S., 'A case of mixed feelings: ambivalence and the logic of emotion' in Amélie Rorty, ed., *Explaining Emotions*, Berkeley: University of California Press, 1980, pp. 223–250.

Grimes, Ronald, 'Ritual Studies: A Comparative Review of Theodor Gaster and Victor Turner' , *Religious Studies Review*, vol. 2, no. 4, October 1976, pp. 13–25.

Guardini, Romano, *Sacred Signs*, trans. G. C. H. Pollen, London: Sheed & Ward, 1930.

Guardini, Romano, *The Spirit of the Liturgy*, trans. Ada Lane, London: Sheed & Ward, 1930.

Guinness, Alec, *Blessings in Disguise*, London: Fontana/Collins, 1986.

Habermas, Jurgen, 'A Review of Gadamer's *Truth and Method*' in Frederick Dallmayr and Thomas McCarthy, eds, *Understanding and Social Inquiry*, Notre Dame, Indiana: University of Notre Dame Press, 1977, pp. 335–363.

Habgood, John, *Church and Nation in a Secular Age*, London: Darton, Longman & Todd, 1983.

Haight, M. R., *A Study of Self-Deception*, Sussex: The Harvester Press, 1980.

Halttunen, Karen, *Confidence Men and Painted Women. A Study of Middle-class Culture in America, 1830–1870*, New Haven: Yale University Press, 1982.

Hamlyn, D. W., and H. O. Mounce, 'Self-Deception', *The Aristotelian Society*, vol. 45, 1971, pp. 45–72.

Hammond, Peter C., *The Parson and the Victorian Parish*, London: Hodder and Stoughton, 1977.

Hamnett, Ian, 'Ambiguity, classification and change: the function of riddles', *Man*, vol. 2, no. 3, September 1967, pp. 379–391.

Hamnett, Ian, 'Sociology of Religion and Sociology of Error', *Religion*, vol. 3, Spring 1973, pp. 1–12.

Hamnett, Ian, 'Idolatry and Docetism: Contrasting Styles of Proclamation' in Denise Newton, ed., *Liturgy and Change*, University of Birmingham: Institute for the Study of Worship and Religious Architecture, 1983, pp. 21–37.

Hamnett, Ian, 'Durkheim and the study of religion' in Steve Fenton, *Durkheim and Modern Sociology*, Cambridge: Cambridge University Press, 1984, pp. 202–218.

Hamnett, Ian, 'A Mistake about Error', *New Blackfriars*, vol. 67, no. 788, February 1986, pp. 69–78.

Hans, James S., 'Hermeneutics, Play, Deconstruction', *Philosophy Today*, vol. 24, Winter 1980, pp. 299–317.

Harré, Rom, 'Social rules and social rituals' in Henry Tajfel, ed., *The Social Dimension. European developments in social psychology*, vol. 1, Cambridge: Cambridge University Press, 1984, pp. 300–313.

Hart, Rob van der, *The Theology of Angels and Devils*, Cork: The Mercier Press, 1972.

Haweis, H. R., 'Bowing', *Belgravia*, vol. 4, 1881, pp. 185–187.

Hawthorn, Geoffrey, *Enlightenment & Despair. A history of sociology*, Cambridge: Cambridge University Press, 1976.

Hayes, Francis, 'Gestures: a working bibliography', *Southern Folklore Quarterly*, vol. 21, no. 4, 1957, pp. 218–317.

Heelas, Paul, 'Semantic Anthropology and Rules' in Peter Collett, ed., *Social Rules and Social Behaviour*, Oxford: Basil Blackwell, 1977, pp. 109–131.

Hekman, Susan, 'Action as a Text: Gadamer's Hermeneutics and the Social Scientific Analysis of Action', *Journal for the Theory of Social Behaviour*, vol. 14, no. 3, October 1984, pp. 333–354.

Hekman, Susan J., *Hermeneutics & the Sociology of Knowledge*, Cambridge: Polity Press, 1986.

'Hell: what it means not to be saved', *New Blackfriars*, vol. 69, no. 821, November 1988.

Helman, Cecil, *Culture, Health and Illness*, Bristol: Wright, 1985.

Herzlich, Claudine, *Health and Illness. A Social Psychological Analysis*, trans. Douglas Graham, London: Academic Press, 1973.

Herzlich, Claudine and Pierret, Janine, *Illness and Self in Society*, trans. Elborg Forster, Baltimore: The Johns Hopkins University Press, 1987.

Hesser, Garry and Weigert, Andrew J., 'Comparative Dimensions of Liturgy: A Conceptual Framework and Feasibility Application', *Sociological Analysis*, vol. 41, no. 3, Fall 1980, pp. 215–229.

Hildebrand, Dietrich von, *Liturgy and Personality*, New York: Longmans, Green and Co., 1943.

Hinman, Lawrence M., 'Quid Facti or Quid Juris? The Fundamental Ambiguity of Gadamer's Understanding of Hermeneutics', *Philosophy and Phenomenological Research*, vol. 40, June 1980, pp. 512–535.

Hirst, Paul and Penny Woolley, *Social Relations and Human Attributes*, London: Tavistock Publications, 1982.

Hitchcock, James, *The Decline and Fall of Radical Catholicism*, New York: Image Books, 1972.

Hitchcock, James, *The Recovery of the Sacred*, New York: The Seabury Press, 1974.

Hochschild, Arlie Russell, *The Managed Heart. Commercialization of Human Feeling*, Berkeley: University of California Press, 1983.

Hodgkin, L. Violet, *Silent Worship. The Way of Wonder*, London: Headley Bros. Publishers Ltd, 1919.

Holden, Tony, *Explaining Icons*, Welshpool, Powys: Stylite Publishing, Ltd, 1985.

Hollinger, Robert, ed., *Hermeneutics and Praxis*, Notre Dame, Indiana: University of Notre Dame Press, 1985.

Holmes, Urban T., 'Liminality and Liturgy', *Worship*, vol. 47, no. 7, 1973, pp. 386–397.

Horn, Marilyn J., *The Second Skin: An Interdisciplinary Study of Clothing*, Boston: Houghton Mifflin, 1968.

Horton, Robin and Ruth Finnegan, eds, *Modes of Thought. Essays on Thinking in Western and Non-Western Societies*, London: Faber & Faber, 1973.

Huber, Georges, *My Angel will go before you*, trans. Michael Adams, Dublin: Four Courts, 1983.

Huels, John M., 'The Intepretation of Liturgical Law', *Worship*, vol. 55, no. 3, May 1981, pp. 218–237.

Huizinga, Johan, *Homo Ludens. A Study of the Play-Element in Culture*, London: Routledge & Kegan Paul, 1949.

Humes, Joy Nachod, *Two Against Time. A Study of the very present worlds of Paul Claudel and Charles Péguy*, Chapel Hill: University of North Carolina, 1978.

Huysmans, J.-K., *The Cathedral*, trans. Clara Bell, London: Kegan Paul, Trench, Trubner & Co., Ltd, 1898.

Huysmans, J.-K., *En Route*, trans. C. Kegan Paul, London: Kegan Paul, Trench, Trubner & Co., Ltd, 1918.

Huysmans, J.-K., *The Oblate*, trans. Edward Perceval, London: Kegan Paul, Trench, Trubner & Co. Ltd, 1924.

Hyland, Drew A., *The Question of Play*, Lanham, Md.: University Press of America, 1984.

Ignatieff, Michael, *A Just Measure of Pain*, London: Macmillan, 1978.

James, E. O., *Christian Myth and Ritual*, London: John Murray, 1933.

James, Henry, *The Turn of the Screw and Other Stories*, London: Penguin, 1969.

James, Nicky, 'Emotional labour: skill and work in the social regulation of feelings', *The Sociological Review*, vol. 37, no. 1, February 1989, pp. 15–42.

Johnson, Peter, *Politics, Innocence, and the Limits of Goodness*, London: Routledge, 1988.

Johnson, Samuel (possibly), *The Rambler*, in A. Chalmers, ed., *The British Essayists*, vol. 17, London: C. and J. Rivington *et al.*, 1823, pp. 38–43.

Johnston, Robert K., *The Christian at Play*, Grand Rapids, Michigan: William Eerdmans, 1983.

Jone, Heribert, *Moral Theology*, trans. Urban Adelman, Cork: The Mercier Press, 1948.

Jones, Cheslyn, Wainwright, Geoffrey and Yarnold, Edward, eds, *The Study of Liturgy*, London: SPCK, 1978.

Joseph, Nathan, *Uniforms and nonuniforms. communication through clothing*, London: Greenwood Press, 1987.

Jungmann, Joseph A., *The Mass of the Roman Rite*, trans. Francis A. Brunner, London: Burns & Oates, 1959.

Kapferer, Bruce, 'Ritual Process and the Transformation of Context', *Social Analysis*, no. 1, February 1979, pp. 3–19.

Kavanagh, Joseph William, *The Altar Boys' Ceremonial*, New York: Benziger Brothers, Inc., 1956.

Kay, Jeffrey, 'Hans Urs von Balthasar, a Post-critical Theologian?' in Gregory Baum, ed., *Neo-Conservatism: social and religious phenomenon*, Concilium, Edinburgh: T. & T. Clark, 1981, pp. 84–89.

Kearney, Richard, *Dialogues with contemporary Continental thinkers. The phenomenological heritage*, Manchester: Manchester University Press, 1984.

Kearney, Richard, 'Religion and Ideology: Paul Ricoeur's hermeneutic conflict', *The Irish Philosophical Journal*, vol. 2, Spring 1985, pp. 37–42.

Kehl, Medard and Werner Loser, eds, *The von Balthasar Reader*, trans. Robert J. Daly and Fred Lawrence, Edinburgh: T. & T. Clark, 1982, introduction by Medard Kehl, pp. 1–54.

Kerman, Joseph, *Musicology*, London: Collins, 1985.

Key, Mary Ritchie, *Nonverbal Communication: a research guide*, Metuchen, N. J.: The Scarecrow Press, 1977.

Kipp, David, 'Self-Deception, Inauthenticity, and Weakness of Will' in Mike Martin, ed., *Self- Deception and self-understanding*, Kansas: University Press of Kansas, 1985, pp. 261–283.

Klauser, Theodor, *A Short History of the Western Liturgy. An account and some reflections*, 2nd edn, trans., John Halliburton, Oxford; Oxford University Press, 1979.

Klemm, David E., *The Hermeneutical Theory of Paul Ricoeur. A Constructive Analysis*, London: Associated University Presses, 1983.

Koenker, Ernest Benjamin, *The Liturgical Renaissance in the Roman Catholic Church*, Chicago: University of Chicago Press, 1954.

König, Joseph, 'Serving at the Altar' in Alfons Kirchgaessner, ed., *Unto the Altar. The Practice of Catholic Worship*, London: Nelson, 1963, pp. 138–146.

Krolick, Sanford, 'Through a Glass Darkly: What is the phenomenology of religion?', *International Journal for Philosophy of Religion*, vol. 17, 1985, pp. 193–199.

Kuhn, Reinhard, *Corruption in Paradise. The Child in Western Literature*, London: University Press of New England, 1982.

Kwatera, Michael, *The Ministry of Servers*, Collegeville, Minnesota: the Liturgical Press, 1982.

Labarre, Weston, 'The Cultural Basis of Emotions and Gestures', *Journal of Personality*, vol. 16, September 1947, pp. 49–68.

Ladrière, Jean, 'The Performativity of Liturgical Language' in Herman Schmidt and David Power, eds, *Liturgical Experience of Faith*, New York: Herder and Herder, 1973, pp. 50–62.

Last, Carl A., ed., *Remembering the Future. Vatican II and Tomorrow's Liturgical Agenda*, New York: Paulist Press, 1983.

Latourelle, René, *Man and his problems in the light of Jesus Christ*, New York: Alba House, 1983.

Laver, James, *The First Decadent. Being the strange Life of J. K. Huysmans*, London: Faber & Faber, 1954.

Leach, Arthur F., 'The Schoolboy's Feast', *The Fortnightly Review*, vol. 59, n.s. January–June 1896, pp. 128–141.

Leclerq, Jean, *The Love of Learning and the Desire for God. A Study of Monastic Culture*, trans. Catherine Misrahi, New York: Fordham University Press, 1961.

Leclerq, Jean, 'Influence and noninfluence of Dionysius in the Western Middle

Ages' in Pseudo-Dionysius, *The Complete Works*, trans. Colm Luibheid with Paul Rorem, London: SPCK, 1987.

Leeuwen, T. M. van, *The Surplus of Meaning. Ontology and Eschatology in the Philosophy of Paul Ricoeur*, Amsterdam: Rodopi, 1981.

Lepenies, Wolf, *Between Literature and Science: the Rise of Sociology*, trans. R. J. Hollingdale, Cambridge: Cambridge University Press, 1988.

Lesage, Robert, *Vestments and Church Furniture* , London: Burns & Oates, 1960.

Levine, Donald N., *The Flight from Ambiguity. Essays in Social and Cultural Theory*, Chicago: The University of Chicago Press, 1985.

Lewis, C. S., *Prayer: Letters to Malcolm*, London: Collins, 1977.

Lewis, Gilbert, *Day of Shining Red. An Essay on Understanding Ritual*, Cambridge: Cambridge University Press, 1980.

Lewis, R. W., *The American Adam: Innocence, Tragedy and Tradition in the Nineteenth Century*, Chicago: The Chicago University Press, 1955.

Li, Dun J., *China in Transition: 1517–1911*, New York: Van Nostrand Reinhold Company, 1969.

Liturgical Commission of the General Synod of the Church of England, *Patterns for Worship*, Church House Publishing, 1989.

Lofland, John, 'Early Goffman: Style, Structure, Substance, Soul' in Jason Ditton, ed., *The View from Goffman*, London: Macmillan, 1980, pp. 24–51.

Lofland, John, 'Erving Goffman's Sociological Legacies', *Urban Life*, vol. 13, no. 1, April 1984, pp. 7–34.

Lossky, Vladimir, *The Mystical Theology of the Eastern Church*, London: James Clarke & Co. Ltd, 1957.

Louth, Andrew, *Denys the Areopagite*, London: Geoffrey Chapman, 1989.

Lukes, Steven, *Emile Durkheim. His Life and Work*, London: Allen Lane, The Penguin Press, 1973.

Lukes, Steven, *Power. A Radical View*, London: Macmillan, 1974.

Lurie, Alison, *Imaginary Friends*, London: Heinemann, 1967.

L., V.G., *Manners at Mass. The Movements and Gestures of Public Worship*, London: Burns & Oates, 1955.

Lynd, Robert S., *Knowledge for what? The Place of Social Science in American Culture*, Princeton: Princeton University Press, 1970.

Madison, G. B., 'Text and Action: The Hermeneutics of Existence', *University of Ottawa Quarterly*, vol. 55, no. 4, 1985, pp. 135–145.

Malcolm, Janet, *In the Freud Archives*, London: Fontana, 1986.

Maldonado, Luis, 'The Church's Liturgy: Present and Future', in David Tracy, Hans Kung and Johann B. Metz, eds, *Toward Vatican III. The work that needs to be done*, Dublin: Gill and Macmillan, 1978, pp. 221–237.

Mâle, Emile, *Religious Art in France. The Late Middle Ages. A Study of Medieval Iconography and Its Sources*, trans. Marthiel Mathews, Princeton: Princeton University Press, 1986.

Maltz, Daniel N., 'Joyful Noise and Reverent Silence: The Significance of Noise in Pentecostal Worship' in Deborah Tannen and Muriel Saville-Troike, eds, *Perspectives on Silence*, Norwood, New Jersey: Ablex Publishing Corporation, 1985, pp. 113–138.

Manly, George, 'Experiments in a Group Mass', *Studia Liturgica*, vol. 8, no. 4, 1971–72, pp. 244–253.

Mars, Gerald and Nicod, Michael, *The World of Waiters*, London: George Allen & Unwin, 1984.

Marshall, Gordon, 'The Workplace Culture of a Licensed Restaurant', *Theory, Culture and Society*, vol. 3, no. 1, 1986, pp. 33–47.

Martimort, Aimé Georges, ed., *Introduction to the Liturgy*, New York: Desclée Company, 1968.

Martimort, Aimé *The Church of Prayer, vol. 1 Principles of the Liturgy*, trans. Matthew J. O'Connell, London: Geoffrey Chapman, 1987.

Martin, David, *A General Theory of Secularisation*, Oxford: Basil Blackwell, 1978.

Martin, David, 'Profane Habit and Sacred Usage', *Theology*, vol. 82, no. 686, March 1979, pp. 83–95.

Martin, David, *The Breaking of the Image. A Sociology of Christian Theory and Practice*, Oxford: Basil Blackwell, 1980.

Martin, Judith, *Miss Manners' Guide to Excrutiatingly Correct Behaviour*, London: Penguin, 1984.

Martin, Mike, *Self-Deception and Morality*, Lawrence: Kansas University Press, 1986.

Matthews, Gareth, 'Ritual and the Religious Feelings' in Amélie Rorty, ed., *Explaining Emotions*, Berkeley: University of California Press, 1980, pp. 339–353.

May, Rollo, *Power and Innocence*, London: Collins, 1976.

Mayo, Janet, *A History of Ecclesiastical Dress*, London: B. T. Batsford Ltd, 1984.

McAllister, Ronald J., 'Theology Lessons for Sociology' in William H. Swatos, ed., *Religious Sociology. Interfaces and Boundaries*, New York: Greenwood Press, 1987, pp. 27–39.

McDannell, Colleen and Lang, Bernhard, *Heaven. A History*, London: Yale University Press, 1988.

MacIntyre, Alasdair, *After Virtue. A Study in Moral Theory*, London: Duckworth, 1981.

McKenna, John H., 'Ritual Activity', *Worship*, vol. 50, no. 4, July 1976, pp. 347–352.

MacKenzie, Mr, *The Mirror*, in A. Chalmers, ed., *The British Essayists*, vol. 5, London: C. and J. Rivington *et al.*, 1823, pp. 206–210.

MacKenzie, Compton, *Sinister Street*, London: Penguin, 1960.

McLellan, David, *Simone Weil. Utopian Pessimist*, London: Macmillan, 1989.

Mead, Margaret, *Twentieth Century Faith, Hope and Survival*, London: Harper & Row, 1972.

Melville, Herman, *Billy Budd, Sailor & Other Stories*, London: Penguin, 1970.

Merton, Robert, *Social Theory and Social Structure*, New York: The Free Press, 1968.

Middleton, John, ed., *Magic, Witchcraft & Curing*, London: University of Texas Press, 1967.

Miles, Clement A., *Christmas in Ritual and Tradition Christian and Pagan*, London: T. Fisher Unwin, 1912.

Millard, James Elwin, *Historical Notices of the office of Choristers*, London: James Masters, 1848.

Miller, Arthur, 'Death of a Salesman', *Collected Plays*, London: Secker & Warburg, 1967, pp. 128–222.

Miller, Thomas, 'Goffman, Social Acting, and Moral Behaviour', *Journal for the Theory of Social Behaviour*, vol. 14, 1984, pp. 141–163.

Miller, Thomas G., 'Goffman, Positivism and the Self', *Philosophy of Social Science*, vol. 16, 1986, pp. 177–195.

Mills, C. Wright, *White Collar*, New York: Oxford University Press, 1956.

Mills, John Orme, 'God, Man and Media: on a problem arising when theologians speak of the modern world' in David Martin, John Orme Mills and W. S. F. Pickering, eds, *Sociology and Theology: Alliance and Conflict*, Brighton: The Harvester Press, 1980, pp. 136–150.

Miri, Mrinal, 'Self-Deception', *Philosophy and Phenomenological Research*, vol. 34, September 1973– June 1974, pp. 576–585.

Mitchell, Duncan G., *A Dictionary of Sociology*, Chicago: Aldine Publishing Company, 1968.

Mitzman, Arthur, *The Iron Cage. An Historical Intepretation of Max Weber*, New Brunswick: Transaction Books, 1985.

Mixon, Don, 'A Theory of Actors', *Journal for the Theory of Social Behaviour*, vol. 13, 1983, pp. 97–109.

Molière, Jean Baptiste, 'The Would-be gentleman', trans. John Wood, London: Penguin Books, 1953.

Moolenburgh, H. C., *A Handbook of Angels*, trans. Amina Marix-Evans, Saffron Walden: C. W. Daniel, 1984.

Moorhouse, Geoffrey, *Against all Reason*, London: Weidenfeld and Nicolson, 1969.

Morris, Brian, *Anthropological Studies of Religion. An Introductory Text*, Cambridge: Cambridge University Press, 1987.

Morris, Herbert, *On Guilt and Innocence. Essays in Legal Philosophy and Moral Psychology*, Berkeley: University of California Press, 1976.

Myerhoff, Barbara, 'Rites of Passage: Process and Paradox' in Victor Turner, ed., *Celebration. Studies in Festivity and Ritual*, Washington D. C.: Smithsonian Institution Press, 1982, pp. 109–135.

Napoli, George A. De, 'Inculturation as Communication' in Arij A. Roest Crollius, ed., *Effective Inculturation and Ethnic Identity*, Rome: Pontifical Gregorian University, 1987, pp. 71–98.

Nash, Arnold S., 'Some Reflections upon the Sociological Approach to Theology', *International Yearbook for the Sociology of Religion*, vol. 2, 1966, pp. 185–197.

Neitz, Mary Jo, *Charisma and Community. A Study of Religious Commitment within the Charasmatic Renewal*, New Brunswick, U.S.A.: Transaction Books, 1987.

New Catholic Encyclopedia, Washington D.C.: The Catholic University of America, 1967.

Newman, John Henry, *The Idea of a University*, New York: Image Books, 1959.

Nichols, Aidan, *The Art of God Incarnate. Theology and Image in Christian Tradition*, London: Darton, Longman & Todd, 1980.

Nichols, Aidan, 'Balthasar and his Christology', *New Blackfriars*, vol. 66, no. 781–782, July–August 1985, pp. 317–324.

Nichols, Aidan, *The Theology of Joseph Ratzinger. An Introductory Study*, Edinburgh: T. & T. Clark, 1988.

Nisbet, Robert A., *The Sociological Tradition*, London: Heinemann, 1967.

Nisbet, Robert A., *The Quest for Community*, Oxford: Oxford University Press, 1969.

North, Richard, *Fools for God*, London: Collins, 1987.

Nouwen, Henri J. M., *Behold the Beauty of the Lord. Praying with Icons*, Notre Dame, Indiana: Ave Maria Press, 1987.

O'Brien, Flann, *The Third Policeman*, London: Picador, 1974.

O'Connell, J. B., *The Celebration of Mass*, Milwaukee: The Bruce Publishing Company, 1956.

O'Connor, Flannery, *Mystery and Manners*, London: Faber & Faber, 1972.

O'Connor, Flannery, *The Habit of Being*, ed., Sally Fitzgerald, New York: Farrar, Straus, Giroux, 1979.

O'Connor, Flannery, *Everything that Rises Must Converge*, London: Faber & Faber, 1980.

Olson, Alan, M., 'Myth, Symbol and Metaphorical Truth' in Alan M. Olson, ed., *Myth, Symbol and Reality*, Notre Dame, Indiana: University of Notre Dame Press, 1980, pp. 99–125.

O'Meara, T. F., 'Notes of Art and Theology: Hans Urs von Balthasar's systems', *Theological Studies*, vol. 42, 1981, pp. 272–276.

Ong, Walter J., *Hopkins, the Self, and God*, Toronto: University of Toronto Press, 1986.

Orme, Nicholas, 'The Medieval Clergy of Exeter Cathedral. II. The Secondaries and Choristers', *Devonshire Association for Advancement of Literary Science. Report and Transactions*, vol. 115, December 1983, pp. 79–100.

Orwell, George, *Down and Out in Paris and London*, London: Penguin, 1975.

Otto, Rudolf, 'Towards a Liturgical Reform. 1. The Form of Divine Service' in *Religious Essays. A Supplement to 'The Idea of the Holy'*, trans. Brian Lunn, Oxford: Oxford University Press, 1931, pp. 53–67.

Otto, Rudolf, *The Idea of the Holy*, trans. John W. Harvey, Oxford: Oxford University Press, 1958.

Overing, Joanna, ed., *Reason and Morality*, London: Tavistock Publications, 1985.

Palmer, Anthony, 'Characterising Self-Deception', *Mind*, vol. 88, n.s., 1979, pp. 45–58.

Parkin, Frank, *Max Weber*, London: Tavistock, 1982.

Paskow, Alan, 'Towards a theory of self-deception', *Man and World*, vol. 12, 1979, pp. 178–191.

Passmore, T. H., *Durandus on the Sacred Vestments*, London: Thomas Baker, 1899.

Pattison, George, 'Idol or Icon? Some principles of an Aesthetic Christology', *Journal of Literature & Theology*, vol. 3, no. 1, March 1989, pp. 1–15.

Pattison, Robert, *The Child Figure in English Literature*, Athens: The University of Georgia Press, 1978.

Pears, David, 'Freud, Sartre and Self-Deception' in Richard Wollheim, ed., *Freud. A Collection of Critical Essays*, New York: Anchor Books, 1974, pp. 97–112.

Péguy, Charles, *Basic Verities. Prose and Poetry*, trans. Ann and Julian Green, London: Kegan Paul, 1943.

Pelikan, Jaroslav, 'Negative Theology and Positive Religion. A Study of Nicholas Cusanus *de pace fidei*' in Raoul Mortley and David Dockrill, eds, *Prudentia*. *The Via Negativa*, University of Auckland, Supplementary number, 1981, pp. 65–77.

Perham, Michael, *Liturgy, Pastoral and Parochial*, London: SPCK, 1984.

Peterson, Eric, *The Angels and the Liturgy: the status and significance of the holy angels in worship*, trans. Ronald Walls, London: Darton, Longman & Todd, 1964.

Phalp, G. A., ed., *Management of Minor Illness*, London: King's Fund Publishing Office, 1979.

Phillips, C. Henry, *The Singing Church*, London: Faber & Faber, Ltd, 1945.

Picard, Max, *The World of Silence*, trans., Stanley Godman, South Bend, Indiana: Regnery/Gateway, Inc., 1952.

Pichois, Claude, *Baudelaire*, trans. Graham Robb, London: Hamish Hamilton, 1989.

Podkradsky, Gehard, *New Dictionary of the Liturgy*, London: Geoffrey Chapman, 1962.

Postman, Neil, *The disappearance of childhood*, London: W. H. Allen, 1983.

Pottmeyer, Hermann, 'The Church as Mysterium and as Institution' in Guiseppe Albergio and James Provost, eds, *Synod 1985 – an Evaluation*, Edinburgh: T. & T. Clark, Ltd, 1986, pp. 99–109.

Power, David N., 'Unripe Grapes: The Critical Function of Liturgical Theology', *Worship*, vol. 52, no. 5, September 1978.

A prosperous head waiter, *Waiting at Table*, London: Universal Publications, 1937.

Proust, Marcel, *Marcel Proust. A selection from his miscellaneous writings*, trans. Gerard Hopkins, London: Allan Wingate, 1948.

Pseudo-Dionysius, *The Complete Works*, trans. Colm Luibheid with Paul Rorem, London: SPCK, 1987.

Quinn, Patricia A., *Better than the Sons of Kings. Boys and Monks in the Middle Ages*, New York: Peter Lang, 1989.

Rahner, Hugo, *Man at Play*, trans. Brian Battershaw and Edward Quinn, London: Burns & Oates, 1965.

Rahner, Karl, *et al.*, eds, *Sacramentum Mundi*, London: Burns & Oates, 1968.

Rainbow, Bernarr, *The Choral Revival in the Anglican Church (1839–1872)*, London: Barrie & Jenkins, 1970.

Ramsey, Boniface, *Beginning to read the Fathers*, London: Darton, Longman & Todd, 1986.

Rappaport, Roy, 'The Obvious Aspects of Ritual' in *Ecology, Meaning and Religion*, Richmond, California: North Atlantic Books, 1979, pp. 173–221.

Rappaport, Roy, 'Sanctity and Lies in Evolution' in *Ecology, Meaning and Religion*, Richmond, California: North Atlantic Books, 1979, pp. 223–246.

Ratzinger, Joseph Cardinal, with Vittorio Messori, *The Ratzinger Report. An Exclusive Interview on the State of the Church*, trans. Salvator Attanasio and Graham Harrison, Leominster, Herefordshire: Fowler Wright Books Limited, 1985.

Ratzinger, Joseph Cardinal, 'Liturgy and Sacred Music', *Communio*, vol. 13, no. 4, Winter 1986, pp. 377–391.

Ratzinger, Joseph Cardinal, *Feast of Faith. Approaches to a Theology of the Liturgy*, trans. Graham Harrison, San Francisco: Ignatius Press, 1986.

Régamey, Pie-Raymond, *What is an Angel?* trans. Mark Pontifex, New York: Hawthorn Books, 1960.

Richardson, Alan and Bowden, John, eds, *A New Dictionary of Christian Theology*, London: SCM, 1983.

Riches, John, 'Hans Urs von Balthasar' in David Ford, ed., *The Modern Theologians. An Introduction to Christian theology in the twentieth century*, vol. 1, Oxford: Basil Blackwell, 1989, pp. 237–254.

Ricoeur, Paul, *The Symbolism of Evil*, trans. Emerson Buchanan, Boston: Beacon Press, 1969.

Ricoeur, Paul, *Interpretation theory: discourse and the surplus of meaning*, Fort Worth, Texas: The Texas Christian University Press, 1976.

Ricoeur, Paul, 'The model of the text: meaningful action considered as a text' in John B. Thompson, ed. and trans., *Paul Ricoeur. Hermeneutics and the Human Sciences*, Cambridge: Cambridge University Press, 1981, pp. 197–221.

Riezler, Kurt, 'Play and Seriousness', *The Journal of Philosophy,* vol. 38, no. 19, September 1941, pp. 505–517.

Rilke, Rainer Maria, *Selected Works, Poetry*, vol. 2, trans. J. B. Leishman, London: The Hogarth Press, 1960.

Robbins, Thomas, 'The Transformative Impact of the Study of New Religions on the Sociology of Religion', *Journal for the Scientific Study of Religion*, vol. 27, no. 1, 1988, pp. 12–27.

Roberts, Julian, *Walter Benjamin*, London: Macmillan, 1982.

Roberts, Louis, *The Theological Aesthetics of Hans Urs von Balthasar*, Washington: The Catholic University of America Press, 1987.

Roberts, Morley, 'Waiters and Restaurants', *Murrays Magazine*, vol. 7, 1890, pp. 534–546.

Robertson, Dora, *A History of the Life and Education of Cathedral Choristers for 700 years*, London: Jonathan Cape, 1938.

Robinson, John A. T., *But that I can't believe!*, London: Collins, 1967.

Rogers, B. G., *The Novels and Stories of Barbey D'Aurevilly*, Genève: Libraire Droz, 1967.

Rorem, Paul, *Biblical and Liturgical Symbols within the Pseudo-Dionysian Synthesis*, Toronto: Pontifical Institute of Mediaeval Studies, 1984.

Rorem, Paul, 'The Uplifting Spirituality of Pseudo-Dionysius' in Bernard McGinn and John Meyendorff, eds, *Christian Spirituality. Origins to the Twelfth Century*, London: Routledge & Kegan Paul, 1986, pp. 132–151.

Rorty, Richard, *Philosophy and the Mirror of Nature*, Oxford: Basil Blackwell, 1980.

Rose, Gillian, *The Melancholy Science. An Introduction to the Thought of Theodor W. Adorno*, London: Macmillan, 1978.

Rouget, A.-M., 'Participation in the Mass: the theological principles' in Vincent Ryan, ed., *Studies in Pastoral Liturgy*, vol. 2, Dublin: Gill and Son, 1963, pp. 120–137.

Roulin, E. A., *Vestments and Vesture. A Manual of Liturgical Art*, trans. Justin McCann, London: Sands & Co., 1931.

Runciman, W. G., ed., *Max Weber. Selections in translation*, trans. E. Matthews, Cambridge: Cambridge University Press, 1978.

Ryan, Mary, *Introduction to Paul Claudel*, Cork: Cork University Press, 1951.

Ryan, Mary Shaw, *Clothing. A Study in Human Behaviour*, New York: Holt, Rinehart and Winston, Inc., 1966.

Salter, Michael, ed., *Play: Anthropological Perspectives*, New York: Leisure Press, 1978.

Sartre, Jean-Paul, *Being and Nothingness. An Essay on Phenomenological Ontology*, trans. Hazel E. Barnes, London: Methuen & Co. Ltd, 1957.

Saward, John, 'Towards an Apophatic Anthropology', *Irish Theological Quarterly*, vol. 41, 1974, pp. 222–234.

Saward, John, *Perfect Fools. Folly for Christ's Sake in Catholic and Orthodox Spirituality*, Oxford: Oxford University Press, 1980.

Schmemann, Alexander, *Introduction to Liturgical Theology*, London: The Faith Press, 1966.

Schiller, Friedrich von, *Naive and Sentimental Poetry and On the Sublime*, trans. Julius A. Elias, New York: Frederick Ungar Publishing Co., 1966.

Schmitt, Jean-Claude, 'Between text and image: the prayer gestures of Saint Dominic', *History and Anthropology*, vol. 1, 1984, pp. 127–145.

Schneider, Mark A. 'Culture-as-text in the work of Clifford Geertz', *Theory and Society*, vol. 16, 1987, pp. 809–839.

Schreuder O., 'Religious Attitudes, Group Consciousness, Liturgy and education', *Social Compass*, vol. 10, 1963, pp. 29–52.

Schudson, Michael, 'Embarrassment and Erving Goffman's idea of human nature', *Theory and Society*, vol. 13, no. 5, September 1984, pp. 633–648.

Schutz, Alfred, 'Concept and Theory Formation in the Social Sciences' in Dorothy Emmet and Alasdair MacIntyre, eds, *Sociological Theory and Philosophical Analysis*, London: Macmillan, 1970.

Schweiker, William, 'Beyond Imitation: Mimetic Praxis in Gadamer, Ricoeur, Derrida', *The Journal of Religion*, vol. 68, no. 1, January 1988, pp. 21–38.

Seasoltz, Kevin, 'Anthropology and Liturgical Theology: Searching for a Compatible Methodology' in David Power and Luis Maldonado, eds, *Liturgy and Human Passage*, New York: The Seabury Press, 1979, pp. 3–24.

Sennett, Richard, 'Two on the Aisle', *New York Review of Books*, vol. 20, no. 17, 1st November 1973, pp. 29–31.

Sennett, Richard, *The Fall of Public Man*, Cambridge: Cambridge University Press, 1977.

Sharrock, Wes and Anderson, Bob, *The Ethnomethodologists*, London: Tavistock, 1986.

Shaughnessy, James D. ed., *The Roots of Ritual*, Grand Rapids, Michigan: William B. Eerdmans Publishing Company, 1973.

Simmel, Georg, 'Contribution to the Sociology of Religion', *The American Journal of Sociology*, vol. 60, no. 6, May 1955, pp. 1–18.

Simmel, Georg, 'Fashion', *The American Journal of Sociology*, vol. 62, no. 6, May 1957, pp. 541–558.

Simmel, Georg, *Sociology of Religion*, trans. C. Rosenthal, New York: Philosophical Library, 1959.

Simmel, Georg, *Essays on Interpretation in Social Science*, ed. and trans. Guy Oakes, Manchester: Manchester University Press, 1980.

Skorupski, John, *Symbol and Theory. A Philosophical Study of Theories of Religion in Social Anthropology*, Cambridge: Cambridge University Press, 1976.

Smith, Gregory W. H., 'Snapshots "sub specie aeternitatis"': Simmel, Goffman and Formal Sociology', *Human Studies*, vol. 12, nos. 1–2, June 1989, pp. 19–57.

Smith, Pierre, 'Aspects of the Organization of Rites' in Michael Izard and Pierre Smith, eds, *Between Belief and Transgression. Structuralist Essays in Religion, History and Myth*, trans. John Leavitt, London: Chicago University Press, 1982, pp. 103–128.

Smits, Kenneth, 'Liturgical Reform in Cultural Perspective', *Worship*, vol. 150, no. 2, March 1976, pp. 98–110.

Sölle, Dorothee, 'The Repression of the Existential Element, or Why so many People become Conservative' in Gregory Baum, ed., *Neo-Conservatism: Social and Religious Phenomenon*, Concilium, Edinburgh: T. & T. Clark Ltd, 1981, pp. 69–75.

Somerville-Large, Peter, *Cappaghglass*, London: Hamish Hamilton, 1985.

Sontag, Susan, 'The Aesthetics of Silence' in *Styles of Radical Will*, New York: Farrar, Strauss and Giroux, 1976, pp. 3–34.

Staley, Vernon, *The Ceremonial of the English Church*, London: A. R. Mowbray, 1899.

Staley, Vernon, ed., *Hierurgia Anglicana. The Ceremonial of the Anglican Church after the Reformation*, vol. 3, part II, New Edition, London: The De La More Press, 1903.

Stark, Werner, *The Sociology of Religion. A study of Christendom*, London: Routledge & Kegan Paul, 1972.

Steele, Richard, 'Indecorums at Church', *Tatler* in A. Chalmers, ed., *The British Essayists*, vol. 3, London: C. and J. Rivington *et al.*, 1823, pp. 183–184.

Steele, Richard, 'On Dissimulation', *Tatler*, in A. Chalmers, ed., *The British Essayists*, vol. 4, London: C. and J. Rivington *et al.* 1823, pp. 133–134.

Steele, Richard, 'On improper behaviour at Church', *Spectator* in A. Chalmers, ed., *The British Essayists*, vol. 9, London: C. and J. Rivington *et al.*, 1823, pp. 356–357.

Steiner, George, *Language and Silence*, London: Faber & Faber, 1967.

Steiner, George, *Real Presences*, London: Faber & Faber, 1989.

Stone, Gregory P., 'Appearance and the Self' in Gregory P. Stone and Harvey A. Farberman, eds, *Social Psychology through Symbolic Interaction*, Waltham, Massachusetts: Xerox College Publishing, 1970, pp. 394–414.

Strachey, Charles, ed., *The Letters of the Earl of Chesterfield to his son*, 2nd edn, vols. 1 and 2, London: Methuen & Co. Ltd, 1924.

Strauss, Anselm, ed., *George Herbert Mead on Social Psychology*, Chicago: The University of Chicago Press, 1956.

Styan, J. L., *Restoration Comedy in Performance*, Cambridge: Cambridge University Press, 1986.

Surin, Kenneth, '*Contemptus Mundi* and the Disenchanted World: Bonhoeffer's "Discipline of the Secret" and Adorno's "Strategy of Hibernation"', *Journal of the American Academy of Religion*, vol. 53, 1985, pp. 383–410.

Sykes, Stephen, *The Identity of Christianity*, London: SPCK, 1984.

Tambiah, S. J., *A Performative Approach to Ritual*, London: The British Academy, 1981.

Taylor, Denis E., *Serving at the Altar. A Manual for Servers*, Exeter: The Religious Education Press Ltd, 1966.

Taylor, Mark Kline, 'Symbolic Dimensions in Cultural Anthropology', *Current Anthropology*, vol. 26, no. 2, April 1985, pp. 167–185.

Teahan, John F., 'A Dark and Empty Way: Thomas Merton and the Apophatic Tradition', *The Journal of Religion*, vol. 58, 1978, pp. 263–287.

Temperley, Nicholas, *The Music of the English Parish Church*, vol. 1, Cambridge: Cambridge University Press, 1983.

Tenbruck, F. H., 'Formal Sociology' in Lewis Coser, ed., *Georg Simmel*, New Jersey: Prentice Hall, Inc., 1965, pp. 77–96.

Tenbruck, Friedrich H., 'The Cultural Foundations of Society' in Hans Haferkamp, ed., *Social Structure and Culture*, New York: Walter de Gruyter, 1989, pp. 15–35.

Thiselton, Anthony C., *The Two Horizons. New Testament Hermeneutics and Philosophical Description with Special Reference to Heidegger, Bultmann, Gadamer and Wittgenstein*, Exeter: The Paternoster Press, 1980.

Thomas, William I. and Dorothy Swaine Thomas, 'Situations Defined as Real are Real in Their Consequences' in Gregory P. Stone and Harvey A. Farberman, eds, *Social Psychology through Symbolic Interaction*, Waltham, Massachusetts: Xerox College Publishing, 1970, pp. 154–155.

Thompson, Francis, *The Works of Francis Thompson Poems*, vol. 2, London: Burns Oates & Washbourne Ltd, 1925.

Thompson, John B., *Critical Hermeneutics. A study in the thought of Paul Ricoeur and Jurgen Habermas*, Cambridge: Cambridge University Press, 1981.

Thompson, Kenneth, 'How Religious are the British?' in Terence Thomas, ed., *The British. Their Religious Beliefs and Practices 1800–1986*, London: Routledge, 1988, pp. 211–239.

Tomlinson, J. T., *The Craving for Mass Vestments*, London: Robert Scott, 1908.

Touraine, Alain, *Return of the Actor. Social Theory in Postindustrial Society*, trans. Myrna Godzich, Minneapolis: University of Minnesota Press, 1988.

T., R. W. C., 'Waiters', *Dublin University Magazine*, vol. 75, May 1870, pp. 583–590.

Travers, Andrew, 'Ritual Power in interaction', *Symbolic Interaction*, vol. 5, no. 2, 1982, pp. 277–286.

Travers, Andrew, 'Social Beings as Hostages: Organizational and Societal Conduct Answering to a Siege Paradigm of Interaction' in I. L. Mangham, ed., *Organization Analysis and Development*, New York: John Wiley & Sons Ltd, 1987, pp. 223–253.

Trexler, Richard C., 'Legitimating prayer gestures in the twelfth century. The *De Penitentia* of Peter the Chanter', *History and Anthropology*, vol. 1, 1984, pp. 97–126.

Trollope, Anthony, *Barchester Towers*, London: J. M. Dent & Sons Ltd, 1975.

Tugwell, Simon, 'Spirituality and Negative Theology', *New Blackfriars*, vol. 68, no. 805, May 1987, pp. 257–263.

Turner, Victor, *The Ritual Process. Structure and Anti-Structure*, London: Routledge & Kegan Paul, 1969.

Turner, Victor, 'Passages, Margins, and Poverty: Religious Symbols of Communitas', Part 1, *Worship*, vol. 46, no. 7, 1972, pp. 390–452.

Turner, Victor 'Passages, Margins, and Poverty: Religious Symbols of Communitas', Part 2, *Worship*, vol. 46, no. 8, 1972, pp. 482–494.

Turner, Victor, 'Ritual, Tribal and Catholic', *Worship*, vol. 50, no. 6, November 1976, pp. 504–526.

Turner, Victor, 'Frame, Flow and Reflection: Ritual and Drama as Public Liminality' in Michel Benamou and Charles Caramello, eds, *Performance in postmodern culture*, Milwaukee: University of Wisconsin Center for twentieth century studies, 1977, pp. 33–55.

Turner, Victor, ed., *Celebration. Studies in Festivity and Ritual*, Washington, D.C., Smithsonian Institution Press, 1982.

Turner, Victor, *From Ritual to Theatre. The Human Seriousness of Play*, New York: Performing Arts Journal Publications, 1982.

Underhill, Evelyn, *Worship*, New York: Crossroad, 1982.

Vagaggini, Cyprian, *Theological Dimensions of the Liturgy*, trans. Leonard J. Doyle, vol. 1, Collegeville, Minnesota: The Liturgical Press, 1959.

Vattimo, Gianni, *The End of Modernity. Nihilism and Hermeneutics in Postmodern Culture*, trans. Jon. R. Snyder, Cambridge: Polity Press, 1988.

Veblen, Thorstein, *The Theory of the Leisure Class*, London: Unwin Books, 1970.

Vergote, Antoine, 'Symbolic Gestures and Actions in the Liturgy' in David Power, ed., *Liturgy in Transition*, London: Herder and Herder, 1971, pp. 40–52.

Vickers, Hugh, *Great Operatic Disasters*, London: Macmillan, 1979.

Villiers, Marjorie, *Charles Péguy. A Study in Integrity*, London: Collins, 1965.

Wace, Henry and Schaff, Phillip, eds, *Nicene and Post-Nicene Fathers of the Christian Church*, vol. 2, Oxford: James Parker, 1894.

Waldstein, Michael, 'An introduction to von Balthasar's *The Glory of the Lord*', *Communio*, vol. 14, Spring 1987, pp. 12–33.

Walker, Charles, *The Liturgy of the Church of Sarum*, London: J.T. Hayes, 1866.

Walker, Charles, *The Server's Handbook: containing the manner of serving at simple and solemn celebrations of the Holy Eucharist: and at solemn Matins and Evensong, according to the Rubrical Directions of the Sarum and Roman Office-Books: with appropriate devotions*, London: C.J. Palmer, 1871.

Walsh, K.J., 'Northern Humanists and the Negative Way' in Raoul Mortley and David Dockrill, eds, *Prudentia. The Via Negativa*, University of Auckland, Supplementary number, 1981, pp. 79–90.

Wardell, Mark L. and Stephen P. Turner, *Sociological Theory in Transition*, Boston: Allen & Unwin, 1986.

Warnke, Georgia, *Gadamer: Hermeneutics, Tradition and Reason*, Cambridge: Polity Press, 1987.

Wathen, Ambrose G., *Silence. The Meaning of Silence in the Rule of St Benedict*, Washington D.C.: Consortium Press, 1973.

Weakland, Rembert G., 'The "Sacred" and Liturgical Renewal', *Worship*, vol. 49, no. 9, 1975, pp. 512–529.

Weber, Max, *The Sociology of Religion*, trans. Ephraim Fischoff, London: Methuen, 1966.

Webster, Paul, 'Victim of a broken mind', *The Guardian*, 8th October 1988.

Weil, Simone, *Waiting on God*, trans. Emma Craufurd, London: Fontana, 1959.

Weinsheimer, Joel C., *Gadamer's Hermeneutics. A Reading of* Truth and Method, London: Yale University Press, 1985.

Wexler, Mark N., 'The Enigma of Goffman's Sociology', *Quarterly Journal of Ideology*, vol. 8, no. 3, 1984, pp. 40–50.

Whatley, Richard, *Bacon's Essays: with Annotations*, 5th edn, London: John Parker, 1860.

Wheelwright, Phillip, *Metaphor & Reality*, Bloomington: Indiana University Press, 1962.

Whyte, William Foote, 'The Social Structure of the Restaurant', *The American Journal of Sociology*, vol. 54, November 1948, pp. 302–310.

Whyte, William H., Jr, *The Organization Man*, New York: Doubleday, 1957.

Wilde, Oscar, *The Works of Oscar Wilde*, London: Galley Press, 1987.

Wildeblood, Joan and Brinson, Peter, *The Polite World. A Guide to English Manners and Deportment from the Thirteenth to the Nineteenth Century*, Oxford: Oxford University Press, 1965.

Williams, David, 'Flannery O'Connor and the via negativa', *Studies in Religion*, vol. 8, no. 3, 1979, pp. 303–312.

Williams, Robin, 'Erving Goffman: An Appreciation', *Theory, Culture & Society*, vol. 2, no. 1, 1983, pp. 99–102.

Williams, Robin, 'Understanding Goffman's Methods' in Paul Drew and Anthony Wotton, eds, *Erving Goffman. Exploring the Interaction Order*, Cambridge: Polity Press, 1988, pp. 64–88.

Williams, Rowan, 'Balthasar and Rahner' in John Riches, ed., *The Analogy of Beauty. The Theology of Hans Urs von Balthasar*, Edinburgh: T. & T. Clark, pp. 11–34.

Williams, R. G., 'The Via Negativa and the Foundations of Theology: an introduction to the thought of V. N. Lossky' in Stephen Sykes and Derek Holmes, eds, *New Studies in Theology*, 1, London: Duckworth, 1980, pp. 95–117.

Williams, Simon Johnson, 'Appraising Goffman', *The British Journal of Sociology*, vol. 37, no. 3, September 1986, pp. 348–369.

Williams, W. S., *The History of Acolytes and Servers and of what they have done for the Church down the Centuries*, Chatham: Parrett & Neves Ltd, 1938.

Willis, Garry, *Bare ruined choirs: doubt, prophecy, and popular religion*, New York: Delta Books, 1972.

Wilson, Bryan R., ed., *Rationality*, Oxford: Basil Blackwell, 1970.

Winch, Peter, *The Idea of a Social Science and its Relation to Philosophy*, London: Routledge & Kegan Paul, 1963.

Wolfe, Tom, *The Bonfire of the Vanities*, London: Picador, 1988.

Wolff, Kurt H., ed. and trans. *The Sociology of Georg Simmel*, New York: The Free Press, 1950.

Wren, David, 'Abraham's Silence and the Logic of Faith' in Robert L. Perkins, *Kierkegaard's* Fear and Trembling: *Critical Appraisals*, Alabama: The University of Alabama Press, 1981, pp. 154–164.

Wright, Craig, *Music and Ceremony at Notre Dame of Paris 500–1550*, Cambridge: Cambridge University Press, 1989.

Wright, John, 'The concept of mystery in the Hebrew Bible: an example of the via negativa' in Raoul Mortley and David Dockrill, eds, *Prudentia. The Via Negativa*, University of Auckland, Supplementary number, 1981, pp. 13–34.

Yeats, William Butler, *Yeats' Poems*, A. Norman Jeffares, ed., London: Macmillan, 1989.

Yeo, Lester, *The Server's Handbook. The Alternative Service Book, 1980. Rite A*, Exeter: Religious and Moral Education Press, 1984.

Zabel, Gary, 'Adorno on music: a reconsideration', *The Musical Times*, vol. 139, no. 1754, April 1989, pp. 198–201.

Zeitlin, Irving, M., *Rethinking Sociology. A Critique of Contemporary Theory*, Englewood Cliffs, New Jersey: Prentice Hall, Inc., 1973.

Index

Abasements, *see* bows (civil and sacred)
Acolyte, *see* altar server
Adam
　Boulding, Maria, 105
　and clothing, 104–5
　Eve and innocence, 111
　Eve and the choirboy, 72
　Ricouer, Paul, 274
Altar servers
　aura, 335
　cleanliness, 225
　demeanour, 212, 222, 228–9
　functions, 214–16, 224
　and innocence, 214
　and 'liturgical mistakes', 175,
　　229–31
　recollections, 154–5, 212–13
　tact, 232–3
　tradition, 213–15
　Tridentine role, 215, 226–7
　Vatican II, 225–6
　and waiters, 208–12
　Wilde, Oscar, 88
Ambiguities
　and appearance, 123–4
　and innocence, 113–14
　in liturgy, 36, 163–5, 173
　and liturgical detail, 154–5
　productive and unproductive in
　　rites, 71
　sociological significance, 158–64
Angels
　and adults as virgins, 94–6
　and choirboys, 8–9, 84–8, 93–4,
　　308
　Comte, Auguste, 84
　image, 86
　and labelling theory, 88
　Old and New Testament, 90–1
　see also Aquinas, Berger, Cowper,
　　Pseudo-Dioynsius, Rilke,
　　Thompson

Antinomies
　altar servers and waiters, 207–10
　and apophatic theology, 291–2,
　　311–13
　and beauty, 77
　and bows, 205
　and clothing, 99–100
　defined, 71–3
　and liturgy, 73–8, 330
　and silence, 251
　and theology, 65–6
Apophatic theology
　and antinomies, 291–2, 311–13
　Dupré, Louis, 27, 252, 291
　and mystery in rite, 310–12
　Pseudo-Dionyisus, 310–11
　Tugwell, Simon, 291
Aquinas, St Thomas
　angels and the body, 91–2
　beauty and its corruption, 77
　imperfections and religious
　　habit, 143
　lies, 138
Archer, Anthony, 50–1
Aura
　and altar servers, 335
　Benjamin, Walter, 331–2
　and distance, 334–5
　and J.-K. Huysmans, 337
　and the tensive, 290

Babin, David, 'liturgical use', 178
Baudelaire, Charles
　childhood innocence, 59–60
　flâneur, 286–7
　and the 'forest of symbols', 75
　modernity, 59, 286–7
　spirituality of the child, 280
Baumstark, Anton, liturgical laws, 51
Balthasar, Hans Urs von
　domestication of the social in
　　rite, 304–5